LOCKE GENEALOGY

Supplement Volume 1

Including the Families *of*
CAPTAIN JOHN LOCKE
of **Portsmouth and Hampton, New Hampshire**

WILLIAM LOCKE
of **Woburn, Massachusetts**

and
GEORGE LOCKE
of Virginia

The only advantage we have over our ancestors is that of experience and the use of the store of things that accumulate through the ages. —Tallmadge

Donald P. Hayes, Jr.
#11733
Secretary, Locke Family Association

HERITAGE BOOKS
2009

HERITAGE BOOKS

AN IMPRINT OF HERITAGE BOOKS, INC.

Books, CDs, and more—Worldwide

For our listing of thousands of titles see our website
at
www.HeritageBooks.com

A Facsimile Reprint
Published 2009 by
HERITAGE BOOKS, INC.
Publishing Division
100 Railroad Ave. #104
Westminster, Maryland 21157

International Standard Book Numbers
Paperbound: 978-0-7884-0642-3
Clothbound: 978-0-7884-8197-0

DEDICATION

To the memory of the spirit, love
and devotion of:

F2591 GEORGE LOCKE ESQ.

founder of the Locke Family Association;

F4131 JUDGE JAMES WILLIAM LOCKE

first president and principal benefactor;

and most especially in appreciation of
#7816 ARTHUR HORTON LOCKE

whose tireless work and dedication
compiling the Locke genealogy can
never be fully appreciated,

this volume is respectfully dedicated.

TABLE OF CONTENTS

Photographs:

INTRODUCTION

Dear Cousins,

The long awaited supplement to the Locke Genealogy has finally been produced. I have presumed to label this effort "Vol. I" in the hope that there will be other efforts to maintain the genealogy as the Lockes progress through the generations. In fact, with the publication of this volume, I call upon the Locke Association officers and members to begin preparations for Volume II. Certainly, we should not wait fifty more years for another updating of our genealogy.

This project was begun in 1973 because nearly fifty years had lapsed since Arthur Horton Locke's History and Genealogy of Capt. John Locke was published. The need for this project was pitifully obvious to and much desired by the Association membership. Over a three year period genealogy information was submitted by Locke descendants from all over the United States. Another two and a half years were consumed by organizing, editing, coalescing, typesetting, and proofing the material. Finally, a finished manuscript in publishable form was prepared in six months of intensive effort.

I did not limit our work to Capt. John Locke's family as our association has always welcomed descendants of any Locke family into membership. Regrettably, not all information submitted was complete enough to be published but these cases being such a minority, I mention it here only to support my statement that another volume is needed.

Errors are a genealogist's bane but they are inherent in the science. Even original records cannot, at times, be trusted because they were written by fallible human beings. Information handwritten rather than typed is open to misinterpretation. Because this material was submitted by a large number of people, the chance for errors to creep into the work is geometrically enlarged. In any case — and in

\

INTRODUCTION

every case – all material has been carefully proofread by this fallible human to assure as much accuracy as possible.

A project of this type cannot be done by one person alone, and no one person should be given all the credit.

This project was first made possible by the support of the officers of the Locke Family Association who allowed me to present the proposal at the 1973 Annual Meeting. Their encouragement has been invaluable.

The enthusiasm of the individual members is well represented by the amount of material submitted on carefully filled data sheets. Certainly all the letters, phone calls, and individuals who anxiously asked, "When will the supplement be ready?" encouraged us on.

But there are individuals whose contributions must be mentioned individually:

#11575 SHIRLEY HOLMES SHEEHAN and her husband, DONALD SHEEHAN, are responsible for the excellent appearance of this volume. Shirley's skills at typesetting not only transformed difficult handwritten pages to neat typescript but her attention to detail and desire for perfection insured uniformity and accuracy. Donald's skills transformed the typescript to neat, accurate, and numbered pages ready for the printer. Their generous contributions of skills, time, and energy saved the Association considerable expense thereby making the project financially possible.

F3464 EDWARD LOCKE LORD was our largest contributor submitting several hundred entries bringing many branches of the Lockes and Lords up to date.

F9319a LAURENCE EDWARD GOSS actively contacted individuals, collected their material and forwarded it to the Secretary.

INTRODUCTION

Finally, some personal observations:

We have in our genealogy a very interesting group of people who consider themselves "ordinary" and not worthy of attention. That is why so many entries are without biographies or have such sparse biographies. Is it correct for us to feel this way?

We make a great deal of certain individual personalities in history. We accord these great men and women much honor both during and after their lifetimes. At the same time we belittle our own influences on history and consider ourselves unimportant and impotent. Yet, every "great" person needs the support of "ordinary" people like ourselves who create substance where he or she had only an idea. And many a "great" person has lost his influence when he lost our support.

On the pages of the Locke Genealogy you will find the kind of people who put into practice the ideas and ideals of democracy, built the world's most successful republic, and kept it alive. While the Lockes cannot boast any "great" men and women among their number, they are the people who turned vision into reality, idea into substance, and talk into action. It is the Lockes and people like them who fight in the wars, grow the wheat, teach in the schools, work in the industries, and build the communities. And only in genealogies like ours is this ignored fact of history hinted at.

Each of us must remember that, like our ancestors, we are a part of the thread of history. It is the living descendants of old and newer families who maintain and perfect a nation of individual freedom with their day-to-day work and influence. And yet, when the genealogist asks us about our own lives we answer, "Oh, me? Oh, nothing important. "

Best wishes,

Donald P. Hayes, Jr.
Secretary

HOW TO USE THIS VOLUME

To insure uniformity and ease of use, we have followed the patterns and layouts of earlier Locke genealogies. The section on the descendants of Capt. John Locke follows the same numbering system for individuals used by Arthur H. Locke in A History and Genealogy of Capt. John Locke. Similarly, the section on the descendants of William Locke follows the style employed by John Goodwin Locke in his Book of the Lockes. Thus, the older books and the new volume may be used in conjunction.

To locate an entry on an individual, look first in the index for that person's name and page number. When you turn to that page and find the person's entry you will also find the person's number. If there is an "F" preceeding the number, that means the person has his own main entry further on in the book. Since the entries are numbered in sequence, it is a small matter to thumb ahead a generation and find the main entry. If there is no "F" then the person is listed only under his parent's main entry. By using the parent's number you can trace back a generation to where they are listed under their parents and so on back to F1 Capt. John Locke. Try this step by step to see how it works.

Since the material for this book was collected from many individuals from all over the United States the Locke Family Association has not attempted to document each entry. An individual wishing to document his line should use this volume as a guide in acquiring the desired documents.

Town Hall of Rye, New Hampshire where our annual reunions were held from 1891 to 1959.

HISTORY OF THE
LOCKE FAMILY ASSOCIATION

by

#11733 Donald P. Hayes, Jr.

In 1891 the United States was very different from the quick-paced world power of today. There were a little over sixty million people stretched across a continent where the west was still considered open frontier. While the open range was rapidly being civilized with fences and farms, and the hills with "Big Business" mining, the east was in the midst of an industrial revolution which helped absorb over nine million foreign born immigrants. The seeds which would occupy future decades with great social change were being sown.

The average life expectancy of a person born in 1891 was about forty-seven years. Both children and adults died of diseases which were then common but are now conquered or subdued. If you lived in the city you walked or rode the horse drawn trolley wherever you wanted to go. If you lived in a rural area you rode your horse drawn wagon into town once a week for shopping. To travel great distances you bought a railroad ticket or booked passage on a coastal steam packet. Water was carried or pumped by hand, homes were lighted with kerosene or gas, and heat came from wood or coal parlor stoves and fireplaces. The newspaper cost two cents a copy. Entertainment was provided by evening lectures, monthly magazines, county fairs, and you made your own.

In 1891 future Presidents Calvin Coolidge and Herbert Hoover began their college educations and Woodrow Wilson was teaching at Princeton. Thomas Edison applied for a patent on his latest invention, the moving picture camera. In Springfield, Mass. James Naismith named his new indoor game "basketball". Winslow Homer was still painting at Prout's Neck, Maine and Anna Mary Moses had just settled with her new husband in Staunton, Virginia. It would be decades yet before she would be called "Grandma Moses". In April, the famous actor Edwin Booth made his final appearance on the stage playing in "Hamlet".

The Presidential primaries were in full swing during the summer of 1891. President Benjamin Harrison was running hard to be renominated by the Republican Party in spite of James G. Blaine's efforts to stop him. Grover Cleveland was expected to be renominated the candidate of the Democratic Party. The newly formed Populist Party was finding its strength in the largely rural character of the country and the people's desire for political reform. It advocated a graduated income tax, an eight hour work day, direct election of U. S. Senators, the secret ballot, laws allowing initiative petition and referendum, and a federal parcel post system. Although a few western states had given women the vote, the majority of the country's women were not allowed to participate in elections.

Wednesday, August 25th was another fair and very warm day in the farming Village of Rye, New Hampshire. The usually quiet Town Hall was the center of much activity. Carriages carrying people were stopping by the front door, people were climbing off the wagons that had come from the railroad station, and here and there people stepped out of nearby front doors and walked down the dirt road to Town Hall. Inside about sixty people were gathered in small groups and could be heard making introductions and talking family history.

Most active in the talkative crowd were the three men who had brought the meeting about. George Locke of Manchester, N. H. had retired the year before at age 74 and had immediately begun convincing his cousins that a family reunion should be held. Recording names and addresses was twenty-five year old Arthur H. Locke who had been the first to agree with George and had already compiled a considerable amount of genealogical information. Preparing to open the meeting was Judge James Locke who served on the Circuit Court of Appeals in New Orleans, La.

After a few words of announcement by the Judge, the meeting was formally opened with a prayer by Rev. James F. Locke of Pillsbury, Minn., the Judge's father. The Judge was elected President of the meeting and Arthur H. Locke the Secretary. The business of the meeting centered on the question, "Do we wish to create an organization to hold annual reunions?" According to the Secretary's records, "The remarks of the many speakers showed brotherly interest in a common cause and that the spirit of Capt. John Locke was not wanting but prominent in his sixth and eighthth (sic) generations. each speaker was listened to with attention and the applause each received showed that a common chord was touched and needed only time to form a perfect fraternal vibration." There was a vote to hold yearly meeting of the family and after some discussion and voting on the reunion organization, the meeting was adjourned until the next day.

As the meeting broke up no one seemed in a hurry to leave. After all, some were seeing cousins for the first time in many years and had much to catch up on. Others had only just made new friendships with distant relations. But finally, little groups could be seen leaving the hall. Some were staying in the nearby seaside hotels which were popular vacation spots of the time. Others were staying with friends or relatives in Rye. Others had to leave Rye and return home using the Eastern Division of the Boston and Maine railroad.

Thursday, August 26th was the one hundred and ninety-fifth anniversary of the death of Capt. John Locke. To commemorate the event seventy-five of his descendants gathered at the Rye Town Hall in Rye Center. At ten A.M. Judge Locke opened the meeting and the group immediately voted to take up the business of creating a permanent organization. The debate centered on the type, design, name, and standing committees of the new organization. The meeting appointed

a committee to draw up the Constitution and those serving were; Dr.
James F. Locke, Miss Hannah B. Locke, Mrs. Ellen M. Hall, Mrs.
Ellen A. Fowler, and Mr. Arthur H. Locke. The Constitution and By-
Laws were presented and voted on article by article and then a Nomi-
nation Committee was appointed. Those serving were Arthur Locke,
Judge Locke and Ira S. Locke.

At noon the Locke Family held its first family fish chowder dinner. Little did anyone realize that the fish chowder dinner would
become the most enduring Locke tradition. The meal was held in the
lower hall which had been rented for $2.00. Vegetables, probably
grown in Rye, were purchased for $2.00 and the fish for $1.50. A
cook, paid $3.00, prepared the meal and the washerwoman, paid
$1.00, took care of the cleaning.

After dinner the meeting was reopened and the first officers of
the new Locke Family Association were elected:

President	Hon. James W. Locke of Key West, Fla.
Vice Presidents	Mr. George Locke of Manchester, N. H.
	Mr. Augustus W. Locke of North Adams, Mass.
	Hon. Joseph A. Locke of Portland, Maine
	Mrs. Ellen M. Hall of Wells, Maine
	Mr. Irving Locke of Barrington, N. H.
Secretary	Mr. Arthur H. Locke of Portsmouth, N. H.
Treasurer	Miss Hannah B. Locke of Wells, Maine

The standing committees created were; a Correspondence Committee
to publish announcements of the reunion, A Historical Committee
chaired by Arthur H. Locke and a Memorial Committee to erect a
monument to Capt. John Locke in Rye. All living descendants of the
fifth generation were sent the congratulations of the new association
and voted honorary members.

The leisurely pattern of the early reunions was established in
1892. The reunion covered two days, the 25th and 26th of August.
The first day began with the descendants arriving in the late morning
and passing their time in "social discourse" before the family lunch in

the lower hall of the Rye Town Hall. At about 2 P.M. the President convened the meeting in the upper hall and the various articles of business were taken care of.

Besides the usual reports, the early reunions concerned themselves with compiling the genealogy, erecting a monument to Capt. John Locke in Rye, changing the name Straw's Point back to its early name of Locke's Neck, purchasing land in Rye and, paradoxically, passing the hat to pay the bills.

At seven in the evening the descendants met again for the Literary Entertainment, a feature which became a tradition enduring into the 1960's. These entertainments were usually home grown and were typical of the era. Before movies, radio and television made people dependent on technology for entertainment they developed the talents they had and provided entertainment for themselves and each other. The Judge began the entertainment with an address followed by a piano solo. Ira S. Locke also gave an address which was followed by two duets, a piano solo and a reading. Arthur Locke shared what historical information he had collected. A song, a piano solo and community sing concluded the program. While these seem dull to us today we must remember that this was a time when people were more self-reliant and learned to do things like sing and play instruments, and do them well. A reading was really storytelling, now nearly a lost art. And these entertainments often required audience participation thereby spreading the activity and fun.

In 1895 a speaker calling himself "Father Locke" of Chelsea, Mass. held the audience spellbound as he related personal recollections of Lincoln and Grant, amusing anecdotes of the Civil War, and sang patriotic songs of his own composition.

In 1904 a competition was held for the best composition about an historical incident in the life of a Locke descendant. Mr. Ernest N. Bragg, literary editor of The Boston Globe, was judge, and a silver loving cup and two silver medals were donated as prizes. Ursa S.

Dunbar of Brookline, Mass. won the cup for her life of Asa Locke of Rye, N.H. but the winners of the medals were not recorded.

The advent of the radio was recognized at the 1924 reunion with a novelty sketch titled, "Imitation Radio Program". The "program" included songs by the "Locke Chorus", violin and piano solos, White Mountain Current Events, stories and skits.

In 1926 a five dollar prize was awarded to Miss Carolyn Burpee of Rye for being the eighth grader with the best essay on Rye history.

On the second day of the reunion the meetings began around 10 A.M. and then adjourned for a family lunch at noon. During the afternoon session the new officers and committee members were elected. In 1892 an important amendment to the Constitution and By-Laws was passed opening membership to all descendants of any Locke family and making the organization a true Locke association.

The attendance of older family members was always noted in the minutes and the congratulations of the association offered them. In 1893 a Resolutions Committee was created to record and eulogize the passing of individual descendants.

By 1900 the reunion meetings had been shortened to one day, usually the Wednesday closest to the anniversary date of August 26th, and by 1909 the Secretary's minutes, Resolution Committee report, election of officers, and the literary entertainment comprised the Locke Reunion.

From the beginning the Locke cousins wished to erect in Rye a memorial to the progenitor of the family. There were attempts to purchase land on Locke's Neck where this memorial could be placed but no property seemed to be available. There was another attempt to attach a tablet to the boulder on Locke's Neck near the site of Capt. John Locke's murder but a clear title to the land could not be obtained and the boulder was in danger of being washed into the sea. The state legislature was petitioned for funds for the project on the grounds that Capt. Locke was one of New Hampshire's pioneer settlers but the state turned the request down.

REUNION.

The descendants, both male and female, of

Capt. John Locke,

who was killed by the Indians at Rye Point, N. H., Aug.
26, 1696, send your him, send greeting, and earnestly
invite you to meet us on

LOCKES NECK, RYE, N. H.,

AUGUST 25 AND 26, 1891.

to commemorate our ancestor's death, and organize
for a general reunion on Aug. 26, 1896, in commemo-
ration of the

Two Hundredth Anniversary

of that event.

Notice of the first reunion held on August 25 and 26, 1891.

The Bethany Congregational Church in Rye, New Hampshire where many of our reunions have been held since 1961.

But these setbacks did not stop the association. Money for a monument was collected and in 1902 the association purchased a lot in the Rye Central Cemetery for $20.54 and erected the monument for $360. At 7:30 P. M. on August 27, 1902 the monument was dedicated by the association's annual reunion. Besides the address of Judge James W. Locke, which was published in the genealogy, remarks were made by President Arthur H. Locke, a prayer given by George Locke and the singing of "America" and the "Doxology".

The most enduring project of the Locke Family Association was launched even before the association itself existed — the compilation of the genealogy. In 1888, while a sophomore at Dartmouth College, Arthur H. Locke began his work researching the Locke genealogy. As he later wrote, he expected his work to take, at most, only a few years. But as his interest grew, so did the amount of material he compiled. Twenty-nine years later, in 1917, his efforts grew to fruition in the publication of his A History and Genealogy of Capt. John Locke of Portsmouth and Rye, N. H.

In his early research work he was aided greatly by F2501 George Locke. As a result of their conversations and Arthur's work, George began to campaign for the creation of a family association. The reunion meetings themselves provided Arthur with an excellent opportunity to make his work widely known and collect more information from an ever widening circle of descendants. By the mid 1890's he had collected over 600 entries and completed his first blue print of the Locke Family Tree.

By 1913 enough material to fill a four hundred page book was collected but the biggest obstacle to publication was money. The association dues were only 25¢ and all expenses including meals were taken out of them. A deficit for reunion expenses was common and the annual solution was to "pass the hat". While this kept the organization solvent and the reunions going, it left nothing for projects which were usually paid for by "subscription".

At the reunion a Book Guarantee Fund was voted and John A. Lang and Judge James Locke were the first subscribers at $25 each. The fund's goal was $1000 and subscribers would be entitled to copies of the book. Letters to more affluent members were sent suggesting loans for the project and Judge Locke advanced a loan of $200 which he later made a gift.

The author hoped to have his book published for the twenty-fifth anniversary of the association but, as with any such effort, there were delays. In 1917 he reported that 419 copies had been printed at a cost of $2030. Despite the book fund goal of $1000, only $625 had been raised. Arthur had absorbed the remaining balance of $825.80 which he hoped he would be repaid as the books were sold.

The association made three payments on their financial debt to Arthur Locke but on November 7, 1926 he died with the debt still unpaid. How sad that he should have given so much in energy, time, and effort to his Locke cousins but they couldn't repay him the small debt in publishing their genealogy! President Charles E. Locke gave Arthur H. Locke a eulogy that reads in part,

> To our Historian we owe a debt which can never be repaid; a financial debt for the burden assumed by him in publishing (our genealogy) and a moral debt for the unselfish spirit in which he gave himself cheerfully and wholeheartedly to its completion. Certainly Historians are born, not made, and we are fortunate indeed to have been served by such a one.

The first quarter century of the association was marked with little unusual activity. There had been some discussion of a 25th anniversary celebration but there was more interest and effort put into publishing the genealogy. At the 26th reunion in 1916 President Charles E. Locke gave an Anniversary Address listing the association's accomplishments and lecturing the members on the need for support to publish the genealogy.

The Committee on Entertainment was very active at this time. In fact, a group known as "The Locke Entertainers" was a regular feature, producing elaborate novelty sketches complete with costumes and props. The nucleus of the performers was the daughters of F6043 Augustus W. Locke: #9187 Eugenia, F9190 Julia (later Mrs. Arthur O. Dewey), and F9191 Harriet (later Mrs. Lyle S. Drew). These three talented young ladies were the creative force of the entertainers and a picture of them in costume may be seen at the top of the page opposite pg. 551 in the genealogy. They kept their interest in theatrics throughout their lives and as late as the 1960's Julia was still producing and directing charming sketches for the Locke Association.

The entertainments for the 1916 reunion are an example of the novelty sketches that were popular and produced by talented amateurs all over the country before World War I: a fashion show, a solo "Just A-Wearying For You", "Reuben and Rachel", a farce "Crystal Bowl", a solo "Long Ago", and a symphony orchestra playing "Rocky Road to Dublin".

The 1920's and 1930's were a leisurely period for the Locke Reunions. There was little in them to reflect the fast paced, easy money era of the 20's or the depression of the 30's. Attendance at reunions ranged from 100 to 170. A few payments were made to Arthur H. Locke for the genealogy debt owed him. The passing of founder Judge James Locke in 1922 and Historian Arthur H. Locke in 1926 were noted. A commemorative boulder was erected on Meeting House Green in Hampton, N. H. A framed copy of the Jan. 8, 1800 "New Hampshire Gazette" was donated to the Rye Public Library. Mrs. Fred Dinsmore of Kittery, Maine wrote a Greeting Song and a Goodbye Song in 1931 for use at reunions. In 1933 there were eight cousins who had attended the first reunion in 1891. A surprise birthday party for past-President Charles E. Locke was arranged during the 1934 reunion luncheon. A resolution was voted in 1936 to mark the passing of Clara E. Parsons who was Secretary from 1893 to her death. Someone reported that the Locke Association was the oldest incorporated family association in the country.

Rev. George R. Locke was first elected President in 1924 and served in that office for twenty-two years. Reunions under his leadership were marked by brotherly love, hymns, prayers and sermons. He cared for people and always had something to report about the activities of Lockes all over the country. He established the custom of asking everyone to rise and introduce themselves so everyone might know each other and feel more a part of the family. Attendance was high during this period. Maybe the difficult times of the depression caused people to appreciate the security of the family reunion. Even the old-fashioned songs and entertainments made people feel that here was something pleasant and familiar that had not been altered by economic and political turmoil.

The Old Locke Burying Ground on Old Beach Road, Locke's Neck, Rye is, according to tradition, the burial place of Capt. John Locke and his wife, Elizabeth. We can no longer prove this tradition to be correct because the early burial records, if there were any, no longer exist. However, there is no doubt that the Burying Ground is a very early one. The use of common field stones to mark the head and foot of each grave was the method used by Seventeenth Century Americans. The location of the burying ground on Locke's Neck is another indication that it is probably the burial place of early Lockes.

In 1898 the association first became interested in the Burying Ground when a suitable place for a memorial to Capt. John was being sought. A deed was written at that time but one of the abuttors would not sign off his claim to the land so the project lay dormant for a number of years. From time to time the association made enquiries about title to the Burying Ground or erection of a tablet there, without success. In 1934 the matter was again discussed and this time an abuttor had been found who would reset the walls and clear the brush away for the association. Further, on November 26, 1934 the deed was recorded in the Rockingham County records with the Locke Family Association as owner of the Old Locke Burying Ground.

The Old Locke Burying Ground on Locke's Neck, owned by the Association. According to tradition, Capt. John Locke and his wife, Elizabeth, are buried here. Fieldstones are used as head and foot markers proving this to be a very early cemetery.

photo by D. Hayes, Jr.

Tablet on Locke's Neck in Rye.

The association has some very good friends in the Rye Historical Society who cleaned the cemetery of weeds and brush as part of their Bicentennial project. Recently a new neighbor has offered to help keep the brush under control so the cemetery will have a nice appearance and Capt. John's descendants may visit it.

For the Fiftieth Reunion of the Locke Family Association, about two hundred cousins traveled to the Town Hall in Rye to attend the event. The business meeting was opened with the singing of "America" followed by a prayer given by President George R. Locke and two verses of "Blest Be the Tie that Binds". The Treasurer reported that the treasury had a balance of $262.36. The President commented that the record book showed that over 1500 persons had attended the reunions during the last fifty years. New members were introduced, the youngest member present was Kathleen Barrett at five months of age, letters and telegrams of greeting were read, and the resolutions for the recently departed were reported. The Nominating Committee report was accepted and voted and the business meeting closed with the singing of the last two verses of "Blest Be the Tie that Binds".

After a family fish chowder lunch the cousins gathered in the upper hall for a pageant based on the history of John Locke and the Locke family, prepared, directed, and read by F9190 Julia Locke Dewey. Because there was no complete rehearsal the pageant was enlivened by the spontaneity and spirit of cooperation and ingenuity of the twenty cousins who participated. The tableau scenes showed John Locke arriving in Rye with his wife Elizabeth, building the first church in New Hampshire, an Indian attack on the Locke Garrison, the murder of John Locke, a minuet by two little children, the sewing of a quilt made of British red coats, and the first reunion.

President George R. Locke's anniversary address struck the note upon which the existence of any family rests and made it vibrate: Brotherly Love. As an original member of the association he realized that he had become, through the passage of time, a senior member and that his generation had long since ceased to be the younger and had earned itself the adjective "elder". He reflected upon the changes of fifty years, and upon the much loved Locke cousins who had taken energetic part in the reunions and were now gone. He looked upon his brothers and sisters, nieces and nephews, and cousins and declared, "How we have been brought together!" How ties which otherwise would have been unknown or ignored have been rediscovered and strengthened! How we have found that blood is thicker than water and does count! I wouldn't have missed all this for any price!"

World War II with its gasoline rationing, travel restrictions, food rationing and manpower demands threatened an interruption in the annual reunion of Lockes. Undaunted, however, small and enthusiastic groups of cousins gathered in Rye at the Town Hall to maintain the thread of family reunions that was over fifty years long. A picnic lunch replaced the traditional Locke Fish Chowder that had been prepared for many years by Reuben Jenness Locke of Rye. Stories and games replaced the usual entertainment.

But the spirit of the reunion was kept and strengthened. War bonds were purchased. Photos of cousins in the service were displayed and mothers and sisters reported of visits made to their sons and brothers in service. A special closeness to the people of England was felt when the reunion was reminded that John Locke was born there. The annual resolutions for the departed Lockes now included the names of young and heroic defenders of Liberty. The hardships of war made earlier generations seem closer through the common bond of pain, sorrow, and travail.

In 1946 a call was sent out for a reunion which would begin a new era in association history. Attendance was encouraged, new officers elected, the fish chowder dinner revived and the literary and theatrical entertainments resurrected. Rev. George Locke gave a sketch of the association history and the history of Capt. John Locke was reviewed. The thread of annual reunions again seemed strong.

However, the fifties and sixties were not the best era of the association. Society changed after the war and the old-style reunion did not suit the times. The reunions were held in the same manner, observing the same traditions. The main business at reunions seemed to be committee reports, particularly the Resolutions Committee, and sending greetings to the sick and shut-ins. The entertainments continued in the style that was so popular before World War I but had been made archaic by movies, radio, and television. Attendance dropped to between fifty and sixty people.

Also, there seemed little work for the association to do to give it purpose. Sporadic attempts at updating the genealogy failed because no one could be found with the spirit and energy of Arthur H. Locke to carry it through. Suggestions to reprint the genealogy for the benefit of younger generations were usually met with a reply of "too expensive". A coat of arms was published and made available and small donations were made to Crochet Mountain and Strawbery Banke.

Still, the attraction to attend an occasional reunion was there: the chance to visit the town that your ancestors pioneered, see the monument, visit the Old Locke Burying Ground, and meet distant relations who had the same heritage in common with you.

Attempts were made to attract larger gatherings. In 1955 the meeting was changed from Wednesday to the third Saturday of August. Dinners were held at local restaurants and entertainments were changed. But still, the attendance was about the same.

In 1960 a change in use of the Rye Town Hall prevented the association from meeting there as it had done for sixty-nine years. After meeting a year in Hampton, N.H. the meeting accepted the invitation of Rye's Bethany Congregational Church to meet in their Fellowship Hall.

The 75th Anniversary Reunion of the Locke Association was a major event as well as an impressive milestone in the life of such an organization. The reunion notice advertised an historical pageant,

Locke Family Famous Fish Chowder, a huge birthday cake, a group photograph, and a tour of Strawbery Banke in Portsmouth.

The nine tableaux historical pageant, again prepared by F9190 Julia Locke Dewey, displayed the high spots of our ancestor's lives as an inspiration to us to meet our present problems as courageously as they had met theirs. While similar to the 1940 pageant, there were changes and additions. Fortunately, our records contain a complete copy of the pageant that was enjoyed by one hundred and twenty-four cousins. As a member of the audience in 1965, I can say that while the style of the pageant was old-fashioned and some of the music and costumes out of historical context, the result was definitely very enjoyable! Its intent was not ancestor worship but an appreciation of the accomplishments, strength, industry, dedication and integrity of our heritage as a Locke family. For young persons, like myself, the pageant and the anniversary reviewed the Locke history, including stories of more recent members, that helped make an individual realize he or she was part of a larger group with a strong heritage — that must continue.

Tableau one showed John Locke and his wife Elizabeth Berry arriving in Rye to establish their new home. Musical accompaniment was provided by Eleanor Voudy as pianist and Emma Trees as soloist who sang "Memories". The audience participated in the singing of "The Old Oaken Bucket". The association treasurer, John L. Parsons and his wife, Blanche, played the roles of John and Elizabeth Locke.

The second tableau showed John Locke framing the first meeting house in Portsmouth, N. H. As John Locke, dressed in Puritan grey, sawed the timbers with his helpers, the soloist sang "The Church in the Wildwood".

The Locke Garrison described in early records was portrayed in tableau three. The audience sang "Battle Hymn of the Republic" and the soloist "Bless this House". An Indian attack occurred as the curtains closed.

The 50th reunion of the Locke Family Association held in the Rye, N.H. Town Hall on August 28, 1940.

The 75th reunion of the Locke Family Association held at the Bethany Congregational Church in Rye, N.H. on August 28, 1965. Note the costumes used in the pageant. Rev. Arthur O. Dewey and Julia Locke Dewey are seventh and eighth from the left. John L. Parsons, our 16th president, is eighth from the left.

John Locke's death at the hand of an Indian was shown in the fourth tableau. A sickle, the only defensive weapon he had, was prominently displayed while the audience was reminded that the original sickle was at the New Hampshire Historical Society.

Rev. Arthur O. Dewey, as reader, recounted stories of Lockes who served various New Hampshire churches prominently. Tableau five showed Rev. Edward Locke, Elder Tozar Lord and John Sheperd, Esq. founding a religious community in Chesterfield, N. H.

Tableau six, "The Old Quilt", displayed a prized possession of F2806 Gardner T. Locke of Rye. This quilt was made of material taken from Revolutionary War red and blue military coats and is the only one known in existence. Gardner's granddaughter, Julia Locke Dewey, apparently realized that the audience did not grasp the fact that the original quilt was there on stage. She stood up on the stage, and breaking the silence maintained by the other posing actors, announced, "This is the VERY quilt!" A dramatic move which brought the point home.

An old-fashioned dance represented the entertainments people had before technology overshadowed independent activity.

The eighth tableau featured Annie Locke Ellingwood of Rye who, at age 95, was our oldest member. As she sat on stage in a rocking chair dressed in her mother's wedding dress, she was described as "bright and cheerful and full of sweet personality. She never misses a meeting of our association".

The final tableau featured an early New Hampshire church service. Rev. Dewey assumed the minister's place on the stage while the entire cast was his congregation. As the hymn "Faith of our Fathers" was being sung the monitor tapped those who were "dozing off". As the service ended and the congregation left, the soloist sang "O God Beneath Thy Giving Hand", concluding the pageant.

In 1969 special note was taken of the Golden Wedding Anniversary of Rev. Arthur O. Dewey and Julia Locke Dewey. Their wedding

announcement was made at the 1919 annual reunion when their Locke
cousins were invited to witness the event. The Deweys were always
active participants in the Locke Association and did much to keep the
reunions alive during the fifties and sixties. Julia attended the first
reunion as a child and was one of the "Locke Entertainers" in her
youth. Her peppy, cheerful spirit added much to the pleasure of the
meeting. She was often seen and heard energetically reminding the
Reverend during his terms as President and she kept the pace of events
moving. She made a particular effort to greet each new member with
a warm smile and enthusiasm. Their passing left a void of spirit and
enthusiasm in the meetings and it looked for a time as though the reunions might not continue.

But each family produces new generations to continue the thread
of family and history when older generations have completed their
weaving. There are few left who attended the early reunions or who
remember the prominent cousins so much loved in the early days. The
family association records are complete but records of any kind do not
reveal the personalities, the feelings and family love of those people.
But there are the people of present generations; their personalities,
feelings, and love are important. And so the association and the
reunions continue.

In 1972 the association accepted the invitation of Locke Lake
Colony founder F11052 Kent D. Locke to meet at that location where
outdoor activities could be enjoyed. With over a hundred cousins
present the questions about the genealogy were asked again. "Why
don't we reprint the old book? What about updating the genealogy?
What's being done about that? What are we doing to locate other
Locke cousins? Do people know there is a Locke reunion?" The new
officers were given some very specific goals.

The first project undertaken was reprinting the old book so people
could have somewhere to start when tracing their lines. In 1973 two
hundred and nineteen copies were printed by Edwards Brothers in

Michigan for a cost of $1949.31. Money was raised by pre-publication sales, and a $600 loan from Treasurer John L. Parsons. The association's funds covered half the expense. Mr. Parsons, the prime mover behind the reprinting, accepted only half payment of his loan and cancelled the rest. The books were all sold within six years.

The Historical Committee began assembling the association records and found that some originals could not be located, only copies. Some research work led to their location at the New Hampshire Historical Society in Concord "on deposit". They were returned along with the Articles of Incorporation and deed to the Old Locke Burying Ground. In addition, a membership drive was conducted and contact made with prominent regional and national genealogical organizations. Since 1971 our membership has grown seventy-two percent.

In 1973 the proposal to compile and print a supplement to the Locke genealogy was approved unanimously. New data sheets were printed and sent to each member. The Secretary estimated that four years would be needed to compile, edit, and prepare the supplement for printing, but he warned the meeting that it could take longer.

The nation's Bicentennial celebrations had an important impact on the population causing many to reflect upon their family history as well as their national heritage. The televising of Alex Haley's book, Roots, had an explosive effect on interest in family history. Genealogy as an interest and a hobby is again looked upon as a worthy enterprise and not just the boring activity of tired old men and ladies.

The 1976 Locke Reunion topped a hundred again for no other reason than there was a reunion being held by an energetic family organization. Families from all parts of the country made the reunion part of their pilgrimage to early revolutionary sites. At this reunion another long-time interest of the association surfaced: Locke's Neck.

Locke's Neck is a piece of land that sticks out from the Rye coast into the Atlantic. Capt. Locke settled there before 1665 when it was known as Josselyn's Neck by the people of Hampton (Rye did not exist until 1726). He was the first to settle and farm the neck and there his family grew and prospered for several generations. For over two hundred years the inhabitants of Hampton and Rye referred to it as Locke's Neck.

In 1878 New Hampshire governor Straw built several homes on the neck and by the time of the association's founding it was equally well known as Locke's Neck or Straw's Point.

The association, as early as 1895, asked the Town of Rye to formally rename the area as Locke's Neck but the town declined to act. The association kept the name alive by erecting "guide boards" directing people to Locke's Neck and by referring to the area as Locke's Neck as much as possible. Newer descendants often heard the area called Locke's Neck before they ever heard of Straw's Point.

In 1976 Corinne Parsons Macdonald, a Rye resident and Locke descendant, made the motion that the association ask Town Meeting to see that the name Straw's Point be returned to its earlier name. The motion passed unanimously and in 1977 an even stronger motion was passed directing the President and Secretary to enter an article in the Town Warrent for the 1978 Town Meeting to return the area to its former name of Locke's Neck.

The Selectmen of Rye very agreeably allowed the article in the warrent and the chairman read a letter of explanation sent by the Secretary. The Rye Historical Society also lent its support and on March 18, 1978 Article 24 was passed unanimously. Once again, Locke's Neck commemorated one of New Hampshire's pioneer families.

What's next? The future, while unpredictable, is not inscrutable. The reunions will continue — they are a symbol of the American family. There will be new generations of the family to record, and more people are discovering genealogy and their Locke heritage. The need for more supplements is obvious. Our old records, if they are to last another ninety years, need preservation work. Will the association one day own property in the ancestral home town? Are there some old Locke homesites that could be explored by archaeology? What about other Locke families? Can we do more to join with them? And what about John Locke's English heritage? It has never been explored. What about the collection of significant Locke artifacts and their display in a museum? The possibilities seem exciting. All we need do is choose!

PRESIDENTS OF THE
LOCKE FAMILY ASSOCIATION

1891 — 1979

1.	F4131	Judge James W. Locke of Key West, Fla.	1891-95; 1907-08
2.	3684	Hon. Ira S. Locke of Portland, Maine	1895-97
3.	7816	Arthur H. Locke of Portsmouth, N. H.	1897-02 1920-24
4.	F4960	William B. Yeaton of Concord, N. H.	1902-03
5.	7341	C. Carroll Bartlett of Chicago, Ill	1903-05
6.	8472	Norton T. Horr of Cleveland, Ohio	1905-07
7.	F8402	Frank Lovering Locke of Boston, Mass.	1907-09
8.	7861	Prof. Charles E. Locke of Boston, Mass.	1909-18
9.	F5775	G. Scott Locke of Concord, N. H.	1918-19
10.	F5218	John A. Lang of Roslindale, Mass.	1919-20
11.	F8125	Rev. George R. Locke of Boston, Mass.	1924-46
12.	F10041	Ernest S. Locke of Bradford, Vt.	1946-53
13.		Rev. Arthur O. Dewey of Hampton, N. H.	1953-65
14.	F11064	Prescott L. Howard of Biddeford, Maine	1965-69
15.		Lena Levitt Fahlow of Woburn, Mass.	1969-71
16.	F10480	John L. Parsons of Rye, N. H.	1971-72
17.	F11052	Kent D. Locke of Alton, N. H.	1972-76
18.	F10042	Raymond S. Locke of Centreville, Mass.	1976-79
19.	F12373	Dr. J. Frederic Burtt of Lowell, Mass.	1979-

FIFTH GENERATION

<u>F111 MARCIA LEAVITT</u>, born in Hampton Falls, N. H., married Jan. 26, 1738, JOB HASKELL, born in Gloucester, Mass., April 27, 1716, died in New Gloucester, Maine, 1806, son of William and Jemima (Hubbard).

Children in 5th Generation

F10690 CAPT. WILLIAM HASKELL, b. Gloucester, Mass., Mar. 20, 1761, d. Poland, Maine, 1832, m. New Gloucester, Maine, Mar. 7, 1778, REBECCA BRADBURY.

<u>F188a PRUDENCE WEBSTER</u>, born on Dec. 25, 1744, died in St. Andrew's, N.B. Canada, married in Georgetown, Maine, May 7, 1764 TIMOTHY BLAKE, born in Kensington, N.H., Jan. 6, 1740, died in Castine, Maine. He was the fourth child of Moses and Mehitable (Smith). At the age of 20, he enlisted in Capt. Jeremiah Marston's Company, under Col. John Goff, for Crown Point and the invasion of Canada. After nearly a year's service, he returned and settled in the area of Bagaduce (now Penobscot, Maine) in 1762. At that time his origin was described as from Kittery, Maine.

Children in 5th Generation

10691 DANIEL, b. Penobscot, Maine, Sept. 8, 1764, d. Brooksville, Maine, Jan. 9, 1833, baptized Phippsburg, Maine, Nov. 13, 1765, m. in that part of Old Penobscot now called Brooksville, 1784, SARAH (SALLY) BAKEMAN.

10692 ANDREW WEBSTER, b. Georgetown, Maine, June 23, 1766 m. SUSANNAH ———— .

10693 MOSES

10694 TIMOTHY, d. at sea.

<u>F188c CAPT. EBENEZER WEBSTER</u>, born in Hampton Falls, N.H. Oct. 22, 1749, died in Cape Elizabeth, Maine, Oct. 9, 1833, married 1st ———— WESCOTT, died in Deer Isle, Maine, before 1794, daughter of William of Falmouth, Maine; married 2nd in Cape Elizabeth, Maine, Dec. 7, 1794, DEBORAH ELDER.

Capt. Webster and his first wife, ———— (Westcott) had nine children as residents of Deer Isle near what is now called Sunset. His first wife was a sister to Mercy Westcott who married Job Small on Feb. 23, 1764. Ebenezer settled on Deer Isle perhaps thru the influence of Job and Mercy who came to Deer Isle before he did. His second wife,

Deborah, was a daughter of Robert Elder, Jr., of Falmouth and Alice Westcoat of York, Maine. From early documents, it is indicated that he settled Deer Isle in 1767. He sold his Deer Isle interests March 28, 1796 to Job Small, Jr. for $700.

The Revolutionary War records at the City Hall in Portland, Maine described Ebenezer's grave as being located in Mt. Pleasant Cemetery, Cottage Road and Pine Street, Cape Elizabeth, Maine. His marker is a tall, thin slate stone located on the Elder family lot.

Children in 5th Generation

10695   ANDREW, b. Deer Isle, Maine, April 26, 1769, d. Brooksville, Maine, Dec. 17, 1851, m. 1788, CHRISTIANA BATEMAN.

F10696   JOSEPH, b. Deer Isle, Maine, ca. 1770, d. North Haven, Maine, after 1850, m. Deer Isle, Maine, Oct. 16, 1794, SARAH PRESSEY.

10697   ANNA, b. Deer Isle, Maine, ca. 1772, m. Deer Isle, Maine, Jan. 23, 1794, CAPT. EBEN SMALL.

10698   JOHN, b. Deer Isle, Maine, ca. 1774, d. ca. 1815 at sea, m. July 13, 1808, ALICE, his cousin, dau. of Job and Mercy (Wescott) Small.

10699   EBENEZER, JR., b. Deer Isle, Maine, ca. 1776, d. Cape Elizabeth, Maine, age 68, Mar. 1, 1844, m. 1st Sedgwick, Maine, 1799, POLLY EATON, b. ca. 1780, d. Cape Elizabeth, Maine, age 39, Mar. 27, 1819; m. 2nd, Cape Elizabeth, Maine, Oct. 1, 1825, MARY (JORDAN) STANWOOD, b. ca. 1799, d. Cape Elizabeth, Maine, age 90, Aug. 11, 1889.

10700   NATHANIEL, b. Deer Isle, Maine, ca. 1778, m. ——— TORREY. They resided in Cape Elizabeth, Maine.

10701   DEBORAH, b. Deer Isle, Maine, ca. 1780.

10702   MARY, b. Deer Isle, Maine, ca. 1782, m. Mar. 5, 1800, AMOS SNOW. They resided in Penobscot, Maine with three children or more.

10703   SARAH, b. Deer Isle, Maine, ca. 1784.

F188d **DANIEL WEBSTER**, born Feb. 12, 1751, died probably in Penobscot, Maine after 1830 as name appears in census of that year. Only Daniel's first child can be confirmed by record as early vital records of Penobscot, Maine have been lost. He is described in the 1800 census as being from Hampton, N. H. and 45 years of age.

Children in 5th Generation

10704 PATIENCE WEBBER, baptized Deer Isle, Maine, Aug. 20, 1790.

10705 DANIEL, JR., b. ca. 1780, d. July 14, 1867, m. May 8, 1803 LUCY HORN and had: 10706 PATIENCE, b. ca. 1805; 10707 ANDREW, b. 1807, m. MARY HILL; 10708 TAMSON, b. ca. 1811.

10709 JOSIAH, b. ca. 1784 and had 2 wives and 6 children.

10710 BETSY, m. Jan. 8, 1812, JOHN WITHAM.

10711 DAVID, m. Jan. 20, 1803, NANCY HIBBERT.

F259 SARAH BERRY, born in Rye, N. H., 1749, died in Meaderboro, Rochester, N. H., Aug. 16, 1818, age 69, married in Rye or Rochester, N. H., AARON JENNESS, born in Rochester, N. H., Jan. 15, 1746, baptized May 25, 1746, died in Meaderboro, Rochester, N. H., Mar. 20, 1819. He signed Oath of Allegiance April 12, 1776.

Children in 5th Generation

10712 JEREMIAH, b. 1777, d. Sept. 16, 1814, age 37.

F10713 WILLIAM, b. 1780, d. July 8, 1864, m. Oct. 5, 1806, HANNAH SEAVEY.

10714 AARON

10715 LEVI, m. SALLY, not of age 1803.

10716 HANNAH

10717 ELIZA, b. 1811, d. Dec. 30, 1830.

SIXTH GENERATION

F196 MEHITABLE DORE, born in Lebanon, Maine, May 2, 1778, died in Newfield, Maine, Sept. 1865, married, in Newfield, Maine, Oct. 24, 1798, JOSEPH MERROW, born in Shapleigh, Maine, Jan. 4, 1778, died in West Newfield, Maine, May 15, 1856. That this Joseph Merrow lived first in Shapleigh is apparent from two York County deeds. He purchased, Oct. 3, 1798, one hundred and twenty-eight acres from Benjamun Guptill, husbandman. The latter was presumably his brother-in-law. Joseph was described as a yeoman. Joseph Merrow "Labourer" deeded seventeen acres Dec. 10, 1798 to Moses Nasson of Shapleigh, husbandman. This deed is signed by Joseph Merrow and his wife "Maheta Bell Merrow". He was still there in 1801.

Joseph and Mehitable moved to nearby West Newfield, Maine, where they were the pioneers in this new town. He was a farmer there. Lieut. Joseph Merrow ran true to form set by four generations of his ancestors. Each had in turn pioneered a new community.

That he had a military title of Lieutenant is on the authority of Rev. Alonzo Quint and Joseph Merrow is reported to have served in the war of 1812, but no military record has been found. In several York County deeds he was called Deacon Joseph Merrow. The census of 1810 showed him to have been living in Newfield with his wife and two children, both males, one age 10-16 and the other under 10.

Children in 6th Generation

10718 JOSEPH, b. West Newfield, Maine, May 6, 1799, d. West Newfield, Maine, April 6, 1862, m. Newfield, Maine, July 10, 1803, LUCY DAVIS

10719 SALLY, b. West Newfield, Maine, Oct. 11, 1801, d. at a young age.

10720 MEHITABLE, b. West Newfield, Maine, Dec. 23, 1803, m. Newfield, Maine, Oct. 17, 1841, SAMUEL PERKINS.

10721 MARY, b. West Newfield, Maine, Feb. 7, 1806, d. West Newfield, Maine, Aug. 24, 1845, m. MOSES TUTTLE.

10722 PATIENCE, never married and kept house for her brother Ezekiel.

10723 EZEKIEL, never married.

F10724 JAMES, b. West Newfield, Maine, 1810, d. North Shapleigh, Maine, Sept. 9, 1875, m. BETSY MARR.

10725 LYDIA, m. West Newfield, Maine, 1815, d. North Shap-
           leigh, Maine, 1899, m. JOHN MERROW, her cousin,
           son of Abel Merrow and Patience James, daughter of
           John and Lydia (Door) James.

10726 CHARLES, b. West Newfield, Maine, Mar. 3, 1816, d.
           East Wakefield, N. H., May 30, 1899, m. Newfield,
           Maine, Oct. 16, 1842, HANNAH DAVIS.

F550 WARD LOCKE, born in Gilmanton, N. H., 1784, died in
Belgrade, Maine, Nov. 25, 1828, married 1st in Belgrade, Maine,
BETSEY YEATON; 2nd in Belgrade, Maine, BETSEY STEARNS, born
in Belgrade, Maine, Dec. 13, 1793, died April 3, 1873.

Children in 6th Gen. b. in Belgrade, Maine

F10727 JOHN LOCKE, b. July, 1812, d. Poland, Maine, Jan.
           13, 1890, m. Poland, Maine, HANNAH DUNN.

F10728 JESSE LOCKE, b. 1813, d. Poland, Maine, April 30, 1887,
           m. 1st EUNICE STURGIS; 2nd MARY ANN FOSS.

10729 HIRAM WARD LOCKE, d. Oct. 22, 1859 at 40 years.

F887 ALBERT GALLATIN MOULTON, born in Lyman, N. H.,
Mar. 20, 1813, died in Athol, Mass., Sept. 6, 1889, married, in
Athol, Mass., June 22, 1851, ELIZABETH ABAGAIL BYLER, born in
Hinsdale, N. H., June 17, 1830, died in Athol, Mass., Feb. 14, 1877.
      He was employed by the Vermont and Massachusetts Railroad as
Superintendant of Buildings and Bridges. Under his supervision, the
Vermont and Massachusetts Depot was built in Athol, Mass. 1872-73.
Near the Depot, in 1873, he built a two-story hotel with a mansard
roof and stable next to the railroad tracks and named it the "Athol
House", which he soon after sold to Mr. Albert Miller. He later con-
structed a building on South Street, Athol which was to be named the
"Moulton Block". He devoted his time to real estate and lumbering
interests both in Mass. and N. H. after retiring from the railroad and
owned a large farm in Bath, N. H. which was operated by his son
Frank Moulton.
      Mr. Moulton was a man of unblemished character, somewhat re-
served to the general public, but cordial and companionable with
those to whom he was drawn by kindred social ties. He was a true and
faithful friend, and his personal worth was best known to those who
enjoyed his intimate acquaintance.
      He married a second time to the widow Martha (Goodnowe) Risley
in Athol on June 22, 1881. She died in Athol on Dec. 5, 1898.

Children in 6th Generation

10730 FRANK P., b. Athol, Mass., April 13, 1853, d. Wilder,
           Vt., May 3, 1918, m. Lisbon, N. H., July 30, 1878,
           MARCIA ELLA ATWOOD.

10731   ELIZABETH M., b. Athol, Mass., Sept. 21, 1854, d. Athol, Mass., May 30, 1886, m. OTHO F. AMSDEN.

F10732 ARTHUR WOODS, b. Athol, Mass., Feb. 25, 1858, d. Fitchburg, Mass., Oct. 20, 1894, m. Athol, Mass., Jan. 12, 1884, DELLA DULCENA FISKE.

10733   JAMES T., b. Aug. 4, 1859, m. JESSIE BEDELL.

F10690 WILLIAM HASKELL, born in Gloucester, Mass., Mar. 20, 1761, died in Poland, Maine, 1832, married in New Gloucester, Maine, Mar. 7, 1778, REBECCA BRADBURY, born in Salisbury, Mass. Mar. 19, 1760, died in Poland, Maine, 1803, daughter of Benjamin and Jemima (True) Bradbury.

Children in 6th Generation

10734   BENJAMIN, b. New Gloucester, Maine, Jan. 3, 1779, m. HANNAH ———.

10735   WILLIAM, b. New Gloucester, Maine, Nov. 6, 1780, m. Feb. 17, 1805, JANE MEGQUIRE.

10736   JEMIMA, b. New Gloucester, Maine, July 6, 1782.

10737   THOMAS, b. New Gloucester, Maine, Feb. 28, 1784, m. PRISCILLA ———.

10738   REBECCA, b. New Gloucester, Maine, April 1, 1786.

10739   MARY, b. New Gloucester, Maine, Nov. 10, 1788.

10740   COMFORT, b. New Gloucester, Maine, July 6, 1789.

10741   JOSEPH, b. Poland, Maine, July 7, 1791.

10742   JOB, b. Poland, Maine, 1793, d. Oct. 31, 1864 and buried at Haines Corner Cem., East Livermore, Maine. m. 1st Dec. 5, 1820, REBECCA WYER; 2nd April 1822, JERUSHA (HAINES) FOSS.

10743   NATHANIEL, b. Poland, Maine, May 22, 1795, m. DEBORAH ———.

10744   JOHN COTTON, b. Poland, Maine, Mar. 26, 1797.

F10745 MOSES GREENLEAF, b. Poland, Maine, Feb. 28, 1799, d. Dec. 20, 1884, and buried at Haines Corner Cem., East Livermore, Maine, m. Mar. 22, 1821, ROSELLA HAINES.

10746   JABEZ B., b. Poland, Maine, 1802, m. May 9, 1829, HANNAH GRIFFIN.

10747   HANNAH, b. Poland, Maine, Oct. 15, 1803.

F10696 JOSEPH WEBSTER, born in Deer Isle, Maine, ca. 1770, and living in North Haven, Maine according to 1850 census, married in Deer Isle, Maine, Oct. 16, 1794, SARAH (SALLY) PRESSEY, born probably in Deer Isle, Maine, died in North Haven, Maine before 1850.

Deer Isle tax records show Joseph Webster of Deer Isle entered for poll tax for the years 1793 through 1798 and for personal and real estate taxes for 1796-7-8. Before leaving Deer Isle, Joseph, "yeoman", borrowed $500 from his brother, Ebenezer, Jr., who then hailed as a mariner from Cape Elizabeth, Cumberland County, Maine, per Vol. 7, p. 257, Hancock Registry of Deeds. The loan was secured by mortgage dated May 28, 1800 involving a parcel of land in Deer Isle adjoining the property of Chase Pressey and William Weed as well as a house, furniture, barn and farming utensils. Joseph was in Deer Isle that year long enough to be listed in the 1800 Census, then he departed, presumably to settle on North Haven on the northern part of the island. Today, this area is designated on maps as Webster Head.

Joseph does not appear as an owner of record on North Haven but his brother, Ebenezer, Jr. of Cape Elizabeth, does. Joseph's sons, Ebenezer and Andrew, acquire one-half of 110 acres belonging to their Uncle Eben in transactions recorded 1835 and 1837/8 per Knox County deeds, Vol. 3, p. 178 and p. 318.

According to George L. Hosmer's History of Deer Isle, Maine, Sarah (Pressey) Webster's grandfather, John Pressey, one of the "grantees of Deer Island, Maine", and his son, Charles (Sarah's uncle), both served in the Revolutionary War with "Roger's Rangers".

Children in 6th Generation

10748 JOHN, b. Deer Isle, Maine, Dec. 25, 1794, d. Deer Isle, Maine, April 5, 1795.

10749 SALLY, b. Deer Isle, Maine, Mar. 31, 1796, d. Jan. 15, 1839, m. THOMAS HOWARD of Deer Isle: intentions published Oct. 14, 1817 and Nov. 23, 1817.

10750 ANNA, b. Deer Isle, Maine, May 18, 1797, d. North Haven, Maine, Oct. 25, 1865, m. Mar. 18, 1817, ELISHA COOPER.

10751 EBENEZER, b. Deer Isle, Maine, Dec. 3, 1798, d. North Haven, Maine, July 28, 1855, m. North Haven, Maine, Nov. 29, 1824, OLIVE BROOK.

10752 MERCY, b. Deer Isle, Maine, ca. 1800, m. May 9, 1819, THOMAS COOPER.

10753 MARY PAGE, b. Bucksport, Maine, Dec. 20, 1803, m. probably North Haven, Maine, HIRAM PACKARD.

10754 ANDREW, b. probably North Haven, Maine, ca. 1804 and still living 1880 according to census, m. SARAH A. BROOK(S), b. ca. 1805.

F10755 JOSEPH, b. Castine, Maine, ca. 1809, d. Castine, Maine, June 24, 1876, m. Castine, Maine, July 22, 1832, EUNICE BOWDEN.

10756 LYDIA, b. North Haven, Maine, ca. 1814, d. probably in North Haven, Maine, m. Dec. 4, 1839, STEPHEN SAWYER of Vinalhaven.

10757 BETSEY, b. North Haven, Maine, ca. 1817, d. North Haven, Maine, Oct. 8, 1902 at age 85, m. EPHRAIM COOPER, b. ca. 1818.

F10713 WILLIAM JENNESS, born in Rochester, N. H., 1780, died in Rochester, N. H., July 8, 1864 or 1861, married in Rochester, N. H., Oct. 5, 1806, F10758a HANNAH SEAVEY, born in Rye or Rochester, N. H., died in Rochester, N. H. (buried, Meaderboro), May 15, 1847. Her mother was F1013 PRUDENCE P. MARDEN, daughter of F258 HANNAH BERRY and NATHANIEL MARDEN.

Children in 6th Generation

10758 EBENEZER, m. SUSAN HORNE.

10759 KEZIAH MARDEN, d. Feb. 25, 1871, aged 57 years, 9 months and 10 days, unmarried.

10760 PATIENCE, m. JOHN LANE.

F10761 HANNAH MARDEN, m. HAMILTON WENDELL.

10762 WILLIAM, m. SARAH HODGDON.

10763 GIDEON, b. May 8, 1822, d. Feb. 4, 1823.

10764 MARIA, b. Jan. 14, 1824, d. Nov. 13, 1888, unmarried.

SEVENTH GENERATION

F1366 STEPHEN DECATUR LOCKE, born in Falmouth, Maine, July 21, 1836, died in Raymond, Calif., April 16, 1909, married in Dutch Flat, Calif., Dec. 30, 1863, ANNA C. RODGERS, born in Pennsylvania, Aug. 11, 1846, died in Raymond, Calif., Mar. 5,1912.

Children in 7th Generation

F10765 WALTER PRESTON, b. Dutch Flat, Calif., Oct. 27, 1865, d. Napa, Calif., July 21, 1941.

10766 DAUGHTER, d. in infancy.

10767 DAUGHTER, d. in infancy.

10768 FRED, b. 1873, d. Death Valley, Calif., 1880.

10769 FRANK, b. 1875, d. Death Valley, Calif., 1880.

10770 VARA GENEVA, b. Calif., Aug. 20, 1878, d. Calif., Aug. 21, 1899.

F10771 LEON LEONARD, b. Raymond, Calif., Aug. 1, 1881, d. Berkeley, Calif., Jan. 18, 1953.

F1370 ELEANOR HOSMER LOCKE, born in Charleston, Maine, June 22, 1846, died in Arcata, Calif., Aug. 9, 1928, married in Clarence, Iowa, Sept. 27, 1869, WILLIAM LORD, born in Freedom, N.H., Feb. 8, 1840, died in Arcata, Calif., Nov. 12, 1919, son of William and Betsey (Lord) Lord.

He traveled to Calif. by way of the Isthmus of Panama at age 16 in 1857 and was a placer miner on the Klamath River until 1912. He had a grocery store in Orleans and was highly regarded by whites and Indians for his honesty and fairness.

Children in 7th Generation

F3452 OSCAR WILLIAM, b. Jim-ka-nee, nr. Orleans, Calif., Dec. 4, 1870, d. Eureka, Calif, Jan. 30, 1960.

F3453 LEWIS MORSE, b. Jim-ka-nee, nr. Orleans, Calif., Mar. 7, 1872, d. Martinez, Calif, Aug. 29, 1963.

F3457 CHARLES WILBUR, b. Jim-ka-nee, nr. Orleans, Calif., Jan. 23, 1874, d. Whittier, Calif., May 3, 1955.

3460 SARAH BETSEY, b. Savorrum, nr. Orleans, Calif., Mar. 31, 1876, d. Arcata, Calif., Dec. 28, 1971, m. Eureka, Calif., Feb. 6, 1908, SAMUEL HENRY LYTEL, b.

Windsor, Nova Scotia, Aug. 16, 1863, d. Arcata, Calif., Mar. 22, 1941, son of William and Ann Eliza (Redden) Lytel. She was a teacher.

3461   BENJAMIN HARDY, b. Arcata, Calif., July 2, 1878/9, d. Eureka, Calif., Dec. 20, 1959, m. Eureka, Calif., Dec. 10, 1908, LUCY EFFIE HASKINS, b. Halfday, III., June 27, 1885, d. Eureka, Calif., Aug. 19, 1964, daughter of Lewis Gould and Belle (Dayton) Haskins.

F3462   FRANK DANFORTH, b. Arcata, Calif., July 27, 1881, d. Knight's Ferry, Calif., Oct. 18, 1907.

F3464   EDWARD LOCKE, b. Arcata, Calif., Mar. 4, 1884.

F1371   LEONARD MORSE LOCKE, born in Charleston, Maine, July 26, 1849, died in Crockett, Calif., Jan. 2, 1933, married in Osceola, Nebr., Nov. 18, 1879, VIOLA LUCINDA CHASE, born in Portage, Wis., Oct. 22, 1860, died in Garfield, Wash., June 22, 1918, daughter of David and Mary (Briggs) Chase. Married by Simon Barrows, Corporal, Co. K., 32nd Regiment of Wisconsin Infantry.

Children in 7th Generation

F3465   BESSIE JANETTE, b. Wayland, Nebr., Jan. 8, 1881, d. Spokane, Wash., 1964.

F3466   LYDIA SUSANNA, b. Redfield, S.Dak., Sept. 18, 1882, d. Garfield, Wash., Sept. 19, 1917.

F3467   WALTER NORMAN, b. Redfield, S.Dak., Nov. 14, 1884.

F3468   ANTONE CHESTER, b. Redfield, S.Dak., Jan. 7, 1887, d. Rosario, Rep. Argentina, Feb. 15, 1964.

F3469   SARAH ELEANOR, b. Redfield, S.Dak., April 15, 1889, d. Colfax, Wash., Feb. 13, 1968.

F3470   ROBERT EARLE, b. Framington, Wash., Oct. 13, 1891, d. Richmond, Calif., Aug. 6, 1955.

F3471   MARY BELL, b. Garfield, Wash., April 3, 1894, d. Hill City, Idaho, Jan. 7, 1919.

3472   EDNA ULNA, b. Garfield, Wash., May 31, 1899, d. Garfield, Wash., Aug. 1, 1957.

3473   NELLIE, b. Garfield, Wash., Nov. 18, 1902, d. Garfield, Wash., Nov. 24, 1903.

F3474   DAVID ABIJAH, b. Garfield, Wash., Nov. 24, 1905, d. Crockett, Calif., Nov. 23, 1947.

F2398 CHARLES WOODMAN, born in Woodstock, N. H., May 24, 1822, died in Bridgewater, N. H., Nov. 11, 1899, married in Campton, N. H., May 20, 1848, JEMIMA AVERY, born in West Campton, N. H., Mar. 7, 1829, died in Bridgewater, N. H., Mar. 3, 1897, daughter of Jacob and Jemima (Cook) Avery.
He was a schoolteacher and merchant in Thornton, N. H.   Also, Justice of the Peace for 30 years and a Selectman in Woodstock in 1852.   He moved to Bridgewater in 1865 to take up farming.   Buried in Blair Cemetery, Campton, N. H.

Children in 7th Generation

2399 JACOB A.

2400 LYMAN B., d. 1923

2401 CHARLES S., a dentist in Ashland.

2405 ADDIE C., m. SIM BERRY

2406 CORYDON E., d. 1939

2407 Baby CORA, b. 1858 and died at 6 months.   Buried in Thornton, N. H.

F2408 AUSTIN WALLACE, b. Bridgewater or Thornton, N. H., April 5, 1865, d. Plymouth, N. H., Nov. 1939, m. Rumney, N. H., 1894, MARTHA STEVENS FRENCH.

F10724 JAMES MERROW, born in West Newfield, Maine, 1810, died in North Shapleigh, Maine, Sept. 9, 1875, married in Limington, Maine, BETSY MARR, born in Limington, Maine, Dec. 1812, died in Limington, Maine, Sept. 22, 1813, daughter of James and Lydia (Hobson) Marr.   She was a seventh generation descendant of William Hobson who came from England and settled in Rowley, Mass. about 1650.

Children in 7th Gen. b. in West Newfield, Maine

10772 DANIEL, b. April 15, 1837, d. buried North Shapleigh, Maine, Feb. 15, 1850.

F10773 ALMON HOBSON, b. April 22, 1841, d. Cape Neddick, Maine, May 1, 1918, m. York, Maine, Nov. 11, 1862, ELIZABETH LUNT WEBBER.

10774 MARY ABBIE, b. Feb. 1, 1849, buried North Shapleigh, Maine, Oct. 1, 1864.

10775 DANIEL FULLER, b. Mar. 5, 1851, d. Sanford, Maine, Feb. 17, 1919, m. Brookline, Mass., Feb. 15, 1881, NELLIE JANE MANLEY.

F10727 JOHN LOCKE, born in Belgrade, Maine, July, 1812, died in Poland, Maine, Jan. 13, 1890, married in Poland, Maine, HANNAH DUNN, born in Poland, Maine, 1812, died in Poland, Maine, Aug. 1, 1890.

Children in 7th Gen. b. in Poland, Maine

10776 ELVIN, b. 1837, d. 1894.

F10777 ELLEN, b. 1836, d. Poland, Maine, 1920, m. ELVIN D. PULSIFER.

10778 CHESTER, m. CLARA McAFFEE.

F10728 JESSE LOCKE, born in Belgrade, Maine, 1813, died in Poland, Maine, 1887, married 1st EUNICE STURGIS, 2nd MARY ANN FOSS, one of whom was born in Danville, Maine in 1816 and died in Poland, Maine in 1861.

Children in 7th Gen. b. in Poland, Maine

10779 HIRAM WARD, b. Jan. 24, 1845, d. Napa, Calif., Nov. 25, 1929. He never married.

F10780 EDWARD OSCAR, b. Oct. 16, 1850, d. Detroit, Mich., Sept. 14, 1937, m. HATTIE CLIFFORD GOWELL.

F10781 MARY ELIZABETH, b. Mar. 2, 1856, d. Poland, Maine, May, 1918, m. Poland, Maine, WILLIAM H. GOWELL.

F10732 ARTHUR WOODS MOULTON, born in Athol, Mass., Feb. 25, 1858, died in Fitchburg, Mass., Oct. 20, 1894, married in Athol, Mass., Jan. 12, 1884, DELLA DULCENA FISKE, born in Russell, N.Y., 1862, died in Fitchburg, Mass., Feb. 20, 1928.

On Nov. 23, 1880 he bought, in Athol, Mass., Mr. A. A. Ward's Grist Mill and began operation near the freight depot in the building owned by his father Mr. Albert G. Moulton. He moved into the ground floor of this building on July 3, 1883, being the first to employ the use of steam power in Athol for this purpose. On Aug. 13, 1889, due to ill health, he was forced to sell his grist mill to Mr. W. N. Potter of Greenfield, Mass. In an effort to save his health, having suffered a heart condition, he moved to Calif. but soon returned and died in Fitchburg, Mass. at age 36 before his full worth could ever be realized.

His widow married second in Concord, N.H. on Aug. 7, 1902 to Frank E. Kinsman of Fitchburg, Mass.

Children in 7th Gen. b. in Athol, Mass.

F10782 BLANCHE SFA, b. Mar. 6, 1886, d. Fitchburg, Mass., Oct. 11, 1942, m. Fitchburg, Mass., Sept. 25, 1906, EDGAR F. WRIGHT.

10783 MINNIE ELIZABETH, b. Mar. 6, 1886, d. Fitchburg, Mass. Feb. 7, 1951, m. Fitchburg, Mass., Aug. 31, 1918, STEPHEN DUFORT.

F10745 MOSES GREENLEAF HASKELL, born in Poland, Maine, Feb. 28, 1799, died in Livermore, Maine, Dec. 20, 1884, married in Livermore, Maine, Mar. 22, 1821, ROSELLA HAINES, born in East Livermore, Maine, Sept. 4, 1803, died in East Livermore, Maine, Jan. 23, 1892, daughter of Capt. Peter and Hannah (Fuller) Haines.

Children in 7th Generation

F10784 HESTER ANN R., b. Lowell, Mass., Feb. 10, 1822, d. East Livermore, Maine, Oct. 28, 1900, m. June 16, 1849, JOHN G. FRANCIS.

10785 MOSES GREENLEAF, JR., b. Oct. 8, 1823, d. April 15, 1848.

10786 MIRANDA JANE, b. Mar. 29, 1825, d. April 27, 1842.

10787 LOVINA H., b. Nov. 10, 1827, d. July 27, 1829.

10788 LOVINA H., SECOND, b. Feb. 8, 1830, d. June 7, 1853, unmarried.

10789 WILLIAM AUGUSTUS, b. Mar. 18, 1832, d. June 25, 1859.

10790 PETER HAINES, b. Nov. 9, 1833, d. May 23, 1873, m. Dec. 25, 1866.

10791 EDWIN BRADBURY, b. East Livermore, Maine, Aug. 24, 1837, d. Mar. 25, 1907, m. Aug. 29, 1861, CELIA HILL.

10792 ELEANOR ROSELLA, b. Aug. 4, 1839, d. July 19, 1924, m. 1886, CRAIG W. HASKELL.

10793 ARABELLE STANLEY, b. Dec. 9, 1841, d. Oct. 7, 1905.

10794 CLARENCE GLYNDON, b. East Livermore, Maine, Aug. 2, 1843, d. Mar. 30, 1865, unmarried.

10795 CLEMENT CALDWELL, b. April 16, 1847, d. Feb. 17, 1900, m. Nov. 19, 1879.

F10755 JOSEPH WEBSTER, born in Castine, Maine, ca. 1809, died in Castine, Maine, June 24, 1876, married in Castine, Maine, July 22, 1832, EUNICE BOWDEN, born in Castine, Maine, ca. 1805, died in Castine, Maine, May 29, 1880. He was principally a farmer. Probate records list his death as on June 17, 1876.

Children in 7th Gen. b. in Castine, Maine

10796 JOSEPH, JR., b. Sept. 28, 1832, d. Castine, Maine, Jan. 8, 1860.

10797   IRA, b. Mar. 14, 1834, d. Castine, Maine, 1907, m. Castine, Maine, Int. Pub. Sept. 19, 1860, AMANDA WEBSTER, b. Oct. 24, 1845, daughter of Andrew and Mary (Hill) Webster of Penobscot, Maine.

10798   JULIA ANN, b. Feb. 8, 1836, d. prob. Penobscot, Maine, Aug. 10, 1874, m. 1859, HUDSON DEVEREUX of Penobscot, Maine.

10799   LITTLETON, b. April 8, 1838, d. Irish, or Indian Bend, La., May 27, 1863, unmarried. He enlisted Oct. 11, 1862 and served with Co. E of the 26th Reg., Maine Volunteers; wounded on May 8, 1863 at the Battle of New Orleans.

10800   LOIS FRANCES, b. May 1, 1840, m. FRANCIS FARNHAM, b. 1826/7, son of Joseph and Betsy (Binney) Farnham.

10801   ALBERT, b. Oct. 17, 1842, d. Castine, Maine, Aug. 5, 1923, m. 1878, HANNAH (BOWDEN) WEBSTER, widow of his brother, Thomas Hillman. She d. Castine, Maine, Sept. 26, 1883, age 33. Albert served with Co. A of the 14th Reg., Maine Volunteers.

10802   THOMAS HILLMAN, b. Sept. 26, 1844/5, d. Castine, Maine, Nov. 20, 1875, m. Nov. 26, 1868, HANNAH L. BOWDEN, daughter of Thomas Bowden of Orland, Maine. Thomas served in the U. S. Navy during the Civil War.

F10803   EDWARD EUGENE, b. Oct. 12, 1848, d. Castine, Maine, Dec. 1, 1922, m. prob. Penobscot, Maine, Nov. 9, 1878, SARAH HEATH.

F10761   HANNAH MARDEN JENNESS, born in Meaderboro, Rochester, N. H., July 28, 1816, died in Dover, N. H. (buried Pine Hill), Nov. 25, 1889, married in Rochester, N. H., Dec. 29, 1851, HAMILTON WENDELL, born in Dover, N. H., Sept. 7, 1827, died in Dover, N. H., Jan. 24, 1864.

Children in 7th Generation

F10804   CHARLES EDWIN, b. Jan. 17, 1854.

10805   CLARENCE WILLIAM FRANCIS, b. Jan. 7, 1857, d. Mar. 1, 1939, m. ISABEL, daughter of Alexander Frazier of Dover. They are buried on Pine Hill in Dover, N. H.

EIGHTH GENERATION

F2408 AUSTIN WALLACE WOODMAN, born in Thornton or Bridgewater, N. H., April 5, 1865, died in Plymouth, N. H., Nov. 1939, married in Rumney, N. H., 1894, MARTHA STEVENS FRENCH, born in Rumney, N. H., Dec. 1867, died in Plymouth, N. H., May, 1955, daughter of Lorenzo Hastings and Elizabeth (Kelly) French.

They are both buried at Riverside Cemetery, Plymouth, N. H.

He was a student at New Hampton Institute and studied dentistry at Boston Dental College. He graduated in 1891 and opened chambers in Plymouth, N. H. in 1893. A charter member of Baker River Lodge #47, Knights of Pythias, in 1895. President of New Hampshire Dental Society in 1929. First "paid" delegate to American Dental Association from N. H. in 1928. Hunter and woodsman, he built a camp at Campton Bog with two cronies at a pond now known as "Rowbartwood Pond" (for Rowe, Bartlett and Woodman).

His wife was a direct descendant of William French who came to Cambridge, Mass. in 1635 and was one of the first settlers of Billerica, Mass. in 1656.

Children in 8th Gen. b. in Plymouth, N. H.

2402   CHARLES LORENZO, b. July 16, 1896, m. Aug. 9, 1921, MARGUERITE MERRILL.

F2403   ROGER FRENCH, b. April 13, 1898, m. Pepperell, Mass., July 2, 1924, CLARA MEREDITH SMITH.

2404   GEORGE BARTLETT, b. Feb. 2, 1904, m. 1927, MARY ANN MEEHAN.

F2667 FREDERICK ELISHA LADD, born in Atlanta, Georgia, Dec. 20, 1868, died in Fort Payne, Alabama, Nov. 7, 1944, married in Columbus, Georgia, ATLANTA GERTRUDE JOHNSON, born in Taunton, Mass., July 24, 1870, died in Fort Payne, Alabama, March 4, 1961. He attended the North Georgia Agricultural College at Dahlonega, Ga. and St. James College, Annapolis, Md. He spent one year in Nome, Alaska, operating a jewelry store in conjunction with his brother-in-law, A. L. Delkin. He chartered a ship and sailed to Siberia where he traded for fur, whalebone and ivory.

He was a charter member of Piedmont Lodge 447, Free and Accepted Masons, Atlanta, Ga. and was a member of the Old Guard, Gate City Guard, Atlanta.

He moved to Ft. Payne, Ala. in 1908 and was partner in Ladd-Birchy Brick Co.; he later bought Birchy's interest and formed the

Southern Refractories Co., for manufacture of Fire Brick and the Ladd
Fullers Earth Co., for mining clay.

Children in 8th Generation

F10806 FREDERICK ELISHA, JR., b. Atlanta, Ga., Nov. 7, 1901,
d. Fort Payne, Ala., Jan. 19, 1932, m. Muskegon,
Mich., Aug. 11, 1923, OPAL BRAZILIA HILL.

F10807 EDWARD JOHNSON, b. Boston, Mass., Nov. 24, 1906,
m. Fort Payne, Ala., Sept. 15, 1931, WILLIE LEE
GILBREATH.

F3308 WATEA ANN LOCKE, born in Richmond, R.I., April 19,
1835, died in Fairburg, Nebr., Mar. 15, 1899, married in Sangamon
Co., Ill., May 15, 1859, Rev. GEORGE ABEL PEASE, born in Oak
Orchard, N.Y., June 18, 1830, died in Fairburg, Nebr., Mar. 4,
1889.

Children in 8th Generation

6563 GEORGE ALMON, b. New Berlin, Ill., Aug. 10, 1861,
d. New Berlin, Ill., Mar. 2, 1869.

6564 MINNIE MIRIAM, b. near Fidelity, Ill., Oct. 21, 1863,
d. Calif. (?), m. INGRAM L. ARMSTRONG.

6565 WINNIE WINSOME, b. near Fidelity, Ill., Oct. 21, 1863,
d. Fairbury, Nebr., May 31, 1880.

F6566 AUTUMN VINE, b. Fidelity, Ill., Sept. 14, 1866, d. June
12, 1934.

6567 ALICE CAREY, b. Stonington, Ill., Aug. 31, 1871, m. Oct.
14, 1896, CHARLES HESS GROSS.

6568 CICADA LILLY, b. Fairbury, Ill., Nov. 13, 1874, d. Fairbury, Ill., July 30, 1875.

10808 MABEL OLA (adopted), b. Jefferson County, Nebr., Jan.
3, 1876, m. SAM MEYERS.

F3312 CHARLES HORACE LOCKE, born in Kingston, R.I., Mar.
26, 1848, died in Monrovia, Calif., July 2, 1898, married in Stonington, Ill., Feb. 24, 1874, CATHERINE HENRIETTA GARWOOD, born
in Stonington, Ill., Jan. 17, 1855, died in Denver, Colo., July 2,
1901, daughter of William and Catherine (Forrester) Garwood.

Children in 8th Generation

F6580 BERTHA EDITH, b. Cass Co., Iowa, Mar. 4, 1875, d.
Chicago, Ill., Nov. 16, 1957.

F6581 ARTHUR AUSTIN, b. Cass Co., Iowa, Nov. 18, 1884, d. Pontiac, Ill., Aug. 23, 1969.

F6582 CORENA STEWART, b. Long Beach, Calif., Sept. 1, 1896.

F3441 RICHARD FOSS LOCKE, born in Arcadia, Iowa, April 13, 1876, died in Glen Ellyn, Ill., April 25, 1962, married in Byron Co., Ill., July 30, 1903, GRACE TAYLOR HENCH, born in Byron (Ogle Co.), Ill., May 17, 1879, died in Glen Ellyn, Ill., April 10, 1963, daughter of William and Sara Jane (Taylor) Hench.

He was a lawyer giving special attention to school district affairs. He was a past master of the Masons for over 50 years. She had a great interest in genealogy.

Children in 8th Generation

F10809 SARAH DOROTHY, b. Rockford, Ill., Oct. 22, 1904.

F10810 JOHN ROBERT, b. Rockford, Ill., Mar. 8, 1906.

F10811 EDWARD TAYLOR, b. Rockford, Ill., July 3, 1907, d. Woodstock, Ill., April 16, 1948.

F10812 RICHARD FOSS, JR., b. Rockford, Ill., Mar. 23, 1909.

F10813 DONALD STEPHEN, b. Rockford, Ill., Nov. 2, 1910.

F10814 PHILIP FRANCES, b. Rockford, Ill., Aug. 10, 1912.

F10815 FREDERICK NATHANIEL, b. Edison Park, Ill., Oct. 19, 1914.

F10816 HELEN MARION, b. Evanston, Ill., July 19, 1916.

F10817 ELEANOR GRACE, b. Wilmette, Ill., Jan. 4, 1918.

F10818 WILLIAM MORSE, b. Glen Ellyn, Ill., Dec. 27, 1919.

F10819 ELIZABETH BRUCE, b. Glen Ellyn, Ill., Feb. 22, 1922.

F10820 MARJORIE RUTH, b. Glen Ellyn, Ill., Sept. 30, 1924.

F3442 SARAH ELIZABETH LOCKE, born in Arcadia, Iowa, Mar. 27, 1880, died in Rockford, Ill., April 14, 1941, married in Rockford, Ill., Mar. 24, 1904, LESTER WARREN LILLIE, born in Rockford, Ill., June 20, 1878, died in Rockford, Ill., April 23, 1966, son of Julius Newton and Caroline Elizabeth (Beatson) Lillie.

Children in 8th Gen. b. in Rockford, Ill.

F10821 LUMAN LOCKE, b. July 13, 1905.

10822 ROY ELVYN, b. June 12, 1907, d. Rockford, Ill., Jan. 19, 1909.

10823 HAZEL CAROLINE, b. April 20, 1909, d. Rockford, Ill., Jan. 12, 1911.

10824 LUCILLE ETHEL, b. June 23, 1911, m. Rockford, Ill., Nov. 9, 1932, RAYMOND FRANCIS SCHMITT, b. near Ottawa, Ill., Sept. 1, 1904, d. Rockford, Ill., July 10, 1950, son of William and Elizabeth (Sauter) Schmitt.

F3443 JOHN LOCKE HERRICK, born in Charleston, Maine, Oct. 22, 1854, died in Fresno, Calif., June 24, 1944, married 1st in Boston, Mass., Nov. 16, 1880, FANNIE E. LAMSON, born in Atkinson, Maine, April 19, 1863, died in Charleston, Maine, Sept. 13, 1894, daughter of H. A. and Rachael (Lowe) Lamson; 2nd in Charleston, Maine, May 31, 1896, FRANCES OLIVIA PLUMMER, born in Dexter, Maine, July 5, 1865, died in Fresno, Calif., July 27, 1944, daughter of George and Jane (Curtis) Plummer.

Children in 8th Gen. b. in Charleston, Maine

6632 JOHN HENRY, b. Sept. 2, 1881, d. Rutherford, N. J., Aug. 26, 1922, m. Fall River, Mass., Dec. 24, 1919, ALICE HOWE.

F6633 RODNEY LAMSON, b. Oct. 27, 1892, d. Fresno, Calif., Oct. 19, 1936.

Children of 2nd wife.

F6634 GLADYS PLUMMER, b. Oct. 10, 1897.

F10825 GRACIA ELIZABETH, b. July 28, 1899, d. Fresno, Calif., July 15, 1928, m. Madera, Calif., Dec. 23, 1925, FREEMAN B. DYER, b. Saco (?), Maine. A son, 11123, in 9th Gen. b. Fresno, Calif., June 18, 1928 and d. the same day.

F10826 GEORGE LINCOLN, b. Nov. 13, 1905, d. Sacramento, Calif., April 12, 1973.

F3444 MARY JERUSHA HERRICK, born in Charleston, Maine, Nov. 22, 1855, died in Osceola, Nebr., Mar. 7, 1926, married in Charleston, Maine, Feb. 12, 1879, JOHN COLEMAN STONE, born in Brownfield, Maine, July 31, 1854, died in Kezar Falls, Maine, Mar. 10, 1913, son of Warren Norton and Eliza Ann (Quint) Stone.

Children in 8th Generation

6635 MARION ELIZABETH, b. Charleston, Maine, Feb. 12, 1881, d. Greenland, N. H., May 28, 1907.

F6636 ELEANOR HARDY, b. Charlestown, Mass., Mar. 8, 1883, d. Melrose, Mass., Sept. 30, 1958.

F3445 RODNEY IRVING HERRICK, born in Charleston, Maine, Oct. 6, 1857, died in Portland, Ore., Jan. 3, 1931, married in Plankinton, S. Dak., Oct. 5, 1886, ANNAHA RAUGH HONENS, born in Rock Island, Ill., Oct. 5, 1866, died in San Leandro, Calif., May, 1948, daughter of William David and Elizabeth J. (Maxwell) Honens.

He spent several years in Riga, Russia as a Representative of the McCormick Harvester Company.

Children in 8th Generation

F10827 RODNEY LIONEL, b. Plankinton, S. Dak., Aug. 2, 1887, d. San Diego, Calif., June 24, 1963.

10828 WILARD EATON, b. 1896, d. Riga, Russia, April, 1905.

F3446 LINCOLN HERRICK, born in Charleston, Maine, Feb. 18, 1861, died in Los Angeles, Calif., Feb. 27, 1953, married in Madera, Calif., May 1, 1899, MARY ALVERDA HANSEN, born in San Francisco, Calif., July 8, 1880, died in Fresno, Calif., Dec. 26, 1918, daughter of Peter and Mary (Purvis) Hansen.

Children in 8th Generation

F10829 MARY ELIZABETH, b. Madera, Calif., Jan. 23, 1902.

F3447 SUSIE MARIE HERRICK, born in Charleston, Maine, Feb. 6, 1871, died in Bangor, Maine, Nov. 11, 1919, married in Charleston, Maine, Sept. 14, 1890, WALTER ALONZO DANFORTH, born in Bangor, Maine, July 12, 1870, died in Bangor, Maine, July 4, 1948, son of Alonzo T. and Lois (Elden) Danforth.

Children in 8th Generation

F6637 EARLE HERRICK, b. Boyd Lake, Maine, Oct. 16, 1891.

F6638 HELEN LOIS, b. Boyd Lake, Maine, Oct. 9, 1892.

F10830 GORDON WALTER, b. Bangor, Maine, Feb. 9, 1903.

10831 PAUL LORIMER, b. Bangor, Maine, Aug. 17, 1909, m. Elkton, Md., Oct. 29, 1938, HILDA MURIEL STEVENSON, daughter of Henry Joseph and Emmie (Howard) Stevenson.

F3448 DANIEL ABIJAH HERRICK, born in Charleston, Maine, Sept. 16, 1877, died in Charleston, Maine, Mar. 14, 1941, married in Medford Center, Maine, July 2, 1903, LILLIAN IOLA WEYMOUTH, born in Medford Center, Maine, Oct. 27, 1881, died in Marblehead, Mass., Sept. 3, 1969, daughter of Andrew Jackson and Charlotte Prudence (Powers) Weymouth.

Children in 8th Generation

F10832   IRVING WEYMOUTH, b. Medford Center, Maine, May 16, 1904, d. Saco, Maine, Aug. 17, 1966.

F10833   CHARLOTTE ELIZABETH, b. Medford Center, Maine, Jan. 17, 1906.

F10834   DANIEL ARLAND, b. Foxcroft, Maine, June 5, 1908.

F10835   JOHN ANDREW, b. Charleston, Maine, Mar. 10, 1912.

F10836   LILLIAN ROBERTA, b. Stockton Springs, Maine, Sept. 16, 1915.

F10837   PRUDENCE IOLA, b. Bowdoin, Maine, Jan. 2, 1918.

F10838   THEODORE LOCKE, b. Lisbon Falls, Maine, Feb. 3, 1922.

F10839   JOSEPHINE SHIRLEY, b. Lisbon Falls, Maine, Feb. 7, 1923.

F3452   OSCAR WILLIAM LORD, born in Jim-ka-nee, near Orleans, Calif. Dec. 4, 1870, died in Eureka, Calif., Jan. 30, 1960, married in Eureka, Calif., May 17, 1893, LOTTIE LYDIA RIDDELL, born in San Francisco, Calif., Dec. 17, 1872, died in Eureka, Calif., Sept. 3, 1945, daughter of William Swain and Martha (Baskerville) Riddell.

He was superintendent of the Eureka, Calif. water works for several years and later was Mayor for four years. He then entered a real estate and insurance business.

Children in 8th Gen. b. in Eureka, Calif.

6639   CLARENCE WILLIAM, b. July 23, 1894, m. 1st Eureka, Calif., June 19, 1918, VIOLA MONTGOMERY, b. Blue Lake, Calif., Dec. 19, 1895, d. Oakland, Calif., June 17, 1943, daughter of James Allen and Eleanor (McCready) Montgomery; m. 2nd Phoenix, Ariz., April 8, 1944, EDNA AREMENTA RHEW, b. Corpus Cristi, Texas, Oct. 15, 1902, daughter of Frank Henry and Edna Allen (Redus) Rhew, Sr.

F6640   MIRIAM RIDDELL, b. July 7, 1898.

F6641   RUTH, b. Oct. 26, 1905.

6642   ELEANOR, b. Dec. 4, 1907, d. Eureka, Calif., Mar. 22, 1908.

F3453   LEWIS MORSE LORD, born in Jim-ka-nee, near Orleans, Calif., Mar. 5, 1872, died in Martinez, Calif., Mar. 29, 1963, married in Etna, Calif., Nov. 16, 1898, ABBIE ANN DOLL, born in

Etna, Calif., Dec. 9, 1875, died in Martinez, Calif., Aug. 5, 1961, daughter of Josiah and Katherine (Simon) Doll. He was a bookkeeper and assisted his father in the mines on the Klamath River.

Children in 8th Generation

3454 ALICE MAE, b. Orleans, Calif., Oct. 30, 1899.

F3455 CHARLES HERBERT, b. Etna, Calif., Feb. 7, 1901, d. San Francisco, Calif., Sept. 27, 1967.

3456 KATHERINE ELEANOR, b. Eureka, Calif., June 16, 1904.

F3457 CHARLES WILBUR LORD, born in Jim-ka-nee, near Orleans, Calif., Jan. 23, 1874, died in Whittier, Calif., May 3, 1955, married in Eureka, Calif., June 29, 1904, HENRIETTA ROSSINA CAMILLA HANSEN, born in Hamilton, Minn., Feb. 5, 1878, died in Whittier, Calif., Aug. 28, 1956, daughter of Andres D. and Mette Christine (Hansen) Hansen. He was a teacher and bookkeeper.

Children in 8th Generation

F3458 HAROLD WILBUR, b. Eureka, Calif., Aug. 20, 1905.

F3459 ROY STANLEY, SR., b. Samoa, Calif., May 28, 1907.

F10840 METTA FRANCES, b. El Centro, Calif., Nov. 16, 1915.

F10841 EARL MALCOLM, b. San Diego, Calif., Aug. 19, 1917.

F3462 FRANK DANFORTH LORD, born in Arcata, Calif., July 27, 1881, died in Knights Ferry, Calif., Oct. 18, 1907, married in Murphys, Calif., April 23, 1907, IRENE ETHEL McQUIG, born in Murphys, Calif., June 20, 1885, died in Redding, Calif., Nov. 16, 1964, daughter of James and Anna Maria (Curren) McQuig.

Children in 8th Generation

F3463 FRANK DANFORTH, JR., b. Angels Camp, Calif., Mar. 7, 1908.

F3464 EDWARD LOCKE LORD, born in Arcata, Calif., Mar. 4, 1884, married in Berkeley, Calif., June 25, 1914, LILIAN GLADYS THAXTER, born in Machias, Maine, Mar. 21, 1890, died in Albany, Calif., Sept. 10, 1962, daughter of Oscar and Georgia Theresa (Hoar) DeCourcy.

He graduated from the University of California in 1907 with a B.S. degree in electrical engineering. He was employed by Electric Storage Battery Co. (EXIDE) for forty-four years, retiring in 1954. His retirement was anything but retiring. In 1956 he published "The Lord-Locke Genealogy" and he was a significant contributor to this volume. His many hobbies include woodworking and he proudly displays a beautiful grandfather clock he has made with over 600 pieces of wood in it. After his 90th birthday he traveled 9000 miles around the U.S. visiting friends and relatives and attending the 1974 Locke Family Association reunion. Although he refers to himself as "the Old Man", others think of him as the "No-age-arian".

Children in 8th Generation

F10842 MARY ALICE, b. Berkeley, Calif., Sept. 8, 1920.

F3465 BESSIE JANETTE LOCKE, born in Wayland, Nebr., Jan. 8, 1881, died in Spokane, Wash., Mar. 20, 1966, married in Garfield, Wash., Jan. 1, 1900, HENRY WILLIS PEDEN, born in Ohio, July 10, 1872, died in Seattle, Wash., Oct. 10, 1946, son of Henry D. and Louisa Peden.

Children in 8th Generation

F10843 CHESTER FREDERICK, b. Gifford, Idaho, Dec. 10, 1900.

F10844 JESSIE LOUISE, b. Gifford, Idaho, Nov. 6, 1902.

F10845 VERA VIOLA, b. Gifford, Idaho, Jan. 12, 1905.

F10846 ELLA MARIE, b. Gifford, Idaho, Dec. 30, 1906, d. Lebanon, Ore., Oct. 2, 1947.

F10847 MARY IVAL, b. Garfield, Wash., April 2, 1909.

10848 HENRY JORDAN, b. Garfield, Wash., April 20, 1912, d. Riddle, Ore., Oct. 1, 1973, m. 1st Marshfield, Ore., Aug. 22, 1944, LETHA KATHLEEN HAZELTON, b. North Bend, Ore., Sept. 7, 1915, daughter of Lester Louis and Birdie May (Barker) Hazelton; 2nd Reno, Nev. June 16, 1956, THELMA ELIZABETH SEYMOUR, b. Anacortes, Wash., July 4, 1915, daughter of Louis and Julia (Brewster) Seymour.

F10849 EDITH ELDORE, b. Malo, Wash., April 22, 1919.

10850 CHARLES NORMAN, b. Malo, Wash., July 16, 1923, d. South Pacific (navy), Oct. 25, 1943.

F3466 LYDIA SUSANNA LOCKE, born in Redfield, S. Dak., Sept. 18, 1882, died in Garfield, Wash., Oct. 19, 1917, married in Cora, Idaho, Dec. 6, 1902, ROBERT RICHARD DAILEY, born in Ames, Iowa, April 22, 1873, died in Garfield, Wash., Mar. 11, 1944, son of Robert Karr and Eleanor (Hughes) Dailey.

Children in 8th Generation

F10851 LOVELLA EVELINE, b. Garfield, Wash., Feb. 10, 1904, d. Colfax, Wash., Aug. 9, 1948.

F10852 VIOLA VIRGINIA, b. Garfield, Wash., Nov. 12, 1905,
d. Colfax, Wash., Dec. 17, 1974.

F10853 JOE KARR, b. Latah Co., Idaho, July 9, 1909, d. Bellevue, Wash., April 8, 1971.

F10854 WALTER RICHARD, b. Latah Co., Idaho, July 10, 1912.

F10855 DONALD MORRIS, b. Garfield, Wash., Nov. 5, 1914,
d. Potlatch, Idaho, April 1, 1974.

F3467 WALTER NORMAN LOCKE, born in Redfield, S. Dak.,
Nov. 14, 1884, married in Boise, Idaho, Jan. 1, 1924, MABEL
CECILIA ANDERSON, born in Genesee, Idaho, July 4, 1901, daugh-
ter of Charles William and Hannah Olive (Gamberg) Anderson.

Children in 8th Gen. b. in Lewiston, Idaho

F10856 ROBERTA ARLENE, b. Mar. 1, 1930.

F10857 GAIL CLEO, b. Dec. 16, 1934.

F3468 ANTONE CHESTER LOCKE, born in Redfield, S. Dak.,
Jan. 7, 1887, died in Rosario, Rep. of Argentina, Feb. 15, 1964,
married in La Plata, Rep. of Argentina, Nov. 8, 1918, CATALINA
MOLLOY, born in Rep. of Argentina, Nov. 25, 1892, daughter of
Michael and Helen (Kelly) Molloy. Following several years with the
U.S. Marines, he went to Argentina, South America with the Swift
Meat Company.

Children in 8th Generation

F10858 HELEN LIDIA, b. Buenos Aires, Rep. of Argentina, Aug.
3, 1919.

10859 MARIA LORRAINE, b. Rosario, Rep. of Argentina, Feb. 23,
1929, m. Rosario, Rep. of Argentina, Feb. 5, 1952,
LESLIE ALBERTO SHOOBRIDGE, b. Tucumán, Rep. of
Argentina, Nov. 10, 1927, son of Stanley A. and Mar-
garita (Benitz) Shoobridge.

F3469 SARAH ELEANOR LOCKE, born in Redfield, S. Dak.,
April 15, 1889, died in Colfax, Wash., Feb. 13, 1968, married in
Garfield, Wash., Oct. 13, 1907, CHARLES MILES DAILEY, born in
Latah Co., Idaho, Oct. 29, 1877, died in Garfield, Wash., Mar. 7,
1962, son of Robert Karr and Eleanor (Hughes) Dailey.

Children in 8th Gen. b. in Garfield, Wash.

F10860 ELVA LOUISE, b. Nov. 18, 1909.

F10861 CHARLES LEONARD, b. June 17, 1913.

F10862 EDNA ALMA, b. Sept. 20, 1915, d. Pullman, Wash., July 26, 1970.

F10863 ROY ARNOLD, b. Nov. 7, 1923.

F3470 ROBERT EARL LOCKE, SR., born in Farmington, Wash., Oct. 13, 1891, died in Albany, Calif., Aug. 6, 1955, married in Martinez, Calif., Nov. 29, 1922, GAY NELL (MASON) CRAVENS born in Hopkinville, Ky., Mar. 2, 1900, died in Sacramento, Calif., July 27, 1976, daughter of Robert Edward and Virginia (Adcock) Mason.

Children in 8th Gen. b. in Crockett, Calif.

F10864 SUSAN VIOLA, b. Sept. 2, 1923.

F10865 BARBARA ANN, b. Oct. 10, 1924.

F10866 MARGARET LOUISE, b. Sept. 29, 1927.

F10867 ROBERT EARL, JR., b. July 9, 1931.

F3471 MARY BELL LOCKE, born in Garfield, Wash., April 3, 1894, died in Hill City, Idaho, Jan. 7, 1919, married in Hill City, Idaho, Feb. 20, 1915, CECIL RAY FRANCIS, born in Lillian, Nebr., Feb. 8, 1894, died in Hill City, Idaho, Jan. 6, 1919, son of Fred Lincoln and Ellen Leonora (Dupray) Francis.

Children in 8th Gen. b. in Hill City, Idaho

10868 NINA MAY, b. Oct. 8, 1915, m. Malo, Wash., June 16, 1934, LEWIS MELVIN HILDERBRAND, b. Spangle, Wash., July 20, 1909, son of Samuel and Hattie (Rust) Hilderbrand.

F10869 JUNE EVELYN, b. June 28, 1917.

F3474 DAVID ABIJAH LOCKE, born in Garfield, Wash., Nov. 24, 1905, died in Crockett, Calif., Nov. 23, 1947, married 1st in Oakland, Calif., June 29, 1924, ROSE MARIE CAMELLO, born in Denver, Colo., Feb. 5, 1907, died in Oakland, Calif., Jan. 28, 1931, parents unknown except as Dr. Camello; 2nd in Reno, Nev., Oct. 29, 1934, EVA IMARONE, born in San Francisco, Calif., Oct. 12, 1905, daughter of Matteo and Teresa (Gatto) Imerone.

Children in 8th Gen. b. in Oakland, Calif.

10870 VIOLA JUNITA, b. Nov. 9, 1925.

F10871 MYRTA BELLE, b. Jan. 28, 1928.

F10872 ALICE MAY, b. Mar. 30, 1929.

F3722 JOHN F. LOCKE, born in Mt. Vernon, Maine, Feb. 15, 1826, died Nov. 3, 1903, married Aug. 1, 1851, BETSEY P. STARIN of Mt. Vernon, born June 24, 1831, died July or Sept. 22, 1905.

Children in 8th Generation

F10873 EDSON, b. Oct. 21, 1862, d. Jan. 1928, m. Sept. 26, 1888, IDA MAY STEVENS of Mt. Vernon, Maine.

F10874 LELA SYLVINA, b. Dec. 18, 1864, d. May 19, 1948, m. June 7, 1883, EDWARD PAYSON HUSSEY of Augusta, Maine.

F10875 FRED JOHN, b. Mt. Vernon, Maine, Sept. 23, 1867, d. Augusta, Maine, May 3, 1931, m. Mt. Vernon, Maine, Nov. 26, 1894, ELOISE M. FELLOWS.

F3728 BENJAMIN EMERY LOCKE, born in Mt. Vernon, Maine, April 25, 1843, married in Mt. Vernon, Maine, ELIZABETH LORD BEAN, born May 9, 1846, died Oct. 27, 1878.

He was a salesman for United Shoe Machinery Corp. of Beverly, Mass. She was daughter of Jesse K. and Betsy Lord Bean of Mt. Vernon. He married 2nd EDITH A. CHAMBERLAIN at Natick, Mass., Jan. 1, 1882. She died Nov. 15, 1947.

Children in 8th Gen. b. in Mt. Vernon, Maine

F10876 SAMUEL, b. Mar. 13, 1866, d. Nahant, Mass., April 12, 1937, m. Lynn, Mass., May 29, 1890, MINNIE FARMER PATTEN CURRY.

F10877 AURILLA BEAN, b. Feb. 24, 1868, d. Lynn, Mass., June 12, 1957, m. Lynn, Mass., Nov. 14, 1888, FRANK BUTLER REYNOLDS.

F10878 CARROL EMERY, b. Feb. 28, 1870, d. Winthrop, Maine, Dec. 13, 1862, m. Oct. 8, 1890, LUELLA POPE.

F4282 MARY EMMA PHILBRICK, born in Seabrook, N. H., July 15, 1842/43, died in New York City, Dec. 18, 1919, married Seabrook, N. H. (?), Sept. 13, 1866, HORACE A. GODFREY, born in Hampton Falls, N. H., April 7, 1840, died in Hampton Falls, N. H., Oct. 9, 1905. He was a farmer and Postmaster in Hampton Falls. Their house is on Route one and still stands.

Children in 8th Gen. b. in Hampton Falls, N. H.

First two children, John P. and Alida died young.

4284 ADELINE, b. 1875, d. New York City, about 1955, m. ROBERT S. DANA.

4285 PERSIS EMILINA, b. Oct. 23, 1880, d. Providence, R.I.,
Oct. 28, 1956, m. Sept. 9, 1903, PHILIP B. SIMONDS.

4286 SARAH PERKINS (changed name to DOROTHY), b. 1882,
d. Drayden, Md., about 1960.

F4405 JACOB F. LOCKE, married CATHERINE NEWELL, born in
Buckstown, Maine. He is known to have been a sailor.

Children in 8th Generation

F10879 CHARLES WINFIELD, b. Dayton, Maine, Mar. 28, 1850,
d. Yarmouth, Maine, Dec. 21, 1942, m. Fort Fairfield,
Maine ??, MARY ANN JUDKINS.

10880 WILLIAM P.

10881 ELLA, d. Newburyport, Mass., m. GEORGE GOOCH and
had: 10882 LUCY LANOUETTE; 10883 BELLE, m. RAY
LEWIS; 10884 HOWARD; all b. Newburyport, Mass.

F4434 LYDIA L. VARNEY, born in Farmington, N.H., Aug. 12,
1840, died in Farmington, N.H., Mar.30, 1915, married in Barnstead,
N.H., Nov. 23, 1876, JOHN FRANK SCRUTON, born in Strafford,
N.H., Nov. 8, 1841, died in Farmington, N.H., May 11, 1927.
She taught rural school before her marriage. They operated a
working farm in Farmington, N.H. northwest of Blue Job Mt. They
raised three children of his first wife, Sarah Berry Hayes. They were
Clara, Otis and Jessie Hayes. Their farm was prosperous.

Children in 8th Gen. b. in Farmington, N.H.

F4435 EUNIETTA SARAH, b. Oct. 18, 1879, d. Rochester, N.H.,
May 7, 1917, m. Rochester, N.H., Nov. 15, 1905,
ALBERT ELI MEADER.

F4436 ARTHUR GARFIELD, b. Oct. 1, 1881, d. Rochester, N.H.,
early 1970's (buried Crown Point Cemetery, Strafford,
N.H.), m. Farmington, N.H., Feb. 5, 1921, MABEL
C. FARNUM.

4437 ALICE, probably died young.

F4482 NANCIE LOCKE, born in Barnstead, N.H., Oct. 13,
1833, died in Alton, N.H., Dec. 5, 1888, married in Natick, Mass.,
JAMES W. "MARTIN" KIMBALL, born Mar. 28, 1825.
The name of Nancie Locke's husband is given as James W. "Martin" Kimball in the book "John Hayes of Dover, N.H., A book of his
family" Vol. II, page 460 by Katharine F. Richmond. Relatives now
living only remember him being called "Jim" Kimball, a man of short
temper.

Children in 8th Generation

F4483 AMANDA JANE, b. Alton, N. H., Oct. 23, 1854, d. Farmington, N. H., Feb. 7, 1917, m. Pittsfield, N. H., Jan. 1, 1881, FRED ALLISTON GILES.

F4484 LAURA, m. JOHN S. HILL.

F4485 SETH H., b. Feb. 1, 1859, d. Alton, N. H., May 31, 1927, m. Pittsfield, N. H., MARY ELLEN SHAW.

F4486 IDA F., b. Alton, N. H., Aug. 1861, d. Center Barnstead, N. H., Feb. 8, 1932, m. FRANK S. NUTTER.

10885 ADDIE M., b. April 6, 1864, d. July 6, 1866.

10886 infant, b. Mar. 13, 1868, d. July 1, 1868.

F4487 MARTIN LUTHER HAYES, b. Oct. 13, 1869, m. Gilmanton, N. H., Feb. 2, 1895, ALICE MAY HURD, b. 1878, d. May 14, 1935.

F4930 SAMUEL BLAKE LOCKE, born in Deerfield, N. H., April 28, 1822, died in Andover, Mass., Nov. 24, 1901, married in Newmarket, N. H., ANNA HOOK BROWN DAVIS, born in Newmarket, N. H., 1827, died in Andover, Mass., 1926.

Children in 8th Generation

8254 ANNIE LOUISE, b. Malden, Mass., Aug. 12, 1847, d. Andover, Mass., 1909, a teacher, unmarried.

F8255 ABBY CUMMINGS, b. Charlestown, Mass., July 8, 1851, d. Andover, Mass., Dec. 1938, m. Andover, Mass., T. DENNIE THOMSON.

8261 SAMUEL BLAKE, JR.

F8260 CLARA TASH, b. Sept. 2, 1853, d. Baltimore, Md., m. Oct. 29, 1885, FRANCIS JORDAN THOMSEN.

8263 FLORENCE MADELEINE, b. 1858, d. Andover, Mass., 1934, a teacher, unmarried.

8264 MARION, b. Andover, Mass., d. Andover, Mass., m. HENRY CLINTON MORRISON

F5147 FLORA ESTHER LOCKE, born in Epsom, N. H., June 2, 1854, died in Manchester, N. H., May 28, 1937, married Sept. 8, 1825, EDWARD OSCAR SANDERSON, born in Pittsfield, N. H., May 18, 1835, died in Pittsfield, N. H., Sept. 25, 1917.

He operated and owned a dry goods store in Pittsfield, N. H. She was a very good piano player and gave piano lessons. She had a very good voice, wrote both poetry and songs, and she was a very sedate and matronly woman.

Children in 8th Generation

F5148 HELEN LOCKE, b. Epsom, N. H., May 20, 1880, d. Manchester, N. H., Nov. 30, 1963, m. Boston, Mass., May 3, 1905, JOHN EDGAR MARSTON.

F5286 JOHN CALVIN GARLAND, born in Rye, N. H., Nov. 26, 1813, died in North Hampton, N. H., April 28, 1889, married Jan. 4, 1835, ELIZABETH SPEED, born in Durham, N. H., Oct. 11, 1814, died in North Hampton, N. H., Oct. 11, 1851, daughter of William and Mary (Thompson) Speed of Durham and Newmarket, N. H.

Children in 8th Generation

10887 ELIZABETH ROWE, b. April 2, 1836, d. April 3, 1836.

10888 JOHN WESLEY, b. Sept. 2, 1837, d. New Castle, N. H., April 9, 1850.

10889 CALVIN THOMPSON, b. June 15, 1839, d. North Hampton, N. H., July 10, 1898, m. Austin, Texas, May 21, 1877, ELIZABETH MARY EVANS.

10889a MARSHALL W., b. May 17, 1841, d. Olustee, Fla., Feb. 22, 1864, killed in Civil War.

10890 CHARLES WILLIAM, b. April 6, 1843, d. Calif., 1928, m. Jefferson, Texas, July 12, 1871, Mrs. HELEN(JOHNSON) McKEE.

10891 MARY ABBY (twin), b. June 17, 1845, d. Feb. 12, 1848.

10892 ELIZABETH A. (twin), b. June 17, 1845, d. Portsmouth, N. H., May 20, 1909, m. 1st Aug. 10, 1868, JOHN FROST, 2nd C. WOODBURY BROWN, brother to Moses.

F10893 HENRIETTA, b. July 15, 1846, d. Rye, N. H., May 28, 1938, m. Rye, N. H., Dec. 11, 1869, MOSES BROWN, brother to C. Woodbury Brown.

10894 ABBY HANNAH (later called Annah A.), b. Aug. 21, 1849, d. 1898, m. North Hampton, N. H., Nov. 24, 1868, CHARLES N. KNOWLES.

F5622 MARIA H. LOCKE, born in Lee, N. H., Dec. 26, 1838, died in South Berwick, Maine, April 24, 1907, married Dec. 6, 1866, LEVI HOWARD, born in Rochester, N. H., Feb. 25, 1829, died in Belgrade, Maine, Aug. 12, 1890, son of Moses and Rebecca (Welch) Howard of Rochester, N. H.

Attended public schools of Rochester, a carpenter by trade all his life, and took contracts to build houses at the age of 20. He was a violin maker of considerable note. So anxious to serve his country in

F2412 Stephen H. Locke

F5628 Abbie A. Locke

the Civil War that he went to the nearest place, Dover, N. H. and joined Company H, 9th Regiment, New Hampshire Volunteers, taking part in the principal engagements, twice wounded and later captured as a prisoner. At the close of the war, he was mustered out with the 8th Maine Regiment, returning with his own gun which he took with him when he joined up. He was a member of the Independent Order of Odd Fellows and the South Berwick Methodist Episcopal church of South Berwick, Maine where he lived after the war.

Children in 8th Generation

8807 SARAH H. FOOTE, b. Sept 24, 1857, d. May 1, 1882.

8808 ETTA GERTRUDE, b. Rochester, N. H., June 4, 1868, d. Beverly Farms, Mass., Feb. 15, 1934, unmarried. She attended the public schools of Rochester, N. H. and Berwick Academy of South Berwick, Me., studying for a school teacher, but on account of eye impairment, was forced to abandon this vocation and instead became an experienced hand in any and all kinds of work in the stitching room of shoe shops in Somersworth, N. H. and South Berwick and Biddeford, Me. A member of the South Berwick Methodist Episcopal church, organist for that church, and a member of the Locke Family Association for 15 years.

F8809 ARTHUR DAME, b. Rochester, N. H., May 1, 1870, d. Beverly Farms, Mass., Feb. 21, 1937, m. Milo, Maine, Nov. 3, 1890, EMMA WHITNEY. He received his education in the public schools of South Berwick and Berwick Academy. In early life he was a boot black, later had a good knowledge of the cotton industry and was a Second Hand in a factory. He studied telegraphy and, on becoming proficient, accepted a job with the Boston & Maine Railroad as ticket agent and telegrapher at Ipswich, Mass., later at Everett and Beverly Farms, Mass. He was a member of the Knights of Pythias of Ipswich.

F8810 ALBERT OREN, b. Rochester, N. H., Aug. 27, 1874, d. Biddeford, Maine, July 2, 1932, m. Saco, Maine, Oct. 27, 1897, SARAH ELIZABETH OWEN.

F5628 ABBIE A. LOCKE, born in Deerfield, N. H., Jan. 13, 1847, died in East Candia, N.H., Sept. 4, 1915, married in Fremont, N.H., June 1, 1875, JOHN HENRY MOORE(S), of Fremont, born in Hampstead, N. H., 1846, died in Brentwood, N. H., Jan. 24, 1930. She was a hard working soul who earned what little luxury she could afford. He was a farmer and shoe maker and generous to a fault. They inherited a farm in East Candia, N. H. where they lived.

Children in 8th Generation

8817   IOLA A., b. Fremont, N. H., Dec. 7, 1876, d. at age 21 or 22, m. ——TURCOTT, and had: 10895 MAYLAND EARL.

8818   SARAH E., b. Fremont, N. H., June 14, 1880, died young.

8819   FANNIE E., b. Raymond, N. H., Mar. 2, 1882, m. DAVID P. LOVERING, a farmer, and lived in Derry, N. H. Had: 10896 BERTHA; 10897 MYRON.

F8820   GEORGE HENRY, b. Raymond, N. H., April 4, 1886, m. Somerville, Mass., Sept. 4, 1910, ALICE BLANCH MORSE.

10898   BETSY, d. a baby.

F5751 ELIZA JANE HOOK, born in Pembroke, N. H., Oct. 29, 1831, died in Fitchburg, Mass., Mar. 22, 1922, married in Manchester, N. H., Dec. 21, 1850, F5298 EDWARD PERKINS, born in Pembroke, N. H., June 23, 1830, died in Fitchburg, Mass., Nov. 22, 1909.

Children in 8th Generation

10899   ELLA JANE, b. Concord, N. H., June 12, 1853, d. Fitchburg, Mass., Jan. 8, 1926, m. CHARLES N. ORDWAY, no children.

10900   ANNA MAY, b. Concord, N. H., Dec. 19, 1860, d. Fitchburg, Mass., Mar. 16, 1948, unmarried.

F10901   EDWARD EVERETT, b. Feb. 1, 1866, d. Aug. 28, 1938, m. 1st Sept. 24, ?, LOTTIE A. KENT, 2nd, Tunbridge, Vt., May 18, 1904, HARRIETTE F. CHADWICK.

10902   MINNIE BELLE, b. Lowell, Mass., Oct. 30, 1870, d. Fitchburg, Mass., unmarried.

F5752 CHARLES HENRY HOOK, born in Boscawen, N. H., Jan. 12, 1834, died in Sacramento, Calif., April 29, 1920, married 1st FANNIE BRUCE (TAY) MERRILL, born in Bedford, N. H., Jan. 12, 1833, died in Stoneham, Mass., late 1880's, 2nd in Sulphur Springs, Colo., LOIS (KENNEY) HAMLIN.

Children in 8th Generation

F10903   ADDIE BURBANK, b. Dunbarton, N. H., May 23, 1859, d. Dec. 6, 1940, m. 1st 1878, MEBIS BURT, 2nd PERCEY MYRON GODDARD.

F10904   NELLIE ELIZA (SAUNDERS), b. Nov. 15, 1862, d. Gloucester, Mass., May 27, 1930, m. Dr. WILLIAM

ROWLEY. She lived with Dr. and Mrs. Saunders after she was six years old, they called her Nellie Lincoln Saunders but she was never legally adopted.

Child of 2nd wife.

F10905 GEORGE, b. Sulphur Springs, Colo., Sept. 12, 1880, m. SADIE A. PINE.

F5754 ELBRIDGE CARTER HOOK, born in Concord, Mass., April 3, 1836, died in Lynn, Mass., Nov. 6, 1890, married ABBY BUTLER.

Children in 8th Generation

10906 CARRIE ETTA, b. Lynn, Mass., Dec. 3, 1861, d. Lynn, Mass., May 12, 1883.

10907 EDGAR LESLIE, b. Lynn, Mass., Dec. 23, 1865, d. Lynn, Mass., Oct. 10, 1867.

10908 FRED ELMER, b. Lynn, Mass., Oct. 2, 1868, d. Lynn, Mass., May 1, 1920.

F10909 SARAH ABBIE, m. Lynn, Mass., Oct. 1, 1898, FRED DANIELS DODGE.

F5755 MARY FRANCES HOOK, born in Chichester, N. H., Oct. 29, 1842, died in Harvard, Mass., Dec. 4, 1924, married in Manchester, N. H., Jan. 9, 1865, BENJAMIN FRANKLIN COBB, born in Canal Fulton, Ohio, Jan. 24, 1844, died in Chicago, Ill., Aug. 26, 1923.

Children in 8th Generation

10910 GERTRUDE ELIZA, b. Concord, N. H., Oct. 20, 1867, d. Harvard, Mass., Aug. 23, 1912, m. Roxbury, Mass., June 19, 1895, EDGAR WILLIS COTTLE (no children).

F10911 GEORGE FRANKLIN, b. Charlestown, Mass., June 14, 1876, d. St. Augustine, Fla., Mar. 28, 1955, m. Roxbury, Mass., Oct. 7, 1901, GERTRUDE ELISABETH HUMPHRY.

F10765 WALTER PRESTON LOCKE, born in Dutch Flat, Calif., Oct. 27, 1865, died in Napa, Calif., July 21, 1941, married in Fresno, Calif., July 21, 1891, ALMA ESTELLE SEABROOKE, born in Leavenworth, Kans., Jan. 1, 1874, died in Petaluma, Calif., May 31, 1972, daughter of William and Martha (Cowan) Seabrooke.

Children in 8th Gen. b. in Raymond, Calif.

F10912 WILBUR DEE, b. May 19, 1892, d. Newport, Ore., Sept. 26, 1964.

F10913 STEPHEN LeROY, b. Feb. 12, 1895.

F10914 WINNIE AILEEN, b. Dec. 22, 1905, d. Sept. 14, 1972.

F10915 ALMA ANITA, b. June 15, 1907.

F10771 LEON LEONARD LOCKE, born in Raymond, Calif., Aug. 1, 1881, died in Berkeley, Calif., Jan. 18, 1953, married in Fresno, Calif., 1913, GRACE C. MOLTZ, born in Australia, Sept. 16, 1886, died in Modesto, Calif., June 13, 1924.

Children in 8th Generation

10916 ALICE CLAUDINA, b. Raymond, Calif., Dec. 23, 1915.

F10917 LEONA ELIZABETH, b. Modesto, Calif., Aug. 6, 1921.

F10773 ALMON HOBSON MERROW, born in West Newfield, Maine, April 22, 1841, died in Cape Neddick, Maine, May 1, 1918, married in York, Maine, Nov. 11, 1862, ELIZABETH LUNT WEBBER, born in Cape Neddick, Maine, April 22, 1841, died in Cape Neddick, Maine, Nov. 23, 1921.

They lived in Cape Neddick where he first taught school. Later he taught at York and Ogunquit. After teaching he carried on a farm and operated a saw mill. For many years he was selectman of York. Still later he conducted a general store and was postmaster at Cape Neddick. His large white house stands today on the main highway through York (Route 1). The house was owned and occupied by his son Lawrence Everett Merrow until the latter's death there in 1945. This son carried on the farm. Both are buried in a family cemetery on the property along with his parents and grandparents.

Children in 8th Gen. b. in Cape Neddick, Maine

10918 GRACE MAUD, b. Oct. 18, 1863, d. Cape Neddick, Maine, June 24, 1869.

10919 LAWRENCE EVERETT, b. Nov. 8, 1864, d. Cape Neddick, Maine, Dec. 14, 1945, m. Cape Neddick, Maine, Jan. 28, 1925, LAURA GOWEN (WOODWARD) CARD, a widow.

10920 BERTHA TILDEN, b. May 18, 1866, d. Cape Neddick, Maine, April 11, 1879.

10921 RALPH HARTLEY, b. Jan. 24, 1868, d. Saco, Maine, Mar. 26, 1960, m. Saco, Maine, June 1, 1892, SISIE GRANT LEAVITT.

10922 GRACIE, b. Sept. 24, 1868, died in infancy.

10923 ALMON LINCOLN (twin), b. Oct. 3, 1871, d. Cape Neddick, Maine, Aug. 27, 1873.

F10924 ARTHUR SAMUEL (twin), b. Oct. 3, 1871, d. Reading, Mass., Mar. 26, 1960, m. Boston, Mass., June 9, 1908, HELEN GENEVA TOLMAN.

F10777 ELLEN LOCKE, born in Poland, Maine, 1836, died in Poland, Maine, 1920, married ELVIN D. PULSIFER.

Children in 8th Generation

F10925 ROSA, b. Aug. 20, 1860, d. 1946, m. EBEN EVELETH.

10926 ADDIE, b. 1865, d. 1964.

F10780 EDWARD OSCAR LOCKE, born in Poland, Maine, Oct. 16, 1850, died in Detroit, Mich., Sept. 14, 1937, married HATTIE CLIFFORD GOWELL.

Children in 8th Generation

10927 HARVEY WARD, b. Jan. 7, 1886, m. FLORENCE PARSONS.

10928 MERRITT CALDWELL, b. Nov. 12, 1887.

10929 HAROLD AUBREY, b. April 14, 1889, m. MYRTLE SPEEDY.

10930 JESSE SUMNER, b. June 5, 1890.

10931 LIDA MADELINE, b. Dec. 17, 1892, m. LOUIS MILLER.

10932 EUNICE STURGIS, b. April 4, 1894, m. ——— GRANT.

10933 GRACE GOWELL, b. April 25, 1896, m. 1st ——— HOOD, 2nd ——— WATSON.

10934 VERNA VELORA, b. May 6, 1897, m. ——— FULLER.

10935 ARTHUR CURTIS, b. July 16, 1899, unmarried.

10936 HOLLIS BRAY, b. April 18, 1901.

10937 ERNEST GOWELL, b. Oct. 23, 1904, died young.

F10781 MARY ELIZABETH LOCKE, born in Poland, Maine, Mar. 2, 1856, died in Poland, Maine, May, 1918, married in Poland, Maine, WILLIAM HENRY GOWELL.

Children in 8th Generation

F10938 ERNEST EDWARD, b. Dec. 29, 1883, d. 1940.

10939 ROGER LOCKE, b. Nov. 21, 1893, m. ELLA F. SAMPSON. He is living in Poland, Maine on the farm purchased by his grandfather, Jesse Locke, in 1838.

10940 WILMA MAY, b. May, 1897, died young.

F10782 BLANCHE SFA MOULTON, born in Athol, Mass., Mar. 6, 1886, died in Fitchburg, Mass., Oct. 11, 1942, married in Fitchburg, Mass., Sept. 25, 1906, EDGAR FRANCIS WRIGHT, born in Brookline, N.H., July 25, 1881, died in Fitchburg, Mass., Aug. 21, 1942.

He owned and operated a Texaco Service Station in Fitchburg, Mass. from 1933 until his death in 1942, having previously been employed as General Foreman for the Putnam Machine Co. He was a member of the Fitchburg Lodge of Masons for many years attaining the rank of 32nd degree mason.

Children in 8th Gen. b. in Fitchburg, Mass.

10941   GWENDOLYN ESFA, b. June 14, 1908, m. Hoosick Falls, N.Y., June 13, 1928, PAUL SANTELLA.

F10942 ARTHUR MOULTON, b. Oct. 31, 1913, m. Derry, N.H., Dec. 25, 1934, OLIVE VIRGINIA WELLS.

10943   PHYLLIS ILEEN, b. Mar. 13, 1917, m. Derry, N.H., April 3, 1938, GORDON MARTIN.

F10784 HESTER ANN R. HASKELL, born in Lowell, Mass., Feb. 10, 1822, died in East Livermore, Maine, Oct. 28, 1900, married in Lowell, Mass., June 16, 1849, JOHN G. FRANCIS, born in England, May, 1824, died in East Livermore, Maine, Jan. 23, 1893.

Children in 8th Generation

F10944 CHARLES MOSES, b. Lowell, Mass., June 27, 1850, d. East Livermore, Maine, Nov. 14, 1928, m. June 5, 1881, LAURA BLACK WARREN.

10945   HENRIETTA S. "Nettie", b. Concord, N.H., Aug. 7, 1854, d. East Livermore, Maine, Jan. 1, 1929, m. SETH H. WATSON.

10946   WILLIAM A., b. Lenoxville, Quebec, Canada, Sept. 13, 1857, d. East Livermore, Maine, Jan. 13, 1937, never married.

10947   GEORGIA H., b. Canada, June 8, 1859, d. Leeds, Maine, Oct. 12, 1946, m. 1879, WALLACE LANE FRANCIS.

F10803 EDWARD EUGENE WEBSTER, born in Castine, Maine, Oct. 12, 1848, died in Castine, Maine, Dec. 1, 1922, married prob. Penobscot, Maine, Nov. 9, 1878, SARAH HEATH, born in Penobscot, Maine, 1861, died in Castine, Maine, 1931.

"Capt. Gene" and his son, Emery, were involved in coast-wise trade. Each had at one time his own vessel. Capt. Gene's was a two-master named the "C.M. Gray" (54.6 x 18.9 x 4.8) which was built in

1872 in Sedgwick, Maine, by Capt. Augustus L. Gray, and named for his mother, Charlotte (McKenzie) Gray.

Emery Webster's vessel was the "L. A. Stetser", built in 1864 at Somers Point, New Jersey. The dimensions of the "Stetser" were: 48.1 x 17.6 x 4.9.

A third vessel, the "Inez" (70.0 x 22.5 x 6.3) was built in 1882 at Millbridge, Maine which they operated together from 1905 on. They hauled lime, brick, and products of a Penobscot, Maine cooperage down the Bagaduce River and across Penobscot Bay to Rockland, Maine. From about 1945 to 1965, the main and main top-mast of the "Inez" stood in the northwest corner of the Maine Maritime Academy athletic field in the village of Castine, Maine, used as a flag pole.

Children in 8th Gen. b. in Castine, Maine

F10948 EMERY H., b. Jan. 1, 1880, d. Castine, Maine, 1951, m. MABEL BOWDEN of Penobscot, Maine.

10949   HARVEY, b. ca. 1882, d. Castine, Maine, 1892, age 10.

10950   infant son who died in 1887 before named.

F10804 CHARLES EDWIN WENDELL, born in Dover, N.H., Jan. 17, 1854, died in Dover, N.H., Mar. 23, 1933, married in Dover, N.H., Mar. 22, 1882, ELLEN AUGUSTA SNELL, born in Dover, N.H., Mar. 3, 1860, died in Dover, N.H., April 25, 1933.

He lived at 34 Mt. Vernon St., Dover, N.H. and was a member of Strafford Lodge #29 A.F. & A.M., Mt. Pleasant Lodge I.O.O.F., Board of Aldermen, Board of Trustees of Pine Hill Cemetery, Board of Trustees of Wentworth Home for the Aged and Official Board, St. John's M.E. Church in Dover. Also, he served as the Representative from Ward 1 to the State House of Representatives. She served on the Board of Governors of the Dover Children's Home and was a member of St. John's M.E. Church and Order of the Eastern Star.

Children in 8th Generation

F10951 CHESTER SNELL, b. Aug. 8, 1887.

NINTH GENERATION

F2403 ROGER FRENCH WOODMAN, born in Plymouth, N. H., April 13, 1898, married in Pepperell, Mass., July 2, 1924, CLARA MEREDITH SMITH, born in Concord, N. H., Nov. 10, 1900, daughter of Charles William and Clara (Wennberg) Smith.

He was a sailor in the U. S. Navy in World War I and graduated from the University of Maine at Orono in 1921. He lived and worked in Plymouth, N. H. until 1942, when he moved to Weston, Mass. and was with the War Production Board during World War II. Sales Manager for "Ramset" powder-actuated tool, division of Winchester/Olin until retirement. Member of Weston Golf Club and at one time an active skier, hunter, fisherman. Fifty-year member of the Masonic Lodge, Plymouth, N. H.

Children in 9th Generation

F10952 NANCY, b. West Lebanon, N. H., Feb. 8, 1928, m. Belmont, Mass., Sept. 14, 1963, DONALD P. DRESSLER.

F3455 CHARLES HERBERT LORD, born in Etna, Calif., Feb. 7, 1901, died in San Francisco, Calif., Sept. 27, 1967, married in Berkeley, Calif., May 16, 1925, RITA MAE RUTLEDGE, born in McAlester, Okla., April 6, 1906, daughter of Robert Taylor and Harriett Amanda (Willingham) Rutledge.

Children in 9th Generation

10953 ROBERT LEWIS, b. Berkeley, Calif., Mar. 9, 1926, m. 1st, San Diego, Calif., Jan. 24, 1953, RUTH BRADY; 2nd, San Francisco, Calif., Dec. 24, 1967, GERALDINE LYNCH.

F10954 CHARLES RUTLEDGE, b. Watsonville, Calif., Dec. 19, 1929.

F3458 HAROLD WILBUR LORD, born in Eureka, Calif., Aug. 20, 1905, married in Pasadena, Calif., July 25, 1928, DORIS SHIRLEY HUFF, born in Grand Rapids, Mich., April 10, 1905, daughter of Charles Monroe and Katherine (Van Hoven) Huff.

Children in 9th Generation

F10955 JOANN SHIRLEY, b. Schenectady, N.Y., Dec. 22, 1929.

F10956 ALAN WILBUR, b. Schenectady, N. Y., Mar. 18, 1932.

F10957 NANCY LOUISE, b. Schenectady, N. Y., Oct. 2, 1934.

F10958 HAROLD WAYNE, b. Schenectady, N. Y., Oct. 30, 1942.

F3459 ROY STANLEY LORD, born in Samoa, Calif., May 28, 1907, married in Pasadena, Calif., May 28, 1931, RUTH JANE BONTHIUS, born in Amoy, China, April 22, 1910, daughter of Dr. Andrew and Nellie (DeYoung) Bonthius.

He received a B.S. degree in Civil Engineering from the Calif. Institute of Technology.

Children in 9th Generation

F10959 JAMES MYRON, b. Pasadena, Calif., May 28, 1934.

F10960 ROY STANLEY, JR., b. Pasadena, Calif., Oct. 11, 1939.

F3463 FRANK DANFORTH LORD, JR., born in Angels Camp, Calif., Mar. 7, 1908, married in Castella, Calif., July 2, 1938, MARIAN (JACOX) OLSEN, born in Flint, Mich., Feb. 6, 1908, daughter of Stanley Forbes and Ida Mae (Conger) Jacox.

He received a B.S. from University of California and served in the Navy during World War II.

Children in 9th Generation

10961 ROBERT EDWARD, b. Redding, Calif., April 2, 1945, m. Toledo, Ohio, Dec. 11, 1976, SONYA MARIE JUN- KINS, b. Toledo, Ohio, June 4, 1951, daughter of Charles Thomas and Opal (Maples) Junkins.

F10962 FRANCES MARIAN, b. Redding, Calif., May 5, 1948.

F4285 PERSIS EMELINA GODFREY, born in Hampton Falls, N.H., Oct. 23, 1880, died in Providence, R.I., Oct. 28, 1956, married in Hampton Falls, N.H., Sept. 9, 1903, PHILIP BALDWIN SIMONDS, born in Lexington, Mass., Nov. 3, 1879, died in Providence, R.I., Feb. 19, 1961.

She made many rugs to her own design including braided and hooked rugs. Also enjoyed needlepoint. She devoted much of her life to her family and grandchildren.

He was successful in the investment business and retired at age 38 due to dissatisfaction with the ethics of his business partners. Spent the rest of his life in civic work and served many years as President of the Providence Boys' Club.

Children in 9th Generation

10963 GODFREY BALDWIN, b. Belmont, Mass., Aug. 13, 1904, d. Providence, R.I., Nov. 26, 1952, m. Providence, R.I., Feb. 22, 1930, MARY CAROLYN VAIL.

F10964 PHILIP BALDWIN, JR., b. Belmont, Mass., Sept. 1, 1906, m. Providence, R.I., June 7, 1935, ESTHER MERRIMAN.

10965 BARBARA CLARKE, b. Providence, R.I., May 19, 1913,
    m. Providence, R.I., Aug. 2, 1947, JOHN A. GAY-
    NOR.

10966 ADELINE COLE, b. Providence, R.I., July 20, 1914, m.
    1st, Providence, R.I., May 1, 1936, LAURENCE LISLE;
    2nd, Providence, R.I., April 30, 1948, JOHNS HOP-
    KINS CONGDOR II.

F10967 CLARKE, b. May 1, 1917, m. 1st, Little Compton, R.I.,
    Sept. 16, 1941, DEBORAH SNOW; 2nd, Providence,
    R.I., June 16, 1967, MARY V. HATCH.

F4435 EUNIETTA SARAH SCRUTON, born in Farmington, N.H.,
Oct. 18, 1879, died in Rochester, N.H., May 7, 1917 in childbirth,
married in Rochester, N.H., Nov. 15, 1905, ALBERT ELI MEADER,
born in Rochester, N.H., Mar. 10, 1875, died in Holyoke, Mass.,
May 17, 1974.
She attended Dover Business School and was a rural school teacher
before her marriage. She was sociable, played piano, and did fancy
work and sewing. Albert and his brother Dana operated a dairy farm
and apple orchard. He was a rural mail carrier and was active in the
Meaderboro Quaker Church. He was able to care for himself into his
90's and died "in his 100th year of bronchitis".

Children in 9th Generation

F10968 ALICE GERTRUDE, b. Rochester, N.H., Nov. 22, 1906,
    m. Holyoke, Mass., June 15, 1939, O. LENARD
    MOQUIN.

F10969 LEON BURTON, b. Rochester, N.H., Nov. 27, 1908.

F10970 LEOLA MAE, b. Rochester, N.H., Aug. 1, 1910.

F10971 EDITH ARLINE, b. Rochester, N.H., Jan. 29, 1914.

10972 unnamed son, stillborn, May 7, 1917.

F4436 ARTHUR GARFIELD SCRUTON, born in Farmington, N.H.,
Oct. 1, 1881, died in Rochester, N.H.(hospital), early 1970's, buried
Crown Point Cemetery, Strafford, N.H., married 1st, ETHEL LA-
POINTE and divorced (no children); 2nd, MABEL C. FARNUM in
Farmington, N.H., Feb. 5, 1921. She was born in Ossipee, N.H.,
1881, the daughter of William and Amanda (Mills) Kendall. She died
in 1961.

Children in 9th Generation

F10973 FRANK JOHN, b. Farmington, N.H., Feb. 13, 1922, m.
    Webster, N.H., PAULINE PHELPS.

F4483 AMANDA JANE KIMBALL, born in Alton, N.H., Oct. 23, 1854, died in Farmington, N. H., Feb. 7, 1917, married in Pittsfield, N. H., Jan. 1, 1881, FRED ALLISTON GILES, born May 1, 1858, died in Farmington, N. H., Feb. 9, 1948.

Children in 9th Generation

10974 CLARA INEZ, b. Barnstead, N.H., Aug. 7, 1884, d. Dover, N. H., June 26, 1970, m. Everett, Mass., April 8, 1921, ARTHUR BUZZELL WENDELL, b. Augusta, Maine, Feb. 5, 1872, d. Cambridge, Mass., April 3, 1935.

10975 PEARL NANCY, b. Farmington, N. H., July 9, 1892, d. Rochester, N. H., July 16, 1979. She was valedictorian of her high school graduating class and went to Dover Business College. Worked at Portsmouth Shipyard for 38 years. While there she struck the first arc in the laying of the keel of the submarine USS Grudgeon.

F10976 EVERLYN MARIE, b. Farmington, N. H., Feb. 6, 1895.

F4484 LAURA KIMBALL, married JOHN S. HILL. They both died sometime before 1932.

Children in 9th Generation

10977 ADDIE M., m. 1st, —— HUCKINS who was drowned; 2nd, Oct. 14, 1922, HARRY I. HAYES.

10978 LORING, m. ADA COLBATH.

10979 WILLEY, m. twice

10980 NELSON, m. 1st, RUBY HERSAM; 2nd, FLORENCE HURD KIMBALL.

F4485 SETH H. KIMBALL, born Feb. 1, 1859, died in Alton, N. H., May 31, 1927, married in Pittsfield, N. H., MARY ELLEN SHAW, died in Alton, N.H., 1931.

Children in 9th Generation

10981 FANNIE

10982 RALPH HAYES, m. FLORENCE HURD.

10983 HELEN

10984 RUBY, d. 1975, m. BRANDON HALL

F4591 RAYMOND FELLOWS, born in Bucksport, Maine, Oct. 17, 1885, died in Bangor, Maine, Sept. 3, 1957, married probably in Bucksport, Maine, 1909, MADGE GILMORE, born in Dedham, Maine, Dec. 15, 1884, died in Bangor, Maine, June 25, 1966.

He was educated in Bucksport public schools, the Eastern Maine Conference Seminary there, and the University of Maine, Orono, and the University of Maine Law School in Bangor. He entered law practice with his father, Hon. Oscar F. Fellows, in Bucksport and Bangor, Maine. After the retirement of Oscar, and subsequent death in 1921, the law firm of Fellows & Fellows continued with him and his brother, F4592 Frank Fellows. In 1925, he was named Attorney General of the State of Maine. After he was appointed a Judge of Superior Court, and Frank was elected to Congress, the firm continued several years with their lawyer sons, Frank F10987 and Oscar F10989. Judge Raymond Fellows was appointed later an Associate Justice of the Maine Supreme Judicial Court, and 1954-1956, served as Chief Justice.

She was educated in Bucksport public schools and the Eastern Maine Conference Seminary there, and at the National Park Seminary in Washington, D.C. She was the daughter of Pascal Pearl Gilmore of Dedham, Maine, b. June 24, 1845, and his wife, Alma Maria Hart of Holden, Maine, b. July 28, 1859.

Children in 9th Generation

F10985 MARGARET, b. Bangor, Maine, Nov. 22, 1909, m. Verona Island, Maine, JOHN W. WHITE.

10986 ROSALIE, b. Bangor, Maine, May 10, 1913, m. 1st, WOODROW W. PIERCE of Bucksport, Maine, who died in 1956 in Boston, Mass.; 2nd, ARTHUR CARL RANDALL of Richmond, Maine, who saw action on board a destroyer in the South Pacific serving with the U.S. Navy during World War II. She was educated in Bangor public schools and the Maine State Teachers College, Farmington.

F10987 FRANK, b. Bangor, Maine, Nov. 26, 1914, m. MARIANNE RUSSELL.

F4592 FRANK FELLOWS, born in Bucksport, Maine, Nov. 7, 1889, died in Bangor, Maine, Aug. 27, 1951, married in Bucksport, Maine, June 27, 1910, GEORGIE ELEANOR MALING, born in Brewer, Maine, May 14, 1889, died in Bangor, Maine, Jan. 2, 1964.

He attended public schools and the Eastern Maine Conference Seminary in Bucksport, Maine, and the University of Maine, Orono, Maine, and the University of Maine Law School, Bangor, Maine; admitted to the bar in 1911. Removed to Portland, Maine to practice law; clerk of the United States District Court of Maine in Portland, Maine, 1917-1920. In the following 20 years, he resided in Bangor, Maine, where he practiced law with his brother F4591 Raymond. In 1940, he was elected to represent the then Third Congressional District of Maine in the 77th U.S. Congress, and re-elected to the 78th, 79th, 80th, 81st and 82nd Congresses until his death Aug. 27, 1951.

She was a trained nurse, housewife and mother of the five children and was a daughter of Melvin E. Maling (April 1, 1856–Feb. 6, 1946) and his wife, Georgie Anna Gilmore (Sept. 3, 1856–Oct. 29, 1903), both of Brewer, Maine.

Children in 9th Generation

F10988 ELIZABETH, b. Bangor, Maine, April 7, 1911, d. Bridge-port, Conn., Jan. 31, 1964, m. Utah, July 8, 1943, STANLEY B. NICHOLS.

F10989 OSCAR, b. Portland, Maine, Jan. 13, 1913, m. 1st, Tops-ham, Maine, June 16, 1934, ANGELA JOHNSON; m. 2nd, CAROLINE ALLEN.

F10990 JOAN, b. Portland, Maine, Dec. 6, 1917, m. 1st, in Maine, Sept. 1934, EDWARD S. McLAUGHLIN; 2nd, PAUL A. KLINE.

F10991 RAYMOND, b. Bangor, Maine, April 17, 1922, d. Bangor, Maine, May 17, 1974, m. Bangor, Maine, Aug. 21, 1943, FAITH ST. GERMAIN.

F10992 WILLIAM ALBERT, b. Bangor, Maine, Nov. 23, 1925, m. Bucksport, Maine, June 18, 1960, LUCILLE ARLENE WEBSTER.

F5148 HELEN LOCKE SANDERSON, born in Epsom, N.H., May 20, 1880, died in Manchester, N.H., Nov. 30, 1963, married in Boston, Mass., May 3, 1905, JOHN EDGAR MARSTON, born in Chichester, N.H., June 15, 1870, died in Manchester, N.H., Feb. 13, 1958.

He attended elementary and high school in Pittsfield, N.H., went to Veterinary College, Chicago, Ill., 1914–1916. He never missed a day or was late and was forty-four years old when he started college. Before that he was owner, trainer, driver of harness race horses, had his own stable and one-half mile track in Pittsfield, N.H. He practiced being a veterinarian for forty years in Manchester, N.H. He was also a thirty-second degree mason.

She went to elementary and high school in Pittsfield, N.H. and attended Mount St. Mary's finishing school in New Hampshire.

Children in 9th Generation

F5149 JOHN BENETTE, b. Pittsfield, N.H., July 23, 1908, m. Manchester, N.H., July 27, 1929, ELIZABETH LOUISE CLOUGH.

F10993 EDWARD DEARBORN, b. Manchester, N.H., Jan. 1, 1916, m. ?Sylacauga, Ala., June 1, 1938, SARA JEAN GRIFFIN.

F5536 DANIEL WINGATE HORNE, born in Rochester, N. H., May 4, 1823, died in Lowell, Mass., April 1, 1903, married in Windham, N. H., Nov. 9, 1848, MARY SMITH, born in Windham, N. H., Jan. 5, 1827, died in Lowell, Mass., July 3, 1891.

Children in 9th Generation

F10994 FRANCES, b. Lowell, Mass., Mar. 21, 1852, d. Manchester, N. H., July 9, 1943, m. Lowell, Mass., Jan. 9, 1876, JOSEPH ALMY FLINT.

10995 CLARA BELL

10996 KATE WINGATE

F5659 MABEL GERTRUDE FRENCH, born in Cincinnati, Ohio, Aug. 24, 1880, died in Detroit, Mich., July 21, 1966, married in Burnside, Ky., Nov. 16, 1904, NORMAN INGRAHAM TAYLOR, born in Burnside, Ky., Nov. 10, 1881, died in Somerset, Ky., Sept. 6, 1961.

Children in 9th Generation

F10997 GEORGE PARKER, b. Burnside, Ky., Aug. 19, 1907, m. Mt. Pleasant, Mich., Mar. 4, 1949, ELMA JEAN BRIEN.

F10998 ROBERT FRENCH, b. Burnside, Ky., Jan. 14, 1912, m. Detroit, Mich., Nov. 12, 1938, MARY WARD SAVAGE.

F6224 EMMA MASON, born in Lawrence, Kans., Mar. 10, 1889, married July 14, 1917, B. STANLEY JORDAN, JR., born in Marlboro, Mass., July 22, 1888, died in Brookline, Mass., Nov. 6, 1944. They resided in Brookline, Mass.

Children in 9th Generation

F10999 DOROTHY, b. Jamaica Plain, Mass., Nov. 25, 1920, m. Brookline, Mass., Feb. 2, 1946, WARREN W. PETERMAN.

F6566 AUTUMN VINE PEASE, born in Fidelity, Ill., Sept. 14, 1866, died in Calif. (?), June 12, 1934, married Nov. 19, 1894, SARAH ELIZABETH BROWN, born Aug. 13, 1869.

Children in 9th Generation

11000 daughter

11001 GEORGE GILBERT, b. Nov. 11, 1903, d. Jan. 28, 1904.

F6577 CLARENCE PARDON LOCKE, born in Des Moines, Iowa, June 11, 1884, died in Portland, Ore., June 20, 1968, married in

Fairfield, Ill., Jan. 4, 1906, BESSIE MAY ROLLINGS, born in Neoga, Ill., Sept. 9, 1886, died in Des Moines, Iowa, Nov. 22, 1965.

Children in 9th Generation

11002 HERMAN ROY, b. Fairfield, Ill., April 11, 1910, d. Fairfield, Ill., June 20, 1910.

11003 FLORENCE MAY, b. Fairfield, Ill., April 11, 1910, m. Des Moines, Iowa, Aug. 29, 1934, REV. JOSEPH HENRY COCHRANE, JR., son of Joseph Henry and Myrtle Rosanna (Davis) Cochrane.

F11004 NONA JEANETTE, b. Fairfield, Ill., Nov. 29, 1911.

F11005 JAMES RICHARD, b. Arkansas City, Kans., Feb. 12, 1917.

F11006 MABLE MARGARET, b. Des Moines, Iowa, Mar. 17, 1921, d. Richmond, Calif., 1968.

F6580 BERTHA EDITH LOCKE, born in Atlantic, Iowa, Mar. 4, 1875, died in Chicago, Ill., Nov. 16, 1957, married in Taylorville, Ill., Nov. 16, 1904, JOHN WESLEY GRIFFIS, born in Tenn., Feb. 12, 1873, died in McKinney, Texas, Feb. 8, 1926.

Children in 9th Generation

11007 MARY LOUISE, b. Italy, Texas, Sept. 4, 1905.

11008 EVELYN, b. Honda, Texas, June 11, 1908.

11009 ROBERT ARTHUR, b. Honda, Texas, Jan. 12, 1910.

11010 HENRIETTA LOCKE, b. Honda, Texas, May 18, 1914.

F6581 ARTHUR AUSTIN LOCKE, born in Cass Co., Iowa, Nov. 18, 1884, died in Pontiac, Ill., Aug. 23, 1969, married in Taylorville, Ill., Feb. 18, 1914, ELLEN POWEL, born in Taylorville, Ill., June 17, 1887, died in Pontiac; Ill., Sept. 13, 1973, daughter of Richard McLean and Emma (Catherwood) Powel.

Children in 9th Generation

F11011 RUTH CORENA, b. Taylorville, Ill., June 4, 1916.

F11012 CHARLES RICHARD, b. Taylorville, Ill., Feb. 9, 1918.

F6582 CORENA STEWART LOCKE, born in Long Beach, Calif., Sept. 1, 1896, married in Taylorville, Ill., Aug. 16, 1922, ARTHUR BUCKLEY CLOSE, born in Chicago, Ill., May 12, 1896, son of Dorr Ralph and Helen Elizabeth (Withrow) Close.

Children in 9th Generation

F11013 DOROTHY LOUISE, b. Taylorville, Ill., Feb. 11, 1924.

64   LOCKE GENEALOGY

F11014   STEWART ARTHUR, b. Taylorville, Ill., May 17, 1928.

11015   MARY ELIZABETH, b. Taylorville, Ill., May 17, 1928.

F6585   HERMAN EARL PARK, born in Cass Co., Iowa, Oct. 9, 1881, died in Pasadena, Calif., Sept. 17, 1973, married 1st, Long Beach, Calif., Mar. 16, 1902, BELLA CHARLOTTE COOK, born in Marsworth, England, Jan. 2, 1881, died in Arcadia, Calif., July 19, 1946, daughter of Albert and Annie (Newman) Cook; 2nd, in Santa Ana, Calif., Oct. 9, 1947, Mrs. MAUDE EDNA GREEN, born in Exeter, Nebr., Dec. 5, 1884, died in Hemet, Calif., Dec. 1, 1960, daughter of Frank E. and Suzanne (?) Russell.

Children in 9th Generation

F11016   THELMA LILLIAN, b. Los Angeles, Calif., Dec. 2, 1902.

F6589   MARY ESTELLA LOCKE, born in Marne, Cass Co., Iowa, April 20, 1882, died in Des Moines, Polk Co., Iowa, July 20, 1955, married in Atlantic, Cass Co., Iowa, Dec. 30, 1903, ROBERT WALTER ALLEN, born Aug. 24, 1881, died in Atlantic, Cass Co., Iowa, Dec. 2, 1941. She lived in Cass County, Iowa her entire lifetime and is buried with her husband at Atlantic City Cemetery, Atlantic, Iowa. She was the daughter of John Edwin (F3314) and Mary Lovica (Barnes) Locke. Her husband was a U.S. Postal carrier.

Children in 9th Generation

6590   GERTRUDE ESTELLA, b. Atlantic, Iowa, Feb. 15, 1910, d. Atlantic, Iowa, Feb. 24, 1912.

F6591   MARY VIRGINIA, b. Atlantic, Iowa, Aug. 31, 1913, m. Grinnell, Poweshiek Co., Iowa, Sept. 11, 1937, PARKE WALCOTT BURROWS, b. Davenport, Scott Co., Iowa, June 25, 1914.

F6593   JESSIE EDNA LOCKE, born in Marne, Cass Co., Iowa, Dec. 10, 1887, died in Perry, Dallas Co., Iowa, Jan. 15, 1975, married in Atlantic, Cass Co., Iowa, Aug. 30, 1911, MATT H. SMILEY, born in Malcom, Poweshiek Co., Iowa, Jan. 2, 1889, died in Perry, Dallas Co., Iowa, Nov. 2, 1973, son of William and Mary Asenath (Dunn) Smiley. Her parents were John Edwin (F3314) and Mary Lovica (Barnes) Locke.

Children in 9th Generation

F6594   ROBERT LOCKE, b. Malcom, Iowa, Dec. 14, 1912, m. Dallas Center, Iowa, Oct. 9, 1937, JUNE GERTRUDE CADWELL, b. Dallas Center, Iowa, June 1, 1915.

F6595   MARY LOCKE, b. Malcom, Iowa, Jan. 3, 1915, m. Dallas

Center, Iowa, Aug. 8, 1937, BENN HOYT NELSON, b. Redfield, Iowa, April 19, 1910.

F6633 RODNEY LAMSON HERRICK, born in Charleston, Maine, Oct. 27, 1892, died in Fresno, Calif, Oct. 19, 1936, married in North Augusta, S.C., April 10, 1915, VERA GLADYS GUTHRIE, born in Grand Manan, N. B., North Head Is., Canada, June 8, 1893, died in Los Angeles, Calif., Feb. 17, 1963, daughter of Loren and Ella (Russell) Guthrie.

Children in 9th Generation

F11017 JOHN CLAYTON, b. Augusta, Ga., Feb. 12, 1916.

F6634 GLADYS PLUMMER HERRICK, born in Charleston, Maine, Nov. 10, 1897, married in Fresno, Calif., June 19, 1926, ROCCO EUGENE GRUBBS, born in Nimshew, Calif., Oct. 7, 1900, died in Fresno, Calif., Oct. 2, 1963, son of Rocco and Belle (Brooks) Grubbs.

Children in 9th Generation

11018   son, b. Fresno, Calif., Sept. 8, 1927, d. Sept. 8, 1927.

F11019 ROCCO NEAL, b. Fresno, Calif., May 9, 1929.

11020   GLADYS JO ANN, b. Fresno, Calif., Jan. 11, 1932, m. Fresno, Calif., June 11, 1955, BILL McCORMICK b. Azalea, Ore., Feb. 9, 1923, son of Jack and Naomi (Findley) McCormick.

F6636 ELEANOR HARDY STONE, born in Charlestown, Mass., Mar. 18, 1883, died in Melrose, Mass., Sept. 30, 1958, married in Bangor, Maine, Aug. 30, 1905, ANGIER LOUIS GOODWIN, born in Fairfield, Maine, Jan. 30, 1881, son of Albert and Ruby (Hoxie) Goodwin. He was a member of the U. S. House of Representatives 1942-1954.

Children in 9th Generation

F11021 ROGER LOUIS, b. Melrose, Mass., Sept. 6, 1906.

F11022 MARY ELEANOR, b. Melrose, Mass., July 7, 1908.

11023   ELIZABETH LOCKE, b. Melrose, Mass., Aug. 25, 1911, d. Melrose, Mass., Mar. 5, 1913.

F11024 BARBARA LUCILLE, b. Malden, Mass., Jan. 9, 1925.

F6637 EARLE HERRICK DANFORTH, born in Boyd Lake, Maine, Oct. 16, 1891, married in Gardiner, Maine, Sept. 25, 1919, MAE ELLEN HAMLIN, born in Gardiner, Maine, April 9, 1893, daughter of Frank and Nellie E. (Mooers) Hamlin.

66   LOCKE GENEALOGY

Children in 9th Generation

F11025 RICHARD HAMLIN, b. Gardiner, Maine, April 17, 1922.

F11026 MARGARET LOIS, b. Gardiner, Maine, Aug. 17, 1926.

F11027 MARJORIE FRANCIS, b. Gardiner, Maine, Aug. 20, 1928.

F6638 HELEN LOIS DANFORTH, born in Boyd Lake, Maine,
Oct. 9, 1892, married in Bangor, Maine, Nov. 2, 1916, WILLIAM
FRANCIS WEST, SR., born in Jonesboro, Maine, Mar. 14, 1894, son
of William T. and Clara (Crocker) West.

Children in 9th Generation

F11028 WILLIAM FRANCIS, JR., b. Lyndonville, Vt., April 5,
1917.

F11029 DANFORTH EMERSON, b. Bangor, Maine, Dec. 16, 1920.

F11030 ELIZABETH JANET, b. Bangor, Maine, May 18, 1924.

F11031 ROBERT GORDON, b. Bangor, Maine, Aug. 12, 1926, d.
Bangor, Maine, Sept. 5, 1954.

11032 STUART ELDEN, b. Bangor, Maine, Aug. 13, 1930, m.
Cornish, Maine, Aug. 27, 1955, PRISCILLA DRAPER,
b. Cornish, Maine, May 29, 1936, daughter of Charles
and Jean (Davis) Draper.

F6640 MIRIAM RIDDELL LORD, born in Eureka, Calif., July 7,
1898, married in Grant's Pass, Ore., Sept. 17, 1927, FRANK HARRY
MARKS, born in San Francisco, Calif., May 22, 1896, son of John
and Margaret (McIntyre) Marks.

Children in 9th Generation

F11033 MARGARET ANNE, b. Eureka, Calif., June 16, 1928.

F11034 CHARLOTTE JEAN, b. Klamath Falls, Ore., Mar. 27,
1930.

F6641 RUTH LORD, born in Eureka, Calif., Oct. 26, 1905, married in Reno, Nev., April 23, 1927, McKEAN CARTER, SR., born in
Kingston, Mo., Mar. 14, 1904, died in Gorham, Kans., July 24, 1971,
son of Ebenezer Ulysses and Susan Gilbert (Hooper) Carter.

Children in 9th Generation

11035 McKEAN, JR., b. Reno, Nev., Jan. 21, 1928, d. Gorham,
Kans., Aug. 5, 1945.

F11036 WILLIAM KEHEO, b. Russell, Kans., April 27, 1929.

F11037 SUSAN GILBERT, b. Mitchell Co., Kans., May 6, 1932.

F6949 BARRY LOCKE, born in Lockeport, N. S., died Jan. 6, 1891, married about 1869, CATHERINE MacKAY, died May, 1904. He was named for his grandmother's family.

Children in 9th Generation

F9608 JOSEPHINE JONES, b. Middle Ohio, N. S., Dec. 10, 1870, d. North Abington, Mass., circa Nov. 1940, married Nov. 1901, ERNEST ROBERTSON.

11038 EDWARD COLIN, b. c. 1872, d. young.

F9606 JOHN HUGH, b. Middle Ohio, N. S., July 12, 1873, d. Arlington, Mass., May 18, 1964, m. 1st, Nashua, N. H., Nov. 29, 1905, EFFIE MILDRED MacKAY, d. Mar. 6, 1935; 2nd, 1939, BESSIE ANN (HARRIS) HEATH, divorced 1956.

9607 ANN MAY, b. N.S., c. 1875, d. N.S., unmarried.

F11039 THOMAS MacKAY, b. Locke's Island, N. S., Mar. 25, 1880, d. Arlington, Mass., c. 1957, m. 1st, BERTHA ROBERTSON; 2nd, Aug. 11, 1915, ANNIE LOUISE HILTZE.

11040 JAMES WILLIAM, b. Locke's Island, N. S., c. 1881, d. Boston, Mass. (res. Fla.), July, 1967, m. c.1918, BELLE McLOUD.

11041 PERCY, died young.

F11042 ESSIE EDNA, b. Locke's Island, N.S., c. 1884, d. East Boston, Mass., c. 1955, m. 1st, DAN SUCKMAN; 2nd, ALEC McGILVERY, d. Mar. 23, 1967.

F11043 DAVID ROY, b. N.S., Mar. 2, 1889, d. N.S., April 17, 1951, m. Mar. 2, 1920, SARAH BLANCHE SEABOYER b. May 10, 1899, d. June 1, 1965.

F7016 FRANKLIN LOCKE, born in Lockeport, N. S., July 10, 1846, died in Lockeport, N.S., 1926, married 1st, LOUISA KEMPTON; 2nd, MARY EMMA MacMILLAN, born in Louis Head, Shelburne Co., May 27, 1862, died in Barss' Corners, N.S., Nov. 3,1935.

Children in 9th Generation

9658 FREDERICK OSGOOD, by first wife, b. St. Charles, Ill., April 28, 1878, d. Ray, Ariz., Dec. 5, 1935.

9659a MARION FISKE, by second wife, b. Lockeport, N. S., April 23, 1891, d. Bridgewater, N.S., Aug. 6, 1955.

9659b IOAN, b. Lockeport, N. S., April 23, 1891, d. Field, B.C., Dec. 1940.

F11044   FRANCES ALBERTA, b. Lockeport, N.S., Feb. 25, 1893, m. Lockeport, N. S., Aug. 24, 1922, HAROLD B. VERGE.

F7050   JONATHAN LOCKE, born in Lockeport, Nova Scotia, Sept. 13, 1964, died in San Antonio, Texas, 1933, married in San Antonio, Texas, 1891, BRENT ROBINSON, born in Wilson County, Texas, 1862, died in San Antonio, Texas, May, 1959.

He left school in Lockeport at about age fourteen and served as a seaman for two years on a sailing ship to the West Indies. In 1884 a magazine article on Texas attracted him to that state in search of new opportunities and he took part in the last big cattle drive from Texas to Kansas in 1885. Settled in San Antonio, he had a series of jobs, starting with washing dishes at the Maverick Hotel, selling flour, and finally into oil, mining, ranching and real estate, where he became highly successful. He was a man of great warmth, humor and vitality, well-liked and respected by a wide circle of friends and a skilled hunter.

Children in 9th Generation

F9681   DAVID ROGER, b. San Antonio, Texas, Mar. 7, 1892, d. Corpus Christi, Texas, Jan. 19, 1960, m. El Paso, Texas, LUCIE HARRIS.

F9682   JOHN ROBINSON, b. San Antonio, Texas, Feb. 10, 1894, m. San Antonio, Texas, Oct. 25, 1921, GRACE WALKER.

F9683   MIGNON, b. San Antonio, Texas, Aug. 9, 1897, m. New York, N. Y., Oct. 10, 1929, WILLIAM DAVID KNIPE.

F9684   COLIN CAMPBELL, b. San Antonio, Texas, July 16, 1902, m. 1st, San Antonio, Texas, Oct. 2, 1934, ANNELISE BOSE, b. Bremen, Germany, Oct. 1, 1908, d. San Antonio, Texas July 12, 1960; 2nd, San Antonio, Texas, Oct. 17, 1962, MARGARET JOHNSON, b. July 1, 1921. He graduated in 1926 from the University of Texas with a degree in Electrical Engineering. He was a member of the University's first band and champion boxer, bantam weight division. His first love was music and he studied the clarinet in Paris, 1931-33. He was a rancher and wine connoisseur and fluent in French and Spanish.

F7251   ARTHUR ROBERT FORD, born in Danbury, N.H., June 14, 1863, died in Danbury, N. H., Nov. 12, 1940, married in Danbury, N. H., Jan. 28, 1894, JENNIE FANNIE RAND.

He attended New Hampton Literary Institution, now New Hampton School for Boys. He was a farmer all his life in Danbury, N. H. He farmed to supply his family with the necessities of life and a few luxuries which meant his farm was self-sustaining. He was a member of the State Legislature, a Selectman in Danbury, a member of the school board and a staunch Granger.

Children in 9th Gen. b. in Danbury, N. H.

11045 MARY HAZEL, b. July 18, 1894, d. Laconia, N. H. nursing home, Sept. 28, 1971. She was single and lived in Danbury, N. H.

11046 ROBERT, b. Aug. 4, 1896, m. Vermont, July 24, 1925, BARBARA HUNT.

F11047 RAND CURRIER, b. Oct. 14, 1898, d. Danbury, N. H., Jan. 15, 1971.

11048 LYDIA HELEN, b. Sept. 10, 1900, d. Portland, Maine, Jan. 9, 1926, m. Danbury, N. H., June 1925, CHESTER CURTIS.

11049 REUL ARTHUR, b. Aug. 18, 1906, m. Danbury, N. H., Jan. 27, 1927, BEULAH GOSS.

F7322 FREDERICK JAMES CURRIER, born in River Falls, Wis., Feb. 13, 1860, died in San Francisco, Calif., Nov. 25, 1935, married 2nd, Saratoga, Calif., April 11, 1918, JEAN BILTON SMITH, born in Rawdon, England, died in San Jose, Calif., Dec. 7, 1971.

This entry covers his second marriage and child by his second wife. See his entry P541 of the "Locke Genealogy".

Children in 9th Generation

F11050 AMY JUNE, b. Saratoga, Calif., June 11, 1920, m. Saratoga, Calif., May 22, 1943, JOHN GEORGE JORGENSEN.

F7574 GEORGE EVERETT LOCKE, born in Barnstead, N. H., Sept. 9, 1872, died in Barnstead, N. H., Oct. 8, 1936, married in Alton, N. H., Sept. 16, 1897, MABEL F. KELLEY, born in Gilmanton, N. H., May 19, 1878, died in Pittsfield, N. H., Dec. 26, 1935.

She taught school when only sixteen years old. Together, they ran a country inn in North Barnstead, which was very successful for many years. It was almost entirely a family affair as all helped. Their clientele came from all over New England and Mabel became famous for her extraordinary skill as a cook and both were appreciated for their hospitality.

Children in 9th Gen. b. in Barnstead, N.H.

9831   JAMES STERLING, b. July 16, 1898, d. Barnstead, N.H.
       Worked with his father in the lumber business.

9832   MARJORIE (twin), b. June 12, 1900, d. Barnstead, N.H.,
       July 16, 1901.

9833   MARGARET (twin), b. June 12, 1900, d. Barnstead, N.H.,
       May 25, 1901.

F11051 GEORGE MALCOLM, b. Nov. 6, 1904, m. Durham,
       N.H., April 5, 1931, ELVA PEARL HOLLAND.

F11052 KENT DREW, b. April 17, 1909, m. Alton, N.H., April 9,
       1933, MARGARET JOHNSTON.

11053 KATHLEEN FRANCES, b. Aug. 14, 1910, m. Belleville,
       N.J., Mar. 31, 1946, HOWARD THOMAS WEST, b.
       Middleburgh, N.Y., Aug. 29, 1912, d. Stamford, N.Y.,
       Dec. 16, 1966.
           She graduated from Laconia General Hospital with
       an R.N. degree in nursing 1932. She worked the fields
       of general nursing, home nursing care in the Ossipee
       area and industrial nursing with nitrogen and gunpowder
       plants in Virginia. She entered the Army Nurse Corps,
       was commissioned a second lieutenant, and worked at
       the Valley Forge General Hospital with patients who
       were blind and had plastic surgery. She returned to the
       nursing profession after her husband's death and has re-
       tired. She lives in N.H. near her brothers and sisters.
       He ran a retail bakery business with his father in Stam-
       ford, N.Y. He was a technical instructor in the Asiatic
       Theater of operations during WWII.

F11054 MARY KELLEY, b. Oct. 29, 1911, m. Sugar Hill, N.H.,
       Dec. 14, 1907, HENRY CHESTER LANE.

F7617 ALBRO WELLS, born in Bristol, N.H., July 26, 1860, died
in Bristol, N.H., April 21, 1914, married in Bristol, N.H., Sept. 15,
1885, HARRIET ANN ROBIE, born in Bristol, N.H., May 12, 1867,
died in Bristol, N.H., June 11, 1945.
   He was educated in the Bristol, N.H. public schools and took
correspondence courses in architecture at International Correspondence School. He was associated with his father, Benjamin Locke
Wells, as a carpenter and builder under the firm name of B. L. & A.
Wells. He was a highly respected businessman of Bristol, where he
always lived. He served the town as selectman for three years, in
1905 was its representative in the state legislature, and for 19 years
was a member of the school board. He was also a member of the official board of the Methodist Episcopal church of Bristol.

Children in 9th Gen. b. in Bristol, N. H.

7618 MARY BERNICE, b. July 17, 1886. She was educated in Bristol, N. H. public schools and graduated from Tilton Seminary in Tilton, N. H., class of 1907. She also took summer courses at Plymouth, N. H. and Keene, N. H. normal schools and taught for several years in Bristol, New Hampton, Tilton, Rochester, Danville, and Jefferson, N. H.

For 20 years she worked as bookkeeper, proofreader, etc., in the office of the "Bristol Enterprise", and from 1945 until her retirement in 1960 she was clerk and treasurer of the Bristol Water Works.

She is a member of Bristol Federated Church and has served it in several capacities; a member of Bristol Historical Society and XYZ (senior citizens) club. She is interested in needlework, local history, and genealogy. She resides in Bristol, N. H.

F7619 HARRY DANIEL, b. April 6, 1888, d. Northfield, N. H., Nov. 18, 1956, m. Tilton, N.H., Aug. 21, 1912, MABEL HELEN DRAKE.

7620 SARA ELIZABETH, b. June 21, 1895. She attended Bristol, N. H. public schools, graduated from Tilton Seminary, Tilton, N. H., class of 1914, and was a teacher for a short time. For about 30 years she was employed as compositor and linotype operator in the office of the "Bristol Enterprise". For about ten years she assisted in the insurance office of the Frank N. Gilman Agency, Bristol, retiring in 1961.

She is a member of the Bristol Federated Church, Bristol Historical Society, and XYZ (senior citizens) club. She is interested in local history and genealogy. She resides in Bristol, N. H.

F7950 EDWIN ERASTUS BOWDEN, born in Kittery, Maine, Sept. 18, 1874, died in Portsmouth, N. H., May 29, 1945, married in Kittery, Maine, Jan. 8, 1902, ANNIE J. LOCKE, born Jan. 20, 1878, died in York, Maine, Aug. 8, 1956.

Children in 9th Generation

7951 SADIE LOCKE, b. Kittery, Maine, Jan. 8, 1903, m. Kittery, Maine, Nov. 7, 1942, CEDRIC C. BROOKS.

She was graduated from Traip Academy and Plymouth Business Schools. Was a bookkeeper for Kittery Water District for 48 years and Treasurer of the Town of Kittery

for 41 years and was active in several organizations in-
cluding the Rebekahs, Order of the Eastern Star, Pythian
Sisters, Grange and the Daughters of the American
Revolution and was a member of the American Legion
Auxiliary.

He was graduated from Traip Academy. He was self-
employed as a carpenter, boat builder and contractor.
He was a veteran of World War II serving in Company A
111th Medical Battalion as a private. He was a member
of the Knights of Pythias, the Masonic Bodies including
the Scottish Rite and Kara Temple of the Shrine and was
a member of the American Legion.

F7982 PHEBE L. WOODMAN, born in 1865, died in 1892, married, July 1885, GEORGE W. McDUFFEE. He later married his wife's
twin sister (#7983), Jennie L. who brought up his son. Jennie died in
November, 1953.

Children in 9th Generation

F11056 FRED, b. Waits River, Vt., April 9, 1887, d. Nov. 2, 1965,
m. Corinth, Vt., May 15, 1912, NETTIE PAGE.

F8000 ABBIE J. EMERY, born in Topsham, Vt., June 18, 1870,
died in Topsham, Vt., May 24, 1891, married in Topsham, Vt., 1889,
WILLIAM BEEDE, born in Topsham, Vt., died in Barre, Vt.

Children in 9th Generation

F8001 HARRY EDWARD, b. Waits River, Vt., July 2, 1889, d.
Lynn, Mass., Feb. 1, 1967, m. 1910, SARAH JANE
BOYD.

F8125 GEORGE REUBEN LOCKE, born in E. Concord, N. H.,
Jan. 1, 1864, died in S. Braintree, Mass., April 14, 1950, married 1st,
FANNIE S. GORDON, died in E. Brookfield, Mass., June 16, 1924;
2nd, 1939, LORA E. B. COURSER.

A Methodist minister. He served appointments, first in the New
Hampshire Conference and then in the New England Southern Conference. In 1909 he was a member of the New Hampshire legislature.

After his retirement he devoted time and effort to Masonry, taking
all the rites through the Commandery and the 32nd degree.

He was elected president of the Locke Family Association in 1924,
and he served in that office for twenty-two years. He took great
pleasure in planning and attending the annual sessions, and much of
the achievement of the Association was due to his leadership.

Children in 9th Generation

10084 MARGARET SARAH, b. Tilton, N.H., Aug. 10, 1888. She was educated in Tilton Seminary and Boston University with A.B. from the College of Liberal Arts and M.A. from the Graduate School. For many years she was the Librarian of the College of Business Administration of Boston University.

10085 HELEN FRANCES, b. Chichester, N.H., April 8, 1893, d. Westboro, Mass., 1935.

F8126 REV. WILLIAM BENJAMIN LOCKE, born in Bristol, N.H., Oct. 10, 1867, died in Derry, N.H., Sept. 2, 1955, married Merrimac, Mass., Aug. 16, 1893, MARY FRANCES ROWELL, born in Merrimac, Mass., June 16, 1870, died in Derry, N.H., July 2, 1966.

He was a graduate of Tilton Seminary and Boston University (CLA) and he studied one year in Boston University School of Theology. An ordained minister of the Methodist (Episcopal) Church, he served pastorates in the New Hampshire Annual Conference until his retirement in 1933. After retirement he lived in Derry, N.H.

Children in 9th Generation

F10086 JUDITH MAY, b. Seabrook, N.H., May 24, 1897, d. Milford, Mass., Aug. 16, 1928, m. Lancaster, N.H., April 14, 1925, LEWIS AINSLEY BENNETT.

10087 MILDRED SARAH, b. Seabrook, N.H., June 10, 1897, d. Seabrook, N.H., Sept. 27, 1897.

F10088 MARY RUBENA, b. Newfields, N.H., June 15, 1901, m. Derry, N.H., May 28, 1930, LEWIS AINSLEY BENNETT.

F11057 WILLIAM ROWELL, b. Manchester, N.H., Nov. 20, 1907, m. Portsmouth, N.H., Sept. 4, 1934, CHARLOTTE M. CLARK.

F8136 ARTHUR TRUE CASS, born in Tilton, N.H., April 9, 1865, died in Northboro, Mass., married in Boston, Mass., May 16, 1894, MARY WALLACE PACKARD, born in Boston, Mass., died in Newton, Mass.

He was a banker, Representative to the State Legislature, held several town offices and was President of the Tilton School Alumni Association. She was a graduate of Lasell Jr. College and Emerson College where she majored in elocution. She was President of the Northfield's Women's Club and member of the Liberty Chapter, DAR.

Children in 9th Generation

F8137 KINGMAN PACKARD, b. Tilton, N.H., April 1, 1895,

d. Winchester, Mass., m. Boston, Mass., May 10, 1919,
MARY FRANCES FISKE.

F8138 WILLIAM TRUE, b. May 27, 1899, d. Albuquerque, N. M.,
Jan. 22, 1976, m. Tilton, N. H., IRENE ELIZABETH
METZ.

8139 ESTHER ELIZABETH, b. Tilton, N.H., April 10, 1903, m.
San Diego, Calif., VICTOR A. WELTON.

F8180 ALICE I. LOCKE, born in Dalton, N. H., July 13, 1852,
died in Huntington Beach, Calif., July 17, 1914, married in Old
Town, San Diego, Calif., July 9, 1874, WILLIAM WALLACE, born in
County Cork, Ireland, May 12, 1840, died in San Luis Rey, Calif.,
Oct. 3, 1893.
He had a store, saloon and stage stop in San Luis Rey, Calif. in
partnership with his father-in-law Elbridge Gerry Locke (#F4917). He
and his father were brought to New England by Henry Wadsworth
Longfellow as gardeners. Young William was apprenticed to a printer
but at age 12 he ran away and made his way to California working
with a wagon train.
Elbridge Locke settled in San Luis Rey Valley about 1868 having
traveled to California by land and sea twice before. He was a Civil
Engineer and laid out his new home town in lots.

Children in 9th Gen. b. in San Luis Rey, Calif.

F10196 WILLIAM LEE, b. Feb. 17, 1875, m. San Luis Rey, Calif.,
JOSEPHINE STEIGER.

F10197 ELBRIDGE HALE, b. Mar. 24, 1876, d. Corona, Calif.,
m. KATE BAKER.

F10198 EDNA J., b. Dec. 12, 1878, d. San Diego, Calif., m. 1st,
WILL ADAMS; 2nd, E. ALVIN WILBUR.

F10199 ROBERT L., b. April 19, 1880, d. Oregon, m. MAY——.

F10200 PEARL, b. June 5, 1883, d. Oceanside, Calif., April 16,
1973, m. San Luis Rey, Calif., Jan. 5, 1907, DAVID
LESLIE JONES.

F10201 ALICE FLORINDA/RIX, b. Feb. 28, 1886, d. Encinitas,
Calif., Oct. 1, 1972, m. Los Angeles, Calif., Sept. 11,
1916, GEORGE RINGO WILSON.

F10202 HUGH, b. Mar. 3, 1888, d. Oakdale, Calif., m. CARO-
LINE STEIGER.

F1023 ANNE ROSE, b. July 17, 1891, m. April 3, 1918, WILLIAM
JESSE WHEAT.

F8185 SARAH ELLA ANNA LOCKE, born in Titusville, Penna.,
April 23, 1862, died in Alameda, Calif., Sept. 2, 1908, married Fall-
brook, Calif., Mar. 18, 1885, MILLARD FILLMORE NEFF, born in
Marysville, Calif., Jan. 24, 1860, died in Biggs, Calif., 1933.

Children in 9th Gen. b. in Fallbrook, Calif.

8186 CLARENCE WILSON, b. Mar. 18, 1886, d. Alameda,
Calif., Oct. 24, 1959. He was an orthodontist.

F8187 EDITH EUNICE, b. Nov. 28, 1887, m. Alameda, Calif.,
Aug. 17, 1914, ROLLO MORTON KELLOGG.

F8188 BENJAMIN GERRY, b. Dec. 9, 1893, d. Alameda, Calif.,
Jan. 12, 1973, m. 1st, San Francisco, Calif., 1918,
ELEANOR DOUGLAS, d. Alameda, Calif., April, 1921;
2nd, Alameda, Calif., 1924, HELEN BEEBEE.

F8255 ABBY (CUMMINGS) LOCKE, born in Charlestown, Mass.,
July 8, 1851, died in Andover, Mass., 1938, married in Andover,
Mass., 1874, THOMAS DENNIE THOMSON, born Sept. 8, 1849,
died in Andover, Mass., 1929.

Children in 9th Gen. b. in Andover, Mass.

F8256 ELEANOR JAFFRAY, b. Mar. 24, 1878, m. Andover,
Mass., April 21, 1908, ALFRED LUCIUS CASTLE.

8257 PHILIP WINGATE, b. April 6, 1880, d. Andover, Mass.,
1968, unmarried.

8258 CLARA LOCKE, b. Mar. 30, 1882, d. Boston, Mass., 1950,
m. 1st, CHARLES M. BLACKFORD; 2nd, HUGH S.
KNOX.

8259 ROSAMOND MEANS, b. Sept. 1, 1884, d. Brookline,
Mass., April (5?), 1950, m. Andover, Mass., DR.
JOSEPH HERSEY PRATT, b. 1872, d. 1956.

F8459 GEORGE FRANK LOCKE, born in Irasburg, Vt., Mar. 9,
1877, died in South Paris, Maine, April 12, 1953, married in West-
more, Vt., Oct. 20, 1899, MARY LILLIAN CHENEY, born in Albany,
Vt., Aug. 16, 1876, died in Chicago, Ill., June 1946.

Children in 9th Gen. b. in Irasburg, Vt.

11058 LLOYD GRANVILLE, b. Nov. 22, 1903, d. Kezar Falls,
Maine, April 5, 1947, m. DORIS STANLEY.

F11059 MADALEINE DALE, b. May 3, 1907, m. Chapel Hill,
N.C., May 24, 1930, J. PAUL CHOPLIN.

F11060 SHIRLEY MAE, b. Aug. 11, 1908, m. Evanston, Ill.,
April 14, 1934, JOHN A. BODKIN.

F8792 FRANK MORTON PRESCOTT, born in Newton, N. H.,
Sept. 28, 1863, died in Amesbury, Mass., Jan. 25, 1946, married in
Amesbury, Mass., June 30, 1887, EMMA FRANCIS TAYLOR.

He was a highly regarded executive of the Merrimac plant of the
Walker Body Co. of Amesbury, Mass. He was active in the planning
and construction of the Amesbury Hospital, a member of the Main St.
Congregational Church, Powow River Lodge of the Odd Fellows and
served as Judge of the 2nd District Court of Essex Co.

Children in 9th Generation

F11061 RUTH CAROLINE, b. Amesbury, Mass., Mar. 18, 1892,
d. Haverhill, Mass., Feb. 5, 1949, m. Amesbury, Mass.,
Oct. 3, 1916, ARTHUR CLARENDON WRIGHT.

F8810 ALBERT OREN HOWARD, born in Rochester, N. H., Aug.
27, 1874, died in Biddeford, Maine, July 2, 1932, married Oct. 27,
1897, SARAH ELIZABETH OWEN, born in Portland, Maine, Nov. 8,
1872, died in Biddeford, Maine, Aug. 19, 1966.

He attended the schools of South Berwick and Berwick Academy.
In his very early years he drove cattle each morning at 6 A. M. from
the village to a location known as Slygo, a distance of a mile; driving
them back after school each afternoon, and receiving a wage of fifty
cents a month. Later he became newsboy on the Mountain Division of
the Boston & Maine Railroad from Portsmouth to North Conway and
return. Nights he studied telegraphy, and when he was 18 years of
age, was telegrapher, station agent, train dispatcher, baggage master, transfer agent and freight clerk on this same line at Conway
Junction. Then he was transferred to the Superintendent's office in
Boston, only to accept a job a few years later as Manager of the Postal Telegraph office in Biddeford, Maine. In April 1897 he joined the
Associated Press as telegrapher and sent to Lewiston, Maine to open
an office for the A. P. at the Lewiston Journal, later the Lewiston Sun
newspaper. On August 15, 1907 he was transferred to the Biddeford
Journal as Associated Press representative and remained until November 26, 1927 at which time he was sent to the Press Herald building in
Portland where he was Superintendent of all A. P. wires in Maine,
rounding out 35 years with the Associated Press, receiving from them
in 1912 the prize award for the best story writer. His hobby was baseball and a member of a professional team which included many well-
known players of the day. He was a member of the Congregational
Church at Biddeford.

She was daughter of Edwin Cotton Owen and Annie Elizabeth
(Bradbury) Owen. Her parents died when she was very young and she
lived with her uncle and aunt, Mr. and Mrs. Thomas Bradbury of Biddeford. A graduate of Biddeford High School, and a schoolteacher in
Biddeford and Saco. She was a member of the Congregational Church
at Biddeford.

F8820 George Henry Moore

Alice Blanch (Morse) Moore

Children in 9th Generation

11062 MARION BELLE, b. Lewiston, Maine, Mar. 6, 1899, d. Biddeford, Maine, Dec. 3, 1965, unmarried.

She was a graduate of Biddeford High School, accomplished musician, Sunday school teacher, and a proficient person in the shoe manufacturing industry in all its phases. At the time of her death, she was Superintendent in charge of all manufacture at Songo Shoe Co. at Portland, Maine. Member of the Congregational Church at Biddeford.

F11063 STANTON BRADBURY, b. Newport, R.I., July 16, 1900, d. Dallas, Texas, Aug. 31, 1967, m. Pittsburg, Penna., Oct. 26, 1928, GERTRUDE REID.

F11064 PRESCOTT LOCKE, b. Newport, R. I., May 7, 1907, m. Biddeford, Maine, June 20, 1936, ADA MARIE GILKS.

F8820 GEORGE HENRY MOORE, born in Raymond, N.H., April 4, 1886, married in Somerville, Mass., Sept. 4, 1910, ALICE BLANCHE MORSE. She was born March 13, 1891 in Bridgewater, Mass., the daughter of Robert Franklin and Sarah Atlanta (Pratt) Morse. They lived at 14 Pearl St. in Somerville, Mass. for over thirty years. He was an engineer for the Boston and Maine Railroad for forty-two years. Although he had only a 5th grade education, he was adept at many crafts and trades which he taught himself. He received many citations from the railroad because he had natural ability in repairing mechanical breakdowns. In his spare time he made furniture, did carpentry, plumbing, electrical wiring, masonry work and automobile repairing. He developed a reputation in his neighborhood for being the man who could fix anything and his neighbors called on him frequently to fix, repair, rebuild, or build things for them. He possessed unlimited energy and drive and had just finished building a new home at 72 Sunset Rock Road in Andover, Mass. when he died there on March 3, 1951, a victim of cancer.

She attended the public schools of Raynham, Mass. and graduated from the Bristol County Business School with a Combined Course Diploma in the Commercial and Stenographic Course in 1907. She died June 9, 1951 in her new home in Andover, a victim of lukemia, and is buried in the Spring Grove Cemetery in Andover with her husband.

Children in 9th Gen. b. in Boston, Mass.

F11065 HAZEL ALICE, b. Jan. 27, 1917, m. Medford, Mass., Sept. 19, 1941, CHARLES ESDALE PROUDFOOT.

F11066 GRACE ESTHER, b. June 2, 1920, m. Somerville, Mass., Dec. 10, 1944, DONALD PAUL HAYES.

F8824 ORIN M. LUCY, born in Nottingham, N. H., July 17, 1871, died in Amesbury, Mass., 1945, married in Amesbury, Mass., Dec. 25, 1897, MATTIE E. HAM, born in Durham, N. H., July 6, 1877, died in Haverhill, Mass., May, 1955.

He was a 2nd Lieutenant in the Militia, Spanish American War. His trade for the rest of his life was machine woodworking and cabinet making.

Children in 9th Gen. b. in Amesbury, Mass.

F11067 GEORGE EARLE, b. Jan. 22, 1899, m. Amesbury, Mass., June 11, 1927, ADA R. FOLLANSBEE.

F11068 ALFRED KENNETH, b. Sept. 21, 1905, m. Mar. 18, 1943, EMMA E. WHITE.

F8868 IRVING M. LOCKE, born in Barrington, N. H., Feb. 13, 1864, died in Boston, Mass., July 31, 1930, married in Barrington, N. H., Feb. 1, 1897, LINNA M. BUZZELL, born in Barrington, N.H., July 2, 1878, died in Barrington, N.H., Dec. 13, 1962.

Children in 9th Gen. b. in Barrington, N. H.

F8869 CLARENCE BRYAN, b. Mar. 10, 1898, d. Barrington, N. H., Oct. 2, 1955, m. 1st, East Boston, Mass., 1921, LILLIAN FRANCES MORRISON; 2nd, Dover, N. H., EVA MAY CLOW FORSYTHE.

F8870 EVA MARY, b. June 9, 1901, m. Salisbury, Mass., Dec. 12, 1928, DOUGLAS McLEOD STEVENSON.

F8876 MILDRED LOCKE, born in Barrington, N. H., Nov. 11, 1895, married in Barrington, N.H., Oct. 2, 1920, CLARENCE L. CALEF, born in Barrington, N. H., Feb. 8, 1894.

Children in 9th Gen. b. in Rochester, N. H.

F11069 ROGER LOCKE, b. July 24, 1924, m. Barrington, N.H. June 6, 1948, ALBERTA M. WITHAM.

F11070 MARILYN, b. Feb. 9, 1933, m. Barrington, N. H., Sept. 24, 1954, GLENN R. ORDWAY.

F9189 AUGUSTUS LOCKE, born in North Adams, Mass., Aug. 22, 1883, married 1st, Brookline, Mass., Dec. 18, 1915, HELEN ALMA LINCOLN, born in Brookline, Mass., Mar. 11, 1883, died in Palo Alto, Calif., Nov. 25, 1961; 2nd, in Carson City, Nev., Sept. 8, 1964, ALICE BRADLEY BOSWELL.

His engineering talents surfaced at an early age when he built a series of pulleys and ropes to feed his father's chickens. He received a Ph.D. at Harvard University, 1913, and his career in mining geology took him to the western U.S., British Columbia, and Mexico. He has written on geological subjects.

Children in 9th Generation

11071 CAROLINE, b. Brookline, Mass., Oct. 20, 1916, d. Washington, D. C., m. Nov. 29, 1946, CHRISTOF A. WEGELIN.

F11072 GARDNER LINCOLN, b. Oakland, Calif., April 9, 1919, m. Santa Rosa, Calif., May 7, 1947, TAPPAN KIMBALL.

11073 ELIZABETH GARLAND, b. Oakland, Calif., June 25, 1921.

F9190 JULIA GARLAND LOCKE, born in North Adams, Mass., July 20, 1887, died in Hampton, N. H., Aug. 3, 1970, married in Hampton, N. H., ARTHUR O. DEWEY, born in Murray, Iowa, Jan. 6, 1884, died in Hampton, N. H., June 12, 1971.

She was a graduate of Wellesley College, Class of 1909 and a teacher and social welfare worker prior to her marriage. Active in church and community affairs, college and cultural organizations. Interests and enthusiasms ranged from all kinds of handcrafts, music, theater, wide ranges of reading, youth group leadership. She was a dedicated and enthusiastic worker for the Locke Family Association for many years.

He attended Iowa State College and received his B.A. from Simpson College in Iowa. He received his degree (STB) in 1918 from Boston University School of Theology. He was an Army chaplain during World War I. Did YMCA work and served as superintendent of the City Mission Settlement House in New Bedford, Mass. for many years. Served the last fourteen years prior to retirement as minister of the Provincetown Methodist Church. In 1968 he was honored at the completion of 50 years as an ordained Methodist minister and member of the New England Methodist Conference. He was active in church and community affairs in New Bedford, Mass., Provincetown, Mass. and, in retirement, in Hampton, N. H. He took an active interest and part in the Locke Family Association, serving as its president for many years. He was chaplain of the Hampton St. James Lodge, A. F. and A. M., and the King Hiram's Lodge, A. F. and A. M. of Provincetown. He and Julia were both active in the Golden Age Club of Exeter, serving as president and in other capacities.

Children in 9th Generation

F11074 JANE MARTINDALE, b. Boston, Mass., Sept. 2, 1921, m. Provincetown, Mass., Jan. 6, 1945, JAMES WALLACE ALCOCK.

F9191 HARRIET ESTHER LOCKE, born in North Adams, Mass., Mar. 14, 1889, died in Union, N. H., Aug. 8, 1960, married in Hampton, N. H., Sept. 18, 1920, LYLE STEVENS DREW, born in Union, N. H., Feb. 13, 1891, died in Union, N. H., Oct. 4, 1961.

She was an active supporter of the Locke Family Association, serving in many capacities.

Children in 9th Gen. b. in Union, N. H.

11075 ERNEST LOCKE, b. Sept. 21, 1921, d. June 29, 1945. He attended the University of New Hampshire, then was called into the U. S. Air Force where he served as a Navigator on a B-29 until his death over Okajama, Japan.

F11076 ESTHER STEVENS, b. Jan. 30, 1923, m. Union, N. H., June 12, 1954, DAVID GALE EASTMAN.

F10806 FREDERICK ELISHA LADD, JR., born in Atlanta, Ga., Nov. 7, 1901, died in Ft. Payne, Ala., Jan. 19, 1932, married in Muskegon, Mich., Aug. 11, 1923, OPAL BRAZILIA HILL, born in Elk Rapids, Mich., Dec. 13, 1902, died in Chattanooga, Tenn., Oct. 20, 1972, buried at Ft. Payne, Ala.

He graduated from DeKalb County High School, Fort Payne, Ala. (1921) and attended Georgia Tech and Auburn University. He was a Resident Engineer for the City of Grand Rapids, Mich. for three years on a sewer project. He worked most of his life for Southern Retractories Co., Ft. Payne, Ala., a company founded by his brother. He was a member of Ft. Payne Lodge 437 Free and Accepted Masons and was also a member of the Chapter of Knight Templers.

Children in 9th Generation

F11077 FRANCES ELAINE, b. Grand Rapids, Mich., April 22, 1924, m. Ft. Payne, Ala., Mar. 14, 1946, RANDOLPH EARL NEAL.

F11078 GERTRUDE LOUISE, b. Ft. Payne, Ala., June 13, 1928, m. Ft. Payne, Ala., June 10, 1950, MATTIE ZACHARIAL HITCHCOCK.

F10807 EDWARD JOHNSON LADD, born in Boston, Mass., Nov. 24, 1906, married in Ft. Payne, Ala., Sept. 5, 1931, WILLIE LEE GILBREATH, born in Ft. Payne, Ala., Sept. 17, 1909.

He graduated from DeKalb County High School, Ft. Payne, Ala. (1922) and from Georgia Tech. (1930, B.S. in Ceramic Engineering). He worked as an Inspector for the City of Grand Rapids, Mich. for two years on a sewer project. He worked five years for Southern Retractories Co., Ft. Payne, Ala. He has been president of Ladd Engineering Associates, Consulting Engineers, since 1940.

He is a member of Ft. Payne Lodge 437, Free and Accepted Masons and a member of the following organizations: Sons of American Revolution, New England Historical and Genealogical Society, American Society of Civil Engineers, American Public Works Association, Association of Communication Engineers, Consulting Engineers Council. He is a Registered Engineer and Land Surveyor in ten states. They reside at 503 Gault Ave. S., Ft. Payne, Ala. 35967.

Children in 9th Generation

11079 PHOEBE ANN, b. Ft. Payne, Ala., Jan. 28, 1933, d. Ft. Payne, Ala., June 28, 1934.

F11080 MARGARET DALE, b. Gadsden, Ala., July 7, 1937, m. Ft. Payne, Ala., June 17, 1961, GERE FRANKLIN GAINER.

F10809 SARAH DOROTHY LOCKE, born in Rockford, Ill., Oct. 22, 1904, married in Beaver, Penna., April 25, 1928, RALPH WAYNE ALLISON, born in Nebo, Ill., May 9, 1904, son of Emerson Elwood and Lily Alma (Shelby) Allison.

Children in 9th Gen. b. in Geneva, Ill.

F11081 DOROTHY TAYLOR, b. Nov. 17, 1936.

F11082 DANIEL SHELBY, b. July 11, 1941.

F10810 JOHN ROBERT LOCKE, born in Rockford, Ill., Mar. 8, 1906, married in Marion, Ohio, July 3, 1929, JOSEPHINE LAWRENCE, born in Marion, Ohio, July 3, 1904, daughter of George Preston and Mae (Owen) Lawrence.
He is a 1933 graduate of the University of Wyoming and is a retired Colonel in the Army Reserve. He served in the South Pacific during WW II and is a member of the American Legion, the Masons and was a Real Estate Broker and Insurance Agent. His hobbies include restoring antique cars and lecturing on the Civil War. She is a graduate of the National College of Education in Evanston, Ill. They built their own home complete to prove it can be done!

Children in 9th Generation

11083 JOANNA, b. Marion, Ohio, July 14, 1934, m. 1st, Stockton, Calif., July 4, 1959, MALCOLM A. STONE, b. Hollywood, Calif., Aug. 5, 1934; 2nd, San Andreas, Calif., June 3, 1972, DONALD ARTHUR TOMPKINS, b. Groton, N.Y., April 8, 1924, d. Stockton, Calif., July 30, 1973, son of Grant A. and Anna A. (Knapp) Tompkins.

F11084 SARAH MORSE, b. Sandusky, Ohio, Dec. 28, 1937.

F10811 EDWARD TAYLOR LOCKE, SR., born in Rockford, Ill., July 3, 1907, died in Woodstock, Ill., April 16, 1948, married in Woodstock, Ill., Aug. 12, 1933, EDITH MAY HOLLARBUSH, b. Greenwood, Ill., June 7, 1910, daughter of Alva and Annetta (Norton) Hollarbush.

Children in 9th Generation

F11085   EDWARD TAYLOR, JR., b. Woodstock, Ill., April 25, 1935.

11086   JAMES RICHARD, b. Elgin, Ill., June 18, 1937.

F11087   JANET MARIE, b. Elgin, Ill., July 11, 1938.

F10812 RICHARD FOSS LOCKE, JR., born in Rockford, Ill., Mar. 23, 1909, married 1st, in Waukegan, Ill., Jan. 21, 1932, ALBERTA WARD MILLER, born in Geneva, Ill., Aug. 2, 1910, died in Los Angeles, Calif., Jan. 1959, daughter of Benjamin A. and Lolita (Beardsley) Miller; 2nd, in Washington, D.C., Feb. 15, 1947, LOUISE L. ANDERSON, born in Lewes, Del., Oct. 16, 1910, daughter of Charles O. and Lillian (Owens) Anderson.

He served in the U. S. Army and was discharged a Colonel. He attended Command and General Staff College at Ft. Leavenworth, Kansas.

Children in 9th Generation

F11088   PATRICIA WARD, b. Battle Creek, Mich., Oct. 1, 1936.

F11089   MARY BRUCE, b. St. Paul, Minn., Aug. 25, 1940.

F11090   CAROL ANNE, child of 2nd wife, b. Palo Alto, Calif., Jan. 12, 1948.

F10813 DONALD STEPHEN LOCKE, born in Rockford, Ill., Nov. 2, 1910, married 1st, in Belvedere, Ill., Jan. 20, 1934, RUTH BELLE FRENCH, born in Riley, Ill., Oct. 20, 1917, daughter of William and Iva Janette (Russell) French; 2nd, in Portage, Wis., July 11, 1943, JUANITA MILDRED WOODYATT, born in Sterling, Ill., April 5, 1923, daughter of Albert and Lulu (Archer) Woodyatt.

Children in 9th Generation

F11091   JOHN GORDON, b. Woodstock, Ill., Jan. 15, 1935.

F11092   JUDITH ANNE, b. Elgin, Ill., May 3, 1936.

Children by 2nd wife.

F11093   DOROTHY JEAN, b. Tulsa, Okla., June 5, 1944.

F11094   SHARON RAY, b. Sterling, Ill., July 29, 1945.

F11095 VALERIE LYNN, b. Morrison, Ill., Oct. 11, 1946.

F11096 DONALD STEPHEN, JR., b. Peoria, Ill., July 6, 1950.

11097 RICHARD ARCHER, b. Highland Park, Mich., June 17, 1953.

F11098 MARY ANITA, b. Royal Oak, Mich., Aug. 8, 1956.

F10814 PHILIP FRANCIS LOCKE, SR., born in Rockford, Ill., Aug. 10, 1912, married in Meridian, Miss., May 4, 1943, MARJORIE ELISABETH (CHALFANT) RYAN, born in Aurora, Ill., Sept. 13, 1917, daughter of Wm. Edward and Maude (Lapsley) Chalfant.
He graduated with a B.A. from North Central College in Napierville ?, Ill. and a LL.B. from John Marshall Law School. He was a Captain in the Navy during WWII and served as Justice of the Peace in Glen Ellyn, Ill.

Children in 9th Generation

F11099 PHILIP FRANCIS, JR., b. Colorado Springs, Colo., Aug. 16, 1944.

11100 JANICE LYNNE, b. Geneva, Ill., Oct. 22, 1948, d. near Wausau, Wis., Mar. 20, 1970.

F10815 FREDERICK NATHANIEL LOCKE, born in Edison Park, Ill., Oct. 18, 1914, married in Twin Falls, Idaho, Oct. 18, 1939, MARTHA ALICE BYRAM, born in Bend, Ore., Mar. 14, 1916, daughter of Sidney and Elma (Benser) Byram. He served in the U.S. Navy during WWII on the Aleutian Islands.

Children in 9th Generation

11101 WALTER FREDERICK, b. Twin Falls, Idaho, Nov. 20, 1940, m. Twin Falls, Idaho, Dec. 2, 1967, MARLENE KATHRYN (CARAWAY) SMITH, b. Rupert, Idaho, Dec. 5, 1939, daughter of Chester Delmas and Elsie Ella (Boldt) Caraway.

F11102 EVELYN LOUISE, b. Gooding, Idaho, Aug. 21, 1943.

F11103 ROBERT BRUCE, b. Gooding, Idaho, April 29, 1949.

F10816 HELEN MARION LOCKE, born in Evanston, Ill., July 19, 1916, married in Clinton, Iowa, Oct. 9, 1937, CAPT. GEORGE ARTHUR WRIGHT, born in Salix, Penna., Oct. 18, 1913, son of George Forrest and Helen Frances (Davis) Wright.
He was a Chaplain in U.S. Navy 1944. Member Evangelical Church, Evangelical United Brethren Church and the United Methodist Church. In 1973, held rank of Capt., Chaplain Corps, U.S.N.

Children in 9th Gen. b. in Johnstown, Penna.

F11104 JAMES ARTHUR, b. Oct. 13, 1938.

F11105 HELEN GRACE, b. Aug. 10, 1941.

11106 MARJORIE ELIZABETH, b. Feb. 17, 1945.

F10817 ELEANOR GRACE LOCKE, born in Wilmette, Ill., Jan. 4, 1918, married in Gulfport, Miss., May 9, 1942, ROBERT JENNINGS ARLEN, born in Wabash, Ind., Sept. 27, 1920, son of Dr. Homer and Maisie (Jennings) Arlen.

He graduated with a B.S. in Physical Education from North Central College and M.S. from Northwestern University. Spent three years in the European Theater during WWII as an Air Force Technical Sergeant.

Children in 9th Generation

11107 KATHRYN GRACE, b. Geneva, Ill., June 25, 1947.

11108 ROBERT EDWARD, b. Elmhurst, Ill., July 12, 1949.

F10818 WILLIAM MORSE LOCKE, born in Glen Ellyn, Ill., Dec. 27, 1919, married in Maumee, Ohio, July 10, 1945, ROSE MARY BETTS, born in Maumee, Ohio, Sept. 19, 1925, daughter of Dr. Charles T. and Mary Emma (Jones) Betts. Is a Ph.D., University of Toledo and served in the European Theater as a Technical Sergeant in the Air Force.

Children in 9th Gen. b. in Toledo, Ohio

F11109 WILLIAM MORSE, JR., b. Aug. 4, 1946.

11110 REBECCA ALLISON, b. April 29, 1948.

11111 BENJAMIN ROSS, b. Feb. 14, 1950.

11112 JESSICA ELIZABETH, Aug. 13, 1951.

F11113 JOSEPH ARTHUR, b. Dec. 28, 1952.

11114 JUSTIN CHARLES, b. April 13, 1955.

F10819 ELIZABETH BRUCE LOCKE, born in Glen Ellyn, Ill., Feb. 22, 1922, married in Elmhurst, Ill., Oct. 16, 1943, WILLIAM GUEN-THER AHLT, born in Hamburg, Germany, Feb. 1, 1922, son of William and Anna (Therkorn) Ahlt (Ahlf?).

He graduated from Elmhurst College with a B.A. and DePaul University with a Jur.D.D. He was a private in the 95th Infantry 1942-45 and distinguished himself earning two bronze stars and the Purple Heart.

Children in 9th Generation

11115 LISA DOROTHY, b. Altendorf, Germany, Feb. 19, 1954,
       m. Dundee, Ill., May 3, 1975, ROY LESTER HANSON,
       b. Coral Gables, Fla., Feb. 3, 1950, son of Glen and
       Eleanor (Mackey) Hanson.

11116 THOMAS PETER, b. Elmhurst, Ill., Oct. 20, 1955.

11117 WILLIAM BRUCE, b. Elmhurst, Ill., June 6, 1957.

F10820 MARJORIE RUTH LOCKE, born in Glen Ellyn, Ill., Sept.
30, 1924, married in Wheaton, Ill., June 7, 1947, HARRY THAYER
MAHONEY, born in Oak Park, Ill., June 19, 1922, son of Harry P.
and Evelyn (Waters) Mahoney.
She graduated from Elmhurst College with a B.A. degree. He also
graduated from Elmhurst and holds a Jur.D. from Northwestern Univ.

Children in 9th Generation

11118 ELIZABETH EVELYN, b. San Jose, Calif., Nov. 26, 1955.

11119 PAUL RICHARD, b. Mexico, D.F., Aug. 31, 1956.

11120 MATTHEW LOCKE, b. Mexico, D.F., Mar. 2, 1959.

11121 SARAH THAYER, b. Washington, D.C., Sept. 25, 1960.

F10821 LUMAN LOCKE LILLIE, born in Rockford, Ill., July 13,
1905, married 1st, Rockford, Ill., Sept. 10, 1930, ALICE GARRETT,
born in Rockford, Ill., Aug. 3, 1910, died in Rockford, Ill., Nov. 16,
1946, daughter of John and Mamie (O'Cleary) Garrett; 2nd, in Rockford, Ill., Nov. 24, 1947, LILY (MILLER) WEAVER, born in Shirland,
Ill., Jan. 29, 1900, daughter of Charles A. and Harriett (Blackmere)
Miller.

Children in 9th Generation

F11122 JOHN LESTER, b. Rockford, Ill., May 15, 1935.

F10826 GEORGE LINCOLN HERRICK, born in Charleston, Maine,
Nov. 13, 1905, died in Sacramento, Calif., April 12, 1973, married
in Fresno, Calif., Feb. 24, 1927, MYRA FRANCES HALL, born in
Hot Springs, Ark., July 24, 1907, daughter of Harry C. and Ethel
(Connell) Hall.

Children in 9th Generation

F11123 MARJORIE IRENE, b. Fresno, Calif., Aug. 14, 1928.

F10827 RODNEY LIONEL HERRICK, born in Plankington, S.Dak.,
Aug. 2, 1887, died in San Diego, Calif., June 24, 1963, married in

Portland, Ore., June 26, 1915, ANNA AMELIA MEISTER, name later
changed to Anita Miller, born in Toledo, Ohio, Dec. 16, 1886, died
in San Leandro, Calif., Dec. 22, 1961, daughter of Charles Karl and
Charlott Louisa (Miller) Meister.

Children in 9th Gen. b. in Portland, Oregon

11124 VEDA ANN (DAY), b. Oct. 18, 1917.

11125 ROBERT KING EATON, b. Mar. 26, 1919, d. Oakland,
       Calif., Oct. 29, 1942.

11126 ELIZABETH JANE, b. Jan. 31, 1921.

F11127 CAROLYN JEAN, b. Nov. 2, 1922.

F10829 MARY ELIZABETH HERRICK, born in Madera, Calif., Jan.
23, 1902, married in Gen. Grant National Park, Calif., Aug. 3,
1924, WILLIAM ARTHUR DANIEL, born in Fresno, Calif., Feb. 4,
1899, son of Robert and Annie (Jagger) Daniel.

Children in 9th Gen. b. in Los Angeles, Calif.

F11128 RICHARD HERRICK, b. July 31, 1927.

F11129 BARBARA ANN, b. Nov. 18, 1928.

F10830 GORDON WALTER DANFORTH, born in Bangor, Maine,
Feb. 19, 1903, married in Bangor, Maine, June 24, 1939, HELEN
MARY RICHARDSON, born in Bangor, Maine, April 28, 1914, daugh-
ter of Endymion C. and Martha (Lansil) Richardson.

Children in 9th Gen. b. in Bangor, Maine

11130 CHRIS HERRICK, b. Jan. 31, 1944.

11131 LINDA SUE, b. Aug. 13, 1945.

F10832 IRVING WEYMOUTH HERRICK, SR., born in Medford
Center, Maine, May 16, 1904, died in Saco, Maine, Aug. 17, 1966,
married in Lisbon Falls, Maine, June 23, 1929, FLORENCE ELIZABETH
HUDGKINS, born in Lisbon Falls, Maine, Sept. 22, 1902, daughter
of Melvin Simonds and Elizabeth (Mulhall) Hodgkins.
He served in U.S. Army 1922-25.

Children in 9th Generation

F11132 ELIZABETH ANN, b. Biddeford, Maine, Dec. 11, 1930.

F11133 IRVING WEYMOUTH, JR., b. Biddeford, Maine, Nov. 7,
       1932.

11134 ROBERT EARLE, b. Saco, Maine, Feb. 6, 1935.

F10833 CHARLOTTE ELIZABETH HERRICK, born in Medford Center, Maine, Jan. 17, 1906, married in Lisbon Falls, Maine, Aug. 24, 1929, PERRY LEE BURBANK, born in Flagstaff, Maine, April 3, 1906, son of James Eugene and Ruth Phoebe (Williamson) Burbank.

Children in 9th Generation

F11135 LOEN HERRICK, b. Lisbon Falls, Maine, Dec. 19, 1930.

F11136 AUIS RUTH, b. Stratton Village, Maine, April 23, 1932.

F11137 GILBERT EATON, b. Stratton Village, Maine, Mar. 26, 1939.

F10834 DANIEL ARLAND HERRICK, born in Foxcroft, Maine, June 5, 1908, married in Lebanon Springs, N. Y., Oct. 5, 1929, SUSIE BELLE FACE, born in Nassau, N.Y., April 29, 1911, daughter of Adolphus Gustavis and Mary May (Bartlett) Face.

Children in 9th Generation

F11138 ROY ARLAND, b. Pittsfield, Mass., May 30, 1930.

F11139 ROBERT DANIEL, b. Stephentown, N.Y., April 4, 1936.

F11140 DEAN GORDON, b. Stephentown, N.Y., Feb. 3, 1938.

F10835 JOHN ANDREW HERRICK, born in Charleston, Maine, Mar. 10, 1912, married in Lynn, Mass., July 20, 1946, PRISCILLA BATCHELDER, born in Lynn, Mass., Mar. 28, 1915, daughter of Ezra Norman and Bertha Florence (Ames) Batchelder.

Children in 9th Generation

F11141 MARTHA IOLA, b. Salem, Mass., July 1, 1947.

11142 CAROL AMES, b. Marblehead, Mass., Jan. 28, 1949.

F10836 LILLIAN ROBERTA HERRICK, born in Stockton Springs, Maine, Sept. 16, 1915, married in Charleston, Maine, Aug. 27, 1939, SAMUEL CROWELL III, born in Boston, Mass., Feb. 24, 1917, son of Samuel and Helen B. (Josselyn) Crowell, Jr.

Children in 9th Generation

F11143 LILLIAN BARSTOW, b. Boston, Mass., Mar. 15, 1940.

F11144 JO NANCY, b. Portsmouth, N.H., Jan. 2, 1942.

F11145 MARCIA WASHBURN, b. Portsmouth, N.H., Feb. 1, 1943.

F11146 DEBORAH HERRICK, b. Richmond, Va., Aug. 30, 1948.

F11147 SAMUEL CROWELL IV, b. Richmond, Va., July 1, 1950.

11148   ERRICA JOSSELYN, b. Saugus, Mass., Oct. 7, 1954.
She graduated from Franklin Pierce College, summa cum
laude, May, 1976 with honors in History and is employed
at Strawberry Banke, Portsmouth, N. H.

F11149   KRESTEN LOCKE, b. Portsmouth, N. H., Sept. 8, 1956.

F10837   PRUDENCE IOLA HERRICK, born in Bowdoin, Maine,
Jan. 2, 1918, married in Cincinnati, Ohio, Oct. 8, 1954, EUGENE
STANTON, born in Eufaula, Ala., son of Winfield and Katherine
(McLeod) Stanton.
  She holds B.M. and M.M. from Cincinnati Conservatory of Music.

Children in 9th Generation

11150   KATHERINE ALICE, b. Cincinnati, Ohio, May 8, 1956.

F10838   THEODORE LOCKE HERRICK, born in Lisbon Falls, Maine,
Feb. 3, 1922, married in Marblehead, Mass., Jan. 18, 1946, BARBARA
BUTT, born in Swampscott, Mass., May 19, 1925, daughter of Henry
Archibald and Kathleen (Doane) Butt.
  He served in U.S. Navy during WW II and holds a B.S. degree from
the University of Maine in Agronomy.

Children in 9th Generation

11151   SUSAN BARBARA, b. Bangor, Maine, Nov. 12, 1946.

F11152   JOHN LOCKE, b. Bangor, Maine, Nov. 1, 1948.

11153   DAVID ALAN, b. Charlestown, Mass., July 24, 1951.

11154   DONALD BUTT, b. Fort Kent, Maine, Dec. 4, 1953.

11155   DANIEL CARL, b. Fort Kent, Maine, Mar. 3, 1956.

11156   DARRELL CHARLES, b. Fort Kent, Maine, Mar. 3, 1956.

F10839   JOSEPHINE SHIRLEY HERRICK, born in Lisbon Falls,
Maine, Feb. 7, 1923, married in Marblehead, Mass., June 15, 1945,
WESLEY RUSSELL WYNN, born in Brimley, Mich., June 21, 1921,
son of Frank Marshall and Marie (Russell) Wynn.

Children in 9th Generation

11157   SHIRLEY MARIE, b. Chelsea, Mass., Naval Hospital, Mar.
5, 1946, m. Marblehead, Mass., Mar. 16, 1968, DANIEL
WEBB GOODWIN, b. Marblehead, Mass., Aug. 25,
1941, son of William Knowland and Ruth (Elder)
Goodwin.

F11158   PATRICIA JEAN, b. Salem, Mass., Dec. 16, 1949.

F10840 METTA FRANCES LORD, born in El Centro, Calif., Nov. 16, 1915, married in Pasadena, Calif., July 2, 1939, DONALD BRIGGS DYER, born in El Centro, Calif., Dec. 18, 1915, son of Clyde Webster and Bertha Mary (Rhoades) Dyer.

He has a B.E. from U.C.L.A.

Children in 9th Generation

11159 FRED WILBUR, b. Santa Monica, Calif., Sept. 8, 1943.

11160 RICHARD CLYDE, b. Pasadena, Calif., Jan. 23, 1945.

F10841 EARL MALCOLM LORD, born in San Diego, Calif., Aug. 19, 1917, married in Pasadena, Calif., Aug. 30, 1941, STELLAMAY FRENCH, born in Pasadena, Calif., May 6, 1923, daughter of Benjamin S. and Opal (Shaner) French.

He holds an A.B. from San Jose State College, M.S. from Univ. of Southern California and was in the U.S. Army Air Force 1943-46.

Children in 9th Generation

11161 WILLIAM EARL LORD, b. Los Angeles, Calif., Aug. 4, 1943, m. 1st, Los Angeles, Calif., June 13, 1965, SHARON LEE SCHROEDER, b. Cleveland, Ohio, Oct. 10, 1943, daughter of George Robert and Genevieve Schroeder; 2nd, Boulder, Colo., April 3, 1970, SUSAN ELAINE SPLEET, b. Detroit, Mich., Oct. 11, 1945, daughter of Sterling Joseph and Ruth Elizabeth (Boomhower) Spleet.

11162 CLARA KATHLEEN, b. Santa Monica, Calif., June 16, 1947, m. Rocky Mountains of Colo., Sept. 30, 1972, BROCK ASHLOCK HAINES, b. Santa Monica, Calif., Jan. 17, 1948, son of Richard Charles and Leonora (Stevens) Haines.

F10842 MARY ALICE LORD, born in Berkeley, Calif., Sept. 8, 1920, married 1st, in Glenside, Penna., Aug. 30, 1947, KENNETH MERLE HARDING, born in Binghamton, N.Y., Sept. 25, 1922, son of Earle Merle and Effie Louise (Kelley) Harding; 2nd, in Redondo Beach, Calif., June 12, 1973, DR. RICHARD LAMBSON CASSELL, born in Anderson, Calif., Aug. 10, 1912, son of Ernest Vincent and Erma Iona (Tabler) Cassell.

She holds a B.S. degree from Ursinus College, Collegeville, Penna. and a Masters of Nursing from Yale Univ. She served as an Ensign in U.S.N.R. during WWII.

Children in 9th Generation

F11163 NANCY ELAINE, b. Philadelphia, Penna., Dec. 24, 1949.

11164 ELIZABETH JANE, b. Abington, Penna., Aug. 22, 1951.

11165   JUDITH ANNE, b. Abington, Penna., Oct. 28, 1953, m. Mason, N. H., April 30, 1976, GERALD ERNEST ANDERSON, son of Robert and Isabelle Anderson.

11166   DONNA JEAN, b. Santa Monica, Calif., Oct. 10, 1957.

F10843   CHESTER FREDERICK PEDEN, born in Gifford, Idaho, Dec. 10, 1900, married in Myrtle Point, Ore., Dec. 13, 1924, MARY AGNES TRIPP, born in Myrtle Point, Ore., Oct. 14, 1902, daughter of Francois Gasper and Charlett Anna Tripp.

Children in 9th Gen. b. in Myrtle Point, Ore.

F11167   WILLIAM FREDERICK, b. Sept. 9, 1926.

F11168   GORDON GENE, b. Nov. 19, 1928.

F11169   BARBARA JANE, b. Sept. 28, 1939.

F10844   JESSIE LOUISE PEDEN, born in Gifford, Idaho, Nov. 6, 1902, married in Colfax, Wash., Dec. 25, 1926, ELLSWORTH CORNELIUS YARWOOD, born in Deertrail, Wash., Oct. 8, 1904, son of William Henry and Theresa M. (Himmelspach) Yarwood.

Children in 9th Generation

F11170   ELIZABETH LOUISE, b. Colfax, Wash., Feb. 8, 1929.

F11171   WILMA NADINE, b. Pullman, Wash., Feb. 28, 1930.

F11172   JANET JEANNE, b. Colfax, Wash., April 7, 1933.

F10845   VERA VIOLA PEDEN, born in Gifford, Idaho, Jan. 12, 1905, married 1st, in Malo, Wash., May 24, 1924, RAY JOHNSON, born in Seattle, Wash., May 30, 1904, son of Olaf and Emma (Traaen) Johnson; 2nd, in Ione, Wash., Mar. 11, 1938, ROBERT GREGG HOLT, born in Deer Lodge, Mont., Mar. 1, 1914, son of Walter and Francis (Gregg) Holt.

Children in 9th Generation

11173   DONALD LeROY, b. Malo, Wash., June 7, 1925, d. Cambridge, England (WW II), Jan. 27, 1945.

F11174   DORIS MILDRED, b. Republic, Wash., Jan. 22, 1927.

F11175   DERALD CLIFFORD, b. Republic, Wash., July 1, 1929.

F10846   ELLA MARIE PEDEN, born in Gifford, Idaho, Dec. 30, 1906, died in Lebanon, Ore., Oct. 2, 1947, married in Wenatchee, Wash., Nov. 12, 1926, CLAIR RODERICK CALDWELL, born in Alexandria, Nebr., Mar. 30, 1905, son of Thomas and Ethel (Demary) Caldwell.

Children in 9th Generation

F11176 VIVIAN ELAINE, b. Malo, Wash., Sept. 7, 1927.

F11177 CLARA LOUISE, b. Hermiston, Ore., Aug. 8, 1930.

F10847 MARY IVAL PEDEN, born in Garfield, Wash., April 20, 1909, married in Republic, Wash., Sept. 2, 1930, CLARENCE MILO HILDERBRAND, born in Spangle, Wash., Dec. 30, 1901, son of Samuel and Hattie (Chase) Hilderbrand.

Children in 9th Gen. b. in Malo, Wash.

F11178 HELEN IRENE, b. Aug. 30, 1931.

F11179 MILDRED JEANNETTE, b. Feb. 4, 1934.

F11180 CLIFFORD EUGENE, b. July 24, 1935.

F11181 LARRIE SAMUEL, b. Mar. 19, 1937.

F10849 EDITH ELDORE PEDEN, born in Malo, Wash., April 22, 1919, married in Republic, Wash., Mar. 19, 1938, DELBERT HAZEN RUMSEY, born in Malo, Wash., July 21, 1916, son of Elver and Lelia (Cull) Rumsey.

Children in 9th Generation

11182 DENNIS HOWARD, b. Colville, Wash., Oct. 10, 1938, m. Coeur D'Alene, Idaho, Dec. 24, 1974, ZOE ANN CLINTON, b. Valentine, Nebr., July 10, 1937, daughter of Everett Holt and Jennie (Teachout) Clinton.

F11183 JUDITH COLLEEN, b. Okanogan, Wash., Sept. 1, 1940.

F10851 LOVELLA EVELIN DAILEY, born in Garfield, Wash., Feb. 10, 1904, married in Colfax, Wash., July 6, 1926, RICHARD LEE WILHELM, born in Colfax, Wash., Oct. 22, 1907, son of Frank E. and Mathilda (Bing) Wilhelm.

Children in 9th Generation

F11184 RICHARD FRANK, b. Colfax, Wash., Nov. 12, 1926.

F11185 SUSAN JOYCE, b. Colfax, Wash., Nov. 6, 1928.

F11186 THELMA MAE, b. Moscow, Idaho, Dec. 29, 1934.

F10852 VIOLA VIRGINIA DAILEY, born in Garfield, Wash., Nov. 12, 1905, died in Colfax, Wash., Dec. 17, 1974, married 1st, in Colfax, Wash., Oct. 27, 1925, CHESTER BOYD McCOWN, born in Garfield, Wash., Feb. 4, 1896, died in Garfield, Wash., May 29,

1949, son of George M. and Elizabeth (Boyd) McCown; 2nd, in Spokane, Wash., April 9, 1950, JAMES C. BYRNE, born in Garfield, Wash., May 9, 1898.

Children in 9th Generation

F11187 ROBERT RAYMOND, b. Madera, Calif., Mar. 31, 1926.

F11188 JANE EVELIN, b. Latah County, Idaho, Oct. 29, 1927.

F11189 RAY CHESTER, b. Garfield, Wash., Dec. 3, 1932.

F11190 SUE ANN, b. Garfield, Wash., Nov. 4, 1942.

F10853 JOE KARR DAILEY, born in Latah County, Idaho, July 9, 1909, died in Bellevue, Wash., April 8, 1971, married in Colfax, Wash., Sept. 21, 1935, HATTIE MARY MITCHELL, born in Mary St. John, Wash., Oct. 29, 1910, daughter of Ezra C. and Sadie (Harmon) Mitchell.

Children in 9th Generation

11191 KAREN SUE, b. Potlatch, Idaho, June 29, 1942, d. same day.

11192 CONNIE JO, b. Spokane, Wash., Nov. 3, 1948.

F10854 WALTER RICHARD DAILEY, born in Latah County, Idaho, July 10, 1912, married in Colfax, Wash., June 5, 1937, JESSIE MAUD TOLAND, born in Gifford, Wash., Dec. 26, 1917, daughter of John and Maud (Anderson) Toland.

Children in 9th Gen. b. in Garfield, Wash.

F11193 DIXIE LOU, b. Dec. 4, 1937.

F11194 JOHN HUGH, b. Jan. 23, 1939.

F11195 BARBARA ANN, b. May 4, 1941, d. Moscow, Idaho, July 9, 1966.

F10855 DONALD MORRIS DAILEY, born in Garfield, Wash., Nov. 5, 1914, died in Potlatch, Idaho, April 1, 1974, married in Coeur D'Alene, Idaho, April 22, 1942, LOUISE MOULSTER, born in Hanford, Wash., Oct. 29, 1920, daughter of Lewis and Lena (Morgan) Moulster.

Children in 9th Generation

11196 DONALD MORRIS, JR., b. Pasco, Wash., Oct. 20, 1944.

11197 LEWIS RICHARD, b. Colfax, Wash., April 6, 1948.

F10856 ROBERTA ARLENE LOCKE, born in Lewiston, Idaho, Mar. 1, 1930, married in Bozeman, Mont., Sept. 9, 1950, DONALD EDWIN REICH, SR., born in Butte, Mont., Feb. 2, 1926, son of Herbert Frank and Inez Cornelia (Rogers) Reich.

He served 2½ years in the Navy as a Petty Officer in the Signal Corps.

Children in 9th Generation

11198 DONALD EDWIN, JR., b. Tacoma, Wash., Sept. 14, 1951, d. Edmonds, Wash., Jan. 3, 1952.

11199 KIMBERLEY DAWN, b. Seattle, Wash., June 7, 1954.

11200 KATHI DIANE, b. Tacoma, Wash., Oct. 25, 1956.

F10857 GAIL CLEO LOCKE, born in Lewiston, Idaho, ca. 1935, married in Lewiston, Idaho, Feb. 19, 1955, THEODORE EDMOND HAALAND, born in Bellingham, Wash., Dec. 13, 1931, son of Edwin Gerhard and Thelma (Wolden) Haaland.

Children in 9th Generation

11201 SHANNON RAE, b. Pasco, Wash., Dec. 31, 1955.

11202 SHERILEE KAY, b. Pasco, Wash., April 24, 1958.

11203 STEVEN LOCKE, b. Yakima, Wash., Aug. 26, 1964.

F10858 HELEN LIDIA LOCKE, born in Buenos Aires, Rep. of Argentina, S.A., Aug. 3, 1919, married in Rosario, Rep. of Argentina, S.A., Jan. 8, 1944, MAXIMO ANTONIO SCHMIDT D.D.S., born in Tucumán, Rep. of Argentina, S.A., July 23, 1918, son of Maximo H. G. and Zulema (Mañay) Schmidt.

Children in 9th Generation

F11204 PATRICIA HELEN, b. Buenos Aires, Rep. of Arg., S. A., Aug. 17, 1947.

11205 MARCIA CECELIA TERESSA, b. Rosario, Rep. of Arg., S.A., Oct. 15, 1950.

11206 MAXIMO ANTONIO JOSE, b. Entre Ríos, Rep. of Arg., S.A., Dec. 19, 1958.

F10860 ELVA LOUISE DAILEY, born in Latah County, Idaho, Nov. 18, 1909, married in Steptoe, Wash., April 25, 1932, LESLIE LeROY CALHOUN, born in Spokane County, Wash., July 24, 1908, son of Lieudaman L. and Viola A. (Roberts) Calhoun.

He served in the Army Air Force during WWII.

Children in 9th Generation

F11207 DONALD LeROY, b. Garfield, Wash., Sept. 21, 1933.

11208 MAX GERALD, b. Potlatch, Idaho, Aug. 9, 1936, d. Spokane, Wash., Feb. 23, 1955.

F10861 CHARLES LEONARD DAILEY, born in Garfield, Wash., June 17, 1913, married in Potlatch, Idaho, July 12, 1942, BERTHA ADELIA TIETZ, born in Steele, N. Dak., Nov. 18, 1919, daughter of Michael and Ottilia (Zerbst) Tietz.

Children in 9th Gen. b. in Colfax, Wash.

11209 CHARLES WILLIAM, b. Nov. 25, 1943.

11210 LEONARD WAYNE, b. Oct. 15, 1949.

F10862 EDNA ALMA DAILEY, born in Garfield, Wash., Sept. 20, 1915, died in Pullman, Wash., July 26, 1970, married in Garfield, Wash., June 1, 1941, ORVIN MARVIS LARSON MIKKELSEN, born in Easby, N. Dak., May 1, 1914, son of Jans Peter Marvis and Clara Josephine (Larson) Mikkelsen.

Children in 9th Generation

F11211 LOIS EVELYN, b. Cashmere, Wash., Mar. 14, 1942.

F11212 LINDA KAYE, b. Colfax, Wash., Sept. 9, 1947.

11213 LARRY MILES, b. Colfax, Wash., Sept. 18, 1951.

F10863 ROY ARNOLD DAILEY, born in Garfield, Wash., Nov. 7, 1923, married in Vancouver, B. C., Canada, Oct. 27, 1945, PHYLLIS RETA BEARD, born in Cochrane, Alberta, Canada, April 26, 1925, daughter of Walter A. and Alice Hilda Marguerite (Green) Beard. She served as a parachute packer in the RCAF during WW II.

Children in 9th Generation

11214 DAVID ALLEN, b. Colfax, Wash., Nov. 28, 1947, m. Leavenworth, Wash., Dec. 20, 1972, DIANA SHREVE, b. Portland, Ore., May 21, 1943.

F10864 SUSAN VIOLA LOCKE, born in Crockett, Calif., Sept. 2, 1923, married 1st, Richmond, Calif., June 21, 1941, RAYMOND GEORGE GOLDEN, born in Richmond, Calif., Jan. 3, 1921, son of Frank and Florence (Ohl) Golden; 2nd, Dakota City, Nebr., July 8, 1949, DERREL JOHN JUELFS, born in Correctionville, Iowa, May 19, 1924, son of John and Anna (Klahn) Juelfs.

Children in 9th Gen. b. in Richmond, Calif.

F11215 EILEEN KAY, b. Oct. 8, 1942.

11216 MICHAEL GEORGE, b. Oct. 12, 1947.

11217 GRANT LAWRENCE, b. Jan. 6, 1951.

11218 KAY FRANCIS, b. Aug. 14, 1953.

F10865 BARBARA ANN LOCKE, born in Crockett, Calif., Oct. 10, 1924, married 1st, Richmond, Calif., April 5, 1942, PAUL ALBERT CIABATTARI, born in Mich., Mar. 8, 1917, son of Theodore and Caroline (Yoahs) Ciabattari; 2nd, in Reno, Nev., Nov. 24, 1953, FRANK ALFRED MARI, born in San Francisco, Calif., July 29, 1924, son of Alfred and Clementine Mari.

Children in 9th Gen. b. in Richmond, Calif.

11219 PAUL ALBERT, JR., b. Mar. 24, 1943.

11220 ARDELLA GAY, b. Feb. 2, 1948

F10866 MARGARET LOUISE LOCKE, born in Crockett, Calif., Sept. 29, 1927, married 1st, Gardnerville, Nev., July 10, 1942, EDWARD JOSEPH FREDERICK, SR., born in Worcester, Mass., May 11, 1916, died in Richmond, Calif., Aug. 14, 1971, son of Albert Anthony and Caroline (Welke) Frederick; 2nd, Carson City, Nev., June 29, 1975, WILLIAM EDWARD PARKER, born in Portland, Ore., Oct. 25, 1918.

Children in 9th Generation

11221 EDWARD ANTHONY, b. Berkeley, Calif., July 8, 1945, d. Oakland, Calif., July 16, 1945.

F11222 EDWARD JOSEPH, JR., b. Bell, Calif., Mar. 4, 1947.

11223 GLEN ALLEN, b. Richmond, Calif., Oct. 10, 1949, m. Las Vegas, Nev., Mar. 19, 1972, DAWN ELAINE BUNTEN, b. Miami, Fla., June 9, 1954, Divorced, no children.

F10867 ROBERT EARL LOCKE, JR., born in Crockett, Calif., July 9, 1931, married 1st, Reno, Nev., Jan. 7, 1950, PEARL DeBRAY, born in Havre, Mont., Aug. 7, 1931, daughter of John and Nancy Marie (Malatere) DeBray; 2nd, in Sacramento, Calif., May 24, 1958, NADYNE WARD, born in Norton, Kansas, Mar. 16, 1931, daughter of Thoma J. and Margaret (Steele) Ward.

Children in 9th Generation

11224 DARLENE MARIE, b. Richmond, Calif., Aug. 20, 1952.

11225   RENEE GAY, b. Sacramento, Calif., Jan. 30, 1954.

11226   JOHN ROBERT, b. Sacramento, Calif., May 12, 1955.

11227   JULIA ANN, b. Covina, Calif., Dec. 5, 1955.

11228   THOMAS PATRICK, b. Sacramento, Calif., Nov. 17, 1962.

11229   JAMES DAVID, b. Sacramento, Calif., Dec. 18, 1964.

F10869   JUNE EVELYN FRANCIS, born in Hill City, Idaho, June 28, 1917, married in Fairfield, Idaho, Nov. 17, 1935, GUY PLANK SKYLES, born in Corral, Idaho, June 16, 1913, son of John Miscal and Eudora Adell (Plank) Skyles.

Children in 9th Generation

F11230   MARGERY ADELL, b. Hill City, Idaho, Sept. 14, 1936.

F11231   EUNICE MAY, b. Fairfield, Idaho, April 13, 1938.

F11232   EUGENE MISCAL, b. Fairfield, Idaho, Aug. 23, 1940.

F11233   BARBARA JEAN, b. Republic, Wash., Aug. 6, 1942.

F11234   GUY DOUGLAS, b. Portland, Ore., Oct. 3, 1944.

F10871   MYRTA BELLE LOCKE, born in Oakland, Calif., Jan. 28, 1928, married in Minden, Nev., Mar. 10, 1946, LEONARD EARL DAUSY, born in Richmond, Calif., Mar. 20, 1927, died in Antioch, Calif., Jan. 26, 1970, son of Louie and Mamie (Craven) Dausy.

Children in 9th Generation

F11235   LENORE ERLEEN, b. Oakland, Calif., Aug. 28, 1947.

F11236   MICHAEL LEWIS, b. Richmond, Calif., July 30, 1949.

11237   MARK WESLEY, b. Richmond, Calif., July 30, 1949.

F11238   DEBORAH ANN, b. Richmond, Calif., May 17, 1952.

11239   VALRI JEAN, b. Walnut Creek, Calif., Sept. 30, 1954.

F10872   ALICE MAY LOCKE, born in Oakland, Calif., Mar. 30, 1929, married in Tahoe Township, Nev., Mar. 30, 1950, GERALD AUGUSTUS MERRICK, born in Oakland, Calif., Sept. 27, 1930, son of James and May (Mesch) Merrick.
He served 2 years in U.S. Army. No overseas duty.

Children in 9th Generation

11240   GERALD DAVID, b. Hayward, Calif., Oct. 30, 1951.

11241   JUDY ANN, b. El Paso, Texas (Army Hosp.), July 5, 1953.

11242   KEITH TODD, b. Hayward, Calif., May 5, 1961.

F10873 EDSON LOCKE, born Oct. 21, 1862, died Jan. 1928, married Sept. 26, 1888, IDA MAY STEVENS of Mt. Vernon, Maine, died Jan. 29, 1941.

Children in 9th Generation

11243 HERBERT EDSON, b. April 6, 1891, d. Jan. 1, 1962, m. May 24, 1916, MARGUERITE LOWELL of Augusta, Maine and had: 11244 NANCY.

F11245 BESSIE RACHEL, b. Aug. 15, 1894, d. Thomaston, Maine, 1956, m. Dec. 29, 1915, HAROLD PERRY VANNAH.

F10874 LELA SYLVINA LOCKE, born Dec. 1864, died May 19, 1948, married June 7, 1883, EDWARD PAYSON HUSSEY of Augusta, Maine, died Dec. 2, 1932.

Children in 9th Generation

11246 JOHN FRED, b. Mar. 21, 1884, d. April 25, 1958, m. June 24, 1912, DORA M. VICKAH of Salem, Mass., no children.

F10875 FRED JOHN LOCKE, born in Mt. Vernon, Maine, Sept. 23, 1867, died in Augusta, Maine, May 3, 1931, married in Mt. Vernon, Maine, Nov. 26, 1894, ELOISE M. FELLOWS, born in Mt. Vernon, Maine, Nov. 10, 1876, died in Augusta, Maine, April 17, 1965.
He was a farmer. She made braided rugs and crocheted. She was the daughter of Fernand Cortez and Ellen (Blake) Fellows.

Children in 9th Gen. b. in Mt. Vernon, Maine

11247 JOHN FERNANDO, b. Sept. 11, 1895, m. Bellows Falls, Vt., Feb. 20, 1917, MARGARET ALLEN WOOD, b. Calais, Maine, May 17, 1894.

F11248 FRED RAYMOND, b. Oct. 26, 1900, m. Augusta, Maine, Sept. 15, 1923, EUNICE HEWINS.

F10876 SAMUEL LOCKE, born in Mt. Vernon, Maine, Mar. 13, 1866, died in Nahant, Mass., April 12, 1937, married in Lynn, Mass., May 29, 1890, MINNIE FARMER PATTEN CURRY, born Mar. 13, 1864, died Dec. 11, 1931. He was a shoemaker in Lynn, Mass.

Children in 9th Generation

11249 EMERY RUSSELL, b. Lynn, Mass., Nov. 13, 1896, d. Lynn, Mass., April 1, 1944, m. Feb. 21, 1917, FLORENCE HOLMSTROM, b. Sept. 22, 1894, d. Jan. 7, 1948. He worked for General Electric Co., in Lynn and Cleveland, Ohio.

F11250 MARJORIE SYLVIA, b. Aug. 27, 1920, m. Mar. 28, 1932, CLARENCE MacKINNON.

11251 VIRGINIA ARLINE, b. Sept. 15, 1921, m. 1st, July 25, 1942, EARL P. GORMAN, killed April 23, 1944; 2nd, Feb. 9, 1946, ROBERT S. NEWHALL, had: 11252 ROBERT ALLEN, b. Sept. 12, 1947; 11253 MEREDITH JEAN, b. Jan. 22, 1954.

F10877 AURILLA BEAN LOCKE, born in Mt. Vernon, Maine, Feb. 24, 1868, died in Lynn, Mass., June 12, 1957, married in Lynn, Mass., Nov. 14, 1888, FRANK BUTLER REYNOLDS. He ran a plumbing and steamfitting establishment in Lynn.

Children in 9th Generation

11254 ABBIE ELIZABETH, b. Dec. 17, 1890, d. Dec. 18, 1963, unmarried.

11255 ETTA FRANCES, b. May, 14, 1892. She graduated from Lynn Classical High School and Burdett College and worked up through the ranks to retire as Head Administrative Clerk of the Mass. State Police at Boston. She is very interested in genealogy.

11256 FRANK WARREN, b. Nov. 22, 1894, d. Nov. 22, 1964, m. Dec. 20, 1928, MARGARET SAGER of Swampscott, Mass., daughter of Charles Anton and Lillian Graham Sager. He was a master plumber, working for his father and inherited the business.

F11257 WESLEY GOODWIN, b. Mar. 23, 1903, m. Portsmouth, N. H., May 16, 1931, ETHEL MILDRED EKSTROM.

F11258 ANDREW ELLSWORTH, b. July 31, 1907, m. Seabrook, N. H., Mar. 29, 1935, ELECTA MARIE LEWIS, daughter of Jacob and Minnie Lewis.

F10878 CARROL EMERY LOCKE, born in Mt. Vernon, Maine, Feb. 28, 1870, died in Winthrop, Maine, Dec. 13, 1962, married Oct. 8, 1890, LUELLA POPE. He was a shoemaker in Lynn until he retired because of ill health to Mt. Vernon, Maine.

Children in 9th Gen. b. in Lynn, Mass.

F3729 AURILLA FRANCES, b. Aug. 27, 1893, m. Lynn, Mass., June 26, 1911, ARTHUR ROY TARBOX.

F11259 ELSIE, b. Mar. 7, 1898, d. 1956, m. Mt. Vernon, Maine, Sept. 24, 1918, CLYDE LEE HALL.

F11259a WESTON THEODORE, b. Mar. 18, 1904, d. Dec. 14, 1935, m. Auburn, Maine, DOROTHY PERKINS.

F10879 CHARLES WINFIELD LOCKE, born in Dayton, Maine, Mar. 28, 1848, died in Yarmouth, Maine, Dec. 21, 1942, married in Ft. Fairfield, Maine, MARY ANN JUDKINS, born in Ft. Fairfield, Maine, May 26, 1859, died in Yarmouth, Maine, Oct. 24, 1940, adopted daughter of Daniel and Sarah (Mitchell) Judkins.

He was a market gardener. Grew his vegetables in Yarmouth and hauled them by horses to Portland's Market Square, sold them all day, and back home again at night. Said by relatives not to be "overloaded with ambition".

Mary Ann Judkins, after moving to Yarmouth, with another woman, cleaned school buildings. Long after her husband retired, she cleaned school buildings and offices, walking to and from work.

Children in 9th Gen. b. in Fort Fairfield, Maine

F11260 JAMES DANIEL, b. May 23, 1882, d. Ft. Fairfield, Maine, Mar. 20, 1959, m. MARGARET JANE DYER.

11261 GEORGIA EDNA, b. Sept. 3, 1884, d. July 28, 1928, m. HUGH MURPHY.

11262 HENRY, b. April 19, 1886, m. SADIE REDIKER.

11263 FRANK JACOB, b. July 3, place and year unknown, d. Portland, buried, Cornish, Maine, m. FLORENCE ——.

11264 EVA, b. July 24, 1894, m. —— NELSON.

F10893 HENRIETTA GARLAND, born July 15, 1846, died in Rye, N.H., May 28, 1938, married in Rye, N.H., Dec. 11, 1869, MOSES BROWN, born in Rye, N.H., Mar. 23, 1835, died in Rye, N.H., Aug. 8, 1918.

Children in 9th Gen. b. in Rye, N.H.

11265 SARAH ALICE, b. Mar. 30, 1871, d. Rye, N.H., Dec. 10, 1893, m. Nov. 29, 1888, FRANK L. GRAVES.

11266 MARTHA ANNAH, b. July 7, 1872, d. Cambridge, Mass., June, 1926, m. July 18, 1889, FRANK F. BOYCE.

11267 DANIEL WARREN, b. July 15, 1874, d. Boston, Mass., Feb. 19, 1953, m. Oct. 21, 1899, JENNIE TRAVIS.

11268 JOHN WESLEY, b. July 23, 1877, d. Lakewood, Ohio, April 26, 1958, m. Galesburg, Ill., Aug. 11, 1904, JULIA T. TERRY.

F11269 MARIETTA, b. Mar. 10, 1880, d. Portsmouth, N.H., Aug. 13, 1974, m. June 28, 1916, DAVID EASTMAN.

11270 CHARLES T., b. May 21, 1882, d. July 8, 1909.

11271 HARRISON, b. Mar. 1, 1889, m. Aug. 12, 1929, MILDRED A. LANE.

<u>F10901</u> EDWARD EVERETT PERKINS, born in Concord, N. H., Feb.
1, 1866, died Aug. 28, 1938, married 1st, Sept. 24,——, LOTTIE A.
KENT, (divorced); 2nd, in Tunbridge, Vt., May 18, 1904, HARRIETTE
F. CHADWICK.

Children in 9th Gen. b. in Waltham, Mass.

11272 EDWARD HAROLD, b. Oct. 21, 1894, d. St. Petersburg,
Fla., June 21, 1915, unmarried.

11273 ROYAL CHANDLER, b. Sept. 13, 1897, d. Cambridge,
Mass., Aug. 9, 1899.

<u>F10903</u> ADDIE BURBANK HOOK, born in Dunbarton, N. H., May
23, 1859, died Dec. 6, 1940, married 1st, 1878, MEBIS BURT; 2nd,
in Stoneham, Mass., April, 1892, PERCEY MYRON GODDARD, born
in Fitchburg, Mass., 1859.

Children in 9th Generation

11274 ALFRED TAY, b. Woburn, Mass., Jan. 14, 1880, d. Feb.
25, 1880.

F11275 CLIFTON MERRILL, b. Stoneham, Mass., April 11, 1883,
m. FLORENCE HILLER of Saugus, Mass.

F11276 PEARL FANNIE, b. Wakefield, Mass., July 30, 1893, m.
July 20, 1918, RICHARD CARLTON STICKNEY.

<u>F10904</u> NELLIE ELIZA (SAUNDERS) HOOK, born in Stoneham,
Mass., Nov. 15, 1862, died in Lanesville, Mass., May 27, 1936,
married DR. WILLIAM ROWLEY, born in Oreston, England, and died
in Lanesville, Mass., about 1950 at age 58.

She lived with Dr. and Mrs. Saunders after she was 6 years old.
They called her Nellie Lincoln Saunders but she was never legally
adopted.

Children in 9th Generation

F11277 PHILIP WILLIAM, b. Gloucester, Mass., Oct. 1, 1893,
m. RUTH HOLMES of N. H.

11278 PRESTON, d. at 11 months.

11279 CONSTANCE, d. at 6 months.

11280 DOROTHY, adopted.

<u>F10905</u> GEORGE HOOK, born in Sulphur Springs, Colo., Sept.
12, 1880, married SADIE A. PINE.

Children in 9th Generation

11281 GEORGE, d. at age 7 years.

F10909 SARAH ABBIE HOOK, born in Lynn, Mass., Nov. 11, 1873, married Oct. 1, 1898, FRED DANIELS DODGE, born in Stoneham, Mass., Feb. 13, 1873.

Children in 9th Gen. b. in Lynn, Mass.

11282 RAYMOND ORIN, b. Nov. 18, 1899.

11283 NORMAN HOOK, b. Jan. 4, 1905.

F11284 FRED DANIELS, JR., b. Jan. 9, 1901, m. Lynn, Mass., Oct. 1, 1923, ALICE ELIZABETH SVERKER.

F10911 GEORGE FRANKLIN COBB, born in Charlestown, Mass., June 14, 1876, died in St. Augustine, Fla., Mar. 28, 1955, married in Roxbury, Mass., Oct. 7, 1901, GERTRUDE ELISABETH HUMPHRY, born in Brooklyn, N.Y., July 3, 1877, died in St. Augustine, Fla., Mar. 14, 1969.

Children in 9th Generation

F11284a EDGAR HUMPHRY, b. Boston, Mass., Aug. 6, 1903, m. Harvard, Mass., Mar. 2, 1936, KATHERINE VARNUM DENNY.

11285 PAUL, b. Feb. 22, 1909, d. Everett, Mass., Feb. 23, 1909.

11286 MILDRED FRANCES, b. Harvard, Mass., Dec. 6, 1910, m. 1st, Brookline, Mass., June 29, 1932, ROBERT BURINGAME CHILTON; 2nd, Boston, Mass., ROBERT DAWSON; 3rd, Hingham, Mass., WILLIAM PERKINS.

F11287 RICHARD, b. Boston, Mass., Feb. 28, 1914, m. Los Angeles, Calif., June 20, 1942, MARIAN VAN VORST COLWELL.

F10912 WILBUR DEE LOCKE, born in Raymond, Calif., May 19, 1892, died in Newport, Ore., Sept. 26, 1964, married 1st, in Merced, Calif., Mar. 20, 1919, BERNICE ZELMA HARRIS, born in Summer Lake, Ore., Oct. 30, 1897; 2nd, in San Rafael, Calif., Oct. 24, 1935, EVELYN BELLE WAGNER, born in Glendive, Mont., Nov. 11, 1913, died in Castro Valley, Calif., June, 1965, daughter of David Augustus and Barbara Agnes (Schantz) Wagner.

Children in 9th Generation

F11288 ALTHEA LENAIRE, b. Paisley, Ore., Dec. 23, 1920.

11289 RICHARD D., b. Florida, Aug. 10, 1934.

F10913 STEPHEN LeROY LOCKE, born in Raymond, Calif., Feb. 12, 1895, died in Fairfield, Calif., July 19, 1975, married 1st, in

Bakersfield, Calif., Sept. 1, 1919, STELLA LORRAINE JENKINS, born in Salinas, Calif., Nov. 23, 1890, daughter of —— and Caroline O. (Purcel) Jenkins; 2nd, in Oakland, Calif., 1937, RAMONA IRENE DESMOND, born in Denver, Colo., Aug. 31, 1900, daughter of Louis and Minnie Desmond.

Children in 9th Generation

F11290 BARBARA LORRAINE, b. Chowchilla, Calif., Sept. 4, 1921.

F11291 CAROL MARGUERITE, b. Fresno, Calif., Dec. 24, 1923.

F10914 WINNIE AILEEN LOCKE, born in Raymond, Calif., Dec. 22, 1905, died in Granger, Wash., Sept. 14, 1972, married in Chowchilla, Calif., June 16, 1923, ALMAR SCOTT BROWN, born in Coffee County, Ga., May 16, 1901, daughter of Rufus Cheney and Hattie Irene (Shepherd) Brown.

Children in 9th Generation

F11292 CLIFFORD ALMAR, b. Chowchilla, Calif., Aug. 9, 1924.

F11293 HAROLD SCOTT, b. Placerville, Calif., Jan. 17, 1926.

F11294 WINNIE ESTELLE, b. Chowchilla, Calif., Mar. 4, 1930.

F11295 ROBERT VINES, b. Petaluma, Calif., Nov. 4, 1933.

11296 DARYL ALVIN, b. San Rafael, Calif., Oct. 6, 1938, d. Fallon, Nev., Dec. 22, 1945.

F10915 ALMA ANITA LOCKE, born in Raymond, Calif., June 15, 1907, married in San Rafael, Calif., July 20, 1936, JOEL IVA MILLER, born in Sparta, Tenn., Mar. 5, 1910, son of Fred E. and Essie (Randolph) Miller.

Children in 9th Generation

F11297 JONITA LAURE, b. Oakland, Calif., Aug. 23, 1937.

F11298 PEGGY JANICE LEE, b. Oakland, Calif., Sept. 22, 1939.

F11299 DON KIRK, b. San Anselmo, Calif., Jan. 1, 1950.

F10917 LEONA ELIZABETH LOCKE, born in Modesto, Calif., Aug. 6, 1921, married in Concord, Calif., Aug. 2, 1940, MARVIN ARLLETTE LEE, born in Modesto, Calif., Feb. 25, 1918, son of Arthur and Mathilda (Johansen) Lee.

Children in 9th Gen. b. in Modesto, Calif.

F11300 ARLEN MORRIS, b. May 17, 1941.

11301 CAROL JEAN, b. Dec. 18, 1943, m. 1st, —— GRATIY; 2nd, —— DOWNS.

F10924 ARTHUR SAMUEL MERROW, born in Cape Neddick, Me.,
Oct. 3, 1871, died in Reading, Mass., Mar. 26, 1960, married in
Boston, Mass., June 9, 1908, HELEN GENEVA TOLMAN, born in
Union, Maine, Mar. 6, 1877, died in Beverly, Mass., Jan. 12, 1969,
daughter of Issac and Florence (Wight) Tolman.

As a young man he worked on his father's farm. From there he
moved to Boston, Mass. in 1895 and worked at Rhodes Brothers Store
on Mass. Ave., where he had charge of the creamery and egg department for over fifty years. He and his wife lived in Dorchester, Mass.,
on the same street for forty years before they moved to Reading where
they lived with their daughter Dorothy and her husband.

Children in 9th Gen. b. in Boston, Mass.

11302 DOROTHY TOLMAN, b. Oct. 7, 1909, m. Dorchester,
Mass., Sept. 7, 1946, ROBERT WOODBERRY LOVETT.
After graduating from Radcliffe College she earned a
degree in library science from Columbia Univ. She
worked in the Boston Public Library System in the Kir-
stein Business Branch and was head librarian at the time
of her retirement. He is an archivist at the Baker Memorial Library of Harvard University. He is a Harvard
graduate and they both are interested in history and are
active in the Beverly, Mass. Historical Society.

F11303 ARTHUR SAMUEL, JR., b. Mar. 31, 1916, m. East Aurora,
N.Y., Nov. 14, 1942, LETA ADELE LEONARD.

F10925 ROSA PULSIFER, born Aug. 20, 1860, died 1946, married
EBEN EVELETH, born 1858, died 1945.

Children in 9th Generation

11304 NORRIS, m. ——— FERNALD.

11305 ROGER, m. EVELYN TOWNSEND, had: 11306 MAX.

11307 HAROLD F., b. April 20, 1897, d. Dec. 8, 1957, m.
DOROTHY PAUL and had: 11308 DOROTHY who
married EDWIN E. CROCKER and has 3 children.

F10938 ERNEST EDWARD COWELL, born Dec. 29, 1883, died
1940, married RUBY RANDALL, born May 7, 1885.

Children in 9th Generation

F11309 EARLE RAYWORTH, b. Sept. 7, 1907, m. HELEN JARVIS.

F11310 RALPH RANDALL, b. Jan. 3, 1911, m. CHARLOTTE
INGALLS.

11311 JOHN ROBERT, b. 1915.

F10942 ARTHUR MOULTON WRIGHT, born in Fitchburg, Mass.,
Oct. 31, 1913, married in Derry, N. H., Dec. 25, 1934, OLIVE
VIRGINIA WELLS, born in Fitchburg, Mass., Mar. 22, 1915.

He continued operation of his father's business for a few years and
then went into the used car business in Fitchburg, Mass. When his
health failed, he moved to Orlando, Fla. where he is employed by the
Martin Marietta Company.

Children in 9th Gen. b. in Fitchburg, Mass.

11312   RODNEY CURTIS, b. June 28, 1935, m. Leominster,
Mass., June 13, 1959, JEANNE MARY LEHOUX.

11313   ARTHUR MOULTON, JR., b. Aug. 12, 1954.

F10944 CHARLES MOSES FRANCIS, born in Lowell, Mass., June
27, 1850, died in East Livermore, Maine, Nov. 14, 1928, married
June 5, 1881, LAURA BLACK WARREN, born in Jay, Maine, April
27, 1863, died in Auburn, Maine, Sept. 24, 1952, daughter of Moses
and Lucinda (Blackwell) Warren.

Children in 9th Generation

F11314   FORREST HERBERT, b. Fayette, Maine, May 11, 1883, d.
Lewiston, Maine, Feb. 1, 1952, m. Dec. 31, 1904,
JESSIE EDWINA COX.

11315   MAUDE, b. Lewiston, Maine, April 7, 1885, d. E. Millinocket, Maine, April 9, 1965, m. CYRIL CYR.

11316   BESSIE, b. May 21, 1888, m. 1st, ——— BRACKETT; 2nd,
JOHN OTIS REYNOLDS.

11317   MAIDIS, b. E. Livermore, Maine, May 12, 1891, d. E.
Livermore, Maine, July 20, 1949, m. JOHN FITZ-
GERALD.

11317a WINIFRED B., b. E. Livermore, Maine, April 6, 1901, d.
Lewiston, Maine, July 25, 1966, m. 1st, JESSE LEE
EMMONS; 2nd, LEONARD FISH.

F10948 EMERY H. WEBSTER, born in Castine, Maine, Jan. 1,
1880, died in Castine, Maine, 1951, married MABEL F. BOWDEN,
born in Penobscot, Maine, 1884, died in Castine, Maine, 1953.

He supported his large family of thirteen boys and girls by farming,
fishing and through the operations of coast-wise trade using two-
masted schooners in the Penobscot Bay area. His wife, Mabel, was
the daughter of Uriah and Lucy J. (Farnham) Bowden of Penobscot.

Children in 9th Gen. b. in Castine, Maine

11318   HARRY, b. Oct. 9, 1902, m. EDITH CARLSON, lived in

Hartford, Conn. and Portland, Maine and had one son,
11318a ARTHUR.

11319 OWEN, b. Mar. 31, 1904, d. Bucksport, Maine, 1965,
m. MADELINE DODGE, lived in W. Penobscot, Maine
and had no children.

11320 LINNIE, b. July 30, 1906, m. WILBUR ROBINSON, lives
in W. Pensobscot, Maine, no children.

11321 HOWARD, b. Dec. 23, 1908, m. GENEVA THOMBS, lives
in North Castine, Maine, no children.

11322 BEULAH, b. Mar. 16, 1910, m. KENNETH COLE, lives in
East Sumner, Maine; three children: 11323 FRANCES,
11324 EDNA, 11325 DAVID.

F11326 DWIGHT RODERIC, b. Sept. 3, 1911, m. ARLENE C.
BOWDEN.

F11327 DONALD, b. July 8, 1914, m. RUTH CROCKETT, lives
in New Sharon, Maine with eight children.

11328 THOMAS FARNHAM, b. Sept. 21, 1915, m. MINA YORK,
lives in Bucksport, Maine, no children.

11329 NINA, b. Jan. 26, 1917, m. OTHA COREY, lives in
Hampden, Maine; four children: 11330 RICHARD,
11331 BRUCE, 11332 STEPHEN, 11333 GARY.

11334 MARTHA, b. May 6, 1919, m. 1st, JAMES BURNS and
had: 11335 JAMES, JR.; 2nd, ROBERT WHITNEY and
lives in Brewer, Maine with twin daughters, 11336
CINDY and 11336a KATHY.

11337 LEWIS, b. April 8, 1922, m. DOROTHY HUTCHINS, lives
in W. Penobscot, Maine, no children.

11338 LLOYD, b. Feb. 24, 1925, m. 1931, JUNE BRIDGES, lives
in Penobscot, Maine; three children: 11339 CHERYL,
b. Nov. 2, 1950; 11340 VICKIE, b. Aug. 28, 1954;
11341 JACQUELINE, b. Nov. 18, 1956.

11342 ARTHUR, b. Aug. 28, 1928, m. FLORA TOWERS of Belfast,
Maine. They live in Bucksport, Maine with three chil-
dren: 11343 LORRE JEAN, b. Dec. 24, 1959; 11344
DAVID ART, b. Nov. 8, 1963; 11345 ERIC TY, b.
Aug. 21, 1966.

F10951 CHESTER SNELL WENDELL, born in Dover, N. H., Aug.
8, 1887, died in Darien, Conn., Aug. 18, 1975, married 1st in Canter-
bury, Conn., Dec. 10, 1918, ALBERTA HOPE VEASEY, born in Boston, Mass., Nov. 1, 1889, died in Darien, Conn., Nov. 3, 1949.

He graduated 1909 University of New Hampshire with B. S. degree and 1911 Howard University Graduate School of Applied Science with M. E. E. degree. He was noted for his community work spanning three decades. This included Chairmanship of the Darien, Conn. Police Commission 1940-1953, Tax Assessor, Plan and Zoning Commission in Darien. History and genealogy were his life hobby and he was active in the Huguenot Societies of Vermont, Canada, London (where he was a Fellow) and Connecticut (where he served as Treasurer). He was also Registrar of the Piscataqua Pioneers (N. H.) and a member of Lodge #107 A. F. & A. M. in Darien. He was a licensed Professional Engineer in Conn., N. Y. and Vt.

She was a career newspaper writer of note and active in the D.A.R.

He married 2nd, BEATRICE RAY (METCALFE) OSBORNE of Windsor, Conn. at Glenbrook, Conn., May 18, 1952. She was active in the D. A. R.

Children in 9th Generation

11346 MARY VEASEY, b. Mar. 12, 1921, d. Oct. 3, 1961, m. ROBERT W. RICE.

11347 RUTH ELLEN, b. Mar. 26, 1924, m. ROBERT W. WEBB.

11348 CHESTER ALBERT, b. Aug. 26, 1929, m. 1st, AUDREY VIVIAN SNYDER and had: 11349 JEFFREY CHARLES; 2nd, BOBBIE JEAN MITCHELL, no children.

11350 STEPHEN EDWARD, b. Dec. 17, 1942, m. PATRICIA ELLEN MAGUIRE and had: 11351 HEATHER ANNE; 11352 SEAN MICHAEL.

TENTH GENERATION

F3729 AURILLA FRANCES LOCKE, born in Lynn, Mass., Aug. 27, 1893, married in Lynn, Mass., June 26, 1911, ARTHUR ROY TARBOX, died in Winthrop, Maine, Aug. 22, 1965.

Children in 10th Gen. b. in Lynn, Mass.

3730 ROY EMERY, b. July 17, 1914, m. ESTHER and had: 11990 ROY EBEN, b. May 27, 1937; 11991 RALPH WESTON; 11992 ROBERT; 11993 GILBERT; 11994 KENNETH.

11995 ERNEST THEODORE, b. Nov. 10, 1916, m. DOROTHY and had: 11996 KAREN.

11997 MARCIA ZELMA, b. April 21, 1918, m. 1st, CARROLL COOPER (divorced); 2nd, ARTHUR NOBIS. Had daughter 11998 CARROLL.

F5149 JOHN BENETTE MARSTON, born in Pittsfield, N. H., July 23, 1908, married in Manchester, N.H., July 27, 1929, ELIZABETH LOUISE CLOUGH, born in Manchester, N.H., Dec. 12, 1906. He attended schools in Chicago, Ill., Manchester, N.H. and the Univ. of New Hampshire. Worked with the trust division of the First National Bank of Boston until 1934, then with the police departments of Manchester, No. Conway, Hanover and Hampton Beach, N.H. Was a security guard for Raytheon, General Electric and Motorola, retiring in 1969 as a Lieutenant. Now living in Mesa, Arizona.
She attended public schools in Manchester, N.H. and graduated from Smith College in 1929 where she was on the soccor team, life guard squad and a cox on the rowing crew.

Children in 10th Generation

F11353 JOHN BENETTE, JR., b. Jamaica Plains, Mass., Nov. 10, 1930, d. Tempe, Ariz., Feb. 7, 1973, m. 1st, Hampton, N.H., Dec. 18, 1953, THELMA INGLIS.

11354 SALLY HELEN, b. Medford, Mass., Dec. 22, 1931, d. Manchester, N.H., Dec. 30, 1945.

F11355 LINDA LOUISE, b. Manchester, N.H., Oct. 6, 1936, m. Hampton, N. H., Mar. 2, 1954, ROBERT SIDNEY PARIZO.

F11356 PAUL EDWARD, b. Manchester, N.H., Mar. 15, 1938, d. Prescott, Ariz., June 9, 1969, m. Hampton, N.H., Nov. 12, 1961, ROSALIND MARIE LUND.

F6536 CORA MELCHER HUMPHREYS, born in Portsmouth, N.H., Oct. 23, 1898, died in Portsmouth, N.H., Aug. 1945, married in Portsmouth, N.H., Feb. 29, 1920, ELWOOD EVERETT ROBERTS, SR., born in Groveland, Mass., Aug. 29, 1898.

Children in 10th Generation

F11357 ELAINE HUMPHREYS, b. Durham, N.H., April 9, 1923, m. Somersworth, N.H., April 3, 1943, RICHARD LEIGH TOWER, SR.

11358 PHYLLIS NORMA, b. Dover, N.H., July 19, 1925, m. Durham, N.H., Mar. 29, 1947, KEITH CHAPIN BIRDSALL.

F11359 ELWOOD EVERETT, JR., b. Dover, N.H., Aug. 6, 1931, m. Franklin, N.H., April, 1966, LINDA ROSE WITHAM.

F6591 MARY VIRGINIA ALLEN, born in Atlantic, Cass County, Iowa, Aug. 31, 1913, married in Grinnell, Poweshiek County, Iowa, Sept. 11, 1937, PARKE WALCOT BURROWS, born in Davenport, Scott County, Iowa, June 25, 1914.

Children in 10th Generation

11360 SUSAN LOCKE, b. St. Louis, Mo., Mar. 7, 1940, m. Manistee, Mich., Mar. 21, 1975, MARVIN L. KIDDER, b. April 15, 1921.

11361 ANNE WALCOT, b. Evanston, Cook County, Ill., Aug. 6, 1942.

11362 VIRGINIA CHERYL, b. Evanston, Cook County, Ill., June 19, 1944.

11363 MARY CAMILLA, b. Evanston, Cook County, Ill., Jan. 17, 1948, m. Evanston, Cook County, Ill., July 4, 1976, DAVID FELLOWS, b. Stubenville, Ohio, Oct. 1, 1947.

11364 ELIZABETH ALLEN, b. Evanston, Cook County, Ill., April 22, 1952.

F6594 ROBERT LOCKE SMILEY, born in Malcom, Poweshiek County, Iowa, Dec. 14, 1912, married in Dallas Center, Dallas County, Iowa, Oct. 9, 1937, JUNE GERTRUDE CADWELL, born in Dallas Center, Dallas County, Iowa, June 1, 1915, daughter of Charles Joseph and Elta Viola (Buterbaugh) Cadwell.

Children in 10th Gen. b. in Des Moines, Polk County, Iowa

F11365 JAMES WAYNE, b. July 30, 1946, m. Des Moines, Polk County, Iowa, May 28, 1967, WANETTE JOANN

SAUNDERS, b. Manchester, Delaware County, Iowa, Nov. 7, 1948.

F11366 JO ANNE, b. Jan. 23, 1949, m. Minburn, Dallas County, Iowa, June 24, 1969, DENNIS DOYLE ROBERTS, b. Perry, Dallas County, Iowa, Sept. 25, 1947.

F6595 MARY LOCKE SMILEY, born in Malcom, Poweshiek County, Iowa, Jan. 3, 1915, married in Dallas Center, Dallas County, Iowa, Aug. 8, 1937, BENN HOYT NELSON, born in Redfield, Dallas County, Iowa, April 19, 1910, son of Mark and Maude Pearl (Johnson) Nelson.

Children in 10th Generation

F11367 WILLIAM HOYT, b. Des Moines, Polk County, Iowa, Nov. 20, 1939, m. Perry, Dallas County, Iowa, Sept. 9, 1967, PENNEE LEE FITZGERALD, b. Dec. 1, 1944. Divorced.

F11368 JOHN LOCKE, b. Dexter, Dallas County, Iowa, Nov. 8, 1944, m. Stratford, Boone County, Iowa, Oct. 24, 1970, CAROL ANN PETERSON.

F7405 JULIA SELMA SCHNIEWIND, born in Whitestone, N. Y., Nov. 3, 1883, died in Garden City, N. Y., Aug. 7, 1960, married in Springfield, Mass., Oct. 19, 1912, WALTER FRED BACHELDER, born in Palmyra, Maine, Nov. 26, 1871, died in Holyoke, Mass., May 23, 1935.

Children in 10th Gen. b. in Holyoke, Mass.

11369 JULIA BLOODGOOD, b. Feb. 6, 1915.

F11370 W. FREDERICK, JR., b. Nov. 12, 1918, m. Northport, N.Y., Feb. 15, 1947, MARGARET ANN GOLDHORN.

F7619 HARRY DANIEL WELLS, born in Bristol, N. H., April 6, 1888, died in Northfield, N.H., Nov. 18, 1956, married at the home of her parents in Tilton, N. H., Aug. 21, 1912, MABEL HELEN DRAKE, born in Bristol, N. H., Feb. 16, 1886, died in Concord, N. H., Dec. 6, 1939; married second, Oct. 10, 1941, MARION AUDREY BEAN LAMB, born May 22, 1890, died Mar. 6, 1968.

He attended Bristol, N. H. public schools and graduated from Tilton, N. H. Seminary, 1907 and took an International Correspondence School Engineering course. He was employed by the New Hampshire Highway Dept. for 39 years retiring 1953. He was active member of Baker Memorial Methodist Church, Concord and was a member of the Masons. She graduated from Tilton Seminary, 1905, and attended Eric Payne School of Art in Boston and taught penmanship in Westbrook, Maine, before her marriage.

Children in 10th Generation

F11371 MALCOLM ROBIE, b. Penn Yan, N.Y., Sept. 16, 1913,
        m. Concord, N.H., Jan. 1, 1939, MARION BUNKER
        FELLOWS.

F11372 WINTHROP ALBRO, b. Bristol, N.H., July 29, 1915, m.
        Concord, N. H., Feb. 1, 1941, BETSY CELINDA
        BASSETT.

F11373 DONALD HASKINS, b. Bristol, N.H., July 3, 1917, m.
        Concord, N.H., Aug. 17, 1940, DOROTHY RACHEL
        COTNOIR.

F11374 DAVID THAYER, b. Concord, N.H., Nov. 29, 1923, m.
        Quincy, Mass., June 18, 1949, ELEANOR JEANNE
        HAMOR.

F8001 HARRY EDWARD BEEDE, born in Waites River, Vt., July
2, 1889, died in Lynn, Mass., Feb. 1, 1967, married in Lynn, Mass.,
1910, SARAH JANE BOYD, born in North Ireland, April 23, 1891,
died in Lynn, Mass., Aug. 24, 1969.

Children in 10th Gen. b. in Lynn, Mass.

11375   ETHEL MAY, b. April 12, 1913, m. Lynn, Mass., July 14,
        1940, JOHN HENRY NYGREN.

F11376 HEZEKIAH MARTIN, b. July 17, 1914, m. Lynn, Mass.,
        Oct. 11, 1941, LOIS RUTH GALEUCIA.

F8137 KINGMAN PACKARD CASS, born in Tilton, N. H., April
1, 1895, married in Boston, Mass., May 10, 1919, MARY FRANCES
FISKE, born in Newton Centre, Mass., Aug. 25, 1898, died in Winchester, Mass., April 11, 1972.
    He graduated from the Tilton School, 1912 and Wesleyan Univer-
sity, 1916. Was 1st Lieutenant, Construction Division of the Army
during WW I. Was Lt. Col. of Mass. Organized Militia during WW II.
Held several town offices in Winchester where he lives and is "fast
getting to be an ornery old cuss !" Was an Insurance Broker before
retirement. She was a devoted housewife and during WW II was an
observer for the Winchester spotting area and Officer of the Day for
women, U.S. Airforce.

Children in 10th Generation

F11377 DONALD CHANDLER, b. Brookline, Mass., May 12, 1923,
        m. Winchester, Mass., Aug. 23, ———, MARION P.
        PHILBROOK.

F8138 <u>WILLIAM T. CASS</u>, born in Tilton, N. H., May 27, 1899, died Jan. 22, 1976, married in Plains, Kansas, May 26, 1926, IRENE E. METZ, born in Perry, Okla., Nov. 20, 1903.

Children in 10th Gen. b. in Boston, Mass.

F11378 RICHARD S., b. July 22, 1928, m. Boston, Mass., Oct. 11, 1952, MARY O'DONNELL.

F11379 EDWARD P., b. June 22, 1933, m. Chicago, Ill., Aug. 27, 1960, JOANN TARCZYNSKI.

F8183 <u>AGNES PADEN</u>, born Oct. 1881, married GUY OWEN FRASER.

Children in 10th Generation

11380 FLORINDA, m. RICHARD MERCER.

11381 JAMES McGREGOR, m. WINNIFRED.

F11382 AGNES MAY, b. San Francisco, Calif., April 7, 1921, m. 1950, MARVIN L. FEHR.

F11383 WILLIAM SAMUEL, b. Sacramento, Calif., Sept. 14, 1923, m. June 1, 1947, BARBARA LOIS WURZBACH.

11384 VIRGINIA ALDRICH, m. ———— BARRYMORE, has 2 boys.

F8187 <u>EDITH EUNICE NEFF</u>, born in Fallbrook, Calif., Nov. 28, 1887, married in Alameda, Calif., Aug. 17, 1914, ROLLO MORTON KELLOGG, died in Bakersfield, Calif., 1974.

Children in 10th Generation

F11385 LOISMARIE EUNICE, b. Bakersfield, Calif., May 20, 1921, m. Bakersfield, Calif., Sept. 5, 1942, ROY MATHEW GUNSOLUS II.

F8188 <u>BENJAMIN GERRY NEFF,</u> born in Fallbrook, Calif., Dec. 9, 1893, died in Alameda, Calif., Jan. 12, 1974, married 1st, 1918, ELEANOR DOUGLAS; 2nd, Alameda, Calif., 1924, HELEN MAY BEEBE, born in Kalamazoo, Mich., July 10, 1899. He was a dentist.

Children in 10th Generation

11386 ELENA MAY, m. ———— DURNEY.

F11387 BENJAMIN GERRY, JR., b. Oakland, Calif., Oct. 14, 1927, m. Sacramento, Calif., Aug. 12, 1967, SUSAN ANN.

11387a ROBERT

F8256 ELEANOR JAFFRAY THOMSON, born in Andover, Mass.,
Mar. 24, 1878, married in Andover, Mass., Jan. 1908, ALFRED
LUCIUS CASTLE, born in Quincy, Ill., Mar. 24, 1875, died in
Andover, Mass., 1951.

Children in 10th Gen. b. in Quincy, Ill.

F11388 ELEANOR JAFFRAY, b. Mar. 7, 1909, m. Quincy, Ill.,
June 15, 1935, ERNEST SIMONTON YOUNG.

11389 ROSAMOND THOMSON, b. Nov. 9, 1911, m. Camden,
Maine, Aug. 10, 1940, DINO OLIVETTI.

11390 ABBY LOCKE, b. Oct. 28, 1913, m. Andover, Mass.,
Dec. 27, 1963, JOHN MASON KEMPER.

11391 ALFRED LUCIUS, JR., b. Oct. 2, 1918, m. Dubuque, Iowa,
Nov. 9, 1939, FRANCES ADELE GOLICK.

F8646 HATTIE CLEAVES KING, born in Framingham, Mass., Feb.
24, 1889, died in Barrington, N.H., Nov. 1, 1966, married Oct. 14,
1911, FRANKLIN MERTON ERCOLINE, born in Boston, Mass., June
17, 1888, died in Barrington, N.H., July 6, 1967.

Children in 10th Generation

F11392 JANET, b. Somerville, Mass., Jan. 26, 1917, m. Dec. 10,
1934, VINCENT FREDERICK BENSON.

F8869 CLARENCE BRYAN LOCKE, born in Barrington, N. H.,
Mar. 10, 1898, died in Barrington, N. H., Oct. 2, 1955, married 1st,
in East Boston, Mass., 1921, LILLIAN FRANCES MORRISON, born in
East Boston, Mass., died in Boston, Mass., Dec. 13, 1963; 2nd, EVA
MAY CLOW FORSYTHE, died in Rochester, N. H., Jan. 6, 1970.
    He served as Town Clerk and as Selectman for the Town of Barring-
ton, and in 1935 was elected as Representative to the General Court
of New Hampshire from the Town of Barrington. January 1, 1943 he
was appointed as Deputy Sheriff of Strafford County. For several years
he was an Engineer at the Sawyer Mills in Dover, N. H.

Children in 10th Gen. b. in Rochester, N. H.

F11393 EVERETT IRVING, son of Clarence and Lillian, b. Oct. 2,
1930, m. East Boston, Mass., June 5, 1955, DOROTHEA
GRACE BOEHNER.

Children of Clarence and Eva

F11394 MARY LINNA, b. Feb. 16, 1943, m. Rochester, N. H.,
1960, ADRIEL SMITH.

F11395 JAMES SAMUEL, b. Feb. 11, 1945, m. Berwick, Maine,
1965, SUSAN HORNE.

F8870 EVA MARY LOCKE, born in Barrington, N. H., June 9, 1901, married in Salisbury, Mass., Dec. 12, 1928, DOUGLAS McLEOD STEVENSON, born in Concord, N. H., July 2, 1904.

She attended Barrington schools and graduated from Rochester High School, 1918 and Bryant & Stratton Business College, 1920. She taught business subjects in high schools in Vermont, New Hampshire and Massachusetts for 45 years, retiring in 1976. She was active in the YMCA, Tri-Hi-Y Club, Future Business Leaders Club and a Girl Scout leader. She is active in several clubs and organizations including several national sororities, garden club, Eastern Star and DAR. Her interests are in Early American arts and crafts.

He attended Concord public schools and graduated from Wentworth Institute and taught woodworking in high schools in Rochester and Portsmouth. He is a Mason and an avid sportsman and serves as Representative to the General Court. They operate a summer campground at the Locke Homestead on Ayers Lake in Barrington, N. H.

Children in 10th Generation

F11396 CAROLYN, b. Barrington, N. H., April 6, 1930, m. Oakland, Calif., Dec. 27, 1951, CLAY PATRICK BEDFORD, JR.

F9174 FLARIA J. LOCKE, born in Exeter, N. H., April 20, 1894, married in Exeter, N. H., Nov. 24, 1918, FRED HOLT PAGE.

Children in 10th Generation

11397 FLORENCE ANN, b. Feb. 9, 1930, d. Exeter, N. H., Aug. 27, 1941.

F9312 REUBEN JENNESS LOCKE, born in Rye, N. H., May 31, 1863, died in Rye, N.H., Oct. 1950, married in North Hampton, N. H., Feb. 23, 1898, BESSIE L. BACHELDER, born in North Hampton, N. H., May 25, 1875, died in Rye, N. H., Aug. 1966.

Known as R. Jenness Locke, because of a dislike for the name Reuben, owned and operated "Locke Lodge", Locke's Pavilion, which is now known as the Rye Beach Club, and the Locke Bath-houses which were located adjacent to the Pavilion, and was noted for its hot salt water baths, with the distinction of being the only salt baths north of Newport, Rhode Island. He was a carpenter by trade and enjoyed duck hunting and fishing.

Children in 10th Gen. b. in Rye, N.H.

F10478 RICHARD JENNESS, b. April 3, 1903, m. 1st, in Rye, N. H., 1924, RUTH S. DRAKE of Bedford, Mass.; divorced, m. 2nd, ROBINA MURRAY of Nova Scotia.

10479 EDWIN BACHELDER, b. April 11, 1908, m. Rye, N. H., HILDRED THOMPKINS of Hallowell, Maine; divorced, m. 2nd, DOROTHY LEONARD of Melrose, Mass.

F9315 CLARENCE ALBERT GOSS, born in Rye, N.H., Feb. 11, 1860, died in Rye, N.H., June 27, 1935, married in Rye, N.H., 1st, Jan. 23, 1876, MARY MACE; 2nd, July 8, 1882, ELLA ELIZA GARLAND, born in Rye, N.H., Jan. 12, 1858, died in Rye, N.H., June 11, 1916.

Children in 10th Gen. b. in Rye, N.H.

F10482 HARRIET DREW, b. June 1, 1888, d. Oct. 14, 1975, m. Rye, N.H., June 1, 1910, ERNEST JENNESS MOULTON.

F10484 ANNIE MARIE, b. Jan. 6, 1890, d. Rye, N.H., Jan. 14, 1926, m. April 30, 1917, RALPH EUGENE BERRY.

F9316 ESTELLE JEWELL GOSS, born in Rye, N. H., Aug. 17, 1861, died in Somerville, Mass., Nov. 28, 1961, married in Rye, N.H., Feb. 28, 1885, EDWARD PAGE PHILBRICK, born in Rye, N.H., Dec. 15, 1858, died in Somerville, Mass., May 25, 1938.

He was educated through the eighth grade, then trained as a cabinet maker. He worked as a carpenter, a mill wright and eventually owned the largest Packard Automobile agency in New England on Commonwealth Ave., Boston. He was the only man in the entire area who installed windshields on Packards. His friends and family considered him "a gentleman through and through". He was proud of his heritage and "a real Yankee at heart". She was educated through the eighth grade and trained as a dressmaker, a craft she practiced through her 101st year. She was a noted cook, showed unusual ability to adapt to conditions beyond her control, possessed a great deal of self-reliance, was generous and a steady church-goer.

Children in 10th Generation

10485 NEIL B., b. Rye, N.H., April 28, 1888, d. Rye, N.H., Nov. 3, 1960, m. July 27, 1907, ANNIE RAND JENNESS. Graduated from Somerville, Mass. High School where he was a good basketball player. Ran a country store in Rye for almost 50 years and was a founder of Rye Volunteer Fire Dept. He was described as a country gentleman and "a constant fellow".

F10486 HESTER, b. Rockport, Mass., June 15, 1890, d. Boston, Mass., Feb. 4, 1966, m. Sept. 15, 1915, ELIAS WILLIAM HENRY WENTZELL.

F9318 GILMAN PICKERING GOSS, born in Rye, N.H., June 6, 1870, died in Portsmouth, N.H., Dec. 9, 1946, married in Rye, N.H., Nov. 3, 1910, LILLIAN GERTRUDE McGANTY, born in West Caledonia, Nova Scotia, Dec. 12, 1888.

He was born on the family homestead, Grove Road, Rye, N. H. and was a lifelong truck gardener, teamster, grower of Grade A McIntosh apples, mover of buildings, and driver for the popular hayrides for the local hotels. He was active in the Jr. OUAM (benevolent society) and town affairs, especially as a long term trustee of the Central Cemetery, where he was buried after his death.

She was active in the community especially in matters of health. She conducted a home laundry and directed the spring opening of many summer estates and resides in Florida.

She was born Lillian G. McGinty.

Children in 10th Gen. b. in Portsmouth, N. H.

9319   RICHARD PICKERING, 2nd, b. Oct. 8, 1912, d. about Oct. 11, 1943 in World War II submarine service in the Pacific. He was educated in the schools of Rye and Portsmouth. After a hitch in the US Navy he returned home and went to work at the Portsmouth Navy Yard. During the Second World War he served as Motor Machines Second on the ill-fated WAHOO, a submarine he had helped build, which was lost in the LaPerouse Strait.

F9319a LAURENCE EDWARD, b. Feb. 17, 1916, m. Rye, N. H., Mar. 20, 1943, ANNA LOUISE OLIVER.

11398   CLIFFORD GILMAN, b. Aug. 26, 1917, d. Sept. 20, 1917.

F11399   PHILIP EUGEN, b. Nov. 24, 1928, m. 1st, JOYCE BUTLER; 2nd, St. Petersburg, Fla., Mar. 31, 1956, LeVAUGHN A. MARSHALL.

F9321   WALTER W. GOSS, born Dec. 11, 1875, died Nov. 3, 1969, married Feb. 14, 1900, FRANCES B. KNOWLES, born Feb. 6, 1877, died Oct. 22, 1911.

Children in 10th Generation

F9322   RICHARD IRWIN, b. Jan. 24, 1901, m. Feb. 14, 1932, LOUISE M. BOOKER.

F9494   ROY HAMILTON LOCKE, born in Somersworth, N. H., Nov. 4, 1872, died in Amesbury, Mass., buried in Somersworth, N. H., Mar. 24, 1930, married in Somersworth, N. H., June 26, 1900, EMMA CHARLOTTE HATCH, born in Somersworth, N. H., May 27, 1873, died in Seabrook Beach, N. H., Aug. 9, 1958, buried in Somersworth, N. H.

He was owner of Lake Gardner Ice Co. from 1909 until his death. He served on the Board of Selectmen of Amesbury, Mass. from 1924 to 1929.

Children in 10th Generation

9495 SARA AGNES, b. Amesbury, Mass., Mar. 1, 1912, m. 1st,
Nov. 27, 1959, JOSEPH ARMAND LEMIRE; 2nd, Sept.
25, 1967, JAMES FARNHAM REDFORD.
She graduated from Amesbury High School, 1930 and
American Univ., Washington, D.C., 1935 with a B.A.
degree. Also earned a Master's degree of Education at
Boston Univ., 1947 and Master of Arts (Spanish) at Univ.
of New Mexico 1960. She taught history and Spanish at
Amesbury High School and retired as head of the Mod-
ern Foreign Language Dept., 1967. In 1968 her History
of Amesbury, Mass. was published. She served in the
U.S. Army, WAC 2nd Signal Service Battalion during
WW II. Also played trumpet in Boston Women's Symphony under Alexander Thiede.

F9499 ANNIE BELLE LOCKE, born in Great Falls, Jan. 23, 1879,
died in Dover, N.H., 1945, married Somersworth, N.H., July 2,
1906, JASON L. MERRILL, died in La Habra, Calif., 1950.

Children in 10th Generation

F9500 JAMES WILLIS, b. Washington, D.C., Nov. 3, 1910, m.
Feb. 8, 1930, ALEXANDRIA WALKER.

F9501 RICHARD NATHAN, b. Mar. 17, 1915, m. April 10, 1953,
BONNIE STENSENG.

F9581 HELENA AUGUSTA PRAY, born Nov. 15, 1878, died in
Westfield, Mass., May 6, 1975, married Jan. 22, 1902, FRED E.
DINSMORE, born May 29, 1879, died in West Palm Beach, Fla.,
Feb. 28, 1956.

Children in 10th Generation

9582 MARIAN, b. Kittery, Maine, July 24, 1904, m. Kittery,
Maine, Aug. 26, 1933, MILO E. CUSHMAN, b. W.
Springfield, Mass., Aug. 8, 1889, d. Westfield, Mass.,
Sept. 26, 1965.

F9583 MAUD ELLA PRAY, born in Kittery, Maine, Oct. 22,
1883, died in Portsmouth, N.H., Jan. 29, 1954, married in Kittery,
Maine, Sept. 1904, STEPHEN BOULTER, born in Kittery, Maine,
1880, died in Kittery, Maine, Aug. 15, 1931.

Children in 10th Generation

F11400 JEAN ELIZABETH, b. Kittery, Maine, April 18, 1915, d.
Dalton, Ga., Oct. 28, 1968, m. HENRY NORCROSS.

F9586 ELMER ONSVILLE PRAY, born Oct. 6, 1886, died 1968, married FRIEDA WETHERBEE, died in Franconia, N.H., 1973.

Children in 10th Generation

9587 SHIRLEY WETHERBEE, b. Melrose, Mass., June, 1913, m. Melrose, Mass., JAMES KEATING, and had: 11401 ROBERT.

11402 LUCIE, b. Melrose, Mass., Sept. 30, 1917, m. Melrose, Mass., VERNON FLETCHER, and had: 11403 MICHAEL, 11404 DONALD.

11405 JOAN, m. HENRY B. MacMILLIAN.

F9608 JOSEPHINE JONES LOCKE, born in Middle Ohio, N.S., Dec. 10, 1870, died in North Abington, Mass., Nov. 6, 1940, married Nov. 1901, ERNEST ROBERTSON, born in Prince Edward Island, died North Abington, Mass., May 18, 1964, buried, Rockland, Mass.
She was named for her aunt.

Children in 10th Generation

F11406 HELEN OLIVIA, b. Somerville, Mass., Aug. 24, 1902, m. 1st, c. 1929, RALPH BLAKE; 2nd, 1967, CHARLES MONEGAN.

F11407 DONALD OSGOOD, b. Somerville, Mass., Dec. 30, 1903, m. GLADYS SNELL.

11408 BARBARA CATHERINE, b. North Abington, Mass., Sept. 10, 1905, m. 1939, ERNEST TREMBLY, divorced, no children.

F11409 DOROTHY ELIZABETH, b. North Abington, Mass., May 20, 1909, m. June 18, 1937, DANNY M. KANE, d. c. 1971.

F11410 FREDERICK ERNEST, b. North Abington, Mass., Dec. 5, 1911, m. 1st, DOROTHY RIDEOUT, d. c. 1958; 2nd, RUTH BAKER.

F11411 ERNESTINE JOSEPHINE, b. North Abington, Mass., Jan. 18, 1913, d. Columbia, S.C., July 17, 1974, m. June 6, 1951, C. CLIFFORD SHEA.

F9606 JOHN HUGH LOCKE, born in Middle Ohio, N.S., July 12, 1873, died in Arlington, Mass., May 18, 1964, married 1st, Nov. 29, 1905, EFFIE MILDRED MacKAY, born in Jordon Branch, N.S., Aug. 26, 1884, died in Somerville, Mass., Mar. 6, 1935; 2nd, 1939, BESSIE ANN (HARRIS) HEATH, divorced 1956.
John left school when eleven years old because his help was much

needed to meet the family expenses. He was strong and hard working. One of the yarns about him was that his first employer paid him $3 a month, until the neighbors forced his boss to raise his pay to $4 a month—because he was doing a man's work and deserved a man's pay!

He spent several winters in the woods as a cook/lumberman, and also drove a team for the Independent Ice Co. of Boston. Later he branched out for himself in the ice business and also range oil.

For several years after retiring he kept active making furniture and doing odd jobs about his children's homes.

His home, while Effie was alive, became a "Hospitality House" for all the family, including in-laws. Often setting table for a dozen to twenty on Sundays and holidays it became a haven for relatives from Down East when they came up to visit.

John's sense of humor was delightful. Once he went down to his work shop in the cellar talking away to himself. Mildred asked him what he said. "How would I know? Remember, I'm deaf as a haddock and can't hear me."

Children in 10th Generation

F11412   MILDRED JOSEPHINE, b. Nashua, N.H., Nov. 4, 1906, m. Nov. 3, 1927, WALTER CROCKER ELLIS, b. Cambridge, Mass., June 25, 1903. They live in Arlington, Mass.

F11413   RICHARD MacKAY, b. Nashua, N.H., Aug. 11, 1910, m. Sept. 14, 1933, RUTH TURNER, b. May 29, 1911.

F11039   THOMAS MacKAY LOCKE, born in Locke's Island, N.S., Mar. 25, 1880, died in Arlington, Mass., c.1957, married 1st, BERTHA ROBERTSON, died c.1909; 2nd, Aug. 11, 1915, ANNIE LOUISE HILTZE, died c.1967.

Tom and Jim were partners in a painting and paperhanging business in Union Square, Somerville, for many years.

A more unlikely partnership would be hard to find. Tom was a cheerful happy extrovert, friendly to all people, even young in-laws. On the contrary Jim was a thrifty scottish introvert, suspicious of everyone, including Tom. A family yarn was that Jim was happy only once —when they reduced the size of the dollar bill. He could then get more money in the barrel down cellar.

None the less they had a successful business until Jim had a bad fall from a ladder and became a bit handicapped. He gave up and retired, soon after going to Florida to live.

Children in 10th Gen. b. in Somerville, Mass.

11414   MABEL ROBERTSON, b. Feb. 25, 1908, d. Arlington, Mass., July 14, 1954, unmarried.

F11415   LEONA, b. June 22, 1918, m. Aug. 11, 1948, WILLIAM LOW MITCHELL.

<u>F11042 ESSIE EDNA LOCKE</u>, born in Locke's Island, N. S., c. 1884, died in East Boston, Mass., c. 1955, married 1st, DAN SUCKMAN; 2nd, ALEC McGILVERY, died Mar. 23, 1967, no issue.

Children in 10th Generation

11416 HARRY, b. c.1913, m. 1st, SALLY KELLY; 2nd, JOAN—.

<u>F11043 DAVID ROY LOCKE</u>, born Mar. 2, 1889, died in Shelburne, N. S., April 17, 1951, married Mar. 3, 1920, SARAH BLANCHE SEABOYER, born May 10, 1899, died June 1, 1965.

Children in 10th Generation

F11417 CATHARINE MAY, b. Shelburne, N. S., Feb. 5, 1921, m. Mar. 7, 1946, HERBERT FLETCHER.

F11418 CHARLES RICHARD, b. Shelburne, N.S., April 17, 1924, m. June 30, 1950, MARILYNE D. NICKERSON.

<u>F9621 CHARLES BILL LOCKE</u>, born in Lockeport, N.S., Jan. 27, 1872, died in Lockeport, N.S., May 16, 1935, married in Lockeport, N.S., April 14, 1897, JERUSHA CROWELL, born in Lockeport, N.S., Oct. 16, 1875, died in Sable River, N.S., Sept. 29, 1957.

He was a school teacher and taught the new Polish immigrants in Manitoba for eight years during the early 1900's. He later taught school for many years in Lockeport, N.S. He also ran a general store for a while and after his death his wife ran a candy store for many years.

Children in 10th Gen. b. in Lockeport, N.S.

11419 SARAH DeWOLFE, b. Jan. 27, 1898, d. Lockeport, N.S., Dec. 15, 1904. She was drowned in the harbour.

F11420 HERMAN CAPSTICK, b. Dec. 8, 1905, d. Windsor, N.S., June 21, 1973, m. Liverpool, N.S., June 20, 1928, GARNETT SYLVIA WIGGLESWORTH.

<u>F9637 CYRIL DURANT LOCKE</u>, born in Lockeport, N.S., 1886, died in Billerica, Mass., 1973, married in Wollaston, Mass., 1915, RUTH LOUISE HARDY, born in Somerville, Mass., 1891.

He graduated from Acadia College in Canada, 1911, where he led his class academically. He won a scholarship to Yale University where he graduated in 1912. For forty two years he was a highly respected member of the education profession. He served 38 years as principal of the Howe High School in Billerica, Mass. where a school and school library are named for him.

Children in 10th Generation

11421 MARIAN HARDY, b. Reddeer, Alberta, 1916, m. LAW-
RENCE WOOLAVER and had: 11422 SUSAN.

11423 NORMAN CHURCHILL, b. 1922. He is a veteran of WW II
and holds a BA and MA from Boston Univ. He is head of
the Audio Visual Dept. at Fitchburg State College.

F9641 LILLIAN MAY LOCKE, born in Lockeport, Nova Scotia,
June 12, 1873, died in Center Conway, N.H., May 4, 1965, married
in Jamaica Plains, Mass., Jan. 6, 1904, JOHN BURNHAM EATON,
born in Center Conway, N.H., July 27, 1881.
They lived in and around Boston, then moving to N.H. she managed Eaton Hall, a summer tourist home until in the 1930's they started an antique business which she operated until her death in 1965.

Children in 10th Generation

F11424 JOHN BURNHAM, JR., b. Center Conway, N.H., Mar.
1, 1913, m. Center Conway, N.H., June 3, 1939,
PAULINE MARION DENNETT.

F9642 ELEANOR ST. CLAIR LOCKE, born in Lockeport, N.S.,
Oct. 3, 1880, died in Phoenix, Ariz., April 18, 1971, married in
Rockland, Mass., Sept. 20, 1904, ROBERT BURNS JOHNSTON, born
in Walpole, Mass., May 12, ?, died in Buckeye, Ariz., Dec. 12,
1961. She was a librarian in Rockland, Mass. for many years.

Children in 10th Generation

F11425 ROBERT ALLAN, b. Rockland, Mass., Nov. 30, 1905, m.
Mar. 12, 1932, DOROTHY MABLE FRASER.

F9681 DAVID ROGER LOCKE, born in San Antonio, Texas, Mar.
7, 1892, died in Corpus Christi, Texas, Jan. 19, 1960, married in El
Paso, Texas, Sept. 1926, LUCIE ELIZABETH TODD HARRIS, born in
Valdosta, Ga., Feb. 22, 1904.
He served as a Lieutenant in the Infantry during World War I.
After graduation from the University of Virginia and the Colorado
School of Mines, he worked as a Mining Engineer in South America
and Mexico. He retired from mine engineering at a relatively early
age, and began to pursue his greatest interest — observing and writing
about the people and the world around him. His journals and letters
have been preserved by his oldest daughter, who will probably turn
them over to a library archives some day as they depict in great detail
a way of life now gone. He was also a wonderful storyteller, scholar
and researcher — and a friend to everyone he met in his travels. He
and his family traveled a great deal over the United States, and his

knowledge about everything they saw or experienced enriched every
trip. He compiled a remarkable genealogy of the Lockes many years
ago, but no one has been able to locate it since his death.

She attended Sophie Newcomb College in New Orleans as an art
student and continued her art work until eye trouble curtailed it in
1976. She has done considerable painting, drawing and sculpture and
has also published several small volumes of illustrated poetry and had
her poetry published in many literary magazines.

Children in 10th Generation

F11426 BRENT ROBINSON, b. San Antonio, Texas, Aug. 18, 1927.

F11427 ELIZABETH HAYGOOD, b. Corpus Christi, Texas, June 19,
1935.

11428 DAVID ROGER, JR., b. Corpus Christi, Texas, Sept. 15,
1950.

F9682 JOHN ROBINSON LOCKE, born in San Antonio, Texas,
Feb. 10, 1894, married in San Antonio, Texas, Oct. 25, 1921, GRACE
WALKER, born in Luling, Texas, Nov. 25, 1896.

He received a L.L.B. from the University of Virginia in 1915, also
attended University of Texas in 1915-16 for additional law studies. He
served in the Field Artillary from 1917-1919 as a First Lieutenant in
WW I. Since that time, he has been a practicing attorney in San
Antonio, and for many years a partner in the law firm of Grace, Locke
and Hebdon. He has been active in many civic organizations and is
still a Director of the Frost National Bank of San Antonio and an
active attorney at age 82.

Hunting, fishing and golf take all his spare time and he is proficient at all these sports.

Children in 10th Gen. b. in San Antonio, Texas

F11428a GRACE WALKER, b. Sept. 18, 1922, m. San Antonio,
Texas, Jan. 25, 1946, FREDERICK BARTON HARVEY, JR.

F11428b JOHN ROBINSON, JR., b. Aug. 2, 1924, m. San Antonio,
Texas, April, 1951, BETTY SUE STACY.

F9683 MIGNON LOCKE, born in San Antonio, Texas, Aug. 9,
1897, married in New York, N.Y., Oct. 10, 1929, WILHAM DAVID
KNIPE, born in New York, N.Y., Nov. 25, 1897, died in San
Antonio, Texas, Dec. 31, 1974.

She attended Gunston Hall, Washington, D.C. in 1915-16. After
some years of travel in Europe and the Orient with her family she
attended the Parsons School of Art, N.Y. in 1922 including three
months of study in Paris.

He was a native of New York and served in the 7th Regiment of

New York City (Infantry) during WWI. He was awarded the Bronze and Silver stars and the Purple Heart. He was an advertising executive with the Mobil Oil Company. They were married in the Brooklyn Navy Yard on board the S.S. Seattle by the Captain who was their friend. They lived in Westport, Conn. until his retirement when they moved to San Antonio, Texas.

Children in 10th Gen. b. in Westport, Conn.

11428c LAURA ELIZABETH, b. Dec. 9, 1931.

11428d CYNTHIA MACLAY, b. Nov. 11, 1933, m. San Antonio, Texas, Oct. 12, 1972, CORNELIUS LOUIS SAROSDY.

F9777 ROGER PUTNAM LOCKE, born in Salem, Mass., Dec. 14, 1904, married in Haverhill, Mass., Oct. 17, 1929, MARGUERITE PAULINE WITHAM, born in Milton Mills, N.H., Sept. 19, 1905.

He is a graduate of Northeastern Univ., Boston, Mass. and was Vice President and Chairman of Engineering at RK Mfg. Co. Also a member of A.F. & A.M. and Allepo Temple. She is a graduate of Haverhill, Mass. High School and McIntosh Business School.

Children in 10th Gen. b. in Salem, Mass.

11429 RICHARD B., b. Nov. 3, 1931. He is a graduate of Northeastern Univ. and Boston Univ. Law School and resides in Seattle, Wash.

F11430 ROBERT WITHAM, b. Nov. 28, 1933, m. Brattleboro, Vt., June 25, 1959, MARJORIE ADAMS.

F9905 MARION C. PHILBRICK, born in Rye Beach, N.H., Dec. 14, 1888, married in Brooklyn, N.Y., June 28, 1911, DOUGLAS LEIGHON KEYS, born in Boulder Creek, Calif., Oct. 11, 1888, died in Norfolk, Va., Sept. 4, 1950.

Children in 10th Generation

9906 CONSTANCE, b. Brooklyn, N.Y., Mar. 19, 1912, m. Washington, D.C., 1950, ALAN G. HERRICK.

11431 NATALIE, b. Brooklyn, N.Y., April 1, 1915, m. Greenville, Miss., Aug. 14, 1938, ROBERT J. CUMMINGS.

11432 DOUGLAS LEIGHON, JR., b. Roanoke, Va., Sept. 26, 1917, m. Angola, Ind., Feb. 19, 1944, MARGARET L. YODER.

F9928 FREDERICK VALENTINE HETT, born in Portsmouth, N.H., Dec. 21, 1886, died in Portsmouth, N.H., Aug. 28, 1948, married in

Portsmouth, N. H., MARGARET GALLAGHER, born in Lawrence, Mass., April 4, 1885, died in Portsmouth, N. H., Dec. 25, 1950.

Children in 10th Gen. b. in Portsmouth, N. H.

F11432a FREDERICK VALENTINE, b. Dec. 8, 1907, d. Portsmouth, N. H., April 19, 1955, m. Portsmouth, N. H., Sept. 30, 1940, ANNA E. SCOTT.

11432b WILLIAM FREDERICK, b. Feb. 8, 1912, d. Portsmouth, N. H., Feb. 20, 1918.

F9929 MARION OLIVE HETT, born in Portsmouth, N. H., June 9, 1889, married in Portsmouth, N. H.; 1st, Nov. 2, 1910, JOHN FRANCIS LATHAM, born in Marlboro, Mass., Sept. 30, 1883, died in Keene, N. H., June 5, 1932; 2nd, Aug. 5, 1933, HARRY TANTON WENDELL, born in Portsmouth, N. H., Mar. 24, 1887, died in Portsmouth, N. H., July 26, 1952.

She was a member of Portsmouth, N. H. High School Girl's Basketball Team, class of 1907, which was undefeated in four years. She was dance chairman of Portsmouth's Tercentenary Celebration in 1923. At age 87 she was still working in the gift shop at the Wentworth Hotel, New Castle, N. H. Her first husband was an Internal Revenue Officer and her second husband was proprietor of Wendell's Hardware Store on Congress Street in Portsmouth.

Children in 10th Gen. b. in Portsmouth, N. H.

F11433 ANNA MARY, b. Dec. 30, 1914, m. Atlanta, Ga., Feb. 4, 1943, LOUIS SHERFESEE.

11434 GRETCHEN, b. May 2, 1916, d. Portsmouth, N. H., Aug. 16, 1916.

F9961 FITZ HARRY LOCKE, born in Lawrence, Mass., Mar. 21, 1888, died in Lawrence, Mass., Nov. 26, 1965, married in Lawrence, Mass., 1910, CARA JOSEPHINE CRAWFORD, born in Lawrence, Mass., May 13, 1886, died in Methuen, Mass., Nov. (?1976).

He and his father operated the firm of L.E. Locke & Son which specialized in industrial construction of mills and hospitals and banks. He had personal knowledge and skills in all facets of the building trades. As with his father, achievement was a way of life and he followed a pace few men could match. He was held in the highest regard by his colleagues, employees and community for both his business and investment acumen. His interests included gardening, landscaping, and farming.

Children in 10th Generation

10609 SHIRLEY CARA, b. Lawrence, Mass., Aug. 29, 1910, m. Methuen, Mass., Mar. 25, 1937, NEAL WESTON

WEBSTER, JR. She attended Methuen Public Schools and Vesper George School of Art, Boston. She is a member of the American Hereford Breeders Assoc. and breeds prize-winning Hereford Breeding Stock at Hidden Springs Farm in Westminister, Vt.

F10610 MARGARET JUNE, b. Methuen, Mass., June 24, 1912, m. Methuen, Mass., Sept. 24, 1934, LEON F. MOWRY.

10611 LANGDON ELVIN II, b. Methuen, Mass., June 19, 1914, d. Methuen, Mass., Oct. 19, 1914.

F10612 JOHN CRAWFORD, b. Methuen, Mass., Oct. 18, 1915, m. Lawrence, Mass., May 15, 1949, RUTHE ROBINSON.

F11435 SHERMAN STANDISH, b. Methuen, Mass., Feb. 2, 1917, m. Frederick, Md., Sept. 28, 1944, BARBARA PHYLLIS KNIGHT.

F11436 RICHARD GORDON, b. Methuen, Mass., Jan. 27, 1918, m. Manchester, N.H., Jan. 2, 1942, EVELYN CASEY.

11437 NANCY ELISABETH, b. Methuen, Mass., Aug. 5, 1919. She is a graduate of Methuen Public Schools and Dana Hall in Wellesley, Mass.; also attended Garland School, Boston, Mass. She served in the Mass. Military Division with the rank of Capt. during WW II and remained active in the Coast Guard Auxiliary becoming a permanent member with the rank of Division Vice-Capt. Her interests include skiing, boating, farming and holds an expert rating in rifle competition. With her sister, Joan, she operates a small farm in Methuen, Mass.

11438 JOAN CONSTANCE, b. Methuen, Mass., Jan. 31, 1922. She is a graduate of Methuen Public Schools and Lasell Jr. College in Newton, Mass. She shares an interest in farming with her sister.

F11439 ANNE MARISE, b. Methuen, Mass., July 8, 1923, m. Three Oaks, Mich., Sept. 20, 1946, HOWARD HAMAN, JR.

F9980 EMERSON CURTIS LOCKE, born in Portsmouth, N. H., Jan. 15, 1890, died in Portsmouth, N. H., 1934, married in Portsmouth, N. H., 1921, FANNY THATCHER KELLEY, born in South Dennis, Mass., Mar. 16, 1889, died in Painesville, Ohio, Oct. 19, 1969.

Children in 10th Gen. b. in Portsmouth, N. H.

F11440 FLORENCE JEANETTE, b. Jan. 21, 1923, m. Covington, Ky., Jan. 30, 1943, RALPH GEORGE DAVIS.

F11441 PHYLLIS THATCHER, b. Sept. 16, 1924, m. Dec. 30, 1945, FRED ETHELBERT ELDER.

F10039 WILLIAM ORIN HUTCHINSON, M.D., born in East Orange, Vt., Sept. 5, 1880, died in Richmond, Vt., Mar. 26, 1955, married in Washington, Vt., July 7, 1906, ILA MAUDE DOWNING, born in Washington, Vt., Sept. 7, 1883, died in Richmond, Vt., Sept. 5, 1943.

Children in 10th Generation

F10040 NITA ALICE, b. Washington, Vt., June 9, 1910, m. Richmond, Vt., Mar. 7, 1941, LELAND ALBERT TOWNE.

F10041 ERNEST STANDLICK LOCKE, born in Corinth, Vt., Nov. 13, 1879, died in Bradford, Vt., Oct. 15, 1966, married in West Topsham, Vt., Oct. 7, 1907, ESTHER SANBORN LOCKE, born in West Topsham, Vt., Feb. 5, 1884, died in Bradford, Vt., July 1964.

He and his father operated a water powered lumber mill in Waits River as well as several farms. In March 1919 the dam at the mill was washed out. In August 1919 he purchased the country store in Waits River, Vt. which he operated for twenty five years. He was town clerk and treasurer for sixteen years, a justice of the peace for over fifty years, a lister, and school director for several years. Always active in town politics he represented the Town of Topsham, Vt. in the State Legislature in the 1927-1929 session.

He was a member of the Masons for over sixty years, and an active supporter of the Locke Family Assoc.

She was very active in educational and church activities. She also represented the Town in the State Legislature and at the time of her death in 1946, was President of the Vermont State Parent-Teacher Association.

Children in 10th Gen. b. in Waits River, Vt.

F10042 RAYMOND SANBORN, b. Jan. 4, 1911, m. Moretown, Vt., June 20, 1935, RUTH ELLEN KINGSBURY.

11442 CATHRYN CHRISTINE, b. April 16, 1917, d. Waits River, Vt., Oct. 1918.

F10045 JOHN BERRY LOCKE, born in Chandlerville, Ill., June 20, 1887, died in Westville, Okla., June 10, 1965, married in Kansas City, Mo., 1914, MARY C. HARGIS, born in Springfield, Mo., Nov. 2, 1889, died in Boynton, Okla., Jan. 26, 1950.

Orphaned at an early age, John and his sister Nita Gail spent some of their childhood years living with their father's relatives in Vermont and Mass. Later they moved to Kansas City, Mo., living with maternal relatives. John graduated from the Kansas City school of pharmacy. As a young man, he had an excellent tenor voice and sang in various choirs. He moved his family to Oklahoma, possibly in 1917, and continued his career in the drug business. In 1964, he received a certificate from the Missouri Board of Pharmacy for recognition of fifty years as a druggist.

Children in 10th Generation

11443 WILLIAM BERRY (BILL), b. Kansas City, Mo., July 28, 1915, d. Westville, Okla., Jan. 1962, unmarried.

11444 BEVERLY B., b. Boynton, Okla., July 2, 1919, now living in Downey, Calif., m. Bellflower, Calif., Mar. 25, 1961, PAUL L. HOGENMILLER, d. Feb. 2, 1976.

11445 BETTE FLO, b. Vian, Okla., Sept. 10, 1921, now living in Hemet, Calif., m. Whittier, Calif., Nov. 25, 1954, DANIEL F. JORDAN and had: 11446 DANIELLE, b. Nov. 10,1955, m. PAUL SELEGEAN and had, 11448 CRAIG ALLEN; 11447 JOHN MICHAEL, b. Feb. 6, 1958.

10044 NITA GAIL LOCKE, sister of John Berry Locke. She was born in Chelsea, Vermont on April 17, 1885 and died unmarried in East Topsham, Vermont, Aug. 9, 1962. She was an accomplished pianist and taught music for many years in Kansas City. Later in life, she made her home with her brother John and his family in Oklahoma. She returned to New England and spent the last fifteen years of her life there. She was a lovely lady, but, perhaps too gentle a person for her own good. She was buried beside her father in the Corinth Center Cemetery.

F10049 ALLEN WINCH LOCKE, born in Winchendon, Mass., Nov. 22, 1894, married in Rochester, N. Y., FLORENCE ELIZABETH HENRY, born in Rochester, N. Y., Oct. 24, 1896.

He graduated from Rutland, Vermont High School, 1913 – B.A. Dartmouth College, 1917–M.D. Harvard Medical School, 1921. After internship and residency at Worcester City Hospital spent more than 50 years in medical practice, first as a general practitioner and later as an internist being certified by the American Board of Internal Medicine. For many years on the active staff of Newton-Wellesley Hospital, member of Mass. Medical Society, American Medical Society, American College of Physicians.

She was a member of first class and graduate of the Army School of Nursing, Walter Reed Hospital, 1918-1921. Did public health nursing in Rochester, N.Y. and on staff of Henry Haywood Hospital, Gardner, Mass. 1922-24.

Children in 10th Generation

11449 DOROTHY MARY, b. Worcester, Mass., April 16, 1926,

m. Florida, 1958, THOMAS D. GOLDSWORTHY, b. Schenectady, N. Y., Sept. 27, 1910.

She attended Wellesley schools. For 15 years raised over 50 litters of Irish Terriers and Scottish Terriers, several of which completed their championships at top Eastern Shows. For the past 5 years has been doing Antique shows featuring country antiques, under the name The Wooden Duck. Member of West Suburban Antique Dealers Association.

He was a railroad passenger agent for New York Central, Atlantic Coast Line and Baltimore & Ohio Railroads. Supervisor in Radar Plant during World War II. Had dog shop in Wellesley and worked for Jordan Marsh Company. Hobby, boats. Former member, Nobscot Power Squadron and United States Power Squadron.

F11450   DAVID HENRY, b. Boston, Mass., Aug. 4, 1927, m. 1952, BARBARA BLOOD.

F11451   JOHN ALLEN, b. Boston, Mass., Nov. 9, 1928, m. Brookfield, Mass., 1949, EVELENE KILMAIN.

F11452   ALLEN WILLIAM, b. Waltham, Mass., Aug. 24, 1938, m. Washington, D.C., 1966, ELIZABETH HEUN.

F10067   GERTRUDE WOODMAN CUNNINGHAM, born Sept. 23, 1874, married July 1892, ERNEST BATTEN.

Children in 10th Generation

10068   BERNICE, b. 1893.

10069   ERWIN, b. Corinth, Vt., 1896, d. Waits River, Vt., Feb. 9, 1972, m. 1917, HELEN PARKS, d. Boston, Mass., 1964.

F11453   KENNETH A., b. Corinth, Vt., April 14, 1899, m. Corinth, Vt., Oct. 27, 1921, ANNABELLE (CHALMERS) WOODCOCK, her 2nd marriage.

11454   OLIVE, b. 1901, d. 1963.

11455   ARDEN, b. 1904, d. 1918.

F10086   JUDITH MAY LOCKE, born in Smithtown, N.H., May 24, 1896, died in Milford, Mass., Aug. 16, 1928, married in Lancaster, N.H., April 14, 1925, L. AINSLEY BENNETT.

Children in 10th Gen. b. in Milford, Mass.

F11456   LEWIS WILLIAM, b. Nov. 17, 1926, m. Stamford, Conn., May 5, 1957, MARY LOUISE ODISEOS.

F11457 MARY EVELYN, b. Aug. 16, 1928, m. Grafton, Mass.,
June 9, 1956, WARREN SCAMMAN.

F10088 MARY RUBENA LOCKE, born in Newfields, N. H., June
15, 1901, married in Derry, N. H., May 28, 1930, L. AINSLEY
BENNETT, born in Malden, Mass., April 2, 1900.
    She is a graduate of Mt. Holyoke College, 1923 and attended Bos-
ton Univ. School of Religion and was trained in Nursery School education. She was a Nursery School teacher for many years. She is
active in church work and Women's Club and historical society.
    He is a graduate of Tufts College School of Dentistry and practiced
dentistry for forty years. He sang professionally as a baritone soloist.

Children in 10th Generation

F11458 FRANCES ALICE, b. Worcester, Mass., April 20, 1936,
m. Grafton, Mass., Nov. 23, 1962, FREDERICK C.
LAING.

F11057 WILLIAM ROWELL LOCKE, born in Manchester, N. H.,
Nov. 20, 1907, married in Portsmouth, N. H., Sept. 4, 1934,
CHARLOTTE M. CLARKE, born in Kittery, Maine, Sept. 6, 1907.
    Wm. Locke, author of No Easy Task, the first 50 years of High
Point College, High Point, N. C. A. B., Wesleyan University; S. T. B.
and Ph. D., Boston University; Pastor of Methodist churches in New
Hampshire and Ohio; Assistant Professor, Mount Union College, Alli-
ance, Ohio, 1943-48; Professor of Religion and Philosophy, High Point
College, High Point, North Carolina, 1950-73.
    Charlotte Locke: A. B., Bates College; Laboratory Technician, Bos-
ton, Mass., 1930-34; Instructor in Woman's College, Univ. of North
Carolina in Greensboro, 1959-63.

Children in 10th Generation

F11459 MARGARET JEAN, b. Manchester, N. H., Nov. 12, 1936,
m. High Point, N. C., Aug. 27, 1957, J. LAWRENCE
McCOLLOUGH.

F11460 MARJORIE SARAH, b. Whitefield, N. H., Sept. 28, 1941,
m. High Point, N. C., June 14, 1963, DAVID ROBERT
BROOKS.

F10195 ROBERT ALLISON LOCKE, born in Titusville, Pa., June
7, 1892, died July 31, 1971, married Sept. 6, 1916, MARGARET
CHASE, born in Titusville, Pa., July 16, 1894, died Haverford, Pa.,
June 20, 1978, buried in Titusville, Pa.

Children in 10th Generation

11461 MARGARET CHASE, JR., b. Titusville, Pa., April 28,

1924. She graduated Earlham College, Richmond, Ind. 1947 with a B.A. degree; Smith College, Northampton, Mass. 1949 with M.S. in Phys. Ed. and Springfield College, Mass. 1959 with a doctorate in Phys. Ed. She is Assoc. Professor of Physical Education at Elmira College, N.Y. She is active in the Red Cross water safety programs and a member of Delta Kappa Gamma and professional organizations. She taught in Delhi, India 1967–68 under the Danforth and Fulbright Program, State Dept.

F11462 ELIZABETH CHASE, b. Coatsville, Pa., Jan. 17, 1928, m. Oakland, Md., Oct. 27, 19—, BYRON EARL BESSE, JR.

F10196 WILLIAM LEE WALLACE, born in San Luis Rey, Feb. 17, 1875, married in San Luis Rey, Calif., JOSEPHINE STEIGER.

Children in 10th Generation

11463 MARGARETE, d. Aug. 1975, m. 1st, —— BARNIER and had: 11464 WILLIAM J. and 11465 JOHN F.; 2nd, WILLIAM LAHEY.

11466 KATHRYN, m. FORREST BEASLEY and had: 11467 KATHRYN.

11468 JACK

11469 LOUISE, m. AUGUST SASSARINI.

F10197 ELBRIDGE HALE WALLACE, born in San Luis Rey, Calif., Mar. 24, 1876, died in Corona, Calif., married KATE BAKER.

Children in 10th Generation

11470 WILLIAM LEE, m. MARY ——.

11471 MAXINE, m. 1st, RONALD STAHL and had: 11472 THOMAS RONALD, m. MARTHA LOU who had 11473 CHRISTOPHER and 11474 SUSAN, b. 1955; 2nd, EARL SEXTON.

11475 ELBRIDGE ROBERT, m. MARNE —— and had: 11476 ROBERT and 11477 WILLIAM.

F10198 EDNA J. WALLACE, born in San Luis Rey, Calif., Dec. 12, 1878, died in San Diego, Calif., 195?, married 1st, WILL ADAMS; 2nd, E. ALVIN WILBUR.

Children in 10th Generation

11478 EARNEST ADAMS, m. FRANCES ——, had: 11479 MARY.

11480 MYRTLE WILBUR, m. ROBERT SHARP, had: 11481 Wm, 11482 WALLACE, 11483 EMMA, 11484 JOHN.

11485 ALVA WILBUR, m. JACOB SCHILLENBERG.

11486 WALLACE WILBUR

11487 MABLE WILBUR, m. JAMES FIELDS, had: 11487a RALPH, 11487b DAVID.

11488 GRACE WILBUR, m. CLARK HEWITT, had: 11488a RICHARD.

11489 JUNE WILBUR

11490 ALVIN WILBUR

F10199 ROBERT L. WALLACE, born in San Luis Rey, Calif., April 19, 1880, died in Oregon, married MAY ——— who died in Oregon.

Children in 10th Generation

11491 MILDRED, m. ———CARROTHERS, had: 11492 LESLIE, 11493 ALICE.

11494 GUS

11495 WILLIAM

11496 HUGH, had: 11497 EVERETT, 11498 JERRY, 11499 JOSE-PHINE.

11500 RIX

F10200 PEARL WALLACE, born in San Luis Rey, Calif., June 5, 1883, died in Oceanside, Calif., April 16, 1973, married in San Luis Rey, Calif., Jan 5, 1907, DAVID LESLIE JONES.

Children in 10th Generation

11501 JOSEPH ELI, b. Sept. 7, 1908, m. OLGA ———.

F11502 DAVID LESTER, b. July 14, 1912, m. HELEN ELIZABETH STARR.

F10201 ALICE FLORINDA (RIX) WALLACE, born in San Luis Rey, Calif., Feb. 28, 1886, died in Encinitas, Calif., Oct. 1, 1972, married in Los Angeles, Calif., Sept. 11, 1916, GEORGE RINGO WILSON, born in Mulberry Grove, Kans., Jan. 11, 1885, died in Alameda, Calif., June 11, 1938.

She was a teacher in Corona, Calif. and Riverside, Calif. She attended Univ. of Calif. at Berkeley and San Diego State College. He was an entomologist with the State Dept. of Agriculture.

Children in 10th Generation

F11503 BARBARA JEAN, b. Riverside, Calif., Aug. 19, 1917, m.
        Las Vegas, Nev., April 16, 1954, AUGUSTUS LEE
        RENNER, JR.

11504 DANIEL KING, b. San Francisco, Calif., Jan. 15, 1919.
       He received a M.A. degree from Stanford Univ. 1950
       and is a teacher at Ventura High School.

11505 CONSTANCE JANE, b. Alameda, Calif., June 27, 1924.
       She graduated with A.B. degree from Univ. of Calif. at
       Berkeley and is Senior Administrative Analyst at the
       Berkeley Campus. Her interests include genealogy and
       she was a significant contributor to this volume.

F10202 HUGH GRIFFIN WALLACE, born in San Luis Rey, Calif.,
Mar. 12, 1888, died in Oakdale, Calif., Oct. 20, 1956, married in
Bard, Calif., Nov. 25, 1924, CAROLINE STEIGER, born in San Luis
Rey, Calif., Feb. 12, 1899, died in La Crescenta, Calif., Aug. 20,
1969.
        He was raised until 14 in San Luis Rey, Calif. Graduated from
Corona, Calif. High School. Worked on San Diego Eastern Railroad
until 1906. Homesteaded at Bard, Calif. 1908, joined U.S. Cavalry
in 1915, was released to join Canadian Army in 1916. Served in
France until 1919. Returned to homestead at Bard. Farmed there until
1935 then moved family to Oakdale, Calif. Had dairy ranch there
until death in 1956. Belonged to Yuma, Ariz. Oddfellow Lodge, was
Arizona Grand Master of Lodge 1927-1928. In later years was president of local telephone company and an active member of the Oakdale, Calif. Grange.
        She was raised in Pala and Temecula, Calif. Graduated from High
School in Oceanside, Calif. Attended San Diego State College, became a teacher in Yuma, Ariz. in 1919, moved to Bard, Calif. and
taught at Bard School. Was principal at Imperial Dam School 1934-
1938. Moved to Oakdale, taught 5th and 6th grades at Riverbank
School, Riverbank, Calif. Was named nad honored as the Stanislaus
County, Calif. Teacher of the Year on two occasions.

Children in 10th Generation

F11506 HUGH DANIEL, b. Bard, Calif., May 26, 1925, m. Fort
        Worth, Texas, June 27, 1950, EVELYN WILLIAMS.

F11507 ROBERT JERI, b. Glendale, Calif., Nov. 13, 1931, m.
        Bemidji, Minn., Nov. 28, 1959, BEVERLY JOANNE
        BLUTH.

F10203 ANNE ROSE WALLACE, born in San Luis Rey, Calif.,
July 17, 1891, married in Globe, Ariz., April 3, 1918, WILLIAM
JESSE WHEAT, died in Escondido, Calif., 1973.
  She received Nurse's training in Los Angeles and was part of the
Army Nurse Corps in WWI.

Children in 10th Generation

11508 WILLIAM JESSE, b. Ariz., Mar. 7, 1919, m. Jan. 1944,
       CHARNILCIE ROBBINS.

11509 RICHARD, b. New Mexico, Aug. 12, 1921, m. April 5,
       1947, GLADYS SMITH.

F11510 PHYLLIS ANNE, b. Fulton, Mo., Oct. 30, 1925, m.
       Feb. 8, ——, EDWARD STARR.

F10286 GRACE WINIFRED LOCKE, born in St. Johnsbury, Vt.,
Oct. 18, 1892, married in St. Johnsbury, Vt., Feb. 22, 1915, OREM
NEWCOMB JENNE, born in Derby Center, Vt., Jan. 19, 1890, died
in Windsor, Vt., Oct. 9, 1924.
  She is a graduate of St. Johnsbury Academy and worked as a Secretary, at one time had a hair-dressing business. In later years she
worked for the State of Massachusetts.
  He was a graduate of Derby Academy and went briefly to Peddie
Institute at Hightstown, N.J. leaving to help on the farm during his
father's illness. He worked for the telephone company in St. Johnsbury and during WWI he worked as a machinist at National Auto-
matic Lathe Co., Windsor, Vt.

Children in 10th Generation

11511 CHARLES EDWIN, b. St. Johnsbury, Vt., Feb. 4, 1916,
       m. Plaistow, N.H., Jan. 30, 1944, RUTH ELIN DUS-
       TON WARNER.

11512 MALCOLM LOCKE, b. St. Johnsbury, Vt., Aug. 16, 1918,
       m. Wareham, Mass., Nov. 6, 1943, MARGARET L.
       HOUDLETTE.

11513 ELIZABETH MARION, b. Windsor, Vt., Mar. 13, 1921,
       m. Allston, Mass., June 12, 1948, ROBERT SWANSON
       Dw. HAROLD BABCOCK.

11514 PRISCILLA LOUISE, b. Windsor, Vt., May 2, 1922, m.
       Brighton, Mass., Nov. 28, 1942, WILLIAM BABCOCK.

F10287 WILLIAM GIFFIN LOCKE, born in St. Johnsbury, Vt.,
Nov. 10, 1894, died in Canandaigua, N.Y., Dec. 2, 1969, married
in St. Johnsbury, Vt., Jan. 20, 1915, GLADYS MAY REED, born in
Sheldon, Vt., May 3, 1896, died in Canandaigua, N.Y.., Dec. 2,

1969. He was a graduate of St. Johnsbury Academy and spent his life as a professional artist in the Boston, Mass. area. He was a self-taught artist who passed his talent to his five children and to his grandchildren. He was also an avid gardener and nature lover.

Children in 10th Generation

F11515   GRAYDON REED, b. St. Johnsbury, Vt., Aug. 20, 1915, m. Sharon, Mass., Feb. 23, 1940, ELEANOR MAY ROFFE.

F11516   KERMIT ALBION, b. St. Johnsbury, Vt., Aug. 28, 1916, m. Arlington, Mass., Feb. 14, 1942, VIRGINIA MAR-GARET KEEFE.

F11517   MAURICE SINCLAIR, b. St. Johnsbury, Vt., May 27, 1918, m. Newton Highlands, Mass., Sept. 3, 1940, DOROTHY LOIS BANKS.

F11518   CORINNE LUCILLE, b. Medford, Mass., Aug. 13, 1920, m. Needham, Mass., Oct. 1, 1942, KENNETH WILLIAM GLAZEBROOK.

F11519   WILLIAM GIFFIN, JR., b. Medford, Mass., April 29, 1929, m. 1st, MARY MARTINEZ; 2nd, ANN SWIGART SWAIN.

F10288   EMMA URSULA LOCKE, born in St. Johnsbury, Vt., Mar. 25, 1898, died in Natick, Mass., Feb. 15, 1974, married in St. Johnsbury, Vt., Oct. 11, ?, EUSTIS EARLE BEATTIE, born in Sherbrooke, Que., Canada, Aug. 4, 1894, died in Boston, Mass., May 16, 1956.

She spent two years at St. Johnsbury Academy then going to Malden, Mass. and to the Weltman Conservatory where she studied violin. During the war she worked at the Waltham Watch Factory. After marriage they moved to Boston, Mass. Emma worked at the Sears Store in Boston for several years.

He had a grammar school education. Went to the States and worked in Lyndonville, Vt., as a short order cook at one time. Went to Fort Devens to train and then overseas during WW I. After his return he took out Naturalization Papers. He worked for Metropolitan Ins. Co. and his last years he was store keeper at the Fernald State School. He was a Mason.

Children in 10th Generation

11520   EUSTIS EARLE, JR., b. Lyndonville, Vt., April 12, ?, m. Natick, Mass., May 27, 1944, BARBARA CLEMENT.

11521   WILLIAM LOCKE, b. Lyndon Center, Vt., Nov. 26, ?, m. Boston, Mass., June 29, 1946, ELIZABETH ———.

F10443 MARGARET LOCKE, born in Rye, N.H., Sept. 11, 1896, died in Portsmouth, N.H., 1939, married in Portsmouth, N.H., 1916, ELMER KLINE WENHOLD, born 1894, died 1977.

Children in 10th Generation

F11522 ELMER GEORGE, b. Portsmouth, N.H., April 19, 1917.

F10952 NANCY WOODMAN, born in West Lebanon, N.H., Feb. 8, 1928, married in Belmont, Mass., Sept. 14, 1963, DONALD P. DRESSLER, M.D., born in Cambridge, Mass., Oct. 3, 1929.

She graduated Phi Beta Kappa in 1949 from Radcliffe College with a B.A. in Romance Languages. Has held executive positions with Jordan Marsh Co., and Filene's, now owner of Topsy Turvey, Inc. in Winchester, Mass., a children's specialty shop. Her interests include genealogy, needlepoint, choral singing, skating and biking. He is a physician and Brigidier General, Air Force, Retired.

Children in 10th Gen. b. in Cambridge, Mass.

11523 AMY MEREDITH, b. Feb. 4, 1965.

11524 ELIZABETH DANA, b. Sept. 17, 1966.

11525 FREDERICK LAWRENCE, b. Aug. 14, 1968.

F10954 CHARLES RUTLEDGE LORD, born in Watsonville, Calif., Dec. 19, 1929, m. 1st, San Francisco, Calif., Sept. 9, 1951, MERRILYN JOYCE KEELEY, born in Bakersfield, Calif., Nov. 25, 1930, daughter of Raymond Dale and Janice Burton (Cameron) Keeley; 2nd, in Atlanta, Ga., May 5, 1973, KATHERINE CLARKE SKOGSTAD, born in Eau Claire, Wis., Nov. 18, 1931, daughter of Samuel Lawton and Katherine Bringhurst (Clarke) Skogstad.

Children in 10th Gen. b. in San Francisco, Calif.

11526 KAREN RENEÉ, b. Mar. 23, 1952.

11527 KATHY DENISE, b. Feb. 7, 1956, m. Berkeley, Calif., Sept. 26, 1976, DANIEL JAMES COLES, b. Bridgeport, Calif., Feb. 27, 1955, son of Richard and Margaret (Falletti) Coles.

F10955 JOANN SHIRLEY LORD, born in Schenectady, N.Y., Dec. 22, 1929, married in Schenectady, N.Y., Aug. 11, 1951, Rev. CARL COOK DISBROW, born in Prattsville, N.Y., July 15, 1928, son of Raymond A. and Ruth (Nelson) Disbrow.

She holds a B.M. degree from Houghton College and he has an A.B. from Houghton and a B.D. from Eastern Baptist Seminary.

Children in 10th Generation

F11528 NANCY RUTH, b. Schenectady, N. Y., April 6, 1953.

11529 DEBORAH JOANN, b. Schenectady, N. Y., Dec. 16, 1955, m. Mill Valley, Calif., Aug. 14, 1976, JOHN HYRUM DALLINGA, b. Fort Campbell, Ky., Aug. 29, 1954, son of Hyrum and Mary (Stuart) Dallinga.

11530 DANIEL CARL, b. Ransomville, N. Y., Nov. 3, 1957.

11531 STEPHEN ERIC, b. Ransomville, N. Y., Dec. 31, 1959.

F10956 ALAN WILBUR LORD, born in Schenectady, N. Y., Mar. 18, 1932, married in Rotterdam, N. Y., May 1, 1955, SARAH JOSE-PHINE MASLAND, born in Amsterdam, N. Y., Aug. 26, 1934, daughter of Floyd Aldrich and Charlotte (Ruff) Masland.
He attended U. S. A. F. Cadet Program.

Children in 10th Generation

11532 KATHLEEN ANN, b. Larson Air Force Base, Moses Lake, Wash., April 3, 1956.

11533 KAREN LOUISE, b. Dennison, Texas, April 25, 1957.

11534 DAVID ALAN, b. Naha Air Force Base, Okinawa, June 17, 1959.

11535 DEAN MICHAEL, b. Stillwater, Okla., May 17, 1961.

F10957 NANCY LOUISE LORD, born in Schenectady, N. Y., Oct. 2, 1934, married in Schenectady, N. Y., June 21, 1958, LESLIE CRANDALL, born in Berlin, N. Y., Aug. 1, 1932, son of Leslie Frank and Alice May (Merrills) Crandall.

Children in 10th Generation

11536 KEVIN EARL, b. Cobleskill, N. Y., April 5, 1959.

11537 MARK LESLIE, b. Cobleskill, N. Y., Aug. 14, 1960.

11538 COLLEEN LOUISE, b. Niskayuna, N. Y., Sept. 8, 1962.

F10959 Dr. JAMES MYRON LORD, born in Pasadena, Calif., May 28, 1934, married in Oakmont, Pa., June 22, 1957, BETTY JEAN JACOBSON, born in Oakmont, Pa., Nov. 13, 1934, daughter of Eugene W. and Miriam (Stewart) Jacobson.

Children in 10th Generation

11539 STEWART KIRK, b. Philadelphia, Pa., Nov. 13, 1959.

11540 WILLIAM ANDREW, b. Cleveland, Ohio, Feb. 4, 1961.

11541 JENNIFER, b. China Lake, Calif., Jan. 15, 1964.

11542 JAMES DUNCAN, b. Frankfort, Ky., May 8, 1972.

F10960 ROY STANLEY LORD, JR., born in Pasadena, Calif., Oct. 11, 1939, married in Oakland, Calif., Sept. 26, 1958, LEANNA KLEEBERGER, born in Oakland, Calif., Dec. 16, 1940, daughter of Edward Virden and Dorothy Ruth (Ashland) Kleeberger.

Children in 10th Generation

11543 GARRY ANDREW, b. Berkeley, Calif., April 27, 1959.

11544 TERI LYNN, b. San Jose, Calif., Jan. 10, 1962.

11545 EDWARD MATTHEW, b. San Jose, Calif., May 5, 1969.

F10962 FRANCES MARIAN LORD, born in Redding, Calif., May 5, 1948, married in Upland, Calif., July 12, 1969, DENNIS SAMUEL POND, born in Fort Collins, Colo., Jan. 11, 1947, son of William Samuel and Marian (Jackson) Pond.

Children in 10th Generation

11546 MARIAN FRANCES, b. Riverton, Wyo., April 26, 1972.

11547 SAMUEL EUGENE, b. Calexico, Calif., Aug. 29, 1975.

10964 PHILIP BALDWIN SIMONDS, JR., born in Belmont, Mass., Sept. 1, 1906, married in Providence, R.I., June 7, 1935, ESTHER MERRIMAN.

He graduated class of 1913 Phillips Academy, Andover, Mass. and Yale College, class of 1927 with B.A. degree. Attended Columbia Business School and worked in the Trust Dept. of R.I. Hospital Trust Co. retiring as Vice President in 1971. Has held numerous civic and business offices including Boys Club, Family Services, Providence Public Library and others in Providence and Little Compton, R.I.

Children in 10th Gen. b. in Providence, R.I.

F11548 WHITNEY, b. April 28, 1935, m. July 25, 1959, LEONARD AUGUSTUS YERKES III.

11549 EDITH GODFREY, b. Oct. 23, 1948, m. Little Compton, R.I., Mar. 28, 1970, DAVID VAN DYNE BORDEN.

10967 CLARKE SIMONDS, born May 1, 1917, m. 1st, Little Compton, R.I., Sept. 16, 1941, DEBORAH SNOW; 2nd, Providence, R.I., June 16, 1967, MARY V. HATCH.

Children in 10th Generation
11550 CHRISTOPHER CLARKE, b. Tuscaloosa, Ala., Oct. 8, 1942, m. Philadelphia, Pa., Feb. 16, 1968, BARBARA BABRICK.

11551 ROBERT HUNT, b. Providence, R.I., Nov. 3, 1946.

11552 PHILIP BALDWIN III, b. Providence, R.I., Mar. 3, 1949.

11553 JENNIFER S., b. June 27, 1955.

F10968 ALICE GERTRUDE MEADER, born in Rochester, N. H., Nov. 22, 1906, married in Holyoke, Mass., June 15, 1939, O. LEONARD MOQUIN, born in Hartford, Conn., Feb. 15, 1909.
She graduated from Rochester, N.H. High School, 1924 and attended Gorham Normal School, Maine. After teaching a short time she studied at the N.E. Deaconess Hospital School of Nursing graduating 1929. In 1939 she graduated from Columbia University nursing education dept. She taught sciences in nursing schools in Maine, New York and Mass. for 22 years. She was a chemist at Strathmore Paper Co. for 21 years. He was employed at Holyoke Public Library for forty years. They are active in church work, gardening, reading and travel. She is a member of DAR and Hampshire Co. Genealogical Society.

Children in 10th Gen. b. in Holyoke, Mass.

F11554 PRISCILLA LILLIAN, b. June 7, 1940, m. Holyoke, Mass., June 30, 1962, ROLAND J. B. GODDER.

11555 SUSANNE EUNIETTA, b. April 18, 1942. She graduated 1964 from University of Mass. with a Master's Degree in microbiology. She has been a research assistant in microbiology in Boston, Frederick, Md., and currently at Tufts — N. E. Medical Center Hospital.

F10969 Rev. LEON BURTON MEADER, born in Rochester, N. H., Nov. 27, 1908, married Vassar, Mich., MARY JACOBUS.
He is a graduate of Wheaton College, Ill. and the University of Maine, M.A. He is an ordained Baptist minister and served parishes in Maine and taught mathematics at Higgins Institute, Charleston, Maine and Principal of Monson, Maine Academy. For several years he was mathematics instructor at Waltham, Mass. High School and head of the department when he retired in June '76. His hobbies are skiing and white water canoeing. His wife was an elementary school teacher in Littleton, Mass. for ten years. She also graduated from Wheaton (Ill.) College.

Children in 10th Gen. b. in area of Charleston, Maine

F11556   LEON B., JR., b. 1940, m. West Acton, Mass., RUTH
         LEE GRAY, daughter of Clyde and Leola (Meader) Gray.

11557   DAVID, m. MARY JO ———. He is a chemist in the Los
         Angeles area. He has two children: 11558 DEBORAH,
         11559 DANIEL.

11560   NEIL ALBERT, m. South Sudbury, Mass., Oct. 23, 1975,
         BARBARA ELLEN McKEE. He is a graduate of Clark
         University, Worcester, Mass.

F10970   LEOLA MAE MEADER, born in Rochester, N. H., Aug. 1,
1910, married in Dover, N. H., April 16, 1930, CLYDE SAMUEL
GRAY, born in Rochester, N. H., Nov. 2, 1901.
   They owned a farm in Strafford, N. H. for decades. He has been a
Selectman for the town of Strafford for twenty-four years and a substitute rural mail carrier in Rochester for forty-four years. The couple
belong to the Meaderboro Community Church. Besides their own two
children, they have "brought up" two other children, one of whom
they adopted.

Children in 10th Generation

11561   RUTH LEE, b. Rochester, N. H., July 15, 1944, m. Acton,
         Mass., LEON B. MEADER, JR., her first cousin.

11562   PHILIP CLYDE, b. Rochester, N. H., June 27, 1947, m.
         MARGARET (Peggy) ———. Their children are girls:
         11563 LISA, 11564 MICHELE. He is a Vietnam War
         veteran. Now he is a technician for dental equipment
         and lives in Wilmington, Mass. During Vietnam War
         he was an air plane mechanic.

11565   JOYCE, (adopted), m. GILBERT GRAY.

F10971   EDITH ARLINE MEADER, born in Rochester, N. H., Jan.
29, 1914, married in Rochester, N. H., May 30, 1941, ISAAC RICH
KELLEY, born in Dennisport, Mass., Sept 23, 1910.
   She is a graduate of New England Deaconess Hospital School of
Nursing, Boston, Mass. class of 1936. Also graduate of Simmons Col-
lege Public Health Nursing Course. Before marriage she was super-
visor of The Falmouth, Mass. Visiting Nurses Association. Her hus-
band had a life-time career in managerial positions with the Western
Union, the last position in the office of the Vice-President in New
York City.

Children in 10th Gen. b. in Boston, Mass.

11566   MALCOLM EBEN, b. Feb. 25, 1947, m. Manassas, Va.,
         Dec. 28, 1970, NANCY JEAN DRAKE, b. Elgin, Ill.,

June 20, 1948. He graduated from Newark, N.J. School
of Engineering.   He was a comissioned officer in the
U.S. Army, last (Captain) in England.   He and his wife
have an import business in St. Paris, Ohio.   She is a
college graduate, majoring in physics.   Her hobby and
business is training and managing horses.

11567 NANCY ALICE, b. Oct. 2, 1948, m. Chatham, N.J.,
April 19, 1975, WILLIAM ROBERT ROEMER, JR., b.
Hoboken, N.J., Jan. 2, 1946.

F10973 FRANK JOHN SCRUTON, born in Farmington, N. H.,
Feb. 13, 1922, married in Webster, N.H., PAULINE PHELPS.
   He owns the Scruton Dairy in Farmington.   He is a graduate of the
University of New Hampshire school of agriculture.   One of his hob-
bies is raising and showing prize oxen.   His three sons are partners in
the dairy.

Children in 10th Generation

11568   Rev. JOHN FRANK

11569   ANNE

11570   ARTHUR W.

11571   RUTH

11572   DANIEL

11573   BARBARA

F10976 EVERLYN MARIE GILES, born in Farmington, N.H., Feb.
6, 1895, married in Haverhill, Mass., Aug. 23, 1916, CHARLES
LESLIE HOLMES, born in Farmington, N.H., Oct. 19 or 22, 1892,
died in Boston, Mass., Jan. 12, 1966.
   She was educated in Farmington, N.H. schools and, after marriage,
moved to the Boston area, settling in Newton, N.H. in 1932.   She
has been active in the Red Cross, Village Improvement Society and a
woman's club.   Her hobbies have been needlework and cooking.
   He attended Farmington schools, received a degree in accounting
from Boston Univ., a law degree from Northeastern Univ., was a Certified Public Accountant and a member of the Mass. and Federal Bar
Associations.   He specialized in accounting for the wool industry and
tax law.   Wrote numerous articles and co-authored books on taxes.   At
his death he was retired as a senior partner in a Boston accounting
firm.

Children in 10th Generation

11574   DOROTHY LOUISE, b. Haverhill, Mass., 1917, d. Boston,
Mass., 1920.

11575 SHIRLEY, b. Malden, Mass., Aug. 7, 1926, m. Newton,
       N.H., Sept. 2, 1956, DONALD MARTYN SHEEHAN,
       b. Melrose, Mass., Dec. 23, 1922. She is a graduate
       of Colby Jr. College, New London, N.H. and Boston
       Univ. (B.S.). Held various positions in magazine and
       textbook publishing and is interested in photography.
       He is a veteran of WWII and Korean conflict. Re-
       tired (Lt. Col.) from Signal Corps Reserve after 29 years.
       Was radio announcer for 23 years before establishing
       own printing business. Hobbies are ham radio and pho-
       tography.
          Their contribution to this volume is significant. She
       spent many hours type-setting from data sheets that were
       often confusing and difficult to read. Her skill and
       efforts gave the volume its professional appearance. His
       skills and efforts in page-finishing further enhanced the
       readability and appearance of this supplement.

F10985 MARGARET FELLOWS, born in Bangor, Maine, Nov. 22,
1909, married in Verona Island, Maine, Sept. 14, 1934, JOHN W.
WHITE, born in Bangor, Maine, July 29, 1907, died in Bangor, Maine,
April 26, 1974.
    She was educated in the public schools of Bangor, Maine, the
University of Maine at Orono, Maine and the Vesper George Art
School of Boston, Mass. He was a manager of the Henry S. Coe Enter-
prises in Bangor and was educated in the Bangor public schools and
Cornell University. His interest in community affairs is evidenced by
his activity as a member of the Katahdin Counsel Boy Scouts of
America, a member and past president of the Bangor Rotary Club,
treasurer of the Bangor Art Society, president and secretary of the
Abanaki Archery Club, as well as a member of the Maine State Archery Association and several other community organizations.

                Children in 10th Gen. b. in Bangor, Maine

11576 JUDITH, b. July 7, 1935, m. Bangor, Maine, Feb. 8, 1958,
       CHARLES L. BOOTHBY. They reside in Winthrop,
       Maine with three sons: 11577 TIMOTHY, b. April 5,
       1961; 11578 ANDREW, b. Mar. 1, 1963; 11579 PAUL,
       b. Oct. 5, 1964.

11580 RALPH FELLOWS, b. June 18, 1937, m. White Plains,
       N.Y., Feb. 26, 1966, THERESE MORENCY. They
       reside in Wappingers Falls, N.Y. with two children:
       11581 JOHN M., b. July 26, 1966; 11582 ANNIK,
       b. Oct. 17, 1968.

F10987 FRANK FELLOWS, born in Bangor, Maine, Nov. 26, 1914, m. East Wilton, Maine, MARIANNE RUSSELL, b. 1919, daughter of John and Velma (Walker) Russell of Phillips, Maine.

He was educated in Bangor public schools, Hebron Academy in Hebron, Maine, the University of Maine, Orono, Maine and the Peabody Law School in Portland, Maine. He was very active in tennis during his college years and at one point he achieved the title of Champion Tennis Player in the State of Maine. He first practiced law in Bangor where he served a term as Assistant County Attorney for Penobscot County Bar Association. Thereafter, he removed to Bucksport, Maine, where he currently operates his law practice.

His wife, Marianne, was educated in the public schools of Phillips, Maine, the University of Maine in Orono, and her interest in children and community affairs is shown in her activities as a member of the Bucksport, Maine School Board.

Children in 10th Generation

11583 PATRICIA, b. April 22, 1942, m. Bucksport, Maine, THOMAS BERRY of Bucksport, Maine where they reside with three children: 11584 CHRISTOPHER H., b. Sept. 15, 1966; 11585 FRANK FELLOWS, b. Oct. 25, 1968; 11586 JANE, b. April 8, 1970.

11587 FRANCES, b. April 19, 1945, m. Bucksport, Maine, JAMES WILLARD of Orono, Maine. They reside in East Millinocket, Maine with two children: 11588 LISA SUSAN, b. Dec. 21, 1969; 11589 JULIE ANN, b. April 6, 1972.

11590 MARTHA, b. Sept. 23, 1946, m. Jacksonville, Fla., LEO KENNETH LOUNSBERRY of Marshalltown, Iowa. They reside at Otis Air Force Base, Mass. with: 11591 JONATHAN RUSSELL, b. May 27, 1969; 11592 WILLIAM KENNETH, b. Feb. 21, 1973.

11593 ANN, b. Aug. 10, 1955, attending the University of Maine, Orono, Maine (1975).

F10988 ELIZABETH FELLOWS, born in Bangor, Maine, April 7, 1911, died in Bridgeport, Conn., Jan. 31, 1964, married in Utah (prob. Salt Lake City), July 8, 1943, STANLEY B. NICHOLS, born prob. in Fairfield, Conn., 1918.

She was schooled in the public schools of Portland and Bangor, Maine, and the Leslie School in Boston, Mass. School teacher for ten years in South Blue Hill and Bangor, Maine. He, as a member of the U.S. Army Signal Corps, served at several Army and Air Force Bases in Maine, Utah and Alaska during World War II before returning to settle in his home town of Fairfield, Conn.

Children in 10th Generation

11594 ELEANOR, b. Bangor, Maine, Feb. 7, 1944, m. MILES
       SPRINGER and reside in Newtown, Conn., with three
       children: 11595 MARY ELIZABETH; 11596 MILES, JR.;
       11597 RAYMOND JOHN.

11598 RAYMOND, b. Bridgeport, Conn., May 26, 1946.

11599 ROBERT FRANK, d. Bridgeport, Conn., May 16, 1947, age
       2 weeks.

11600 DAVID, b. Bridgeport, Conn., Oct. 3, 1949.

11601 ELIZABETH JANE, b. Bridgeport, Conn., Nov. 24, 1952.

F10989 OSCAR FELLOWS, born in Portland, Maine, Jan. 13, 1913,
married 1st, Topsham, Maine, June 16, 1934, ANGELA JOHNSON,
born in Topsham, Maine, Mar. 18, 1915; 2nd, CAROLINE ALLEN of
Columbia Falls, Maine.
     He was schooled in the public schools of Portland and Bangor,
Maine, the University of Maine, Amherst College and Harvard Law
School. Practiced law in Portland and Bangor, Maine. Served with
the U.S. Navy in World War II, and returned to Bangor where he
served several terms as Assistant County Attorney and County Attorney
and Register of Probate for the County of Penobscot.

              Children in 10th Gen. b. in Bangor, Maine

11602 REBECCA RANDOLPH, b. June 12, 1938, d. Vinalhaven,
       Maine, Mar. 18, 1966, m. KENNETH HOLBROOK of
       Vinalhaven, Maine and had: 11603 HERMANN; 11604
       JENNIFER.

11605 MARY ANGELA, b. Dec. 21, 1951.

11606 JESSICA LEE, b. May 20, 1954, m. DONALD W. McKIN-
       NON, JR.

       Child of second wife.
11607 JOEL OSCAR, b. Feb. 20, 1967.

F10990 JOAN FELLOWS, born in Portland, Maine, Dec. 6, 1917,
married 1st, prob. Bangor, Maine, 1934, EDWARD S. McLAUGHLIN,
born Veazie, Maine, 1914; 2nd, PAUL ARTHUR KLINE of Mahonoy
City, Penna., born 1914.
     She was schooled in the public schools of Bangor, Maine. She re-
sided in Bangor and Millinocket, Maine, and in Oregon. Her first
husband was an auto mechanic and mill worker, and in World War II,
he was employed with Pratt & Whitney in Connecticut and served with
the Royal Canadian Air Force. Her second husband was schooled in
the public schools of Mahonoy City, Penna., the University of Maine,

Orono, Maine, and George Washington University in Washington, D.C. During World War II, he served with the U.S. Army Air Corps in France. Paul adopted Richard and Betsy, children of the first marriage, thus, their last names were changed to Kline. After the war ended, Paul and Joan and family removed to Washington, D.C.

Children in 10th Gen. b. in Bangor, Maine

11608 RICHARD ALBERT McLAUGHLIN KLINE, b. Jan. 19, 1935, unmarried, postal employee in Silver Spring, Md.

11609 BETSY McLAUGHLIN KLINE, b. Aug. 22, 1938, m. 1st, ROY HUSSON and had: 11610 DERRICK, 11611 DEBBIE; 2nd, CHESLEY HUSSON, JR. of Bangor, Maine.

11612 GRETCHEN ELLEN KLINE, b. July 1948.

F10991 RAYMOND FELLOWS, born in Bangor, Maine, April 17, 1922, died in Bangor, Maine, May 17, 1974, married in Bangor, Maine, Aug. 21, 1943, FAITH ST. GERMAIN, born 1919.

He was educated in the public schools of Bangor, Fryeburg Academy in Fryeburg, Maine, and the Bangor Maine School of Commerce. He was a hotel employee and worked for Sears, Roebuck & Co., in Bangor. During World War II, he was a civilian employee for Aluminum Company of America in Mobile, Alabama, and for the U.S. Navy Department in Washington, D.C. Returning to Bangor, he served as manager of an auto and truck parts concern.

She was educated in public schools of Hampden and Bangor, Maine and the State Teachers College in Machias, Maine. She has taught in the school systems of Newport, Brewer, Holden and Eddington, Maine.

Children in 10th Generation

11613 BETH LOUISE, b. Bangor, Maine, Sept. 8, 1944, m. 1963, JOHN F. VETTER of Iowa City, Iowa, have: 11614 JEANNE, b. Mar. 23, 1964. Currently reside North Kingstown, Rhode Island.

F10992 WILLIAM ALBERT FELLOWS, born in Bangor, Maine, Nov. 23, 1925, married in Bucksport, Maine, June 18, 1960, #12075 LUCILLE ARLENE WEBSTER, born in Castine, Maine, Sept. 27, 1939.

He was educated in the public schools of Bangor, the University of Maine, Orono, Maine, the George Washington University and the Benjamin Franklin School of Financial Administration, both located in Washington, D.C. He was a participating musician (trumpet) for seven years with military, marching, and dance bands in the areas of Bangor, Maine and Washington, D.C. He served three years and one day in the U.S. Marine Corps during and after the Korean War; stationed with the Office of the Disbursing Officer, Second Marine Division, Camp LeJeune, North Carolina and with the Department of

Transportation, Headquarters Marine Corps, Arlington, Virginia. Returning to Maine, he served briefly as a sales representative with the
Singer Sewing Machine Company branch office in Bangor. From 1955
to 1962, he resided in Bucksport, Maine, where he was employed with
The Merrill Trust Company. During this period, as assistant manager
of the Bucksport branch, he met and married Lucille A. Webster, hotel
cashier and telephone operator for the Jed Prouty Tavern in Bucksport.
In July of 1962, they moved to Augusta to join Maine State service
and currently is employed as a budget examiner in the Department of
Finance and Administration, Bureau of the Budget.

Children in 10th Generation

11615   MICHAEL WILLIAM, b. Bangor, Maine, April 15, 1961.

11616   LORRAINE ANN, b. Augusta, Maine, Nov. 17, 1964.

11617   LAURA ARLENE, b. Augusta, Maine, June 30, 1971.

F10993   EDWARD DEARBORN MARSTON, born in Manchester,
N. H., Jan. 1, 1916, married Birmingham, Ala., June 1, 1938, SARA
GENE GRIFFIN, born in Birmingham, Ala., Aug. 19, 1918.
   He attended University of Pennsylvania and then Auburn Veteri-
nary College and graduated with a D.V.M. in 1939 from Auburn, Ala.
He later entered the U.S. Army in 1941 and was discharged honorably
after five years as a Lieutenant Colonel in the Veterinary Corps.   He
then entered private practice with his father, who graduated from
Chicago Veterinary College in 1917.
   Entered the Masonic Lodge in Boston, Massachusetts in 1943, and
later transferred to Washington Lodge in Manchester, New Hampshire.
She also went to Auburn University and majored in Home Economics
and belonged to Theta Upsilon sorority.

Children in 10th Gen. b. in Manchester, N. H.

F11618   KENNETH EDWARD, b. Sept. 28, 1940, m. Manchester,
         N. H., Nov. 1959, BETTY JANE SPAULDING.

F11619   JOE RUSSELL, b. Sept. 22, 1942, m. Manchester, N. H.,
         Sept. 16, 1967, LINDA JEANE LECLERC.

F11620   JEFFREY STEPHEN, b. Sept. 24, 1949, m. Manchester,
         N. H., Oct. 3, 1970, LINDA ELIZABETH VIEIRA.

11621   AMY SUE, b. Mar. 9, 1955. "All Manchester, New Hamp-
         shire knew when I was born.   The doctor said 'Look,
         Sara, she's all girl !' because I had 3 older brothers, and
         if I would of been a boy I think my father would of
         died.   As a little girl loved animals. I had many differ-
         ent kinds. I also took baton lessons and tap dancing. I
         was always the 'Teacher's Pet'. My job now is working

in the Superior Court and plan to leave soon cause I am fed up with working in an office with seventeen wacky chicks ! " (Direct quote)

F10994 FRANCES HORNE, born in Lowell, Mass., Mar. 21, 1852, died in Manchester, N. H., July 9, 1943, married in Lowell, Mass., Jan. 9, 1876, JOSEPH ALMY FLINT, born in Lowell, Mass., Sept. 21, 1850, died in Lowell, Mass., Sept 13, 1931.

Children in 10th Gen. b. in Lowell, Mass.

F11622 EDITH FRANCES, b. July 10, 1879, d. Lowell, Mass., Jan. 10, 1965. m. Lowell, Mass., Oct. 21, 1903, WALTER NEEDHAM BURTT.

11623 RACHEL, b. May 7, 1885, d. Manchester, N.H., Jan. 14, 1960, m. Manchester, N.H., July 19, 1913, Dr. ARTHUR FITTS WHEAT.

F10997 GEORGE PARKER TAYLOR, born in Burnside, Ky., Aug. 19, 1907, married in Mt. Pleasant, Mich., Mar. 4, 1949, ELMA JEAN BRIEN, born in Mt. Pleasant, Mich., July 8, 1919.

Children in 10th Gen. b. in Mt. Pleasant, Mich.

11624 RICHARD BRIEN, b. Feb. 27, 1950, m. Tulsa, Okla., Aug. 7, 1971, PATRICIA SUE TESSIER.

11625 LINDA FRENCH, b. Mar. 20, 1951, m. Tulsa, Okla., Aug. 31, 1973, STEVE CASTLE SAUNDERS.

F10998 ROBERT FRENCH TAYLOR, born in Burnside, Ky., Jan. 14, 1912, married in Detroit, Mich., Nov. 12, 1938, MARY WARD SAVAGE, born in Detroit, Mich., Dec. 25, 1913.

Children in 10th Gen. b. in Chicago, III.

11626 MARK LENAGHAN, b. Jan. 19, 1947.

11627 CATHERINE FRENCH, b. Oct. 4, 1948.

F10999 DOROTHY JORDAN, born in Jamaica Plain, Mass., Nov. 25, 1920, married in Brookline, Mass., Feb. 2, 1946, WARREN W. PETERMAN, born in Portsmouth, N.H., July 7, 1918.
    She lived in Brookline, Mass. until she was thirty years old at which time she moved to Concord, N.H. She is a graduate of Colby Junior College, New London, N.H.
    He is a graduate of the University of New Hampshire, served on PT Boat 118 in the So. Pacific in World War II and most of his business life has been spent as an agent for the Internal Revenue Service.

Children in 10th Gen. b. in Boston, Mass.

11628   JANE LAWRENCE, b. July 5, 1947.

11629   JOANNE DOROTHY, b. April 30, 1950, m. Concord, N.H., Mar. 3, 1973, PAUL E. TORRE.

11630   JUDITH JORDAN, b. Dec. 14, 1951.

F11004   NONA JEANETTE LOCKE, born in Fairfield, Iowa, Nov. 29, 1911, married in Des Moines, Iowa, May 12, 1934, JOHN HENRY CALHOUN, born in Nevada, Iowa, Dec. 27, 1909, died in Des Moines, Iowa, Aug. 31, 1957.

Children in 10th Gen. b. in Des Moines, Iowa

F11631   JO ANN JUNE, b. June 11, 1935.

F11632   JOHN RICHARD, b. Dec. 17, 1937.

F11633   LINDA CAROL, b. Dec. 25, 1942.

F11005   JAMES RICHARD LOCKE, born in Arkansas City, Kans., Feb. 12, 1917, married in Laon, France, 1955, MARGERY JEAN BOLES, born in Cottonwood Falls, Kans., Oct. 20, 1935.

Children in 10th Generation

11634   ROBERT JAMES, b. Chateaureoux, France, April 3, 1956.

11635   DONALD RICHARD, b. Laon, France, Sept. 25, 1957.

11636   KATHLEEN ANNE, b. Victorville, Calif., Nov. 23, 1958.

F11006   MABEL MARGARET LOCKE, born in Des Moines, Iowa, Mar. 17, 1921, died in Richmond, Calif., June 9, 1969, married in Albany, Mo., Mar. 30, 1940, RAYMOND P. ELLIS, born in Van Wert, Iowa, Aug. 3, 1914.

Children in 10th Generation

F11637   ELLEN MAY, b. Des Moines, Iowa, July 20, 1943.

11638   RAYMOND CLARENCE, b. Richmond, Calif., Nov. 9, 1951.

F11011   RUTH CORENA LOCKE, born in Taylorville, Ill., June 4, 1916, married in Taylorville, Ill., July 27, 1940, SHERMAN M. BOOTH, born in Chicago, Ill., April 21, 1910, son of Sherman M. and Elizabeth (Knox) Booth.

Children in 10th Generation

F11639   CHARLOTTE, b. Evanston, Ill., Dec. 25, 1941.

11640 JAMES, b. Washington, D.C., July 22, 1944, d. Evanston, Ill., Dec. 1, 1968.

F11012 CHARLES RICHARD LOCKE, born in Taylorville, Ill., Feb. 9, 1918, married in Indianapolis, Ind., Oct. 15, 1944, MARY CATHARINE MILLIGAN, born in Indianapolis, Ind., Mar. 3, 1919, daughter of J. S. and Margaret (Wynn) Milligan.

My wife, whom I met at Great Lakes, was a WAVE officer in 1942-45. She is descended from Samuel Stockton of New Jersey, who represented the U.S. in Russia and whose younger brother, Richard, signed the Declaration of Independence. My mother is descended from Thomas Lloyd, Deputy Governor to Wm. Penn in 1683.

Children in 10th Generation

11641 JOHN STUART, b. Taylorville, Ill., Jan. 23, 1946, d. Lincoln, Ill., April 19, 1966.

11642 MARGARET ELLEN, b. East St. Louis, Ill., Dec. 25, 1947, m. Evanston, Ill., June 2, 1973, RICHARD SCOTT MAYER, b. Chicago, Ill., May 31, 1945, son of Robert and Lois (Herrling) Mayer.

11643 RICHARD MILLIGAN, b. East St. Louis, Ill., Aug. 7, 1950.

F11013 DOROTHY LOUISE CLOSE, born in Taylorville, Ill., Feb. 11, 1924, married in Evanston, Ill., Sept. 10, 1944, ROBERT WILSON HOUSER, born in Chillicothe, Ohio, May 27, 1924, son of Clinton Franklin and Mary Eva (Wilson) Houser.

Children in 10th Generation

F11644 ROBERT KENT, b. Oberlin, Ohio, Nov. 9, 1946.

11645 STEVEN CRAIG, b. Reno, Nev., July 9, 1948, m. Perry, N.Y., June 5, 1972, JANET MARIE NORDOCCI, b. Perry, N.Y., May 30, 1949.

F11646 DAVID CLOSE, b. Vancouver, Wash., Dec. 20, 1950.

11647 CHARLES STEWART, b. Vancouver, Wash., Dec. 5, 1952.

F11014 STEWART ARTHUR CLOSE, born in Taylorville, Ill., May 17, 1928, married in Racine, Wis., June 15, 1957, GLADYS OLGA NEUMANN, born in Racine, Wis., Oct. 7, 1932, daughter of John August and Olga Wilhelmina (Weskum) Neumann.

Children in 10th Gen. b. in Racine, Wis.

11648 KEVIN STEWART, b. Jan. 10, 1960.

11649 THOMAS JOHN, b. Nov. 1, 1962.

11650 TODD ARTHUR, b. Nov. 1, 1962.

F11016 THELMA LILLIAN PARK, born in Los Angeles, Calif., Dec. 2, 1902, married in Pasadena, Calif., Aug. 3, 1922, HOWARD GARNER EDGCOMB, born in Knoxville, Penna., Nov. 26, 1895, died in Claremont, Calif., Oct. 17, 1974, son of James and Meeda (Garner ?) Edgcomb.

Children in 10th Generation

F11651 DORIS THELMA, b. Pasadena, Calif., July 21, 1925.

F11017 JOHN CLAYTON HERRICK, born in Augusta, Ga., Feb. 12, 1916, married in Yosemite Valley, Calif., Sept. 22, 1949, HELEN GENEVIEVE RANKIN, born in Woodbine, Iowa, Feb. 23, 1917, daughter of George Edwin and Stella Maude (Triplett) Rankin.

He holds a Correspondence School Diploma in Civil and Structural Engineering and is a registered Mechanical Engineer in the State of Calif. Was active in the Boy Scouts. She is a graduate of Iowa State College.

Children in 10th Generation

11652 STEVEN LEE, b. Los Angeles, Calif., April 1, 1957.

F11019 ROCCO NEAL GRUBBS, born in Fresno, Calif., May 9, 1929, married in Burbank, Calif., Mar. 5, 1955, DARLENE STEN-QUIST, born in Kaysville, Utah, May 12, 1929, daughter of Edwin Oscar and Mary (King) Stenquist.

Children in 10th Generation

11653 LISA DEE, b. Glendale, Calif., April 7, 1960.

11654 KARL NEAL, b. Burbank, Calif., July 12, 1961.

F11021 ROGER LOUIS GOODWIN, born in Melrose, Mass., Sept. 6, 1906, married in Medford, Mass., June 25, 1937, GERTRUDE CHRISTINE TURCOTTE, born in Boston, Mass., June 20, 1904, daughter of Frederick F. and Margaret A. (Young) Turcotte.

Children in 10th Generation

11655 JANET GLORIA, b. Brockton, Mass., Aug. 20, 1938.

11656 JOYCE PAMELA, b. Newton, Mass., Dec. 7, 1943.

F11022 MARY ELEANOR GOODWIN, born in Melrose, Mass., July 7, 1908, married in Melrose, Mass., Oct. 15, 1932, ROBERT DeWITT CULVER, SR., born in Albany, N.Y., July 17, 1909, son of DeWitt Clinton and Alice (Wright) Culver.

Children in 10th Gen. b. in Melrose, Mass.

F11657 ROBERTA LEE, b. Sept. 17, 1933.

F11658 JUDITH MARILYN, b. Sept. 22, 1936.

F11659 ROBERT DeWITT, JR., b. Dec. 10, 1943.

F11024 BARBARA LUCILLE GOODWIN, born in Malden, Mass.,
Jan. 9, 1925, married in Melrose, Mass., Oct. 2, 1948, ARTHUR
EUGENE FLINT, born in Jersey City, N.J., Mar. 4, 1925, son of
Arthur Jonas and Edith Marion (Estes) Flint, Jr.

Children in 10th Gen. b. in Melrose, Mass.

11660 JEFFREY ARTHUR, b. Oct. 14, 1951.

11661 JILL ELIZABETH, b. Nov. 10, 1953.

11662 JAY THOMAS GOODWIN, b. Feb. 9, 1956.

11663 JOAN CAROL, b. Aug. 11, 1959.

F11025 RICHARD HAMLIN DANFORTH, born in Gardiner, Maine,
April 17, 1922, married in Gardiner, Maine, Sept. 25, 1948,
BEVERLY JOAN HERSOM, born in Gardiner, Maine, Feb. 24, 1927,
daughter of J. Richard and Kathryn (O'Grady) Hersom.

Children in 10th Generation

11664 KATHRYN MARY, b. Gardiner, Maine, July 9, 1949.

11665 DEBORAH HERRICK, b. Gardiner, Maine, Mar. 12, 1951,
       d. Wilmington, Del., Oct. 8, 1951.

11666 MICHAEL RHYS, b. Salem, N.J., Nov. 10, 1952.

11667 PETER HERRICK, b. Augusta, Maine, April 15, 1955.

11668 JOHN RICHARD, b. Augusta, Maine, Jan. 31, 1956.

F11026 MARGARET LOIS DANFORTH, born in Gardiner, Maine,
Aug. 17, 1926, married in Gardiner, Maine, Oct. 15, 1944, RUSSELL
WAKEFIELD GLIDDEN, JR., born in Gardiner, Maine, May 12, 1927,
son of Russell Wakefield and Gladys (Libby) Glidden, Sr.

Children in 10th Generation

11669 RICHARD DANFORTH, b. Gardiner, Maine, Mar. 12, 1945.

11670 RUSSELL LIBBY, b. Lewiston, Maine, Sept. 12, 1948.

11671 GORDON WAKEFIELD, b. Christiansburg, Va., Mar. 12,
       1951.

F11027 MARJORIE FRANCIS DANFORTH, born in Gardiner, Me., Aug. 20, 1928, married in Gardiner, Maine, Sept. 4, 1948, ORICK WESTMAN, born in New Sweden, Maine, April 11, 1926, son of Robert and Dora (Pettingil) Westman.

Children in 10th Gen. b. in Caribou, Maine

11672 JUDITH ELLEN, b. April 22, 1949.

11673 BARBARA MARJORIE, b. Mar. 14, 1950.

11674 MARK ROBERT, b. April 22, 1952.

F11028 WILLIAM FRANCIS WEST, JR., born in Lyndonville, Vt., April 5, 1917, married in Bangor, Maine, Sept. 27, 1941, NAOMI ADAMS BLAKE, born in Lowell, Mass., Aug. 25, 1917, daughter of Clive and Vivian (Cunningham) Blake.
She is a descendent of Pres. Adams.

Children in 10th Generation

11675 WILLIAM CLIVE, b. Milford, Conn., Oct. 2, 1942.

11676 DAVID LEE, b. Dover-Foxcroft, Maine, Jan. 13, 1947.

11677 SUSAN DANFORTH, b. Dover-Foxcroft, Maine, Nov. 29, 1947.

11678 CLIVE EUGENE, b. Concord, Mass., Jan. 6, 1951.

F11029 DANFORTH EMERSON WEST, born in Bangor, Maine, Dec. 16, 1920, married in Bangor, Maine, May 17, 1947, MADELINE LOUISE LeBLANC, born in Boston, Mass., Sept. 21, 1920, daughter of Alfred Damase and Eleanor (Kingman) LeBlanc.

Children in 10th Gen. b. in Bangor, Maine

11679 ELINOR JEAN, b. Mar. 26, 1948.

11680 DANFORTH EMERSON, JR., b. Feb. 27, 1951.

F11030 ELIZABETH JANET WEST, born in Bangor, Maine, May 18, 1924, married in Bangor, Maine, Aug. 6, 1949, SETH BRIGGS, born in Boston, Mass., June 28, 1919, son of Albert Payson and Gertrude (Lyndon) Briggs.

Children in 10th Gen. b. in Boston, Mass.

11681 ANNE MEREDITH, b. June 30, 1950.

11682 ROBERT PAYSON, b. Aug. 10, 1951.

11683 SETH, Jr., b. Mar. 21, 1953.

11684 THOMAS LYNDON, b. June 30, 1954.

11685 JAMES NATHANIEL, b. Aug. 24, 1955.

F11033 MARGARET ANNE MARKS, born in Eureka, Calif., June 16, 1928, married in Arcata, Calif., Feb. 8, 1948, SHEDRICK ALLEN JACKSON, born in Eureka, Calif., July 24, 1927, son of Percy and Ruth (Clark) Jackson. He served on the USS Texas during WW II.

Children in 10th Gen. b. in Arcata, Calif.

11686 KENT WILLIAM, b. June 18, 1949.

11687 ERIK ALLEN, b. May 2, 1962.

11688 PHILLIP DAVID, b. May 2, 1962.

F11034 CHARLOTTE JEAN MARKS, born in Klamath Falls, Ore., Mar. 27, 1930, married in Arcata, Calif., Dec. 20, 1952, PHILIP JOSEPH CRAMMER, born in Redlands, Calif., Mar. 30, 1925, son of Max A. and Augusta (Williams) Crammer.
He was a U.S. Navy Radioman during WW II.

Children in 10th Generation

11689 MARK WILLIAM, b. San Francisco, Calif., Oct. 8, 1954.

11690 LYNN MARIA, b. San Rafael, Calif., Mar. 21, 1956.

11691 JENNIFER ANNE, b. San Rafael, Calif., July 2, 1958.

11692 THOMAS MAXWELL, b. San Rafael, Calif., May 28, 1960.

F11036 WILLIAM KEHEO CARTER, born in Russell, Kans., April 27, 1929, married in Russell, Kans., Aug. 27, 1954, DORISELAINE STALEY, born in Bunkerhill, Kans., Mar. 14, 1930, daughter of Vern M. and Lillie (Missimer) Staley. He attended Kansas State College.

Children in 10th Gen. b. in Russell, Kans.

11693 ANN, b. June 23, 1955.

11694 JANE, b. Sept. 11, 1956.

F11037 SUSAN GILBERT CARTER, born in Mitchell Co., Kans., May 6, 1932, married in Tucumcari, N. Mex., April 23, 1955, LARRY DEAN CURTIS, born in Great Bend, Kans., Oct. 11, 1932.

Children in 10th Gen. b. in Great Bend, Kans.

11695 DAVID WILLIAM, b. June 1, 1957.

11696 STEVEN DEAN, b. Dec. 16, 1959.

11697 PEGGY SUZANN, b. Sept. 24, 1963.

F11044 FRANCES ALBERTA LOCKE, born in Lockeport, N. S., Feb. 25, 1893, married in Lockeport, N.S., Aug. 24, 1922, HAROLD B. VERGE, born in Barss' Corners, N.S., Dec. 30, 1893, died Bridgewater, N.S., Jan. 1955.

Children in 10th Gen. b. in Barss' Corners, N.S.

11698   MARION ELIZABETH, b. Feb. 11, 1919.

F11699   WYLIE FOSTER, m. Sept. 24, 1955, MARGARET Mac-KENNON.

11700   HAROLD FRANKLIN, b. June 7, 1931.

F11047 RAND CURRIER FORD, born in Danbury, N.H., Oct. 14, 1898, died in Danbury, N.H., Jan. 15, 1971, married 1st, Danbury, N.H., April 26, 1919, AGNES LITCHFIELD; 2nd, Danbury, N.H., Sept. 26, 1925, GRACE RUSSELL.

Children in 10th Generation

11701   STANLEY LITCHFIELD, b. Danbury, N.H., Nov. 24, 1919, d. Danbury, N.H., June 6, 1971, m. New London, N.H., Oct. 27, 1946, JEANNE NEWTON.

F11702   ALTHEA LUCILLE, b. Danbury, N.H., April 20, 1921, m. Danbury, N.H., Sept. 22, 1945, ROYCE ALISON HASKELL.

By second wife, Grace:

F11703   CHARLES RUSSELL, b. Harrison, Maine, Jan. 17, 1927, m. Saratoga Springs, N.Y., Mar. 14, 1953, ANNAMAY TAYLOR.

F11704   ARTHUR SUTHERLAND, b. Harrison, Maine, Feb. 17, 1928, m. Barnstead, N.H., July 21, 1951, MARJORIE EQUI.

F11705   JOHN BROOKS, b. Danbury, N.H., Aug. 8, 1932, m. Wilder, Vt., Sept. 15, 1956, JANET LEAVITT.

F11050 AMY JUNE CURRIER, born in Saratoga, Calif., June 11, 1920, married in Saratoga, Calif., May 22, 1943, JOHN GEORGE JORGENSEN, born in Erwin, S. Dak., Jan. 9, 1918.

She graduated from San Jose State College 1941 with A.B. degree in English. She was active in PTA; President of Women's Auxiliary of Saratoga Federated Church, 1958; President Faculty Wives Assoc. of W. Valley College, 1969; President Saratoga Foothill Women's Club, 1973. Member of PEO Sisterhood and lives in Saratoga, Calif.

He graduated from San Jose State College, 1941 and holds MBA degree from Stanford University, 1947. Spent five years in the Mtn.

Infantry during WW II and is a Colonel in the Army Reserve. Professor at West Valley College teaching business subjects and also served four years as Division Chairman. Hobbies are skiing, coin collecting, auto mechanics and gardening.

Children in 10th Gen. b. in San Jose, Calif.

F11706 KIRKE CURRIER, b. July 26, 1945, m. Riverside, Calif., Nov. 1, 1969, VENITA JEAN McPHERSON.

11707 LOCKE CURRIER, b. Aug. 30, 1948. He holds B.S. degrees in Business Administration and Natural Resource Management from California State Polytechnic Univ. Is in the Peace Corps as an agriculturist aide in Liberia, West Africa.

11708 RILLA JEAN, b. June 20, 1951, m. Saratoga, Calif., Sept. 8, 1973, ROBERT STEPHEN DURING.
Holds B.S. and M.A. in home economics from Calif. State Polytechnic Univ. Lives in San Luis Obispo, Calif.

F11051 GEORGE MALCOLM LOCKE, born in Barnstead, N.H., Nov. 6, 1904, married in Durham, N.H., April 5, 1931, ELVA PEARL HOLLAND, born in Pembroke, Maine, Feb. 11, 1906, died in Barnstead, N.H., Feb. 2, 1971.

He graduated from University of N.H., 1924, Thompson School of Agriculture. He was on the Rifle Team, and Champion Light Heavyweight boxer 1924. He is a farmer and noted trapper. In 1945 he trapped 200 Red foxes in 26 days and in 1966-67 earned the World's Record for trapping 206 Fisher. He has written three books on Fox, Fisher and trapping Beaver. He raised hunting dogs and was a carpenter.

Children in 10th Gen. b. in Rochester, N.H.

F11709 JOHN MALCOLM, b. Oct. 15, 1931, m. Dec. 10, 1950, EVELYN TASKER.

11710 STEPHEN JEFFERY, b. Jan. 13, 1941, d. Rochester, N.H., Jan. 16, 1941.

F11711 SHARON KATHLEEN, b. Mar. 7, 1944, m. Barnstead, N.H., Feb. 4, 1964, ROGER TREMBLAY.

F11052 KENT DREW LOCKE, born in Barnstead, N.H., April 17, 1909, married in Alton, N.H., April 9, 1933, MARGARET JOHNSTON, born in Somerville, Mass., Nov. 25, 1910.

He attended a local one-room school and graduated from Alton High School, 1929, with honors. He played baseball and basketball and played on semi-pro teams. He has farmed as a part-time occupation all his life but was the largest shipper of N.H. blueberries at one time and farmed extensively during WW II. He is a master mason by trade having a well-known reputation. In 1966 he started a 2000 acre development project called Locke Lake Colony with 1200 lots for vacation/recreation homes. His sons joined him in this project which expanded to Maine and Florida. He served several years as President of the Locke Family Assoc. He is active in church affairs being a Deacon and incorporator of the Alton Community Church. He has been a sportsman all his life and lives in the family homestead in Alton where he and his brothers and sisters were born.

Children in 10th Gen. b. in Wolfeboro, N.H.

F11712　KENT DREW, JR., b. Sept. 10, 1936, m. Sept. 27, 1958, JEAN AUDREY POWERS.

F11713　JAMES NUTTER, b. Dec. 21, 1937, m. Gilmanton Iron Works, N.H., Nov. 14, 1959, NATALIE JEAN PRICE.

F11714　THOMAS GEORGE, b. Feb. 14, 1940, m. No. Barnstead, N.H., Oct. 15, 1966, JOANNE DEE MEUNIER.

F11054 MARY KELLEY LOCKE, born in Barnstead, N.H., Oct. 29, 1911, married in Sugar Hill, N.H., June 29, 1940, HENRY CHESTER LANE, born in East Swanzey, N.H., Dec. 14, 1907.

She attended Keene State College and graduated from the Univ. of N.H. with a B.S. degree. She taught Home Economics in Keene and Prince George's County, Md. She was the first President of the N.H. School Food Service Assoc., and has participated in national conventions and the National Executive Committee. Many of her students have received state and national honors. She was active in the United Church of Christ, Washington, D.C. and the No. Barnstead Congregational Church.

He attended Keene Public Schools and graduated from the Univ. of N.H. with a Bachelor's Degree, 1931. He was a teacher-coach at Keene High School and then entered the U.S. Army serving in India. He remained in the Army Reserve retiring in 1968 as a Lt. Colonel. He was employed by the U. S. Bureau of the Census, Washington, D.C., retiring in 1972. He has been active in Boy's Club athletics and served eleven years as a Trustee of the United Church of Christ, Washington, D.C. They live in No. Barnstead.

Children in 10th Generation

F11715　DEBORAH, b. Keene, N.H., Aug. 31, 1942, m. Washington, D. C., Nov. 17, 1962, EARL WALTER ESCHBACHER, JR.

F11716　JOHN TIMOTHY, b. Richmond, Va., Feb. 15, 1945, m. Washington, D.C., Aug. 16, 1967, SUZANNE HAIRFIELD.

F11717 PENELOPE, b. Keene, N.H., Sept. 16, 1949, m. Washington, D.C., June 19, 1971, EUGENE WILLIAMS, JR.

F11056 FRED McDUFFEE, born in Waits River, Vt., April 9, 1887, died Nov. 2, 1965, married May 15, 1912, NETTIE PAGE, born Oct. 10, 1889.

Children in 10th Gen. b. in Waits River, Vt.

11718 NATALIE, b. Feb. 15, 1913.

F11719 RONALD, b. April 27, 1915, m. Mar. 10, 1939, DAISY HALL.

F11059 MADALEINE DALE LOCKE, born in Irasburg, Vt., May 3, 1907, married in Chapel Hill, N. C., May 24, 1930, J. PAUL CHOPLIN, born in Winston-Salem, N.C., Mar. 2, 1907.

Children in 10th Generation

11720 JOHN LOCKE, b. Virginia, Nov. 2, 1948, adopted Jan. 1949, m. April, 1971, PAULA LOTT, and had: 11721 JOHN PAUL II, b. Ft. Belvoir, Va., May 9, 1973; 11722 IAN LOCKE, b. Ft. Meade, Md., June 17, 1974.

F11060 SHIRLEY MAE LOCKE, born in Irasburg, Vt., Aug. 11, 1908, married in Evanston, Ill., April 14, 1934, JOHN A. BODKIN, born in Chicago, Ill., Dec. 21, 1907, died in Mountain Home, Ark., April 9, 1976.

Children in 10th Gen. b. in Evanston, Ill.

F11723 CHARLES ARTHUR, b. April 25, 1937, m. Evanston, Ill., Oct. 14, 1961, PRISCILLA JEAN VOIGT.

11723a JOHN LOCKE, b. June 6, 1940.

F11061 RUTH CAROLINE PRESCOTT, born in Amesbury, Mass., Mar. 18, 1892, died in Haverhill, Mass., Feb. 5, 1949, married in Amesbury, Mass., Oct. 3, 1916, ARTHUR CLARENDON WRIGHT, M.D., born in Woolwich, Maine, Nov. 17, 1890, died in Haverhill, Mass., Mar. 1, 1964.

She graduated from Amesbury, Mass. High School in 1909 and Framingham, Mass. Normal School in 1912. She taught home economics at Marblehead, Mass. High School for four years. She was active in charitable organizations in Haverhill, Mass. including The Red Cross, YWCA and Day Nursery and was President of the Women's City Club at the time of her death and a member of the First Congregational Church. He graduated from Howe School, Billerica, 1908, Burdett Business College, Boston, Mass. and Tufts Medical School,

1913. He was a prominent physician in Haverhill, Mass. for over 40 years. He served as a First Lieutenant in WW I, was a member of the American Legion, a Master Mason, and member of the Mass. Medical Society.

Children in 10th Gen. b. in Haverhill, Mass.

11724 DONALD PRESCOTT, b. July 7, 1920, m. Haverhill, Mass., July 7, 1950, BERYL MARY BYRNE.

F11725 DAVID CLARENDON, b. June 28, 1925, m. Haverhill, Mass., Sept. 1, 1946, HARRIET LOUISE PARKS.

F11063 STANTON BRADBURY HOWARD, born in Newport, R. I., July 16, 1900, died in Dallas, Texas, Aug. 31, 1967, married on Oct. 26, 1928, GERTRUDE REID, born in Pittsburgh, Penna., Sept. 5, 1898.

He graduated from Biddeford High School and Worcester Polytechnic Institute in Worcester, Mass., class of 1924, taking part in athletics of both schools. He worked for Western Union as construction lineman, then by the Raymond Concrete Pile Co. where he was made a Superintendent by this firm which installs foundations for large buildings. He was in charge of the Schrafts building in Boston and the Proctor & Gamble plant at Quincy. Following these, he was made Divisional Superintendent with headquarters in Chicago. Here too, he was a member of the Congregational church and a Past Master of the Masonic Lodge. In 1965 he retired to his new home at Port Charlotte, Florida.

Children in 10th Gen. b. in Pittsburgh, Penna.

F11726 DOUGLAS REID, b. June 8, 1931, m. San Francisco, Calif., Dec. 19, 1952, LARUE CREPPS.

F11727 JANET ELIZABETH, b. July 28, 1935. m. Chicago, Ill., Aug. 17, 1957, VERYL DRUMMOND JOHNSON.

F11064 PRESCOTT LOCKE HOWARD, born in Newport, R. I., May 7, 1907, married June 20, 1936, ADA MARIE GILKS, born in Gilks, New Brunswick, Canada, Aug. 26, 1907.

He is a graduate of Biddeford High School and University of Maine at Orono. Employed by the Pepperell Manufacturing Co. where he was promoted through the ranks to Assistant Plant Engineer, rounding out 45 years with one company. In the interim, he was Scoutmaster 10 years, Senior Deacon at the Congregational church, life member of the Masonic order, Vice Pres. of Locke Association 1959 thru 1967 and 1972, President of the Locke Association 1968 thru 1971.

She was graduated from the Doaktown, N. B. High School and the Webber Hospital School of Nursing of Biddeford, followed by post graduate work at the Manhattan Eye Ear Nose and Throat Hospital in

New York and the Graystone Park Mental Hospital of Morristown, N.J. She returned to Biddeford as Supervisor of surgery and pediatrics at the Webber Hospital. She is a member of the United Methodist church and Eastern Star of Biddeford, Eastern District Nurses Association and has been Receptionist for the Locke Association for 13 years.

Children in 10th Gen. b. in Biddeford, Maine

F11728 RONALD ALBERT, b. Mar.16, 1937, m. Brunswick, Maine, Feb. 10, 1962, JOLEEN PATRICIA BARKER.

F11729 BERYL ANN, b. Aug. 17, 1942, m. Biddeford, Maine, June 22, 1963, CHARLES EDGAR HOBART.

F11065 HAZEL ALICE MOORE, born in Boston, Mass., Jan. 27, 1917, married in Medford, Mass., Sept. 19, 1941, CHARLES ESDALE PROUDFOOT, born in Somerville, Mass., April 25, 1914.

She graduated from Somerville High School in 1934 and trained as a nurse at Massachusetts General Hospital for two years. They have lived in Bedford, Mass. at 57 Sweetwater Ave. since 1949. She is active in community organizations including the Bedford Woman's Club, Emerson Hospital Auxiliary, Bedford Historical Society and the Red Cross. She is chairman of the Civic Committee of the Bedford Garden Club which plants and maintains fourteen triangle gardens in Bedford. He graduated from Tufts Univ. in 1933 and worked as an engineer for General Radio in Concord, Mass. For several years they were chairmen of the "Chuck Wagon" which was a fund raiser for the high school music department.

Children in 10th Generation

11730 BRUCE ROBERT, b. Springfield, Mass., Mar. 25, 1944, m. Chelmsford, Mass., Oct. 19, 1973, DONNA LOU GRAY, b. Lowell, Mass., April 11, 1948. He graduated from Bedford High School, 1962 and attended Northeastern Univ. and is an industrial general and cost accountant. They live on a small farm in Rindge, N.H. where they raise prize goats and chickens.

11731 DEAN MOORE, b. Boston, Mass., Mar. 8, 1948, m. New Washington, Ohio, May 27, 1978, VICKIE SUE PHILBRICK. He is a 1966 graduate of Bedford High School and served four years on the USS Enterprize off the coast of Viet Nam during that war as a catapult operator. For several years he ran his own specialty welding and machine shop in Bucyrus, Ohio. They had: 11731a SHELLY LOUISE, b. May 9, 1976 and 11731b SHAWN CHARLES, b. Bucyrus, Ohio, Mar. 24, 1979.

11732 MARILYN CLAIRE, b. Concord, Mass., July 8, 1952, m. Andover, Mass., April 20, 1974, CHARLES EDWARD

PFAFF, b. Rochester, N.Y., Aug. 5, 1952. She is a graduate of Bedford High School and Bay State Jr. College of Business. He graduated from Andover High School and served four years in the U.S. Navy. They are living in Colorado where he attends Colorado State Univ. in Ft. Collins.

F11066 GRACE ESTHER MOORE, born in Boston, Mass., June 2, 1920, married in Somerville, Mass., Dec. 10, 1944, DONALD PAUL HAYES, born in Noank, Conn., Feb. 21, 1919, son of Patrick and Melina (Lussier) Hayes.

She is a 1938 graduate of Somerville High School and Felt and Terrant Comptometer School in 1940. She is employed at the home office of the Andover Companies, Andover, Mass. Her hobbies and interests include sewing, knitting, gardening and rug braiding. She also collects English bone china. She has served as a Den Mother for the Cub Scouts and a Brownie leader for the Girl Scouts.

He attended St. Joseph's Parochial School, Somerville and graduated from Somerville High School in 1936. In 1942 he graduated from Northeastern Univ. with a degree in Chemical Engineering. In May, 1942 he volunteered for military service in the Naval Air Force. He was a pilot in the So. Pacific Command and the Central Pacific Command and attained the rank of full Lieutenant. After the war he worked as a computor analyst for Gillett and Co. In 1948 he started his own business now known as Hayes Last Co. in Haverhill, Mass. His business enjoys a very good reputation in the shoe industry for quality and modern techniques. For thirteen years he was active in the No. Essex Council, Boy Scouts of America serving as Neighborhood Commissioner and in other capacities. They live at 72 Sunset Rock Road, Andover, Mass. in the home built by her father.

Children in 10th Generation

11733 DONALD PAUL, JR., b. Boston, Mass., Aug. 30, 1947, m. Chelmsford, Mass., July 15, 1978, DEBORAH JEAN MOORE, b. Plainfield, N.J., Nov. 28, 1951, daughter of Harold Laurance and Betty Alice (Planck) Moore.

He graduated from Andover High School in 1965 and Salem State College in 1969 with a B.A. degree. He teaches the 6th grade in the Lowell, Mass. public school system. His numerous interests come under the general heading of history. He is currently serving as Secretary of the Locke Family Association and as a member of the Andover Historical Commission. He served on the Andover Bicentennial Committee, Historic District Study Committee, and as President of the Andover Historical Society from 1976 to 1978. During his term as President the historical society built the Susanne Smith Purdon

This picture shows a pleasant group of people who are representative of Locke Descendants. It was taken at the picnic on Odiorne's Point after the 84th reunion in 1974. From left to right are: F11076 Ester Drew Eastman; F11052 Kent D. Locke, our 17th president; Margaret Locke; #11735 Melanie Grace Hayes; #11733 Donald P. Hayes, Jr.; F3464 Edward Locke Lord who at age 90 made the trip from California to attend the reunion.

photo by Charles T. Ganzer

F10042 Raymond Sanborn Locke
18th President of the Association.

museum wing. He was Assistant Director of the Samuel
Parris Parsonage archaeological excavation in Danvers,
Mass. and authored "Andover, Mass., A Guide to Sites
of Historic Interest". He is also a private in the Danvers Alarm List Co., a colonial unit, and his hobbies
include collecting antique watches and clocks, restoring
antique automobiles, photography, bicycling, skiing,
and hiking.

She graduated from Chelmsford High School in 1969
and Lowell State College in 1973 with a B.S. degree.
She was a partner in the Open Door Nursery from 1974
to 1976 and teaches Kindergarden in Lowell, Mass.

F11734 DIANE ALICE, b. Lawrence, Mass., July 23, 1951, m.
Andover, Mass., June 27, 1970, DENNIS MICHAEL
TRAYNOR.

11735 MELANIE GRACE, b. Lawrence, Mass., May 11, 1960.
She is a High Honors student at the high school, plays
trombone in the band, and received the Faculty Award
for Academic Achievement at Andover East Jr. High
School, 1975. She is an avid horsewoman and animal
lover. She entered Cornell University in fall, 1978.

F11067 GEORGE EARLE LUCY, born in Amesbury, Mass., Jan. 22,
1899, married in Amesbury, Mass., June 11, 1927, ADA A. FOL-
LANSBEE, born in Amesbury, Mass., May 9, 1909.

In his early years he was a machine woodworker and bodymaker in
the automobile shops, then was a machinist and toolmaker in the
Navy Yard for 18 years. He was athletic in his youth in spite of a
lame leg, the result of an accident at age 4. During the early 1930's
he sang on radio station WHDH in Boston, Mass. on amateur programs
and with studio orchestras. He was a member of the Merrimac, Mass.
Board of Appeals for three years and has served on the Housing Authority since 1965. He is a 33rd degree Mason.

Children in 10th Gen. b. in Amesbury, Mass.

F11736 GEORGE EARLE, JR., b. July 5, 1928, m. Las Vegas,
Nev., June 15, 1954, GLADYS F. VERGAS.

F11737 BARBARA MAE, b. Oct. 14, 1930, m. Sept. 17, 1949,
LOUIS J. BEAULIEU.

F11068 ALFRED KENNETH LUCY, born in Amesbury, Mass., Sept.
21, 1905, died in Haverhill, Mass., Sept. 23, 1974, married in
Plaistow, N.H., Mar. 18, 1943, EMMA E. WHITE, born in Haverhill,
Mass., Sept. 13, 1909.

Attended grammar school and worked as a chef all his life.

Children in 10th Gen. b. in Haverhill, Mass.

F11738 ELLEN JANE (twin), b. Aug. 9, 1944, m. 2nd, MICHALE WALSH.

F11739 DOROTHY MAY (twin), b. Aug. 10, 1944, m. 2nd, PAUL CHRIONE (divorced 1964)

F11069 ROGER LOCKE CALEF, born in Rochester, N.H., July 31, 1924, married in Barrington, N. H., June 6, 1948, ALBERTA M. WITHAM, born in Exeter, N.H., Jan. 27, 1929.

He graduated from Dover High School, 1941 and attended McIntosh Business College. He served in the U.S. Army during WW II and is owner of Calef's Country Store.

Children in 10th Gen. b. in Rochester, N.H.

F11740 ANDREA ELIZABETH, b. Sept. 16, 1949, m. Rockford, N.Y., July 25, 1970, MARTIN W. CONLEY.

11741   WILLIAM R., b. April 19, 1953, m. Barrington, N. H., Aug. 23, 1975, KAREN TASKER.

11742   JERE CLARENCE, b. July 24, 1958.

F11070 MARILYN CALEF, born in Rochester, N.H., Feb. 9, 1933, married in Barrington, N. H., 1954, GLENN RICHARD ORDWAY, born in Bow, N.H.

She graduated from Dover High School and Concord Hospital School of Nursing 1953. Worked at Concord Hospital in several capacities as an R.N. He is a Clerk at the Concord, N.H. Post Office and they live in Bow, N.H.

Children in 10th Generation

11743   LISA ANNE, b. Concord, N.H., Oct. 6, 1970.

F11072 GARDNER LINCOLN LOCKE, born in Oakland, Calif., April 9, 1919, married in Santa Rosa, Calif., May 7, 1947, TAPPAN KIMBALL, born in Palo Alto, Calif., June 28, 1923.

His character exhibits several New England traits including determination, dedication, dependability, stocism, perseverance and hard work tempered with a dry, wry sense of humor. He graduated from Esmeraldas County High School, Nev., 1937; San Mateo Jr. College, 1939 and Stanford Univ., 1942. He served in the U.S. Marines 1942-45 participating in landings at Guam and Iwo Jima and was discharged a Captain with 2 bronze stars. He earned a Master's Degree in 1947 and Degree of Engineer in Engineering Mechanics 1948. He worked in engineering until 1959 when he began devoting fulltime to his livestock farm in Joseph, Oregon with time off for teaching and

consulting. In April 1972 he and his wife joined the Peace Corps and
worked three years in Ecuador. His wife "Tappy" writes that her phi-
losophies, character and personality are opposite to Gardner's result-
ing in an "idylic life together". She enjoys farming especially horses,
and traveling. She graduated from Sequoia Union High School in
Redwood City, 1940 and Stanford Univ. 1947 majoring in journalism.
She has run a 4-H horse club for 13 years and her letters show her to
be a very interesting, energetic person.

Children in 10th Generation

F11744 BARNEY LINCOLN, b. San Mateo, Calif., Dec. 14, 1947,
m. Cliffside Park, N. J., Aug. 29, 1971, SUSAN
PHILLIPS.

F11745 MARTIN TAPPAN, b. San Mateo, Calif., Oct. 26, 1949,
m. Enterprise, Ore., Dec. 28, 1972, CAPRICE SHORT-
RIDGE.

11746 WILLIAM KIMBALL, b. Richland, Wash., Jan. 9, 1952,
m. London, Ontario, May 25, 1876, MARY MARGARET
BRENNAN, b. Mar. 12, 1955.
He graduated from Joseph, Ore. High School in 1969
and a junior college in London, Ontario, 1976 majoring
in architecture technology. He is now working in
architectural design of farm buildings. He was a champion wrestler in high school and enjoys hiking and
camping. His wife is a ranch-raised horsewoman,
talented in guitar and singing. She is head of a library
in a mental institution in London, Ontario.

11747 STEVEN AUGUSTUS, b. Richland, Wash., Feb. 19, 1953.
Showed an interest in journalism in high school
working half-day as a reporter for the La Grande, Ore.
Observer and attending classes the other half-day. He
was active in sports, music and 4-H, hiking and camping. Has spent some time in Ecuador in the Peace Corps.

11748 SAMUEL GARLAND, b. Enterprise, Ore., Jan. 1, 1962,
d. Enterprise, Ore., Sept. 12, 1967.

11749 TIMOTHY, b. Enterprise, Ore., May 30, 1964. Traveled
to Ecuador with his parents where his personality earned
him the title of "The best good-will ambassador the U.S.
ever had" from his parents.

11750 TERESA, (adopted), b. Seoul, Korea, Dec. 3, 1964.
She was adopted by the Lockes at age six because they
"never were able to push the 'girl'button".

F11074 JANE MARTINDALE DEWEY, born in Boston, Mass., Sept. 2, 1921, married in Provincetown, Mass., Jan. 6, 1945, JAMES WALLACE ALCOCK, born in South Dartmouth, Mass., May 6, 1921. She graduated from Wellesley College with A.B. in 1943. Has worked to date 23 years in education, from psychology at University of Miami to special education class for educable children, to developmental reading program, reading supervisor, assistant principal of an elementary school.

Major interests are family, school, church, skiing and sailing. Sings in the church choir and is at present a Trustee of the church. Active in local theater group.

He graduated from University of Miami with A.B. and M.A. with advanced graduate work at Boston University. Taught in the psychology department, University of Miami. Served in World War II and Korean conflict as Navy pilot. Has been employed in Chatham, Mass., school system for 23 years initially as guidance director and principal, later audio visual director. Active in church and community affairs. Enthusiastic sailor.

Children in 10th Generation

F11751   GARLAND SHAW, b. Coral Gables, Fla., Feb. 10, 1948, m. Tahoe, Calif., June 28, 1975, LAWRENCE PRITCHARD.

11752   GAEL DEWEY, b. Hyannis, Mass., Sept. 23, 1949. She is a 1973 graduate of Bennington College and is a professional cellist and lives in San Francisco.

11753   ARTHUR JAMES, b. Hampton, N.H., Sept. 7, 1950, m. North Chatham, Mass., KATHLEEN CROWELL PETERSON. He graduated from Cape Cod Community College and from Univ. of Mass. with a B.Ed. degree. Presently teaching science in Jr. High School in Barnstable, Mass. His wife is a graduate of Framingham, Mass. College.

F11076 ESTHER STEVENS DREW, born in Union, N.H., Jan. 30, 1923, married in Union, N.H., June 12, 1954, DAVID GALE EASTMAN.

She was graduated from the University of New Hampshire, 1945 with a B.S. degree in Occupational Therapy. She held several positions in this field at hospitals in Maine, N.H., Mass. and N.Y. She was Supervisor of Occupational Therapy at the Univ. of N.H., 1950-54. She lives in Somersworth, N.H. with her husband who is a family physician. They are active in community affairs. She has been an active supporter of the Locke Family Assoc. since childhood.

Children in 10th Generation

11754   DAVID ALAN, (adopted 1958), b. Manchester, N.H.,

Jan. 15, 1948. He received an Associate of Arts degree from Bryant & Stratton Jr. College, Boston, Mass., 1972. Attended Belknap College, Center Harbor, N. H. and Lyndon State College, Vt. Presently working for Rockingham Security Co. in Portsmouth.

11755 SUSAN GALE, (adopted 1959), b. Brookline, Mass., Sept. 26, 1958. She is a graduate of Somersworth High School 1977, and plans to study child care on the college level. She has artistic talent and has received awards for her work at local fairs.

F11077 FRANCES ELAINE LADD, born in Grand Rapids, Mich., April 22, 1924, married in Fort Payne, Ala., Mar. 14, 1946, RANDOLPH EARL NEAL, born in Gardner, Mass., June 9, 1918.
    She graduated from DeKalb County High School, Fort Payne, Ala., (1942) and attended Montevallo College, Montevallo, Ala., and Weselyn College, Macon, Ga. Her husband served with the U. S. Armed Forces during World War II and graduated from Georgia Tech (1952) (B. S. in E.E.). He was an Engineer with the U.S. Government at the Huntsville Space Center.

Children in 10th Generation

11756 RANDOLPH EARL, JR., b. Atlanta, Ga., Oct. 12, 1951.

11757 PAMELA JEANNE, b. Bristol, Va., Feb. 18, 1954, m. Huntsville, Ala., Mar. 13, 1976, JESSE PHILIP McCALL.

F11078 GERTRUDE LOUISE LADD, born in Fort Payne, Ala., June 13, 1928, married in Fort Payne, Ala., June 10, 1950, MATTIE ZACHARIAL HITCHCOCK, born in Douglasville, Ga., Oct. 7, 1918.
    She graduated from DeKalb County High School (1946) and attended Judson College and University of Ala. He was a salesman.

Children in 10th Gen. b. in Chattanooga, Tenn.

11758 FREDERICK LADD, b. May 9, 1953, m. Chattanooga, Tenn., Aug. 25, 1973, PAMELA JEANNE SIVLEY.

11759 CHERYL ELAINE, b. May 26, 1956.

F11080 MARGARET DALE LADD, born in Gadsden, Ala., July 7, 1937, married 1st, in Rising Fawn, Ga., June 30, 1954, GERALD LEDFORD KING, born in Ft. Payne, Ala., Sept. 8, 1935; 2nd, Ft. Payne, Ala., June 17, 1961, GENE FRANKLIN GAINER, born in Panama City, Fla., Jan. 12, 1938.
    She graduated from DeKalb County High School, 1955, and from Edmondson Business College, 1960. Gene Gainer graduated from Bay

County High School and from Florida State University. He worked for Sears, Roebuck and Company and was last employed at the General Office in Chicago, Ill.

Children in 10th Generation

11760 CATHERINE LYNN KING, b. Ft. Payne, Ala., Jan. 31, 1955, d. Elmwood, Ill., Aug. 25, 1974, m. Villa Park, Ill., June 15, 1974, WILLIAM JAMES BENTELL, JR.

11761 TRACY LEE GAINER, b. Clearwater, Fla., May 13, 1963.

F11081 DOROTHY TAYLOR ALLISON, born in Geneva, Ill., Nov. 17, 1936, married in Wilmette, Ill., Aug. 20, 1960, WILLIAM WALFRED MUNSON, born in Peoria, Ill., Dec. 28, 1931, died in Kansas City, Mo., Jan. 27, 1976, son of Lyle and Ruth (Coffman) Munson.
She has a B.S. degree from Purdue Univ., 1958.

Children in 10th Generation

11762 DANIEL STEWART, b. Chicago, Ill., Nov. 19, 1964.

11763 KATHERINE ALLISON, b. Kansas City, Mo., Jan. 5, 1968.

F11082 DANIEL SHELBY ALLISON, born in Geneva, Ill., July 11, 1941, married in Elmhurst, Ill., Aug. 18, 1962, NANCY GAIL STRONG, born in Chicago, Ill., April 1, 1941, daughter of Orville H. and Elsie (Lovgren) Strong.
He is Trust Officer of First Wisconsin Bank of Milwaukee, Wisc.

Children in 10th Gen. b. in Evanston, Ill.

11764 SARAH SHELBY, b. Dec. 9, 1966.

11765 REBEKAH LOVEGREN, b. Mar. 7, 1968.

11766 MATTHEW BENJAMIN, b. Sept. 10, 1971.

F11084 SARAH MORSE LOCKE, born in Sandusky, Ohio, Dec. 28, 1937, married in Castro Valley, Calif., Jan. 31, 1959, ROBIN RAY DRAGOMANOVICH, born in Stockton, Calif., June 15, 1937, son of Ellis Grant and Ethel (Sharp) Dragomanovich.

Children in 10th Generation

11767 BRIAN GRANT, b. San Andreas, Calif., Dec. 3, 1959.

11768 BRUCE GEOFFREY, b. Lodi, Calif., June 22, 1962.

F11085 EDWARD TAYLOR LOCKE, JR., born in Woodstock, Ill., April 25, 1935, married in Woodstock, Ill., June 14, 1958, MARJORIE

LEE HIRONIMUS, born in Volo, Ill., Jan. 2, 1936, daughter of Harry Lee and Genevieve (Behning) Hironimus.

Children in 10th Gen. b. in Woodstock, Ill.

11769 EDWARD TAYLOR III, b. Nov. 30, 1960.

11770 ROBERT TAYLOR, b. Dec. 8, 1966.

F11087 JANET MARIE LOCKE, born in Elgin, Ill., July 11, 1938, married in Woodstock, Ill., Aug. 16, 1958, JOHN KENNETH TURNOW, born in Woodstock, Ill., Dec. 29, 1926, son of John Fred and Mame (Selchow) Turnow.

Children in 10th Gen. b. in Woodstock, Ill.

11771 TERRI LYNN, b. April 21, 1960.

11772 CYNTHIA SUE, b. April 1, 1963.

F11088 PATRICIA WARD LOCKE, born in Battle Creek, Mich., Oct. 1, 1936, married in Moffett Field, Calif., April 28, 1956, JOYE DUANE MILLER, born in Adelphi, Iowa, Feb. 1, 1935, son of Gale Charles and Helen Belle (Curry) Miller.

Children in 10th Generation

11773 COLE DUANE, b. Scotia, Calif., Dec. 7, 1956.

11774 PHIL CHARLES, b. Fortuna, Calif., Dec. 9, 1957.

11775 KERRY-JO, b. Fortuna, Calif., June 12, 1959.

F11089 MARY BRUCE LOCKE, born in St. Paul, Minn., Aug. 25, 1940, married in Los Altos, Calif., Dec. 20, 1961, JOHN WILLIAM HARDESTY, born in Albany, Calif., Aug. 31, 1939, son of Merritt F. and Bernice Isabel (Hayden) Hardesty.

Children in 10th Generation

11776 JOLEEN RAE, b. Mountain View, Calif., Sept. 6, 1967.

11777 JEFFREY SCOTT, b. Chula Vista, Calif., Aug. 1, 1969.

F11090 CAROL ANNE LOCKE, born in Palo Alto, Calif., Jan. 12, 1948, married in Moffett Field, Calif., April 17, 1971, FRANK ANTHONY GAGLIARDI, JR., born in Gainesville, Fla., Dec. 16, 1947, son of Frank Anthony and Margaret Marie (Cosgrove) Gagliardi.

Children in 10th Generation

11778 DAVID MICHAEL, b. Laguna Hills, Calif., Sept. 15, 1975.

F11091 JOHN GORDON LOCKE, born in Woodstock, Ill., Jan. 15, 1935, married 1st, in Chicago, Ill., Mar. 31, 1961, MARY ANN SWENSKI, born in Chicago, Ill., Sept. 27, 1941, daughter of Raymond and Agnes Swenski; 2nd, in Silver Spring, Md., Dec. 6, 1974, ANTJE MARIA SCHULTZ, born in Hamburg, Germany, July 14, 1939, daughter of Arthur E. and Alita F. (Oltmanns) Schultz.

He graduated 1961 from Univ. of Ill. with a B.S. degree in marketing and has worked for 3-M Co. in sales and marketing since then. He served in the Navy for two years and became a Mason in 1960 in Marengo, Ill. He was raised to his 3rd degree by his grandfather (F3441) Richard Foss who was a past master for over 50 years.

Children in 10th Generation

11779 JANE ELLEN, b. St. Paul, Minn., Dec. 28, 1961.

11780 NANCY THERESA, b. Pittsburgh, Pa., May, 24, 1963.

11781 DAVID RUSSELL, b. Pittsburgh, Pa., Mar. 15, 1965.

F11092 JUDITH ANNE LOCKE, born in Elgin, Ill., May 3, 1936, married 1st, in Marengo, Ill., Jan. 24, 1959, WILLIAM CLYDE MILLER, born in Whiteside Co., Ill., Feb. 21, 1930, son of Milo Clough and Amy Ethel (Robinson) Miller; 2nd, in West Chicago, Ill., July 15, 1971, WILLIAM CLYDE LEATHERMAN, born in Pontiac, Ill., April 23, 1927, son of Daniel Orville and Fay Oneva (Ketterman) Leatherman.

Children in 10th Generation

11782 WILLIAM SCOTT, b. McHenry, Ill., July 3, 1964.

F11093 DOROTHY JEAN LOCKE, born in Tulsa, Okla., June 5, 1944, married in Royal Oak, Mich., Oct. 3, 1964, DAVID ALLAN COYLE, born in Highland Park, Mich., Jan. 8, 1942, son of Delmar Guy and Edna (Keithan) Coyle.

Children in 10th Generation

11783 ANDREA LYNN, b. Pontiac, Mich., Dec. 6, 1965.

11784 JOHN KEITHAN, b. Warren, Mich., Aug. 18, 1968.

F11094 SHARON KAY LOCKE, born in Sterling, Ill., July 29, 1945, married in Lansing, Mich., June 29, 1968, DAVID LAWRENCE SHAUB, born in Lansing, Mich., Oct. 23, 1939, son of Dale and Helen Kay (Banfield) Shaub.

They both are graduates of Mich. State Univ. with degrees in Education and he has a Master's degree in Educational Psychology.

Children in 10th Generation

11785 DAVID CHRISTOPHER, b. Southfield, Mich., Oct. 12, 1970.

11786 DARREN LEE, b. Southfield, Mich., Feb. 4, 1972.

11787 DAWN MARIE, b. Pueblo, Colo., Oct. 1, 1976.

F11095 VALERIE LYNN LOCKE, born in Morrison, Ill., Oct. 11, 1946, married April 27, 1964, RICHARD MARLIN GOLINSKI, born in Hamtramck, Mich., Feb. 24, 1944, son of Leonard and Cecilia (Remp) Golinski.

Children in 10th Generation

11788 ROBIN VALERIE, b. Royal Oak, Mich., April 2, 1965.

11789 RENEE VICTORIA, b. Royal Oak, Mich., April 16, 1967.

11790 RICHARD VINCENT, b. Royal Oak, Mich., July 31, 1968.

11791 RYAN VANCE, b. Rochester, Mich., April 11, 1973.

F11096 DONALD STEPHEN LOCKE, JR., born in Peoria, Ill., July 6, 1950, married Aug. 6, 1971, KATHERYN ANN PREVOST, born in Detroit, Mich., Feb. 6, 1953, daughter of Melvin Claude and Dolores (Sobieski) Prevost.

Children in 10th Generation

11792 JOHN STEPHEN, b. North Miami, Fla., Feb. 1, 1972.

11793 SHANNON NICOLE, b. Southfield, Mich., Aug. 4, 1973.

11794 MICHAEL DAVID, b. Southfield, Mich., July 31, 1975.

F11099 PHILIP FRANCIS LOCKE, JR., born in Colorado Springs, Colo., Aug. 16, 1944, married in Watertown, N.Y., Nov. 14, 1954, SHARON SANDERCOCK, born Nov. 17, 1944.

Children in 10th Generation

11795 PHILIP FRANCIS III, b. Allentown, Pa., Feb. 2, 1965.

11796 BRENLEY JOANNE, b. Ithaca, N.Y., April 2, 1967.

F11102 EVELYN LOUISE LOCKE, born in Gooding, Idaho, Aug. 21, 1943, married 1st, ROBERT W. BECK; 2nd, in Coeur d'Alene, Idaho, July 12, 1974, JAMES CHARLES PIERCE, born in Bozeman, Mont.

Children in 10th Generation

11797 RICHARD WALTER, b. St. George, Utah, May 28, 1965.

11798 BENJAMIN FRED, b. Twin Falls, Idaho, May 20, 1968.

F11103   ROBERT BRUCE LOCKE, born in Gooding, Idaho, April 29, 1949, married in Gooding, Idaho, Sept. 4, 1969, KATHLYN ANN STRICKLAND, born in Wendell, Idaho, April 26, 1949, daughter of Richard Bernie and Dorothy Mae (Stickle) Strickland.

Children in 10th Generation

11799   BRIAN SCOTT, b. Fallbrook, Calif., Dec. 10, 1972.

11800   CHRISTINE LOUISE, b. Gooding, Idaho, Sept. 2, 1975.

F11104   JAMES ARTHUR WRIGHT, born in Johnstown, Pa., Oct. 13, 1938, married CHRISTINE ALICE RUBSAMEN, born in Orange, N.J., Dec. 23, 1939, daughter of Robert Brownlee and Grace Alice (Scilipoti) Rubsamen.

He has a B.A. from San Jose State Univ., 1962, is now a major in the U.S. Army.

Children in 10th Generation

11801   REBECCA ELEANOR, b. San Francisco, Calif., June 24, 1963.

11802   COLIN JAMES, b. Tacoma, Wash., Nov. 1, 1964.

11803   LAIRD ANDREW, b. Bethesda, Md., June 15, 1969.

F11105   HELEN GRACE WRIGHT, born in Johnstown, Pa., Aug. 10, 1941, married in Fort Lewis, Tacoma, Wash., Dec. 22, 1964, THOMAS GORDON DAVID EVANS, born in Portland, Ore., Sept. 11, 1944, son of David Elmer and Florence Leona (Mather) Evans.

She has a B.A. from Calif. Western Univ. in San Diego, 1963.

Children in 10th Generation

11804   THOMAS GEORGE, b. Oakland, Calif., Mar. 8, 1968.

11805   DAVID JONATHAN, b. Hayward, Calif., June 29, 1974.

F11109   WILLIAM MORSE LOCKE, JR., born in Toledo, Ohio, Aug. 4, 1946, married in Toledo, Ohio, June 27, 1970, SARA JANE LUMBATTIS, born Aug. 10, 1946, daughter of John Curson and Betty Jane Luis (Carver) Lumbattis.

Children in 10th Generation

11806   JULIE ANN, b. Toledo, Ohio, Sept. 15, 1976.

F11113   JOSEPH ARTHUR LOCKE, born in Toledo, Ohio, Dec. 28, 1952, married in Monroe, Mich., April 7, 1973, BARBARA LYNN HUGHES, born in Oceanside, Calif., Nov. 18, 1951, daughter of Roger Merrill and Margaret Alice (Crum) Hughes.

Children in 10th Generation

11807   OCTAVIA JO, b. Toledo, Ohio, Nov. 17, 1974.

11808   ASTREUS JUSTIN, b. Perrysburg, Ohio, Aug. 25, 1976.

F11122   JOHN LESTER LILLIE, born in Rockford, Ill., May 15, 1935, married in Rockford, Ill., Nov. 9, 1957, JOYCE TRAVIS, born Rockford, Ill., Sept. 29, 1937, daughter of Carl and Ruth Travis.

Children in 10th Gen. b. in Rockford, Ill.

11809   DOUGLAS WILLIAM, b. Nov. 22, 1958.

11810   DENNIS JOHN, b. Aug. 1, 1960.

11811   BARBARA ANN, b. Nov. 8, 1961.

11812   BRENDA KAY, b. Jan. 4, 1964.

11813   BETH S., b. Jan. 25, 1965.

11814   DAVID CARL, b. Feb. 20, 1966.

F11123   MARJORIE IRENE HERRICK, born in Fresno, Calif., Aug. 14, 1928, married in Fresno, Calif., Sept. 7, 1947, KENNETH DEVERE DROULLARD, born in Holoyoke, Colo., Dec. 27, 1923, son of Fred R. and Grace (Powell) Droullard.

Children in 10th Gen. b. in Fresno, Calif.

11815   DANIEL DEVERE, b. Nov. 11, 1949, m. Sacramento, Calif., July 1, 1972, LINDA LOUISE BICKER, b. Sacramento, Calif., June 4, 1949, daughter of Harvey David and Della Irene (Bean) Bicker.

11816   REBECCA ANN, b. Sept. 26, 1952.

F11127   CAROLYN JEAN HERRICK, born in Portland, Ore., Nov. 2, 1922, married in Berkeley, Calif., April 6, 1957, GEORGE WM. HOBBS, born in London, England, Jan. 6, 1922, died in a plane accident, Nov. 8, 1962, son of George and Elizabeth (Fitzgerald) Hobbs.

Children in 10th Generation

11817   MALCOLM GEORGE RODNEY, b. San Francisco, Calif., Nov. 15, 1958.

F11128   RICHARD HERRICK DANIEL, born in Los Angeles, Calif., July 31, 1927, married in Los Angeles, Calif., July 31, 1954, MARY KATHRYN BRYANT, born in Williston, N. Dak., Jan. 22, 1928, daughter of George and Kathryn (Dawalt) Bryant.

Children in 10th Gen. b. in Los Angeles, Calif. .

11818   KAREN LOUISE, b. Feb. 1, 1957.

11819   KELLY ANN, b. June 28, 1961.

F11129   BARBARA ANN DANIEL, born in Los Angeles, Calif.,
Nov. 18, 1928, married in Beverly Hills, Calif., Sept. 5, 1948,
CHARLES EDISON TYNER, JR., born in Modesto, Calif., Aug. 14,
1925, died in Sacramento, Calif., Jan. 9, 1968, son of Charles E. and
Berenice (Browne) Tyner.

Children in 10th Generation

11820   KIMBERLY, b. Oakland, Calif., May 20, 1953.

11821   KRIS PATRICK, b. Bakersfield, Calif., May 29, 1955.

F11132   ELIZABETH ANN HERRICK, born in Biddeford, Maine,
Dec. 11, 1930, married in Saco, Maine, Oct. 15, 1950, FERNAND
EDWARD AUDIE, born in Biddeford, Maine, Oct. 30, 1926, son of
Wm. Joseph and Marie Ann (LaRouche) Audie.

Children in 10th Gen. b. in Biddeford, Maine

11822   MARK EDWARD AUDIE, b. May 31, 1952, m. Allentown,
         Penna., Feb. 5, 1977, NANCY KULBE HARRIES, b.
         Paterson, N.J., Feb. 29, 1952, daughter of Herbert D.
         and Emily (Kulbe) Harries

11823   PETER MELVIN, b. May 8, 1954.

11824   GAYLE ELIZABETH, b. Sept. 24, 1957.

F11133   IRVING WEYMOUTH HERRICK, JR., born in Biddeford,
Maine, Nov. 7, 1932, married in Folcroft, Penna., Aug. 18, 1966,
BERNICE ADELE MORGAN, born in Chester, Penna., Oct. 12, 1931,
daughter of Edward L. and Esther (Dunham) Morgan.

Children in 10th Generation

11825   PATRICIA ANN, b. Baltimore, Md., April 23, 1959.

11826   MICHAEL IRVING, b. Riverdale, Md., Nov. 2, 1961.

F11135   LOEN HERRICK BURBANK, born in Lisbon Falls, Maine,
Dec. 19, 1930, married DONALIE TAYLOR, born in Lexington Town-
ship, Maine, Sept. 8, 1941, daughter of Robert B. and Thelma
(Bachelder) Taylor.

     He graduated from the Northern Conservatory of Music, 1961. She
is a graduate of Farmington State College, 1964.

Children in 10th Gen. b. in Skowhegan, Maine

11827 PERALIE MAY, b. Nov. 14, 1968.

11828 VILIA JEAN, b. Feb. 8, 1971.

F11136 AVIS RUTH BURBANK, born in Stratton Village, Maine, April 23, 1932, married in Solon, Maine, Aug. 27, 1950, RICHARD LOUIS KING, born in Stratton Village, Maine, Nov. 21, 1929, son of Charles E. and Lillian M. King.

Children in 10th Generation

11829 SHERRYL MARIE, b. Skowhegan, Maine, Sept. 6, 1953, m. Jan. 15, 1977, DARRELL LAVOIE.

11830 MARJORIE ELLEN, b. Farmington, Maine, Dec. 19, 1954, m. Dec. 26, 1976, PAUL WELCH.

11831 SUSAN, m. June 26, 1976, WM. MORRISS.

11832 DAVID

F11137 GILBERT EATON BURBANK, born in Eustis, Maine, Mar. 26, 1939, married in Skowhegan, Maine, May 18, 1963, RENA BEGIN, born in Jackson, Maine, July 10, 1943.

Children in 10th Gen. b. in Skowhegan, Maine

11833 CLINT MILES, b. Mar. 1, 1964.

11834 VALERIE LYN, b. Jan. 25, 1966.

11835 CRAIG DANIEL, b. Sept. 4, 1969.

F11139 ROBERT DANIEL HERRICK, born in Stephentown, N.Y., April 4, 1936, married in West Stephentown, N.Y., Sept. 11, 1955, FRANCES LOBDELL, born in Troy, N.Y., June 4, 1936, daughter of Irving and Marguerite (Manley) Lobdell.

Children in 10th Gen. b. in Pittsfield, Mass.

11836 BONNIE LEE, b. Sept. 2, 1956.

11837 SHIELA MARIE, b. July 30, 1959.

11838 ROBERT DANIEL, JR., b. Feb. 20, 1962.

11839 SAMUEL A., b. Nov. 6, 1972.

11840 REBECCA EILEEN, b. Dec. 26, 1976.

F11140 DEAN GORDON HERRICK, born in Stephentown, N.Y., April 4, 1936, married DONNA HEMMING, born in Middleburg, N.Y., Oct. 2, 1942, daughter of Fred E. and Eleanor (Stannard) Hemming.

Children in 10th Gen. b. in Pittsfield, Mass.

11841 DEBORAH SUE, b. April 6, 1962.

11842 DIANE ELEANOR, b. Feb. 9, 1964.

11843 DEANNA LYN, b. Aug. 17, 1973.

F11143 LILLIAN BARSTOW CROWELL, born in Boston, Mass., Mar. 15, 1940, married in Fairbanks, Alaska, Sept. 1, 1964, DONALD MOORE SCHELL, born in New Bedford, Mass., July 3, 1940, son of Charles and Elizabeth (Moore) Schell.
She has a B.S. from New Bedford Inst. of Tech., 1962 and M.S. from Univ. of Alaska, 1971. He has a B.S. from New Bedford Inst. of Tech., 1962 and a M.S. and Doctorate in Marine Science, Univ. of Alaska, 1970.

Children in 10th Generation

11844 SARANA BARSTOW, b. Fairbanks, Alaska, April 19, 1969.

F11144 JO NANCY CROWELL, born in Portsmouth, N.H., Jan. 2, 1942, married in Eliot, Maine, Aug. 6, 1966, CARLETON E. GUNN, born in Manchester, N.H., July 25, 1941, son of Wilfred and Edith (Ericson) Gunn.
She has a B.S. from Aroostook State Teachers College, 1963 and a M.S., Univ. of Maine. He went to Rhode Island School of Design and is a graduate of Bangor Theological Seminary, 1969.

Children in 10th Gen. b. in Bangor, Maine

11845 CARLETON ERIC, b. May 4, 1969.

11846 WILLIAM DANE, b. July 6, 1970.

F11145 MARCIA WASHBURN CROWELL, born in Portsmouth, Va., Feb. 1, 1943, married in Kittery, Maine, May 29, 1965, BRUCE GORDON VIOLANTE, born in New Bedford, Mass., Nov. 6, 1941, son of Manuel and Lillian (Macedo) Violante.
She has a B.S. from New Bedford Inst. of Tech., 1964 and went to Plymouth Teachers College. He received a B.S. from New Bedford Inst. of Tech. in 1965.

Children in 10th Gen. b. in Quincy, Mass.

11847 JOSSELYN ANNE, b. July 18, 1966.

11848 JAN ELIZABETH, b. Oct. 9, 1968.

11849 BRUCE GORDON II, b. April 4, 1973.

F11146 DEBORAH HERRICK CROWELL, born in Richmond, Va., Aug. 30, 1948, married in Hagerstown, Md., Sept. 16, 1966, ELWOOD BRINTON MILLER, JR., born in Hazelton, Penna., July 23, 1943, son of Elwood Brinton and Ruby (Hudson) Miller, Sr.
He was in the U.S. Navy to 1969 and is a descendant of General Robert E. Lee on his mother's side.

Children in 10th Generation

11850 DEBORAH LYNN, b. Kittery, Maine, Jan. 28, 1967.

11851 JOELLE MARIE, b. San Diego, Calif., June 17, 1969.

11852 DANIELLE LEE, b. Portsmouth, N.H., May 23, 1975.

F11147 SAMUEL CROWELL IV, born in Richmond, Va., July 11, 1950, married in Alvin, Texas, Dec. 8, 1972, DONNA JENKINS, born in Houston, Texas, Mar. 28, 1955, daughter of Donald and Ruth (Cotham) Jenkins.
He went to Davis and Elkins College, West Va., and was in the U.S. Coast Guard.

Children in 10th Gen. b. in Galveston, Texas

11853 JANA BETH, b. Aug. 30, 1974.

11854 SHANNON DEE, b. May 28, 1976.

F11149 KRISTEN LOCKE CROWELL, born in York, Maine, Sept. 8, 1956, married in Biddeford, Maine, Dec. 13, 1975, SCOTT TIMOTHY GARDNER, born in Portsmouth, N.H., June 17, 1955, son of Ray and Virginia (Conley) Gardner.

Children in 10th Generation

11855 JAMES JOSHUA, b. Portsmouth, N.H., Nov. 25, 1974.

F11152 JOHN LOCKE HERRICK, born in Bangor, Maine, Nov. 1, 1948, married in Dover Foxcroft, Maine, June 6, 1970, JEAN COFFIN, born in Dover Foxcroft, Maine, Jan. 6, 1950, daughter of Eugene and Pearl Coffin.

Children in 10th Generation

11856 AMY RACHAEL, b. Dunedin, Fla., June 7, 1973.

F11158 PATRICIA JEAN WYNN, born in Salem, Mass., Dec. 16, 1949, married in Marblehead, Mass., Sept. 12, 1970, RICHARD

BOWDEN ATTRIDGE, born in Salem, Mass., May 25, 1947, son of Richard and Ann (Osborne) Attridge.

Children in 10th Gen. b. in Salem, Mass.

11857 CHRISTINE ELAINE, b. Nov. 3, 1972.

11858 ERICK RUSSELL, b. July 12, 1976.

F11163 NANCY ELAINE HARDING, born in Philadelphia, Penna., Dec. 24, 1949, married in Redondo Beach, Calif., Jan. 14, 1972, JOHN ALAN JENKS, born in Glasgow, Mont., Nov. 27, 1949, son of Douglas Allen and Louise Lillian (Ekola) Jenks.

Children in 10th Generation

11859 DOUGLAS ALLEN II, b. Torrance, Calif., July 25, 1972.

F11167 WILLIAM FREDERICK PEDEN, born in Myrtle Point, Ore., Sept. 19, 1926, married in Lebanon, Ore., June 15, 1947, ELIZABETH KATHRYN IRVINE, born in Albany, Ore., July 22, 1927, daughter of James Harold and Esta Katherine (Ryder) Irvine.

Children in 10th Generation

11860 VICKIE JO, b. Lebanon, Ore., May 10, 1951, m. July 31, 1971, GARY LLOYD THOMPSON, b. Oaks, N.Dak., Nov. 26, 1951, son of Harold Lloyd and Roseann (Hildahl) Thompson.

11861 PAMELA SUE, b. Lebanon, Ore., Dec. 3, 1953, m. Junction City, Ore., July 13, 1974, MICHAEL WAYNE JOHNSON.

11862 JEFFREY WILLIAM, b. Eugene, Ore., Nov. 14, 1959.

F11168 GORDON GENE PEDEN, born in Myrtle Point, Ore., Nov. 19, 1928, married in Tacoma, Wash., Nov. 3, 1952, LEOLA ANN DILLON, born in Nampa, Idaho, April 30, 1935, daughter of Martin Jerome and Otha Rea Shirley Iona (Kastillo) Dillon.

Children in 10th Generation

11863 GENEINE ANN, b. Tacoma, Wash., April 4, 1953.

11864 HOWARD ALAN, b. Springfield, Ore., April 1, 1956.

11865 MARY IONE, b. Oxnard, Calif., June 9, 1967.

F11169 BARBARA JANE PEDEN, born in Myrtle Point, Ore., Sept. 28, 1939, married in Leaburg, Ore., July 8, 1956, DAVID ARTHUR SWANKIE, born in Palmer, Alaska, June 14, ——, son of Joseph

Hubert and Mary Maxine (Zimmerman) Wycoff.   Later Mrs. Wycoff married Mr. Swankie and David took his name.

He joined the U. S. Navy in 1955 and later reinlisted with the intention of making the navy his career.

Children in 10th Generation

11866   DEBORAH KAY, b. Springfield, Ore., Oct. 15, 1957.

11867   PATTY ANN, b. Oak Harbor, Wash., Dec. 18, 1958.

11868   RICHARD LEE, b. Oak Harbor, Wash., May 24, 1961.

11869   STEVEN DEE, b. Oak Harbor, Wash., May 24, 1961.

11870   DAVID ALLEN, b. Oak Harbor, Wash., July 12, 1962.

F11170   ELIZABETH LOUISE YARWOOD, born in Colfax, Wash., Feb. 8, 1929, married in Spokane, Wash., May 5, 1950, EDWARD ALBERT ROGERS, born in Spokane, Wash., Dec. 11, 1928, son of Allen A. and Florence (Loughin) Rogers.

Children in 10th Generation

11871   TIMOTHY ALLAN, b. Oceanside, Calif., Dec. 2, 1950.

11872   CHRISTOPHER EDWARD, b. Spokane, Wash., Feb. 3, 1953, m. Seattle, Wash., Sept. 14, 1974, BARBARA CRAW-FORD.

11873   DOUGLAS TODD, b. Spokane, Wash., Feb. 25, 1955.

11874   KELLY SCOTT, b. Springfield, Ore., June 30, 1956.

11875   SHEILA ANN, b. Spokane, Wash., Sept. 15, 1963.

F11171   WILMA NADINE YARWOOD, born in Pullman, Wash., Feb. 28, 1930, married in Spokane, Wash., Feb. 23, 1952, ANTHONY COSTANZO, born in Spokane, Wash., Nov. 8, 1928, son of Emilio and Villoria (Perry) Costanzo.

Children in 10th Gen. b. in Spokane, Wash.

11876   RONALD ANTHONY, b. Sept. 14, 1958.

11877   ELIZABETH MARY, b. Aug. 30, 1960.

F11172   JANET JEANNE YARWOOD, born in Colfax, Wash., April 7, 1933, married in Coeur d'Alene, Idaho, Dec. 28, 1951, MYRLE RALPH NEAD, born in Spokane, Wash., Mar. 31, 1930, son of Ralph Donald and Grace (Alderson) Nead.   Later divorced.

Children in 10th Generation

11878 NICHOLAS ELSWORTH, b. Coronado, Calif., July 27, 1953.

11879 CURTIS LAMONT, b. Spokane, Wash., Aug. 7, 1954.

11880 STEVEN FORREST, b. Spokane, Wash., Nov. 6, 1955.

11881 KENNETH, b. Spokane, Wash., Aug. 5, 1957.

11882 LEESA ANN, b. Spokane, Wash., July 12, 1959.

11883 CHARLES LOREN, b. Spokane, Wash., Aug. 20, 1960.

F11174 DORIS MILDRED JOHNSON, born in Republic, Wash., Jan. 22, 1927, married in Coeur d'Alene, Idaho, Sept. 30, 1946, JAMES WILLIAM GILBERT, born in Little Rock, Ark., Aug. 29, 1925, son of William and Sarah (Campbell) Gilbert.

Children in 10th Generation

11884 TERRY WADE, b. Spokane, Wash., July 27, 1954.

11885 SUSAN MARIE, b. Spokane, Wash., Dec. 17, 1956.

11886 DIANE LYNN, b. Eugene, Ore., June 4, 1958.

F11175 DERALD CLIFFORD JOHNSON, born in Republic, Wash., July 1, 1929, married 1st, in Spokane, Wash., Sept. 1, 1954, DOROTHY MILLS, born in Missoula, Mont., daughter of Clyde and Jessie Mills; 2nd, in Coeur d'Alene, Idaho, Dec. 21, 1957, DIXIE LEE HAGEL, born in Calif., Oct. 4, 1934.

Children in 10th Generation

11887 MARK CLIFFORD, b. Houston, Texas, Jan. 17, 1956.

F11176 VIVIAN ELAINE CALDWELL, born in Malo, Wash., Sept. 7, 1927, married 1st, in Kittanning, Penna., Nov. 28, 1945, CLARENCE PAUL EMMINGER, born in Kittanning, Penna., Mar. 11, 1920, died in Lebanon, Ore., Feb. 9, 1967, son of James Daniel and Anna Jane (Painter) Emminger; 2nd, in Lebanon, Ore., Nov. 26, 1969, JOSEPH R. ABBOTT, born in Butte Falls, Ore., Mar. 14, 1931, son of Archie E. and Hildred (Hereford) Abbott.

Children in 10th Gen. b. in Kittanning, Penna.

F11888 SANDRA PAULINE, b. Aug. 25, 1946.

11889 DANIEL JEROME, b. June 11, 1949.

F11177 CLARA LOUISE CALDWELL, born in Hermiston, Ore., Aug. 8, 1930, married in Lebanon, Ore., Feb. 14, 1947, BUFORD

ULYSSES DAILY, born in Lebanon, Ore., Mar. 19, 1927, son of Edwin Cecil and Amy Mildred (Parsons) Daily.

Children in 10th Gen. b. in Lebanon, Ore.

F11890 SHARON LOUISE, b. Sept. 16, 1947.

F11891 GENE RODERICK, b. July 11, 1949.

11892 VERN STEPHEN, b. April 30, 1956.

F11178 HELEN IRENE HILDERBRAND, born in Malo, Wash., Aug. 30, 1931, married in Seattle, Wash., June 23, 1950, STANTON JAMES SCHERTENLEIB, born in Wauconda, Wash., Aug. 12, 1928, son of Robert and Lillian (Thomason) Schertenleib.

Children in 10th Gen. b. in Tonasket, Wash.

F11893 NORMAN DUANE, b. Mar. 31, 1952.

11894 DAVID BURTON, b. May 24, 1954.

11895 RICKY DEAN, b. April 21, 1961.

F11179 MILDRED JEANNETTE HILDERBRAND, born in Malo, Wash., Feb. 4, 1934, married in Las Cruces, N. Mex., Mar. 8, 1952, JIMMY FLOYD CLARK, born in Siloam Springs, Ark., April 13, 1930, son of Lester and Maxine (Oliver) Clark.

Children in 10th Gen. b. in Republic, Wash.

11896 DANNY WADE, b. Jan. 1, 1954.

F11897 DEBRA MAXINE, b. Oct. 3, 1956.

F11180 CLIFFORD EUGENE HILDERBRAND, born in Malo, Wash., July 24, 1935, married June 9, 1968, DARLENE JOYCE REESE, born Nov. 5, 1948, daughter of Ira and Joyce (Carbin) Reese.

Children in 10th Generation

11898 KELSEY REESE, b. Kwajlein, Marshall Islands, May 31, 1974.

F11181 LARRIE SAMUEL HILDERBRAND, born in Malo, Wash., Mar. 19, 1937, married 1st, Aug. 29, 1964, DIANNE MAY HARRINGTON, divorced, 1969; 2nd, Nov. 19, 1972, ROWENA HARRAH, daughter of Thomas and Virginia Loury.

Children in 10th Gen. b. in Pullman, Wash.

11899 LANCE KANE, b. Nov. 8, 1965.

11900 DARIN KEITH, b. Mar. 30, 1967.

F11183 <u>JUDITH COLLEEN RUMSEY</u>, born in Okanogan, Wash., Sept. 1, 1940, married in Seattle, Wash., June 21, 1968, ROBERT DEAN THOMPSON, born in Webster City, Iowa, Dec. 16, 1946, son of Sidney and Ruby (Stoppelmoor) Thompson.

Children in 10th Gen. b. in Eugene, Ore.

11901 DENNIS ROBERT, b. May 9, 1969.

11902 TERRY DEAN, b. Mar. 3, 1973.

F11184 <u>RICHARD FRANK WILHELM</u>, born in Colfax, Wash., Nov. 12, 1926, married in Colfax, Wash., Sept. 9, 1950, SHIRLEY LORRAINE ESPY, born in Potlatch, Idaho, June 4, 1931, daughter of Wallace and Mattie Pearl (Clyde) Espy.

Children in 10th Generation

11903 CLYDE RICHARD, b. Colfax, Wash., July 26, 1951.

11904 PENNY SUE, b. Lewiston, Idaho, May 21, 1954.

11905 PEGGY ANN, b. Lewiston, Idaho, April 5, 1956, m. Mar. 16, 1973, EDWARD RAY.

F11185 <u>SUSAN JOYCE WILHELM</u>, born in Colfax, Wash., Nov. 6, 1928, married in Colfax, Wash., Nov. 8, 1947, HOWARD JEROME MILLER, born in Colfax, Wash., Dec. 4, 1921, son of Ellery Jerome and Pauline (Kroll) Miller.

Children in 10th Gen. b. in Colfax, Wash.

F11906 JERRY JEROME, b. April 8, 1948.

F11907 THOMAS ELERY, b. Feb. 17, 1950.

F11186 <u>THELMA MAE WILHELM</u>, born in Moscow, Idaho, Dec. 29, 1934, married 1st, in Lewiston, Idaho, Jan. 31, 1951, CLARENCE MAURICE CARLSON, born in Viola, Idaho, Oct. 5, 1927, died in Spokane, Wash., Aug. 10, 1965, son of Harry and Rosie Mae (Gerber) Carlson; 2nd, in Potlatch, Idaho, Nov. 4, 1965, NOBEL LEWIS LaPLANTE, born in Browning, Mont.

Children in 10th Generation

11908 DOUGLAS CLARENCE CARLSON, b. Lewiston, Idaho, Feb. 6, 1954.

11909 STEVEN KENNETH CARLSON, b. Moscow, Idaho, Dec. 11, 1958.

11910 SUSAN LOUELLA CARLSON, b. Colfax, Wash., Nov. 23, 1962.

11911 SHAWN NOBEL LaPLANTE, b. Spokane, Wash., July 25, 1966.

11912 NOLA MAE LaPLANTE, b. Spokane, Wash., Jan. 30, 1969.

F11187 ROBERT RAYMOND McCOWN, born in Madera, Calif., Mar. 31, 1926, married in Colfax, Wash., Oct. 6, 1955, JO ANN GERING, born in Lind, Wash., Dec. 11, 1934, daughter of Frank and Hilda (Fleschliman) Gering.

Children in 10th Generation

11913 MARLA LYNN, b. Colfax, Wash., Dec. 29, 1956.

F11188 JANE EVELIN McCOWN, born in Latah Co., Idaho, Sept. 29, 1927, married in Oakesdale, Wash., Sept. 29, 1947, CLIFFORD WAYNE FRANKS, born in Oakesdale, Wash., Sept. 1, 1922, son of Ray C. and Hazel (Kendall) Franks.

Children in 10th Gen. b. in Spokane, Wash.

11914 CATHE CAE, b. Sept. 16, 1952.

11915 CANDE RAE, b. Feb. 25, 1954.

11916 TAMMIE, b. Oct. 7, 1958.

F11189 RAY CHESTER McCOWN, born in Garfield, Wash., Dec. 3, 1932, married in Garfield, Wash., July 21, 1951, MARJEAN PATRICIA WATSON, born in Moscow, Idaho, Aug. 15, 1934, daughter of Omer and Marjean (Crites) Watson.

Children in 10th Gen. b. in Colfax, Wash.

11917 DEBORAH GAIL, b. Jan. 26, 1952.

11918 RAYMOND CRAIG, b. April 13, 1953, m. Pullman, Wash., June 8, 1974, DEBORAH LYNN CAMP, b. Colfax, Wash., daughter of George Eugene and Patty (Wizemann) Camp.

11919 MARCIA LYNN, b. Feb. 13, 1956.

11920 CAROLYN JILL, b. April 5, 1959.

F11190 SUE ANN McCOWN, born in Garfield, Wash., Nov. 4, 1942, married in Garfield, Wash., Aug. 30, 1959, ROY EDWARD DVORAK, born in Spokane, Wash., Nov. 28, 1939, son of Daniel Vincent and Myrl Dvorak.

Children in 10th Gen. b. in Colfax, Wash.

11921 KELLY KAYE, b. April 13, 1960.

11922 JAMIE ROY, b. Aug. 27, 1961.

F11193 DIXIE LOU DAILEY, born in Garfield, Wash., Dec. 4, 1937, married in Garfield, Wash., June 5, 1956, WALTER E. ROACH born in Ewan, Wash., Dec. 2, 1930, son of Arthur E. and Pauline (Bentley) Roach.

Children in 10th Generation

11923 DARBY LEE, b. Moscow, Idaho, June 2, 1957.

11924 DARWIN MARK, b. Moscow, Idaho, Dec. 29, 1958.

11925 COREY PAUL, b. Colfax, Wash., July 17, 1960.

11926 TROY WALTER, b. Moscow, Idaho, Sept. 19, 1961.

F11194 JOHN HUGH DAILEY, born in Garfield, Wash., Jan. 23, 1939, married in Farmington, Wash., Nov. 1, 1958, CELESTA ANN BENNETT, born in Colfax, Wash., May 11, 1941, daughter of John Clarence and Artha D. (Fisher) Bennett.

Children in 10th Generation

11927 KIRBY JON, b. Colfax, Wash., May 20, 1959.

11928 CARMEN CELESTA, b. Pullman, Wash., Dec. 9, 1961.

11929 KERRY ALISSE, b. Pullman, Wash., Dec. 30, 1963.

11930 CASEY ALAN, b. Pullman, Wash., Feb. 26, 1966.

F11195 BARBARA ANN DAILEY, born in Garfield, Wash., May 4, 1941, died in Moscow, Idaho, July 9, 1966, married Nov. 5, 1960, JOHN STOUT, born Oct. 9, 1935, son of Richard and Kathryn (Springer) Stout.

Children in 10th Generation

11931 TIM DEAN, b. Dec. 19, 1961.

11932 TODD RICHARD, b. April 29, 1963.

11933 TRACI SUSAN, b. Moscow, Idaho, Aug. 2, 1965.

11934 KATHRYN JESSICA, b. Moscow, Idaho, July 9, 1966, d. Moscow, Idaho, July 11, 1966.

F11204 PATRICIA HELEN SCHMIDT, born in Buenos Aires, Rep. of Arg., S. A., Aug. 17, 1947, married RICARDO GARCIA VACCA-LUZZO.

Children in 10th Gen. b. in Rosario, Rep. of Arg., S.A.

11935 GERALDINE ANN, b. Aug. 6, 1954.

11936 CAROL LORRAINE, b. Mar. 11, 1956.

11937 JOHN JOSEPH, b. June 19, 1962.

11938 LORRAINE PATRICIA, b. Jan. 5, 1968.

F11207 DONALD LeROY CALHOUN, born in Garfield, Wash., Sept. 21, 1933, married in Garfield, Wash., Dec. 25, 1955, DONNA MAE HOLDEN, born in Deer Park, Wash., Nov. 4, 1937, daughter of Orval and Beulah Estella (Cofer) Holden.

Children in 10th Generation

11939 CHERYL LYNN, b. Pullman, Wash., Mar. 26, 1959.

F11211 LOIS EVELYN MIKKELSEN, born in Cashmere, Wash., Mar. 14, 1942, married in Seattle, Wash., June 6, 1964, JAMES DAVID GRAHAM, born in Jefferson Co., Ind., Oct. 8, 1939, son of John Wesley and Stella (Johnson) Graham.

Children in 10th Generation

11940 MICHAEL JAMES, b. Ft. Lewis, Wash., Jan. 26, 1965.

11941 BARBARA KAYE, b. Seymour, Ind., Jan. 27, 1967.

11942 MICHELLE GAIL, b. Madison, Ind., Sept. 1, 1971.

F11212 LINDA KAYE MIKKELSEN, born in Colfax, Wash., Sept. 9, 1947, married in Pullman, Wash., June 1, 1966, ROBERT LEROY DAGGETT, born in Wenattchee, Wash., Oct. 28, 1941.

Children in 10th Gen. b. in Seattle, Wash.

11943 CHARLES MILES, b. April 18, 1967.

11944 ROBERT WARREN, b. Jan. 16, 1969.

F11215 EILEEN KAY GOLDEN, born in Richmond, Calif., Oct. 8, 1942, married 1st, June 17, 1961, LLOYD DONALD SEEVERS, born in Fallon, Nev., Jan. 15, 1933, son of Elmer and Edna Seevers; 2nd, April 4, 1967, KENNETH RAYE NEW, born in Checotah, Okla., Jan. 12, 1938, son of Virgal L. New and Nora Bell Brown.

Children in 10th Generation

11945 LLOYD DONALD SEEVERS, JR., b. Reno, Nev., Jan. 26, 1962.

11946 SHERI LYNN SEEVERS, b. St. Helena, Calif., July 11, 1964.

11947 MICHAEL LAWRENCE NEW, b. Oakdale, Calif., Oct. 1, 1969.

F11222 EDWARD JOSEPH FREDERICK, JR., born in Bell, Calif., Mar. 4, 1947, married 1st, in Richmond, Calif., May 4, 1968, DENISE BARKER; 2nd, in Reno, Nev., Dec. 28, 1975, DIANA JOHNSON, born in Sacto, Calif., Nov. 13, 1948, daughter of Charles R. and Betty (Weaver) Johnson.

Children in 10th Generation

11948 TROY ALLEN, b. Berkeley, Calif., Nov. 4, 1968.

11949 MATHEW EDWARD, b. Eugene, Ore., Aug. 7, 1976.

F11235 LENORE ERLEEN DAUSY, born in Oakland, Calif., Aug. 28, 1947, married in Bethel Island, Calif., May 21, 1966, TROY D. TREAT, born in Oklahoma, July 12, 1940, son of Herman and Pearl (Hart) Treat.

Children in 10th Gen. b. in Antioch, Calif.

11950 ERICA LYNNE, b. June 30, 1968.

11951 TRAVIS D., b. July 9, 1969.

F11236 MICHAEL LEWIS DAUSY, born in Richmond, Calif., July 30, 1949, married in Brentwood, Calif., Jan. 23, 1974, DEBRA K. TAULBEE, born May 23, 1956.

Children in 10th Generation

11952 AMY LOUISE, b. Walnut Creek, Calif., Dec. 19, 1975.

F11238 DEBORAH ANN DAUSY, born in Richmond, Calif., May 17, 1952.

Children in 10th Generation

11953 DARREN ROY ELLIS, b. Walnut Creek, Calif., Jan. 2, 1969.

11954 TERRY WILLIAM BUSH, b. Antioch, Calif., July 18, 1976.

F11230 MARGERY ADELL SKYLES, born in Hill City, Idaho, Sept. 14, 1935, married in Vancouver, Wash., Dec. 20, 1954, DOUGLAS DEAN HILDRETH, born in Council Bluffs, Iowa, Jan. 23, 1933, son of Ira Dean and Viola Beatrice (Donahave) Hildreth. Divorced.

Children in 10th Gen. b. in Portland, Ore.

11955 DEANIA MARIE, b. Dec. 4, 1955.

11956 DOREEN ADELL, b. Aug. 5, 1957.

11957 DOUGLAS, b. Sept. 21, 1959.

11958 DAWN EVELYN, b. April 22, 1961, d. Portland, Ore., April, 23, 1961.

11959 DANIEL GUY, b. Sept. 30, 1964.

F11231 EUNICE MAY SKYLES, born in Fairfield, Idaho, April 13, 1938, married in Vancouver, Wash., Aug. 6, 1956, JOHN PAYTON LYNN TRUE, born in Minneapolis, Minn., Mar. 19, 1933, son of George Vaughn and Elizabeth (Tenold) True.

Children in 10th Gen. b. in San Francisco, Calif.

11961 MICHAEL LYNN, b. Sept. 16, 1957.

11962 JANET LYNN, b. July 26, 1959.

11963 STEVEN LYNN, b. Oct. 5, 1960, d. Jan. 29, 1962.

11964 ROBERT LYNN, b. May 20, 1962.

F11232 EUGENE MISCAL SKYLES, born in Fairfield, Idaho, Aug. 23, 1940, married in Portland, Ore., Oct. 26, 1962, CAROL SUE KELLOGG, born in Portland, Ore., Nov. 23, 1944, daughter of Harold G. and Charlotte B. (Smith) Kellogg.

Children in 10th Gen. b. in Portland, Ore.

11965 NICKLAS LEE, b. Feb. 14, 1964.

11966 JEFFREY TROY, b. Feb. 16, 1965.

11967 PAULA RAE, b. Sept. 20, 1969.

F11233 BARBARA JEAN SKYLES, born in Republic, Wash., Aug. 6, 1942, married 1st, in Portland, Ore., Oct. 3, 1961, ALBERT CIRILO SALDIVAR, born in Kearney, Nebr., Mar. 18, 1938, son of Fermin Salvador and Rose Loretha (Appleton) Saldivar; 2nd, in Sun Valley, Nev., July 12, 1974, ISRAEL DEAN BARLOW, born in Burley, Idaho, Dec. 2, 1928, son of Israel Call and Myrtle (Ford) Barlow.

Children in 10th Gen. b. in Portland, Ore.

11968 BARBARA TAVANE SALDIVAR, b. Oct. 30, 1962.

11969 AARON RANDALL SALDIVAR, b. Jan. 16, 1964.

11970 JENNIFER LYNN SALDIVAR, b. Dec. 11, 1969.

11971 ANGELA CHRISTINE SALDIVAR, b. Aug. 28, 1973.

11972 SAMUEL VERRON BARLOW, b. Dec. 20, 1975.

F11234 GUY DOUGLAS SKYLES, born in Portland, Ore., Oct. 3, 1944, married in Vancouver, Wash., July 22, 1966, MARY ISABEL (ESPINOZA) HILTON, born in Grand Junction, Colo., Nov. 19, 1941, daughter of Rupert and Flora (Guillen) Espinoza.

Children in 10th Generation

11973 DARRAN MONTGOMERY, b. Portland, Ore., Jan. 8, 1969.

F11244 BESSIE RACHEL LOCKE, born Aug. 15, 1894, died in Thomaston, Maine, 1956, married Dec. 29, 1915, HAROLD PERRY VANNAH, died in Thomaston, Maine, 1964.

Children in 10th Generation

11974 RICHARD PERRY, b. Sept. 12, 1916, d. Sept. 29, 1916.

11975 BETSEY, b. Sept. 29, 1917.

11976 WILLIAM EDSON, b. Nov. 14, 1919.

11977 MARY, b. Oct. 24, 1921.

11978 HAROLD P., JR., b. Mar. 12, 1923.

F11248 FRED RAYMOND LOCKE, born in Mt. Vernon, Maine, Oct. 26, 1900, died in Augusta, Maine, Jan. 28, 1973, married in Augusta, Maine, Sept. 15, 1923, EUNICE MARSON HEWINS, born in Augusta, Maine, Dec. 17, 1901.

He started dairy farming with his father in Mt. Vernon and continued in Augusta from 1926 to 1950. He then worked at Hudson Pulp and Paper Mill until retirement. He had a great love for the outdoors. She was the daughter of Daniel A. and Helen M. (Marson) Hewins and was known for her fine knitting.

Children in 10th Gen. b. in Augusta, Maine

11979 RICHARD DANIEL, b. Nov. 6, 1928, m. Ft. Bennings, Ga., June 28, 1952, MONA (MORGRAGE) GOODE. He served in the U.S. Army 1945-6 and 1950-4 and is a Colonel in the U.S. Army Reserve. Received a B.S. degree in 1950 and is currently employed by the State of Maine Dept. of Manpower Resources. They had: 11979a JAYNE INEZ, b. Ft. Dix, N.J., Feb. 6, 1953, m. Augusta, Maine, Sept. 25, 1971, GEORGE McLAUGHLIN.

F11980 RACHEL JANE, b. Mar. 28, 1932, m. Augusta, Maine, Sept. 19, 1953, LESTER NICHOLS ODAMS, JR. She is a Registered Nurse, 1953, Central Maine General Hospital, Lewiston, Maine.

F11981 ROBERT HEWINS, b. Augusta, Maine, Mar. 30, 1940, m. Boston, Mass., Sept. 14, 1962, JANICE NANCY HAYDEN.

F11250 MARJORIE SYLVIA LOCKE, born Aug. 27, 1920, married Mar. 28, 1942, CLARENCE MacKINNON.

Children in 10th Generation

11982 JAMES D., b. Dec. 15, 1945.

11983 RICHARD D., b. Aug. 5, 1948.

11984 JEAN L., b. Nov. 15, 1953.

F11257 WESLEY GOODWIN REYNOLDS, born Mar. 23, 1903, married in Portsmouth, N. H., May 16, 1931, ETHEL MILDRED EKSTROM.

He graduated from Boston University and Harvard Graduate School of Business Administration. Taught at Nichols College, Then Univ. of No. Carolina, Raleigh, N. C. until his retirement. She was daughter of Charles and Estelle Fairchild Ekstrom.

Children in 10th Gen. b. in Lynn, Mass.

F11985 JOYCE ELAINE, b. May 6, 1933, m. Marblehead, Mass., Dec. 28, 1954, EDWARD ARTHUR LUDWIG of Gardner, Maine.

11986 ALAN WAYNE, b. Jan. 15, 1939, m. July 1, 1966, MARGERY GERALDINE PATTERSON, and have: 11987 HEIDI, b. June 7, 1967.
   He is a photographer and works for General Electric Company at Lynn.

F11258 ANDREW ELLSWORTH REYNOLDS, born July 31, 1907, married in Seabrook, N. H., Mar. 29, 1935, ELECTA MARIE LEWIS.
He graduated from Tufts College and was an electrical engineer for University Sign Co. of Boston. She was the daughter of Jacob and Minnie Lewis.

Children in 10th Generation

11988 JUDSON LEWIS, b. Boston, Mass., Sept. 21, 1937, d. Waltham, Mass.; June 2, 1962.

F11259 ELSIE LOCKE, born in Lynn, Mass., Mar. 7, 1898, died 1956, married in Mt. Vernon, Maine, Sept. 24, 1918, CLYDE LEE HALL of Auburn, Maine, born Jan. 22, 1898, died 1958.

Children in 10th Generation

11999   ROBERT POPE, b. Feb. 12, 1920.

12000   MERNA LUCILLE, b. Aug. 7, 1922.

12001   MILTON ROY, b. Mar. 15, 1924.

12002   CHARLES EMERY, b. Jan. 6, 1926.

12003   HERBERT LLEWELLYN, b. May 4, 1927.

12004   CLYDE THEODORE, b. April 27, 1929.

12005   DOROTHY LOUISE, b. Jan. 14, 1931,   m. WILLIAM LEIGHTON.

12006   SYLVIA MAE, b. April 10, 1935, m. July 4, 1959, EARL R. TIBBETTS.

12007   AURILLA FRANCES, b. Dec. 18, 1939.

F11259a WESTON THEODORE LOCKE, born in Lynn, Mass., Mar. 18, 1904, died Dec. 14, 1935, married in Auburn, Maine, DOROTHY PERKINS. She married 2nd, Ernest Tarbox and had daughter KAREN.

Children in 10th Generation

12008   WESTON THEODORE, JR., b. Mt. Vernon, Maine, Nov. 5, 1931. He is living in Mt. Vernon, Maine and is interested in genealogy and local history.

F11260   JAMES DANIEL LOCKE, born in Ft. Fairfield, Maine, May 23, 1882, died in Ft. Fairfield, Maine, Mar. 20, 1959, married in River de Chute, N. B., Canada (probably), MARGARET JANE DYER, born in River de Chute, N. B., Canada, Sept. 2, 1883 or 1885, died in Ft. Fairfield, Maine, Aug. 4, 1958.

He was a Fishing and Hunting Maine Guide in the North Woods, Allagash region   He was a great story teller and jokester; but not much of a farmer, which he had his family doing when they were young. His favorite saying was: "The Locke's aren't known for being ambitious. I'm glad I take after the Judkins' side of the family." He was a janitor in later years.

She was famous for her bread and doughnuts in Ft. Fairfield Village. She had a large clientele as long as she was able to cook. She was an avid bridge player.

Children in 10th Gen. b. in Ft. Fairfield, Maine

F12009   JAMES KENNETH, b. Aug. 20, 1903, d. East Corinth, Maine, July 11, 1949, m. Gorham, Maine, April 26, 1926, GERTRUDE PRATT.

F12010 MARY PHYLLIS ANN, b. Sept. 24, 1909, m. Portland, Maine, Nov. 7, 1953, JOEL CARGILL.

12011 JOHN GLENWOOD, b. Jan. 21, 1911, d. Ft. Fairfield, Maine, June 19, 1960, m. ETHEL PRATT.

F12012 CHARLES EUGENE, b. Nov. 22, 1912, d. New Sweden, Maine, Jan. 20, 1969, m. Presque Isle, Maine, May 10, 1930, MARION AVERILL STONE.

F12013 EDGAR CLEMENT, b. Dec. 20, 1913, m. DORIS SEVER-ANCE. Now living in Bristol, Conn. and works at Pratt-Whitney, Southington, Conn.

12014 ANNA FREIDA, b. Sept. 19, 1919, m. DONALD McLAUGHLIN. She graduated from Ft. Fairfield High School, is very clever with handcrafts and sings well.

F11269 MARIETTA BROWN, born in Rye, N.H., Mar. 10, 1880, died in Portsmouth, N.H., Aug. 13, 1974, married in Groton, Vt., June 28, 1916, DAVID ROBERT EASTMAN, born in E. Topsham, Vt., Sept. 10, 1893, died in Exeter, N.H., Sept. 21, 1959.

She attended the West School in Rye and Newburyport High School and was graduated with the Class of 1906 from the State Normal School in Hyannis, Mass. She taught school in Mass. and Vt. She was married at Groton, Vt. and lived in East Topsham for eight years where she and her husband farmed. In 1924, she moved back to West Rye so she could be near her aging mother and lived there the rest of her life.

Children in 10th Gen. b. in Woodsville, N.H.

F12015 EILEEN THOMPSON, b. Aug. 11, 1917, m. Rye, N.H., Oct. 15, 1938, HARRIS MARTIN ROGERS.

12016 RUBY SEAVEY, b. Aug. 12, 1919, m. Rye, N.H., April 12, 1941, GLEN EARL SCHULTZ.

F11275 CLIFTON MERRILL BURT, born in Stoneham, Mass., April 11, 1883, died in Wellfleet, Mass., Aug. 18, 1966, married in Lynn, Mass., 1906, FLORENCE HILLER, born in Saugus, Mass., Sept. 5, 1887 or 8, died Nov. 1956.

Children in 10th Generation

12017 ESTHER FLORENCE, b. Lynn, Mass., Oct. 1907, d. Wellfleet, Mass., June 1971, m. 1939, FRED BELL.

12018 EVELYN CLIFTON, b. Stoneham, Mass., Jan. 30, 1909, m. 1st, EDWARD J. BROWN and had: 12019 JANICE b. Mar. 11, 1931; 2nd, ERNEST TURNER.

F12020 ROBERT CARLTON, b. Melrose, Mass., July 17, 1918, m. Aug. 4, 1939, ELSIE McELROY.

12021 ROY WESTERN, b. Melrose, Mass., Oct. 23, 1920.

F11276 PEARL FANNIE GODDARD, born in Wakefield, Mass., July 30, 1893, died in Concord, N.H., Aug. 15, 1977, married July 20, 1918, Colonel RICHARD CARLTON STICKNEY, USA, born in Gloucester, Mass., died in Stoneham, Mass., Dec. 14, 1952.

Children in 10th Generation

12022 RICHARD CARLTON, JR., b. Manhattan, Kans., April 11, 1920, d. in Pacific in raid over Nagoya, Japan, Jan. 3, 1945, m. Dalhart, Texas, Jan. 6, 1944, MILDRED WEBB.

F12023 MARION GODDARD, b. Ft. Benning, Ga., Feb. 7, 1923, m. Boston, Mass., April 30, 1949, ROBERT H. RENO.

12024 ALFRED, b. Ft. Leavenworth, Kans., Mar. 8, 1929, m. HARRIET HOPPERT, b. Sheboygan, Wis.

F11277 PHILIP WILLIAM ROWLEY, born in Gloucester, Mass., Oct. 1, 1893, died in Dunedin, Fla., about 1965, married RUTH HOLMES, later divorced.

Children in 10th Gen. b. in Gloucester, Mass.

12025 PHYLLIS, b. Sept. 1, 1919, m. ROBERT PUBLICOVER. She is a Wellesley College graduate and Professor at Univ. of Utah.

12026 JANICE, b. Jan. 1925, m. Gloucester, Mass., JOHN A. LINEHAN. She is a Radcliff College graduate.

F11284 FRED DANIELS DODGE, JR., born in Lynn, Mass., Jan. 9, 1901, married in Lynn, Mass., Oct. 1, 1923, ALICE ELIZABETH SVERKER.

Children in 10th Generation

12027 NORMAN DANIELS, b. Lynn, Mass., Aug. 27, 1924.

F11284a EDGAR HUMPHRY COBB, born in Boston, Mass., Aug. 6, 1903, married in Harvard, Mass., Mar. 2, 1936, KATHERINE VARNUM DENNY, born in New York City, Jan. 27, 1910.

Children in 10th Generation

12028 ELISABETH HUMPHRY, b. Ayer, Mass., Mar. 20, 1940.

F12029 GEORGE DENNY, b. Washington, D.C., April 24, 1944, m. New Orleans, La., Mar. 18, 1967, SUZANNE DALLAS CARROLL.

F11287 RICHARD COBB, born in Boston, Mass., Feb. 28, 1914, married in Los Angeles, Calif., June 20, 1942, MARIAN VANVORST COLWELL, born in West Newton, Mass., Jan. 16, 1917.

He was graduated cum laude from Harvard College in 1936. He attended a one year program at Harvard Business School in 1945-1946 and earned his Master of Business Administration degree at Northwestern University in 1960. He was commissioned an Ensign in the Supply Corps U.S. Navy in January 1940 and served in World War II in the Pacific area. His Navy Supply Corps assignments included duty at Pearl Harbor; Boston, Mass.; Wash., D.C.; Paris, France; Harrisburg, Penna. and Chicago, Ill.

He retired from the Navy in 1963 as a Captain and became manager of the Navy Federal Credit Union in Wash., D.C. He was elected to the Board of Directors and appointed Treasurer-Manager of the world's largest credit union in 1972. He also was elected to three terms as Vice President, National Association of Federal Credit Unions.

She was graduated from Wellesley College in 1939. She was active in Wellesley alumni affairs serving as president of two Wellesley Clubs and has been active in many charitable organizations.

Children in 10th Generation

12030 WINTHROP COLWELL, b. Wash., D.C., Jan. 29, 1950.

12031 DIANA VANVORST, b. Paris, France, Mar. 22, 1954.

F11288 ALTHEA LENAIRE LOCKE, born in Paisley, Ore., Dec. 23, 1919, married 1st, in Carson City, Nev., Jan. 29, 1940, MELVIN DONAZEL TRINE, born in Eureka, Calif., July 10, 1901, son of Wilfred and Sadie (Miller) Trine; 2nd, in Chatsworth, Calif., Nov. 5, 1953, ROLLA J. HELDT, born in Macks Creek, Mo., June 10, 1917; 3rd, July 17, 1967, DONALD E. POPE, annulled; 4th, Aug. 20, 1970, RANDALL C. HARDIE, divorced.

Children in 10th Generation

12032 RODERICK STIRLING, b. Eureka, Calif., Nov. 25, 1940, d. Arcata, Calif., April 20, 1959.

F12033 SHARLA LENAIRE, b. Eureka, Calif., Mar. 17, 1942.

F12034 CANDACE SHERRILL, b. Oakland, Calif., June 18, 1944.

F12035 ROBIN LYNNE, b. Eureka, Calif., Oct. 31, 1946.

F11290 BARBARA LORRAINE LOCKE, born in Chowchilla, Calif., Mar. 20, 1916, married in Oakland, Calif., May 20, 1939, CARROLL CLEMENT TERRY, born in Gilroy, Calif., Mar. 20, 1916, son of Royal Roscoe and Gertrude Lavine (Davis) Terry.

Children in 10th Generation

12036 WILLIAM JAMES, b. Oakland, Calif., Dec. 19, 1935.

F11291 CAROL MARGUERITE LOCKE, born in Monmouth, Calif., Dec. 24, 1923, married 1st, in Santa Cruz, Calif., Mar. 7, 1941, BRUCE PHILIP LEE; 2nd, in Reno, Nev., June 27, 1946, GORDON ROLAND FLINN, born in Omaha, Nebr., Oct. 21, 1921, son of Roland and Myra (Jones) Flinn; 3rd, in Brentwood, Calif., Feb. 28, 1953, VERGIL EUGENE SCRIBNER, born in Iowa, April 9, 1918, son of Grayson and Audrey Rose (Wray) Scribner.

Children in 10th Generation

12037 MICHELLE ROXANNE, b. San Francisco, Calif., Oct. 27, 1949.

12038 VICTORIA KELAINE, b. Mar. 12, 1959.

12039 SUSAN LEE SCHADER, b. Sept. 15, 1961.

F11292 CLIFFORD ALMAR BROWN, born in Chowchilla, Calif., Aug. 9, 1924, married 1st, in Santa Rosa, Calif., April 16, 1943, PATRICIA VOYLE, born in Oakland, Calif., Mar. 17, 1927, daughter of Francis Brady and ——— (York) Voyle; 2nd, in Elko, Nev., Mar. 19, 1960, URSULA LOUISE AXT, born in East Berlin, Germany, Dec. 18, 1925.

Children in 10th Generation

12040 PATRICIA ANN, b. San Rafael, Calif., Dec. 27, 1943.

12041 DENNIS BRADLEY, b. Houston, Texas, Jan. 13, 1950.

F11293 HAROLD SCOTT BROWN, born in Placerville, Calif., Jan. 17, 1926, married 1st, in San Rafael, Calif., June 8, 1945, MARY McFETRICK, born in Okla., April 4, 1926; 2nd, in Reno, Nev., Sept. 20, 1947, VERGINE LOUISE SPENCER, born in Buhl, Idaho, Sept. 29, 1930, daughter of Bewley Marion and Louise Pauline (Lee) Spencer.

Children in 10th Generation

12042 HAROLD EUGENE, b. Ventura, Calif., Mar. 7, 1946.

12043 SPENCER SCOTT, b. Fallon, Nev., July 14, 1948.

12044 ROCHANNE LEE, b. Salt Lake City, Utah, Nov., 26, 1952.

F11294 WINNIE ESTELLE BROWN, born in Chowchilla, Calif., Mar. 4, 1930, married in Fallon, Nev., Oct. 12, 1945, MILLARD WARD ALLEN, born in Panguitch, Utah, Sept. 21, 1924, son of John Chancy and Sarah Rebecca (Lister) Allen.

Children in 10th Generation

F12045 PAMELA IRENE, b. Fallon, Nev., Sept. 5, 1945.

F12046 JACQUELYN LYNN, b. Salt Lake City, Utah, May 31, 1948.

F12047 MARCELLA JEAN, b. Salt Lake City, Utah, Mar. 30, 1955.

F12048 APRIL KAY, b. Pocatello, Idaho, Aug. 21, 1956.

F11295 ROBERT VINES BROWN, born in Petaluma, Calif., Nov. 4, 1933, married in Springville, Utah, April 2, 1952, ELLA SINGLE-TON, born in Springville, Utah, Nov. 5, 1934, daughter of Eldon LeRoy and Thersa Vera (Allen) Singleton.

Children in 10th Gen. b. in Salt Lake City, Utah

12049 CRAIG LYNN, b. June 25, 1953.

12050 EDWARD ARNOLD, b. Mar. 18, 1955.

12051 JOY DEAN, b. Sept. 9, 1957.

F11297 JONITA LAUREL MILLER, born in Oakland, Calif., Aug. 23, 1937, married 1st, in Carson City, Nev., May 17, 1953, MICHAEL G. URQUHART, born in San Francisco, Calif., Aug. 1, 1929, son of Roy and Mary (McEntee) Urquhart; 2nd, in Martinez, Calif., Nov. 19, 1965, THOMAS C. SHUCK, born in Oakland, Calif., Aug. 9, 1927, son of Jack and Louise (Costa) Shuck.

Children in 10th Generation

F12052 STEVEN SCOTT, b. San Rafael, Calif., Oct. 28, 1954.

12053 TERESA KIM, b. San Francisco, Calif., Mar. 18, 1956.

F11298 PEGGY JANICE LEE MILLER, born in Oakland, Calif., Sept. 22, 1939, married in Santa Rosa, Calif., Nov. 2, 1956, RUSSELL LEONARD KIMBERLY, born in San Francisco, Calif., July 1938, son of Leonard and Florence (Pedotti) Kimberly.

Children in 10th Generation

12054 MARK STEVEN, b. San Francisco, Calif., April 17, 1960.

F11299 DON KIRK MILLER, born in Ross, Calif., Jan. 1, 1950, married in Reno, Nev., Sept. 14, 1971, JULIE NUNLEY, born in Lafayette, Calif., July 30, 1950, daughter of Thomas and Hazel (McDermott) Nunley.

Children in 10th Generation

12055 JOEL KEATS, b. San Francisco, Calif.

F11300 ARLEN MORRIS LEE, born in Modesto, Calif., May 17, 1941, married 1st, NANCY LOU ELLIS, born in Berkeley, Calif., Sept. 1944; 2nd, NANCY JEAN FERERIA, born in Richmond, Calif., Feb. 19, 1943.

Children in 10th Generation

12056 MORGAN ENDREW, b. Berkeley, Calif., Jan. 26, 1966.

F11303 ARTHUR SAMUEL MERROW, JR., born in Boston, Mass., Mar. 31, 1916, married in East Aurora, N.Y., Nov. 14, 1942, LETA ADELE LEONARD, born in Torrington, Conn., April 6, 1915.

He graduated from Tufts College and received his masters degree from the Massachusetts Institute of Technology in chemical engineering in 1939. He went to work for the Lackawanna Plant of the Bethlehem Steel Corporation near Buffalo, New York. He was active in the Association of Iron and Steel Engineers and served as chairman of the Buffalo Section and the National Combustion Engineering Committee. He served two terms as national Director. He was a member of the Buffalo Area Chamber of Commerce and served as chairman of the Environmental Activities Council of the Chamber. He was also active in both Air and Water Pollution Control organizations. He was active in the work of the Methodist Church and served on boards and committees of the Buffalo District and the Western New York Conference. He retired from the steel plant in 1976 after 37 years of service and is continuing his interest in church activities, international travel and genealogical research. He has recently been accepted as a member of the Society of Mayflower Descendants and the Sons of the American Revolution.

Children in 10th Gen. b. in Buffalo, N.Y.

12057 ARTHUR SAMUEL III, b. Jan. 15, 1945, m. West Bridgewater, Mass., June 22, 1968, SUSAN DITCHETT.
    After graduating from Tufts Univ. he went to work for Pratt and Whitney Corp., div. of United Aircraft in the Research Dept. He received his master of science degree from Renselear Polytechnic Institute Hartford Branch in Mechanical Engineering in a program provided by Pratt and Whitney Corp. He and his wife live on a ten acre farm near Colchester with two horses, two

dogs, numerous cats and a couple of chickens. He is in
the process of restoring a 175 year old Cape Cod House
in which they live. They are both active in the Sierra
Club and Susan has been most recently in charge of the
Hartford Office of the Club.

12058 ELIZABETH CLARK, b. Aug. 15, 1947, d. Buffalo, N.Y.,
Nov. 24, 1956.

12059 CURTIS HENRY, b. Aug. 13, 1952.
He attended Tufts Univ. for two years and is presently studying at the Rochester Institute of Technology,
majoring in the field of photographic process and management.

F11309 EARLE RAYWORTH GOWELL, born Sept. 7, 1907, married
HELEN JARVIS.

Children in 10th Generation

F12060 EARLE RAYWORTH, JR., b. Dec. 24, 1934.

12061 JOHN, b. Feb. 3, 1938.

F11310 RALPH RANDALL GOWELL, born Jan. 3, 1911, married
CHARLOTTE INGALS, born Dec. 27, 1913.

Children in 10th Generation

12062 SARAH JANE, b. Portland, Maine, Sept. 23, 1943.

12063 ERNEST EDWARD, b. Bar Harbor, Maine, Sept. 11, 1945.

12064 MARTHA N., b. Bar Harbor, Maine, Aug. 27, 1947.

12065 RALPH RANDALL, b. Portland, Maine, Feb. 7, 1952.

F11314 FORREST HERBERT FRANCIS, born in Fayette, Maine,
May 11, 1883, died in Lewiston, Maine, Feb. 1, 1952, married in
East Livermore, Maine, Dec. 31, 1904, JESSIE EDWINA COX,
born in Carthage, Maine, Sept. 7, 1888, died in Lewiston, Maine,
Mar. 17, 1963, daughter of Eugene and Mayvilla (Mitchell) Cox.

Children in 10th Generation

12066 MONA GEORGIA, b. East Livermore, Maine, Mar. 4,
1906. m. LESTER O. PRUE.

12067 WALLACE HERBERT, b. East Livermore, Maine, Aug. 2,
1908, m. MABEL KENDRICKS.

F12068 CECIL GEORGE, b. Lewiston, Maine, Dec. 5, 1911, m.
May 29, 1931, MARION ADELAIDE TURNER.

12069 CELIA HATTIE, b. Lewiston, Maine, Dec. 5, 1911.

12070 WILMA MAY, b. East Livermore, Maine, Sept. 30, 1921, d. Lewiston, Maine, 1963, m. WARREN MAILMAN.

F11326 DWIGHT RODERIC WEBSTER, born in Castine, Maine, Sept. 3, 1911, married ARLENE COTTON BOWDEN, born in Orland, Maine, June 9, 1916.

He remembers when a run across Penobscot Bay on Board the Schooner "Inez" to Rockland, Maine, a vessel operated by his grandfather, Capt. Gene Webster, and his father, Emery, usually took 3 to $3\frac{1}{2}$ hours.

He was employed several years with the Seaboard Paper Company, (now St. Regis) at their mill in Bucksport, Maine. During later years, he has operated in the Penobscot and Castine, Maine area as a general contractor in the construction of cellars, wharves, drainage systems and landscaping.

Children in 10th Gen. b. in Castine, Maine

12071 CORINNE FRANCES, b. May 18, 1936, m. 1st, June 20, 1956, WILLIAM ORR of Penna.; 2nd, JOHN SANBORN, b. 1930, a widower, of Ellsworth, Maine, where they reside with three children: 12072 DEBRA ANNE SANBORN (Nee: Orr), b. Aug. 16, 1957; 12073 WILLIAM DWIGHT SANBORN (Nee: Orr), b. June 22, 1959; 12074 GREGORY SANBORN, b. Sept. 30, 1959.

12075 LUCILLE ARLENE, b. Sept. 27, 1939, m. June 18, 1960, F10992 WILLIAM A. FELLOWS. Resides in Augusta, Maine.

F11327 DONALD WEBSTER, born in Castine, Maine, July 8, 1914, married RUTH CROCKETT. They reside in New Sharon, Maine where they own and operate a dairy farm with about forty head of cows.

Children in 10th Generation

12079 MAYNARD, b. July 31, 1941.

12080 BETTY, b. Dec. 22, 1942.

12081 JEANNETTE, b. Dec. 7, 1943.

12082 MARGARET, b. Mar. 30, 1946.

12083 NORMA, b. Oct. 5, 1949.

12084 ROBERT, b. Jan. 30, 1953.

12085 MARIE, b. June 2, 1955.

12086 STANLEY, b. June 22, 1961.

ELEVENTH GENERATION

F9319a LAURENCE EDWARD GOSS, born in Portsmouth, N. H., Feb. 17, 1916, married in Rye, N.H., Mar. 20, 1943, ANNA LOUISE OLIVER, born in Exeter, N.H., Nov. 11, 1922, died Mar. 25, 1974, buried in Rye, N.H.

He was educated in the schools of Rye and Portsmouth and holds degrees from Keene, N. H. Teachers College and Springfield College. He served as teacher, administrator and coach in the public schools of N. H., New York and Mass. for forty years. Active in YMCA as a youth secretary, club leader, camp counselor and camp director. Director of Adult Education in West Springfield, Mass. and principal of the Summer School and Evening Adult Education. Organizer and charter member of the West Springfield Municipal Employees Federal Credit Union. Served as Mass. representative on the New England Council for Crafts. Active in several craft organizations as a weaver. Interested in traveling, especially Freighter Cruises.

She was the daughter of William H. and Louise Lange Oliver of North Hampton. Graduate of the North Hampton schools, valedictorian at Robinson Female Seminary in Exeter and Concord Business School. Executive secretary with several agencies and businesses in New Hampshire and Massachusetts. Certified teacher of sewing with the Mass. Dept. of Occupational Education. Active member of the Business and Professional Women's Association. She was intelligent, industrous, and planned ahead for the success of her husband and three children. It is unfortunate that death from cancer at an early age did not permit her to enjoy the results of her efforts. Still there are many happy memories for her family.

Children in 11th Generation

F12087 LAURENCE EDWARD, JR., b. Greenfield, Mass., Dec. 9, 1944, m. Springfield, Mass., June 9, 1968, SHARON MARGARET RIPP.

12088 LOUISA ANNE, b. Milford, Mass., Jan. 23, 1950.
She was educated in the schools of Leavittown and Westbury, Long Island and West Springfield, Mass. The majority of her summers have been spent in camping in N. H. She has a bachelors degree from Springfield College in teaching and is following a career in nursing with an associate degree from Springfield Technical Community College.

12089 RICHARD PICKERING, 3RD, b. Worcester, Mass., Jan. 15, 1953, m. Easthampton, Mass., May 26, 1973, JEAN

AUGUSTA MECOZZI, b. Sept. 7, 1953.

He had a grammar school education in the schools of West Springfield, Mass. Graduated from Williston Academy, Easthampton, Mass. Enjoyed a concert tour of Europe as a vocalist. Continued his athletic career as a swimmer and middle distance runner at Ithaca College, N. Y. while a music major. Having spent his summers at Camp Belknap on the shores of Lake Winnepesaukee he returned to N. H. and the University of New Hampshire to complete his education with a major in English. Engaged in hotel and restaurant management.

She is the daughter of Dominick and Louise Macozzi of Georgetown, Conn. She attended Ithaca College, N. Y. for two years as a music major. After marriage she transferred to UNH and graduated summa cum laude as a music major. Taught public school music and pursues her career with the flute.

F9322 RICHARD IRWIN GOSS, born Jan. 24, 1901, married Feb. 14, 1932, LOUISE M. BOOKER, born Dec. 19, 1910.

Children in 11th Generation

F12090 CAROLYN FRANCES, b. Oct. 1, 1932, m. June 9, 1957, PETER G. BROOKS.

F9500 JAMES WILLIS MERRILL, born in Washington, D.C., Nov. 3, 1910, married 1st, Feb. 8, 1930, ALEXANDRIA WALKER; 2nd, May 12, 1951, FLORA P. FORBES.

Children of James and Alexandria and of 11th Generation

12091 DIANNA LOCKE, b. Oct. 2, 1934, m. June 30, 1956, EDWIN C. KAINE and had: 12092 STEVEN; 12093 JULIE BETH.

F9501 RICHARD NATHAN MERRILL, born Mar. 17, 1915, married April 10, 1953, BONNIE STENSENG, born April 21, 1923.

Children in 11th Generation

12094 JAMES RICHARD, b. Nov. 17, 1953.

12095 JOHN LOCKE, b. Aug. 8, 1955.

12096 JEFFREY SCOTT, b. Mar. 9, 1957.

F9585 ESTELLE PRAY, born in Portsmouth, N. H., July 23, 1912, married in Portsmouth, N. H., July 18, 1936, ROBERT FRANCISCO ESTES, born in Canton, Mass., Mar. 31, 1913.

She graduated from Portsmouth, N. H. High School, 1930 as Vice President of her class. Then graduated from University of N. H., 1934 with a B. S. degree in Home Economics which she taught before her marriage. She was President of the Madison, Maine Garden Club, Congregational Church Women's Assoc. and active in the No. Anson, Maine Extension Club. She is interested in horses, crafts and ecology. He earned a B. S. degree in accounting and business at Colby College. Worked for Continental Can and Great Northern Paper Co.

Children in 11th Generation

F12097 ROBERT FRANCISCO, JR., b. Boston, Mass., June 11, 1937, m. Farmington, Conn., ANONE PEARL GET-CHELL.

F12098 ELIZABETH PRAY, b. Hodge, La., July 9, 1940, m. Madison, Maine, Sept. 7, 1962, DAVID FRANCIS MARTIN.

12099 ELAINE M., b. Skowhegan, Maine, Feb. 28, 1949, m. Rangeley, Maine, Dec. 27, 1974, CHARLIE THOMAS, b. Plainfield, N. J., June 25, 1951.
Graduated from Madison, Maine High School, 1967 and Univ. of Maine, Orono, 1971 and attended Springfield, Mass. College, 1972. Taught at Ball State Univ. 1972-75. She is a National Honor Society member and was Maine All Around Gymnastic Champion 1967 and College Women's All Around Gymnastic Champion 1970. Interests include raising and breaking horses, scuba diving, hunting, fishing and baseball.

12100 STEPHEN FRED, b. Farmington, Maine, July 30, 1951, m. Rangeley, Maine, Sept. 14, 1974, CYNTHIA DAVIS.

F10040 NITA ALICE HUTCHINSON, born in Washington, Vt., June 9, 1910, married in Richmond, Vt., Mar. 7, 1941, LELAND ALBERT TOWNE, born in Richmond, Vt., July 27, 1900.

Children in 11th Generation

F12101 MARTHA ANNE, b. Burlington, Vt., Mar. 8, 1942, m. Richmond, Vt., Oct. 3, 1962, ROGER LOUIS BOMBARDIER.

F10042 RAYMOND SANBORN LOCKE, born in Waits River, Vt., Jan. 4, 1911, married in Moretown, Vt., June 20, 1935, RUTH ELLEN KINGSBURY, born in Moretown, Vt., May 15, 1909.

He received a B. S. degree from Springfield College, M. A. from the University of Michigan, and C. A. G. S. from Boston University.

Spent forty years in Secondary Education, thirty four as Principal in Vermont, Michigan, Rhode Island and Massachusetts. Summers were spent in various boy's camps as swimming instructor, Director and teacher at Tabor Academy until the position of Principal became a year round job.

A member of Mad River Lodge of Masons since 1935.

She received her B.S. from Lowell State and a M.S. from Boston University. A music teacher in Vermont, Michigan, Rhode Island and Massachusetts for thirty years. She has been a member of the Eastern Star for forty five years, and is very active in the Garden Club and the Association of University Women.

Since retiring four years ago and moving to the Centerville of Cape Cod, the Locke's have been busy with their gardens (her's flowers, his vegetables), bridge, reading, relaxing and enjoying the summers there and the sunshine of Florida in the winter.

Two organizations that he is honored to serve as President of are the Springfield College Alumni Chapter of Cape Cod, and the Locke Family Association.

Children in 11th Generation

F12102   RAYMOND STANDLICK, b. Hillsdale, Mich., Aug. 17, 1938, m. Barrington, R.I., July 15, 1962, SALLY PAGE RAYMOND.

F12103   RANDOLPH KINGSBURY, b. Attleboro, Mass., Oct. 6, 1944, m. Cambridge, Mass., Oct. 16, 1966, MARTHA ANDREWS.

F10478   RICHARD JENNESS LOCKE, born in Rye, N.H., April 3, 1903, married 1st, in Rye, N.H., 1924, RUTH S. DRAKE of Bedford, Mass.; 2nd, in Rye, N.H., ROBINA MURRAY of Nova Scotia.

Children in 11th Generation

Child of Richard and Ruth

F12104   RICHARD JENNESS, JR., b. Portsmouth, N.H., Aug. 1, 1925.

Children of Richard and Robina

12105   SANDRA

12106   STANLEY REUBEN

F10480   DR. JOHN LANGDON PARSONS, born in Rye, N.H., June 3, 1895, married in Watertown, Mass., Oct. 12, 1921, BLANCHE GLADWIN GILLIATT, born in Beverly, Mass., Aug. 27, 1898, daughter of Thos. and Anna Gilliatt.

His achievements in the pulp and paper field covered a span of nearly fifty years and encompassed a broad spectrum of activities—in research, technical management, writing, translation, and as a long-time leader of the Technical Association of the Pulp and Paper Industry. He received the 1971 TAPPI Research and Development Award.

For several years he was an independent consultant as an associate of Calkin and Bayley, Inc., New York City, where he was vice president for pulp and paper.

He graduated from M.I.T. and taught chemistry there and at Boston University. In 1920 he was a research chemist for the Hammermill Paper Company and later became research director. During his early years with Hammermill he won a company fellowship to Yale University, receiving the Ph.D. degree in 1925. In 1945 Dr. Parsons joined the technical staff of Hollingsworth and Whitney Company as research director and later as technical director.

He was a member of the TAPPI Board of Directors, and of its Editorial Board. He is a Fellow of the American Association for the Advancement of Science and of the Institute of Chemists. He is a member of Sigma Xi, Alpha Chi Sigma, Kappa Sigma and the ACS (50 year member), and is holder of the Silver Beaver Award.

His writings include the section on "Paper" in the Encyclopedia Americana and on "Packaging" in the Encyclopedia Brittanica. He is an author of many articles on cellulose and for several years was an abstractor for Chemical Abstracts. He served as a lecturer on subjects relating to pulp and paper manufacture at the University of Maine, Allegheny College, and Colby College.

He has been an active member of the Locke Family Assoc. having served a dozen years as its Treasurer and as President 1971-72. He resides in the family homestead in Rye.

Children in 11th Generation

F12107 ROBERT DECATUR, b. Boston, Mass., Oct. 25, 1923, m. Springfield, Penna., June 21, 1947, ANNA CAROLYN DETZ.

F12108 DONALD GLADWIN, b. Portsmouth, N. H., July 14, 1927, m. Ambler, Penna., May 14, 1955, ETHEL SHIRLAW.

F12109 PRISCILLA LOCKE, b. Erie, Penna., Sept. 9, 1930, m. Rye, N. H., June 6, 1953, ARTHUR ERNEST FINGER, JR.

F10482 HARRIET DREW GOSS, born in Rye, N.H., June 1, 1888, died in Rye, N.H., Oct. 14, 1975, married in Rye, N.H., Mar. 1, 1910, ERNEST JENNESS MOULTON, born in North Hampton, N.H., Jan. 23, 1886, died in North Hampton, N.H., Nov. 2, 1963.

Children in 11th Generation

F10483 WILLIAM ALBERT, b. Rye, N.H., June 7, 1911, m. Hampton, N.H., Dec. 23, 1950, AUDREY E. KING.

12110 MURIEL GERTRUDE, b. Portsmouth, N.H., April 17, 1916, m. Exeter, N.H., Nov. 19, 1941, JOHN DAVIS BARR, b. Mar. 1, 1915.

F10484 ANNIE MARIE GOSS, born in Rye, N.H., Jan. 6, 1890, died in Rye, N.H., Jan. 14, 1926, married April 30, 1917, RALPH EUGENE BERRY, born Jan. 3, 1898, died Dec. 17, 1971.

Children in 11th Generation

F12111 NORMAN EUGENE, b. June 17, 1919, m. Dec. 18, 1942, ELIZABETH ANN GRUBB.

F12112 NANCY ELIZABETH, b. Aug. 27, 1925, m. Oct. 18, 1947, ADOLPH LOUIS BEROWNSKY.

F10486 HESTER PHILBRICK, born in Rockport, Mass., June 15, 1890, died in Boston, Mass., Feb. 4, 1966, married possibly in Somerville, Mass., Sept. 15, 1915, ELIAS WILLIAM HENRY WENTZELL, born in Dartmouth, Nova Scotia, Nov. 7, 1887.

She graduated from Somerville, Mass. High School and Katherine Gibbs Secretarial School in Boston. He was educated in Massachusetts and was a salesman of paperboard to box companies for 53 years. A successful Salesman who won many prizes, he worked for Pioneer-Carmer Co. and Robert Gair Co. He retired at age 80 having enjoyed considerable prosperity throughout his career. He is a long time member of Kiwanis International. He is described as "has the patience of Job and the wisdom of Euripides". In 1921 they built a summer home in Rye which the family still enjoys.

Children in 11th Gen. b. in Somerville, Mass.

12113 HOMER PHILBRICK, b. July 6, 1916, m. Lyndonville, Vt., June 12, 1954, MARALYN E. GRANT, b. Jan. 5, 1923.

He graduated from Somerville, Mass. High School, 1934; Univ. of N.H., 1939 with B.A. degree; Boston Univ., 1951 with M.Ed. degree and Clark Univ., 1954 with M.S. degree. He was a teacher for 24 years and is retired in Florida.

She was born in Lyndon, Vt. and holds a B.S. and M.A. degrees plus 34 credit hours beyond her Master's degree. She taught for many years in public schools in Vermont and held positions at Lyndon State College. In May 1975 she received the Distinguished Alumni Award from Lyndon State College.

F12114 JOHN LLOYD, b. June 1, 1919, m. Boston, Mass., June 28, 1941, ELIZABETH KINSMAN, b. Jan. 18, 1920.

F12115 DOROTHY, b. July 1, 1922, m. Medford, Mass., Sept. 17, 1946, DONALD MARTIN BUTCHER, b. Sept. 9, 1922.

She graduated from Somerville, Mass. High School and Univ. of N.H. They had: 12116 LAURIE; 12117 EDWARD; 12118 CAROLYN.

F10566 EMMIE MARNITA MOORE, born in Rockingham County, N.C., near Reidsville, May 23, 1893, died in Greensboro, N.C., Oct. 22, 1967, married in Reidsville, N.C., Nov. 30, 1911, CHARLES JOSEPH ADAMS, born in Ruffin, N.C., Mar. 30, 1888, died in Greensboro, N.C., June 7, 1942.

She was by unanimous opinion the loveliest of the Moore girls, and she was as sweet as she was lovely. She was the champion "baby spoiler", the family correspondent, keeping distant members of the family posted on what was going on at home. She took care of anyone in the family who was ill and needed her. She delighted in new babies and weddings and all family get-to-gethers. She loved reading and music and art. She always wanted to go up to where "Papa came from" and one of her good friends took her to Maine and she loved every minute of her trip. She was ill for two and a half years and was sweet and patient through it all. Everyone in the family misses her still. She was a lovely, lovely lady.

Charlie was one of four brothers who were very musical. They were born fifty years too soon, as they would have been a television hit, without a doubt. Charlie loved people and travel, and managed a music company for years, then later opened a restaurant, as he was a marvelous cook.

Children in 11th Generation

12116 MARNITA, b. Reidsville, N.C., July 30, 1912. She inherited her Mother's love of books and art, and her father's love of music and travel. She sketches a bit, has written two books and writes lots of poetry. She was associated for 32 years with the Library Department of the Greensboro Public Schools, until retirement due to ill health in 1963. Collects cat books, and cookbooks. Loves to write letters to all "Yankee" relatives and the trip to Maine with her Mother is one of the most memorable times in her life. She loves to cook and makes cookies, cheese straws and candy for her family at Christmas time. She is the genealogist of the family, keeping up with all of the relatives' data, having been the one who gathered all this information for the new Locke volume.

F10567 HARRIDELL LOUILLE MOORE, born in Rockingham Cty., N.C., near Reidsville, N.C., Sept. 6, 1894, married in Graham, N.C., Dec. 31, 1911, OTIS DIXON PHILLIPS, born in Saxapahaw, N.C., June 19, 1890, died in Greensboro, N.C., Jan. 28, 1948.

At 82 "Dell" is still working every day at a local department store where she has worked for many, many years. She is very happy working and gets along beautifully with everyone. He was a stock broker and one of the most intellectual men, an avid reader and corresponded with many of the controversial figures of his time.

Children in 11th Generation

F12117   OTIS DIXON, JR., b. Newport News, Va., Sept. 30,
         1912, d. Atlanta, Ga., Sept. 24, 1966, m. West Palm
         Beach, Fla., Aug. 10, 1937, HATTIE ADA BOURN.

F12118   CHARLES HARRY, b. Statesville, N. C., July 9, 1914,
         m. Greensboro, N. C., Oct. 14, 1939, VIRGINIA
         BEVERLEY REAVES.

F12119   JACK BEVERLY, b. Richmond, Va., Aug. 11, 1917, m.
         Wetumpka, Ala., Sept. 12, 1942, KATHERINE ANN
         RAVESIES.

F10568   HENRY BROWN MOORE, born in Rockingham County, N.
C., near Reidsville, N.C., Nov. 19, 1897, married in Greensboro,
N.C., Nov. 20, 1923, ALLIE AGNES KING, born Jan. 11, 1900.
   He is retired from the Southern Railway and she taught kindergarten for a while before becoming involved in bringing up her own
children. She goes to bridge club and book club and he to a breakfast
club weekly. They like television and both are avid readers. He is
very interested in the Locke genealogy and has made a trip to Maine
to the home of his father and family.

         Children in 11th Gen. b. in Greensboro, N. C.

F12120   MARTHA ANNE, b. Sept. 2, 1925, m. Greensboro, N.
         C., June 4, 1946, CHARLES DAVIS MIZE.

F12121   WILLIAM LOCKE, b. Dec. 18, 1926, m. Reidsville, N.C.,
         Aug. 17, 1957, DOROTHY ELLEN CHEEK.

F12122   ADA JANE, b. Jan. 17, 1929, m. Greensboro, N. C.,
         Mar. 31, 1959, ARMISTEAD WRIGHT SAPP, JR.

F10568a MARY HELEN MOORE, born in Rockingham County, N.C.
near Reidsville, N.C., April 22, 1900, married in Greensboro, N. C.,
Nov. 25, 1922, HUGH GARDNER ARMFIELD, born in Greensboro,
N.C., Aug. 7, 1898.
   They live in a house they built with their own hands. He is retired
but still does work on safes and locks. He enjoys fishing and has built
several boats and sea sleds. They enjoy gardening and reading.

         Children in 11th Gen. b. in Greensboro, N. C.

F12123   ROBERT MOORE, b. Feb. 5, 1927, m. Greensboro, N.C.,
         Sept. 16, 1949, BEVERLEY FRANCES BELL.

F12124   RICHARD LOCKE, b. Nov. 7, 1929, m. Easley, S. C.,
         April 4, 1953, CATHERINE LENOIR DAVIS.

F10569 HELEN DUNBAR, born in Kittery, Maine, Mar. 7, 1893, married in Kittery, Maine, Dec. 1, 1914, GEORGE SHAFFER WOOD born in Kunkle, Pa., Feb. 28, 1886, died in Portsmouth, N.H. Naval Hospital, Oct. 14, 1969.

Children in 11th Generation

F12125 GEORGE SHAFFER, JR., b. Kittery, Maine, Dec. 4, 1915, m. April 24, 1941, NANCY GRAY LEE.

F10570 NORMAN DEAN DUNBAR, born in Kittery, Maine, Feb. 10, 1898, married in Los Angeles, Calif., July 11, 1923, SARAH ELLENA WARNER, both died in Los Angeles, Calif.

Children in 11th Gen. b. in Los Angeles, Calif.

F12126 CALVIN WARNER, b. Dec. 16, 1924, m. Los Angeles, Calif., June 28, 1954, JANICE HORLICK ROMNEY.

F12127 BETTIE LU, b. May 9, 1926, m. Los Angeles, Calif., June 4, 1949, ROBERT OLNEY THORN.

F12128 ADALYN HELEN, b. Aug. 19, 1930, m. Los Angeles, Calif., May 30, 1953, LEONARD EVERETT.

F10571 ARNOLD KENNETH PRAY, born in Hartford, Conn., Nov. 27, 1895, married in Melrose, Mass., MARION JONES.
He was a WWI Veteran of the Army of Occupation N.S. Engineers Div. I.

Children in 11th Generation

12129 KENNETH

12130 JANET

F10572 EARL FRANCIS PRAY, born Jan. 15, 1898, married FLORA LLOYD. He was an M.D. graduate of Tufts Medical School.

Children in 11th Generation

12131 ELIZABETH

F10610 MARGARET JUNE LOCKE, born in Methuen, Mass., June 24, 1912, married in Methuen, Mass., Sept. 25, 1934, LEON F. MOWRY, born in Lawrence, Mass., Feb. 20, 1912, died in Lawrence, Mass., Feb. 18, 1969.
Attended Methuen Public Schools and is a graduate of Katherine Gibbs Secretarial School, Boston, Mass.

Children in 11th Gen. b. in Lawrence, Mass.

12132 DAVID EUGENE, b. Aug. 27, 1936, m. 1st, in Great

Falls, Va., June 25, 1960, SUZANNE TUBAUGH (died);
2nd, in Rye, N.H., May 6, 1972, MAUREEN LYNCH.

12133 GAIL JUDITH, b. Jan. 7, 1942, m. Sept. 30, 1966,
ROBERT M. WILBUR.

F10612 JOHN CRAWFORD LOCKE, born in Methuen, Mass.,
Oct. 18, 1915, married in Lawrence, Mass., May 15, 1949, RUTHE
LAURAE ROBINSON, born in Boston, Mass., July 17, 1921.

He went to Bowdoin College, Mass. School of Radio. Electronics
Engr. Served in Army Signal Corp. during WW II in Pacific Theater.
Joined Philco as Field Engr. to Air Force in Korea and U.S.

She was a W.A.C. Served in U.S. during WW II. Worked as Tax
Examiner for I.R.S. and Real Estate Broker.

Children in 11th Generation

12134 DEBRA MICHELE, b. Lawrence, Mass., Mar. 12, 1951,
m. Methuen, Mass., Oct. 29, 1971, ROBERT J.
RICHARDS, JR.

F11353 JOHN BENETTE MARSTON, JR., born in Jamaica Plains,
Mass., Nov. 10, 1930, died in Tempe, Ariz., Feb. 9, 1973, married
1st, in Hampton, N.H., Dec. 18, 1953, THELMA MABEL INGLIS,
born in Hampton or Exeter, N.H., Oct. 19, 1933; 2nd, in Las Vegas,
Nev., April 19, 1963, ARLENE (PETERSON) HOUSE, born in Boston,
Mass., Dec. 5, 1934.

He was always called "Jack" by his family and friends. Attended
public schools in Manchester and Hampton, N.H. Also studied automobile mechanics at Portsmouth, N.H. trade school. Was member of
DeMolay in Hampton-Exeter, N.H. Also with the Coast Guard
Reserve. First worked for Andrew White Laboratory in Lee, N.H.
One test was driving car into both solid and absorbing barrier to
determine injury to driver and passenger.

He owned-operated a gasoline service station in Nashua, N.H. for
several years. In 1963 he moved his family to Arizona where he became interested in real estate. He then owned and operated a gasoline service station. This he combined with a towing service, covering
three cities with four tow trucks. The night of Feb. 9, 1973, while
cleaning debris in the highway, he was fatally injured when hit by a
vehicle.

Children in 11th Generation

F12135 LISA ANN, b. Exeter, N.H., June 24, 1955, m. Hampton,
N.H., Mar. 10, 1972, RICHARD JOSEPH OSBORN.

12136 TIMOTHY JOHN, b. Exeter, N.H., May 15, 1957.

12137 JASON PAUL, b. Mesa, Ariz., Oct. 19, 1971, d. Tempe,
Ariz., Mar. 17, 1972.

F11355 <u>LINDA LOUISE MARSTON</u>, born in Manchester, N. H., Oct. 6, 1936, married 1st, in Vermont, Mar. 2, 1954, ROBERT SIDNEY PARIZO, born June 27, 1935, (divorced); 2nd, in Hampton Falls, N. H., July 27, 1956, DAVID McLAUGHLIN, born in Haverhill, Mass.; 3rd, in Las Vegas, Nev., Nov. 21, 1964, JAMES NIELSON FINNELL, born in Phoenix, Ariz., Dec. 17, 1935.

She attended public schools in Manchester and Hampton, N. H., graduating from Hampton Academy. Worked as a clerk-cashier at Hampton Beach and Hampton Union Office. Lives in Mesa, Ariz. and works for Thom McAn. Hobbies are camping, hunting and fishing.

James Finnell attended public schools in Phoenix, Ariz. and Arizona State University 1954-1960. Served two years in the United States Army Veterinary Corps. He has worked for U.S. Dept. of Agriculture since 1963. Between 1958 and 1964 he was active in Rodeos riding horses and bulls bareback. He is an avid hunter and fisherman having taken five of Arizona's big ten game animals.

Children in 11th Generation

12138 LAURIE JEAN PARIZO, b. Exeter, N. H., Dec. 18, 1954, m. Mesa, Ariz., Mar. 8, 1974, FAUSTO ARTHUR BETANCOURT.

12139 SALLY ELIZABETH McLAUGHLIN, b. Exeter, N. H., June 18, 1957.

12140 CHRISTINA RUTH FINNELL, b. Mesa, Ariz., Sept. 10, 1965.

F11356 <u>PAUL EDWARD MARSTON</u>, born in Manchester, N. H., Mar. 15, 1938, died in Prescott, Ariz., June 9, 1969, married in Hampton, N. H., Nov. 22, 1961, ROSALIND MARIE LUND, born possibly Bedford, N.H., June 23, 1941.

He attended public schools in Manchester, N. H. and Hampton, N. H. He furthered his schooling at the Trade School in Dover, N. H. He worked at a number of temporary jobs, including police work at Hampton, N. H. (following his father). He spent his honeymoon on a trip to California, via Arizona, where they liked it so well they decided to move out west. He settled in Mesa, Arizona and in 1961 began working at the General Motors proving grounds. His work there consisted of driving new cars over various types of public roads and making numerous tests at intervals. In 1962 he was accepted as an officer for the Phoenix, Arizona police department. His ambition after arriving in Arizona was to become an Arizona highway patrolman therefore, after two years with the Phoenix police, he passed all exams and tests and was accepted as a patrolman in the Arizona highway patrol. His first assignment was working out of Williams, Arizona where some of his time was spent patrolling a section of the infamous "Route 66". Two years later he was transferred to Prescott, Arizona

where he lived for about five years, bringing up his family and enjoying the community. It was on the 7th of June, 1969, his day off and
showing a new officer the area that he became involved in the pursuit
of an escaped state prison convict. Chased into a farm yard, the convict fled into a large building. Paul started for the building, not seeing the convict come out the other end, whereupon the escapee fired
a fatal shot.

Children in 11th Generation

12140 SHERRY LYNN, (adopted), b. June 16, 1964.

12141 BRIAN EDWARD, b. Prescott, Ariz., Jan. 22, 1966.

F11357 ELAINE HUMPHREYS ROBERTS, born in Durham, N. H.,
April 9, 1923, died June 20, 1978, married in Somersworth, N. H.,
April 3, 1943, RICHARD LEIGH TOWER, SR., born in Pelham, Mass.,
May 14, 1923.

Children in 11th Generation

12142 STANLEY LYLE, b. Longbranch, N. J., July 17, 1944,
       d. same day.

12143 CHRISTINE LEIGH, b. and d. Exeter, N. H., Oct., 1950.

12144 DEBORAH ANN, b. Hampton, N. H., Mar. 2, 1953.

12145 RICHARD LEIGH, JR., b. Hampton, N. H., Jan. 27, 1956,
       m. Bradenton, Fla., Feb. 7, 1976, DENISE DOROTHY
       TALBOT.

F11359 ELWOOD EVERETT ROBERTS, JR., born in Dover, N. H.,
Aug. 6, 1931, married in Tilton, N. H., April 17, 1965, LINDA R.
WITHAM, born in Nashua, N. H., Jan. 3, 1946.
   He graduated Portsmouth High School, 1949 and is an electronic
engineering technician. Was a radio operator, United States Air Force
Korean War, 1952-1957, stationed Bedford, England, 1953-1957.
Lived Durham, N. H.; Hopkinton, N. H.; Concord, N. H.; Boston,
Mass.; New London, N. H.; and presently Sutton, N. H. Member,
National Geographic Society, Consumers Union. Hobbies are travel,
hiking and sports.

Children in 11th Generation

12146 KEITH ALLEN, b. Concord, N. H., Feb. 17, 1967.

F11365 JAMES WAYNE SMILEY, born in Des Moines, Iowa, July
30, 1946, married in Des Moines, Iowa, May 28, 1967, WANETTE
JOANNE SAUNDERS, born in Manchester, Iowa, Nov. 7, 1948,
daughter of William J. and Delphine (Yelden) Saunders.
   He was in the National Guard, 1967-1973 and is engaged in landscaping and horticulture.

Children in 11th Generation

12147 MICHELLE LYNN, b. Guthrie Center, Iowa, Feb. 1, 1969.

12148 JILL MARIE, b. Des Moines, Iowa, Dec. 10, 1971.

12149 DARCY SUE, b. Des Moines, Iowa, Mar. 20, 1974.

F11366 JO ANNE SMILEY, born in Des Moines, Iowa, Jan. 23, 1949, married in Minburn, Iowa, June 24, 1969, DENNIS DOYLE ROBERTS, born in Perry, Iowa, Sept. 25, 1947, son of Gaylord and Marjorie E. (Sulgrove) Roberts.

Children in 11th Generation

12150 BRETT JAMES, b. Perry, Iowa, Oct. 4, 1969.

F11367 WILLIAM HOYT NELSON, born in Des Moines, Iowa, Nov. 8, 1939, married in Perry, Iowa, Sept. 9, 1967, PENNEE LEE FITZGERALD, born Dec. 1, 1944, daughter of Edward and Mary (Elder) Fitzgerald, Jr.
He is a captain in the National Guard of Iowa.

Children in 11th Generation

12151 LEE WILLIAM, b. Des Moines, Iowa, Nov. 26, 1973.

F11368 JOHN LOCKE NELSON, born in Dexter, Iowa, Nov. 8, 1944, married Stratford, Iowa, CAROL ANN PETERSON, born in Boone County, Iowa, Sept. 22, 1947, daughter of Joel and Violet Peterson.
He was in the U.S. Army and served in Viet Nam. Later was a captain in the National Guard.

Children in 11th Generation

12152 MICHAEL JOHN, b. Des Moines, Iowa, May 13, 1971.

12152a JAMES ARTHUR, b. Fort Dodge, Iowa, Nov. 4, 1973.

F11370 W. FREDERICK BACHELDER, JR., born in Holyoke, Mass., Nov. 12, 1918, married in Northport, N.Y., Feb. 15, 1947, MARGARET ANN GOLDHORN, born in Northport, N.Y., July 7, 1925.

Children in 11th Generation

12153 SUSAN PARKINSON, b. New York, N.Y., May 23, 1948.

12154 SALLY BLOODGOOD, b. Garden City, N.Y., Feb. 5, 1950.

12155 JOHN HENRY, b. Garden City, N.Y., Feb. 23, 1957.

F11371 MALCOLM ROBIE WELLS, born in Penn Yan, N.Y., Sept. 16, 1913, married in Concord, N. H., Jan. 1, 1939, MARION BUNKER FELLOWS, born in Russell, N.Y., July 5, 1919.

He graduated from Wesleyan University, Middletown, Conn., 1935.

Has been employed by New Hampshire Highway department since 1936 —except for five years with the Army Engineers (civil), 1941-1946 — working on field and office engineering: roads, dams, bridges. Most of work with Highway Department has been in revising road and bridge construction specifications. Is an active member of Wesley Methodist Church in Concord, N. H.

She was employed for ten years by Union School District of Concord, N. H. as pastry cook in cafeteria program. Presently employed by Christian Mutual Life Insurance Co. in home office in Concord. Is an active member of Nazarene Church. Interested in arts and crafts.

Children in 11th Gen. b. in Concord, N. H.

F12156 NANCY ANN, b. April 13, 1941, m. Concord, N. H., Oct. 30, 1965, HOMER VENCIL HORTON.

F12157 HERBERT DANIEL, b. Oct. 17, 1943, m. Wolfboro, N.H., Aug. 26, 1967, BARBARA JEAN PRESTON.

F11372 WINTHROP ALBRO WELLS, born in Bristol, N. H., July 29, 1915, married in Concord, N.H., Feb. 1, 1941, BETSY CELINDA BASSETT, born in Orleans, Vt., Jan. 15, 1919.

He attended Concord, N. H. public schools and graduated from Wesleyan Univ., 1937. He was an engineer for the U.S. Army Corps of Engineers engaged in flood control design and construction and military construction for 31 years, retiring in 1970. He is a Registered Professional Engineer in Mass. and Oregon.

He was a Boy Scout leader, served on various boards and commissions in Portland, Ore., First Congregational Church. His hobbies are photography, wood carving, macrame, candlemaking, rock polishing, jewelry making, hiking, camping and travel.

She attended Orleans, Vt. public schools and graduated from Lasell Jr. College, Auburndale, Mass., 1939. Her occupations have been consumer analysis survey, public school secretary, library aid and homemaker. She has been active in church work, Salvation Army and Boy Scouts of America. Her hobbies include knitting and crocheting, painting and ceramics.

In 1960 they were Oregon delegates to the All-American Family Conference at Lehigh Acres in Florida.

Children in 11th Generation

F12158 PETER HARRY, b. Waltham, Mass., April 19, 1943, m. Portland, Ore., Nov. 22, 1969, ELRAE LOUISE SADRING.

F12159   MICHAEL WINTHROP, b. Newton, Mass., Jan. 8, 1945,
         m. Bremerton, Wash., Sept. 3, 1966, ELAINE MORRIS.

12160   STEPHEN THAYER, b. Waltham, Mass., Feb. 20, 1947,
        m. Portland, Ore., Aug. 24, 1968, NANCY LUCRETIA
        WILES.
              He was educated in Portland, Ore. public schools; is
        a Boy Scouts of America Life Scout; graduated from
        Willamette Univ., Salem, Ore., 1970. He repairs and
        finishes fine furniture. His special interests are living
        an ecologically sound life and photography.
              She graduated from Eugene, Ore. High School and
        from Willamette Univ., 1969. She is a garage mechanic
        and filling station attendant. Her interests are philo-
        sophical reading and study, gardening, and living an
        ecologically sound life.

F11373   DONALD HASKINS WELLS, born in Bristol, N.H., July
3, 1917, married in Concord, N.H. at home of bride's parents, Aug.
17, 1940, DOROTHY RACHEL COTNOIR, born in Dorchester, Mass.,
Dec. 1, 1916.
     He was educated in Concord, N.H. public schools and was gradu-
ated from University of New Hampshire at Durham in 1940. He was
appointed to the engineering section of the U.S. Engineers' office at
the Franklin, N.H. dam. From 1943 to late 1945 he was with U.S.
Naval Reserves, U.S. Navy Construction Battalion as ensign and later
lieutenant junior grade. He was employed as civil engineer draftsman
with Fay, Spofford & Thorndike in Boston and with other firms until
1961 when he became a civilian employee with the Engineering (civil)
Department of the Air Force at office in New Boston, N.H. at the
Satellite Tracking station where he is still employed. He is a member
of National Society of Professional Engineers. He enjoys sailing and
skiing, arts and crafts.
     She was graduated from Penacook, N.H. High School and was em-
ployed at Emmons' store in Concord before her marriage. She has
helped with the school lunch program at Junior High School in Concord, has been a volunteer at New Hampshire Hospital, and has been
active in Merrimack County Extension group and Junior Woman's
Club. She is a volunteer at Concord Hospital and a member of
Madisses Circle, South Congregational Church, Concord, where they
reside. She is a homemaker, enjoys sailing and skiing, and collects
cups and saucers.

Children in 11th Generation

F12161   ANNALEE, b. Franklin, N.H., Dec. 12, 1942, m. Con-
         cord, N.H., Oct. 27, 1962, CARLETON SAGER MACK.

12162 MARILYN, b. Concord, N. H., May 26, 1946, m. Middleboro, Mass., Aug. 24, 1971, ROBERT WILLIAM TRIBOU. She was educated in Concord, N. H. public schools and is a graduate of Plymouth, N. H. State College. She is an elementary school teacher. Interested in gardening, skiing, arts and crafts. He is a student. He is interested in photography and skiing. He is a member of the Elks and they reside in Falmouth, Mass.

12163 DANA DRAKE, b. Concord, N. H., June 2, 1952. He is a graduate of Concord High School and New Hampshire Technical Institute, Concord, with associate degree in electronics engineering and employed as electronic engineer. His hobbies are skiing, sailing and contra dancing.

12164 SCOTT DONALD, b. Concord, N. H., Oct. 16, 1958. He is a senior in Concord High School, plays drums in marching band.

F11374 DAVID THAYER WELLS, born in Concord, N. H., Nov. 29, 1923, married in Quincy, Mass., June 18, 1949, ELEANOR JEANNE HAMOR, born in Bar Harbor, Maine, Sept. 27, 1926.
    He was graduated from Concord, N. H. High School, attended the University of New Hampshire; was an airplane mechanic and corporal in World War II. Since 1950 he has lived in Concord, N. H. where he is employed as a bookbinder by Evans Printing Co. He has been active in Junior Chamber of Commerce and is a member of First Congregational Church. He is interested in music and plays bass viol in a dance orchestra.
    She is a graduate of Children's Hospital Medical Center School of Nursing, Boston, Mass., where she was a head nurse; now is a staff nurse on Pediatrics at Concord Hospital. She is a member of First Congregational Church, currently on Board of Deacons; active in extension work. In 1963 she was chosen Mother of the Year, nominated by her daughter Kathleen. Interests include knitting and needlework.

Children in 11th Generation

12165 CHRISTINE ELAINE, b. Boston, Mass., May 3, 1950, m. Concord, N. H., Aug. 24, 1974, STEPHEN RICHARD ROBERTS. She was educated in Concord, N. H. public schools and a graduate of Forsyth Dental Center, Boston, Mass., is employed as a dental hygienist in Dedham, Mass. Her interests are music (plays flute), painting and sewing.
    He is a graduate of Gardiner, Maine High School and has served in the U. S. Coast Guard. Now enrolled in computer technology at the Control Data Institute of Burlington, Mass. They reside in Braintree, Mass.

12166 KATHLEEN ALISON, b. Concord, N. H., July 7, 1951.
m. Concord, N. H., June 8, 1974, MARK KELVIN
McDONALD. She is a graduate of Concord, N. H. High
School and of Brown University with degree of A. B. in
Psychology. Following her graduation she was employed
as research technician with infants in Brooklyn, N. Y.
Jewish hospital. Presently living in West Lebanon, N.H.
        He is a graduate of Brown University, was a contact
representative with the U. S. Railroad Retirement Board.
At present he is a student at Amos Tuck School of Busi-
ness, Dartmouth College, Hanover, N. H.

12167 BRIAN DAVID, b. Concord, N. H., Mar. 26, 1955. He
is a student at Mass. College of Pharmacy, Boston, Mass.
He is interested in music and sports.

F11376 HEZEKIAH MARTIN BEEDE, born in Lynn, Mass., July 17,
1914, m. 1940, LOIS RUTH GALEUCIA, born in Lynn, Mass.

Children in 11th Generation

12168 DONALD MARTIN, b. Lynn, Mass., Oct. 26, 1942.

12169 ROBERT HENRY, b. Salem, Mass., June 7, 1947, m. Providence, R. I.

12170 RICHARD EDWARD, b. Lynn, Mass., Mar. 6, 1949, m.
Lynnfield, Mass., JEANNIE HILL.

12170a NANCY RUTH

F11377 DONALD CHANDLER CASS, born in Brookline, Mass.,
May 12, 1923, married in Winchester, Mass., MARION P. PHIL-
BROOK.
He was Battalion Sergeant Major in the Third Army during WWII
and wears several combat ribbons. She is a housewife. They live in
Wellesley, Mass.

Children in 11th Generation

12171 BRIAN PHILBROOK, b. Boston, Mass. He was Lance Cpl.
U. S. Marines in the Vietnam War.

12172 BETTINA PHILBROOK, b. Wyoming, Pa.

12173 JANA, b. Wheaton, Ill.

F11378 RICHARD S. CASS, born in Boston, Mass., July 22, 1928,
married in Boston, Mass., Oct. 11, 1952, MARY O'DONNELL.

Children in 11th Generation

12174 NANCY JANE, b. Oct. 10, 1954.

12175   JAMES R., b. June 13, 1956.

12176   ROBERT W., b. May 13, 1958.

F11379   EDWARD P. CASS, born in Boston, Mass., June 22, 1933, married in Chicago, Ill., Aug. 27, 1960, JOANN TARCZYNSKI.

Children in 11th Generation

12177   E. PAUL, b. Aug. 19, 1961.

12178   DIANE, b. Nov. 21, 1962.

12179   JOSEPH E., b. Nov. 20, 1963.

12180   LINDA A., b. Mar. 22, 1966.

F11382   AGNES MAY FRASER, born in San Francisco, Calif., April 7, 1921, married in Clarksburg, Calif., 1950, MARVIN L. FEHR, born in Happy, Texas, Dec. 22, 1918.

Children in 11th Generation

12181   SHIRLEY ALICE, b. Martinez, Calif., Aug. 24, 1953, m. Aug. 8, 1975, JAMES BARKET.

12182   PATRICIA JEAN, b. Albany, Calif., Jan. 3, 1952.

F11383   WILLIAM SAMUEL FRASER, born in Sacramento, Calif., Sept. 14, 1923, married in Sacramento, Calif., June 1, 1947, BARBARA LOIS WURZBACH, born in San Francisco, Calif., April 2, 1924.

He attended Oregon State College prior to serving in the U. S. Army from 1943-1947. He lives in Clarksburg, Calif. where he is a partner in farming with his father, Guy O. Fraser and brother, James. They raise sugar beets, alfalfa, corn, milo, safflower, barley, wheat.

Children in 11th Gen. b. in Sacramento, Calif.

12183   ANNE ELIZABETH, b. July 10, 1948.

12184   ROBERT SCOTT, b. Jan. 19, 1951, m. Orinda, Calif., Sept. 7, 1974, CARY JEAN WATTS.

12185   KATHRYN JO, b. Feb. 12, 1952, m. Sacramento, Calif., Oct. 25, 1975, BRIAN JAMES DONOHUE.

12186   JOHN SAMUEL, b. Dec. 24, 1955.

F11385   LOISMARIE EUNICE KELLOGG, born in Bakersfield, Calif., May 20, 1921, married in Bakersfield, Calif., Sept. 5, 1942, ROY MATHEW GUNSOLUS II, born Feb. 2, 1921.

She graduated from Univ. of Calif. at Berkeley, 1942 with an A. B. degree and was a member of Phi Mu sorority.

Children in 11th Gen. b. in Bakersfield, Calif.

12187 ROY MATHEW III, b. Oct. 25, 1945.

12188 PAMELA SKYE, b. Feb. 9, 1949.

F11387 BENJAMIN GERRY NEFF, JR., born in Oakland, Calif.,
Oct. 14, 1927, married in Sacramento, Calif., Aug. 12, 1967, SUSAN
ANN, born in Sacramento, Calif., Mar. 21, 1944.
     He attended Berkeley public schools and earned a B. A. in Eco-
nomics at the Univ. of Calif. at Berkeley, 1950 and a M. A. in School
Administration from Calif. State Univ., Sacramento, 1956 and Ed. D.
at Nova Univ., Ft. Lauderdale, Fla., 1975. His career has been
public school education. He is active in community affairs and
organizations and hobbies include reading, fishing, camping and sport
activities.

Children in 11th Gen. b. in Sacramento, Calif.

12189 KATHLEEN AMELIA, b. Dec. 9, 1958.

12190 BENJAMIN GERRY, III, b. Feb. 24, 1962.

12191 MARY ANN, b. Nov. 7, 1964.

12192 KRISTIN LYNN, b. Nov. 25, 1965.

F11388 ELEANOR JAFFRAY CASTLE, born in Quincy, Ill., Mar.
7, 1909, married in Quincy, Ill., June 15, 1935, ERNEST SIMON-
TON YOUNG, born in Boston, Mass., Nov. 14, 1901.

Children in 11th Gen. b. in Cambridge, Mass.

F12193 JOSHUA ADAMS SIMONTON, b. June 26, 1939, m.
          Cambridge, Mass., June 15, 1961, MARION HOLLIS
          McCOWN.

12194 TIMOTHY CASTLE, b. Nov. 27, 1946.

F11392 JANET ERCOLINE, born in Somerville, Mass., Jan. 26,
1917, married Dec. 10, 1934, VINCENT FREDERICK BENSON.

Children in 11th Generation

12195 JOAN, b. Medford, Mass., Mar. 22, 1939, married in
          Trinity Church, Boston, Mass., Sept. 11, 1965, KEN-
          NETH HENRY KULESZA.

12196 JANET, b. Medford, Mass., Mar. 22, 1939, m. Sudbury,
          Mass., May 28, 1967, PAUL BOTTAZZI.

12197 BRUCE WILLIAM, b. Waltham, Mass., July 17, 1946.

F12198 PETER RONBECK, b. Everett, Mass., Mar. 28, 1949, m.

Sacred Heart Church, Roslindale, Mass., Oct. 4, 1969,
JUNE ANNE CRAVEN.

F11393 EVERETT IRVING LOCKE, born in Rochester, N. H., Oct.
2, 1930, married in East Boston, Mass., 1955, DOROTHEA GRACE
BOEHNER, born in Gloucester, Mass., Oct. 10, 1933.
  He was educated in the Barrington, N. H. and East Boston, Mass.
schools. When he first went to Boston he worked in a drug store and
later earned his Insurance Broker's License and worked for a Boston
Insurance Broker. His interest is Advanced Amateur Radio Operator.
  She was educated at the Girl's High School of Boston and attended
Simmons College majoring in Science and Education. She later went
to work for a Boston Insurance Agency.

Children in 11th Gen. b. in Boston, Mass.

12199 DAVID CLARENCE, b. July 16, 1959. He attends Boston
       English High School and is interested in science re-
       search, mathematics, computer and advanced amateur
       radio operator.

12200 PAUL WARREN, b. Nov. 13, 1960. He attends Boston
       Latin School and is an all-round student, academically
       and socially.

12201 CLINTON FRANCIS, b. May 20, 1964. He attends Boston
       Latin Academy and is interested in sports and mathema-
       tics.

12202 ROBERT BRYAN, b. Sept. 10, 1967. He attends Hugh Roe
       O'Donnell Elementary School, East Boston, Mass. He is
       interested in amateur radio.

F11394 MARY LINNA LOCKE, born in Rochester, N. H., Feb. 16,
1942, married, 1960, ADRIEL SMITH.
  She was educated in the Barrington and Rochester, N. H. Schools.
She is a Laboratory Control Inspector at Davidson Rubber Company,
Farmington, N. H.

Children in 11th Generation

12203 BETTY ANN, b. Rochester, N. H., April 6, 1961.

F11395 JAMES SAMUEL LOCKE, born in Rochester, N. H., Feb.
11, 1945, married, 1965, SUSAN HORNE, born in Berwick, Maine.
  He was educated in the Barrington and Dover, N. H. schools and
received his college degree while in the United States Army. He is
making the Army his career and now has the rank of SSG.

Children in 11th Generation

12204 JOYCE, b. Rochester, N.H., Mar. 28, 1966.

12205 TERRY, b. Valley Forge, Penna., Dec. 3, 1968.

12206 BRYAN, b. Carmel, Calif., Feb. 4, 1974.

F11396 CAROLYN STEVENSON, born in Barrington, N.H., April 6, 1930, married in Oakland, Calif., Dec. 27, 1951, CLAY PATRICK BEDFORD, JR., born in Glen Cove, N.Y., Dec. 7, 1929.
She was educated in the Rochester, N.H. public schools and graduated from Russel Sage College, Troy, N.Y., 1951 with a B.S. degree and entered Filene's Executive Training Program in Boston. She is a member of DAR and American Women's Club in Montreal and is interested in Eskimo Art and skiing.
He is a graduate of New Mexico Military Institute and Rensselaer Polytechnic Institute, Troy, N.Y. with a B.S. degree in Civil Engineering. He served in the U.S. Navy and is Vice-President of Field Operations for Kaiser Engineers.

Children in 11th Generation

12207 THOMAS ALAN, b. Norfolk, Va., July 21, 1952, m. Concord, N.H., Aug. 25, 1973, CAROLYN BETH DEHLS. He is presently attending Stanford Univ., Calif. having graduated from St. Paul's School, Concord, N.H., 1970 where he received the Valpey and Dickie prizes for Scholastic Achievements. In the summer of 1970 he studied at the Universite d'Aix-en-Marseille, Avingnon, France.

12208 STEVEN McLEOD, b. Norfolk, Va., Oct. 3, 1953. He graduated from St. Paul's School, Concord, N.H., 1971 where he was active in athletics. He attended the University of Nice, France and Rensselaer Polytechnic Institute, Troy, N.Y. graduating 1976 receiving the Ricketts Award for Academic Distinction. He is employed by Educational Facilities Laboratories in New York City.

12209 SUSAN CLAY, b. Baton Rouge, La., Oct. 1957, d. Baton Rouge, La., Nov. 1957.

12210 HILARY SUE, b. Montreal, P.Q., Canada, Oct. 6, 1962.

F11399 PHILIP EUGENE GOSS, born in Portsmouth, N.H., Nov. 24, 1928, married 1st, in Worcester, Mass., JOYCE ANN BUTLER; 2nd, in St. Petersburg, Fla., Mar. 31, 1956, LeVAUGHN A. MARSHALL, born May 5, 1921.

216   LOCKE GENEALOGY

Children in 11th Generation

12211 PHILIP EUGENE, JR., b. St. Petersburg, Fla., Jan. 12, 1959.

F11400 JEAN ELIZABETH BOULTER, born in Kittery, Maine, April 18, 1915, died in Dalton, Ga., Oct. 28, ——, married HENRY NORCROSS, born in 1913, died in Kittery, Maine, 1961.

Children in 11th Gen. b. in Sanford, Maine

12212 JUDITH

12213 STEPHEN, (twin), b. Feb. 14,——, m. KATHY——.

12214 SANDRA, (twin), b. Feb. 15, ——, m. EMMETT WOOD and had: 12215 DEBRA; 12216 LARRY; 12217 CHRIS.

F11406 HELEN OLIVIA ROBERTSON, born in Somerville, Mass., Aug. 24, 1902, married 1st, RALPH BLAKE; 2nd, in 1967, CHARLES MONEGAN, died in Dec. 1967.

Children in 11th Generation

12218 BARBARA ANN BLAKE, b. Dec. 14, 1932, m. 1952, ROBERT ESTES, divorced, no children.

12219 FREDERICK WOODBURY BLAKE, b. 1937.

F11407 DONALD OSGOOD ROBERTSON, born in Somerville, Mass., Dec. 30, 1903, married GLADYS SNELL.

Children in 11th Generation

12220 REX, b. Sept. 1929.

12221 LOIS JEAN

12222 ROBERT

12223 ROY

F11409 DOROTHY ELIZABETH ROBERTSON, born in North Abington, Mass., May 20, 1909, married, June 18, 1937, DANNY MONROE KANE, died, c 1971.

Children in 11th Generation

12224 DIANE ROBERTSON, b. Mar. 9, 1940, m. Mar. 9, 1962, ZIZLS ANDREAS FOROULIS.

12225 SUSAN MUNROE, b. Mar. 9, 1945, m. Nov. 14, 1970, DAVID P. GILLIS.

12226 NANCY ERNESTINE, b. Sept. 29, 1952.

F11410 FREDERICK ERNEST ROBERTSON, born in North Abington, Mass., Dec. 5, 1911, married 1st, in Aug. 1937, DOROTHY
RIDEOUT; 2nd, in 1961, RUTH BAKER.

Children in 11th Generation

12227 RUTH LOCKE, b. 1944.

F11411 ERNESTINE JOSEPHINE ROBERTSON, born in North Abington, Mass., Jan. 18, 1913, died July 17, 1974, married, June 6,
1951, C. CLIFFORD SHEA.

Children in 11th Generation

12228 KAREN MARA, b. April 26, 1953.

12229 DARLENE, adopted, b. July 4, 1958.

F11412 MILDRED JOSEPHINE LOCKE, born in Nashua, N. H.,
Nov. 4, 1906, married, Nov. 3, 1927, WALTER CROCKER ELLIS,
born in Cambridge, Mass., June 25, 1903.
She was named for her mother and a paternal aunt. Her early
youth alternated between Nashua, N. H. and Somerville, Mass. She
attended Forsythe Dental Institute and graduated as a dental hygienist.
He was very interested in genealogy and, despite illness, was a
significant contributor to this volume.

Children in 11th Generation

F12230 ELIZABETH JEAN, b. Somerville, Mass., June 2, 1930,
        m. Oct. 14, 1950, CHARLES LITTLEFIELD SEAMAN,
        b. Melrose, Mass., April 15, 1930.

F11413 RICHARD MacKAY LOCKE, born in Nashua, N.H., Aug.
11, 1910, married, Sept. 14, 1933, RUTH TURNER.

Children in 11th Generation

F12231 RICHARD MacKAY, JR., b. Feb. 24, 1941, m. Nov. 14,
        1970, KATHLEEN E. KEYES.

12232 WENDY RUTH, b. Oct. 18, 1945.

12233 JUDITH ANN, b. Nov. 25, 1948.

F11415 LEONA LOCKE, born June 22, 1918, married Aug. 11,
1948, WILLIAM LOW MITCHELL.
She was in the navy during WW II. She was a medical technician
observing the pilots and crew members during very high altitude
flights, for anoxia, when they might be expected to black out. Highly
hazardous flying. Yet the only injuries she sustained during the war

was in a car crash when off duty.

She has been associated with the Addison Gilbert hospital in Gloucester for many years. She was honored by being selected as "medical technician of the year" in a national survey.

Children in 11th Generation

12234 ADA LOUISE, b. Dec. 8, 1951, m. 1971, DONALD R. WATSON.

F11417 CATHARINE MAY LOCKE, born in Shelburne, N.S., Feb. 5, 1921, married Mar. 7, 1946, HERBERT FLETCHER.

Children in 11th Generation

12235 CAROLYN MAY, b. Feb. 26, 1947.

12236 DAVID WAYNE, b. April 6, 1950.

F11418 CHARLES RICHARD LOCKE, born in Shelburne, N.S., April 17, 1924, married June 30, 1950, MARILYN DORIS NICKERSON.

Children in 11th Generation

12237 GERALD RICHARD, b. Aug. 4, 1955.

12238 DARRELL ROY, b. July 17, 1956.

12239 MICHAEL WAYNE, b. July 29, 1958.

12240 STEPHEN JEFFREY, b. Jan. 17, 1961.

12241 KEVIN SIDNEY, b. Jan. 29, 1962.

12242 HERBERT ALAN, b. Aug. 7, 1963.

F11420 HERMAN CAPSTICK LOCKE, born in Lockeport, N.S., Dec. 8, 1905, died in Windsor, N.S., June 21, 1973, married in Liverpool, N.S., June 20, 1928, GARNETT SYLVIA WIGGLESWORTH, born in Liverpool, N.S., Oct. 18, 1907.

He went to school in Lockeport, later attended Business College and worked as a bookkeeper for a while. He then attended Barber College and worked for a number of years as a barber in Lockeport. In 1940 he became postmaster in Lockeport and continued in this capacity until he retired in 1970. In 1971 he and his wife went to live in Windsor, N.S. He was a master mason for many years and a Past Master of Taylor Lodge, Lockeport.

Children in 11th Generation

F12243 GLORIA JUNE, b. Lockeport, N.S., May 14, 1929, m.

Lockeport, N.S., July 28, 1950, STUART LAWRENCE MORSE.

F12244 PAULA CORRINE, b. Liverpool, N.S., April 10, 1934, m. Toronto, Canada, Dec. 14, 1956, NEIL NIMMO.

F11424 JOHN BURNHAM EATON, JR., born in Center Conway, N.H., Mar. 1, 1913, married in Center Conway, N.H., June 3, 1939, PAULINE MARION DENNETT, born in Eaton, N.H., Sept. 28, 1917.

He attended Fryeburg Academy and managed an A & P store for 25 years. Hobby is collecting and appraising coins. Is a member of Cumberland Lodge A.F. & A.M., Boaz Chapter, Dunlap Council and Lewiston Commandry also Golden Sheaf O.E.S. Also a member of several numismatic associations.

Children in 11th Generation

F12245 CAROL ANNE, b. Center Conway, N.H., Mar. 19, 1940, m. Gray, Maine, Aug. 22, 1958, RUSSELL MAURICE KEENE.

F12246 JAMES LESLIE, b. Gray, Maine, Dec. 9, 1947, m. Gray, Maine, Aug. 5, 1967, SANDRA RAY PARSONS.

F11425 ROBERT ALLAN JOHNSTON, born in Rockland, Mass., Nov. 30, 1905, married in New York City, N.Y., Mar. 12, 1932, DOROTHY MABLE FRASER, born in New Haven, Conn., Sept. 8, 1906.

He is a graduate of Brown University and a teacher by profession.

Children in 11th Gen. b. in Norwood, Mass.

F12247 DONALD LOCKE, b. Oct. 19, 1932, m. Mar. 15, 1958, ROBIN DIXON, (divorced).

F12248 DARYL ANN, b. Aug. 30, 1935, m. Tempe, Ariz., Dec. 2, 1955, CARL BABCOCK.

F12249 ELEANOR FRASER, b. Oct. 30, 1938, m. Tempe, Ariz., Dec. 24, 1958, ROBERT A. HAMILTON.

F11426 BRENT ROBINSON LOCKE, born in San Antonio, Texas, Aug. 18, 1927, married in Albuquerque, N.M., Mar. 25, 1948, CARROLL L. RILEY, born in Summersville, Mo.

She attended Stephens College in Columbia, Mo., then moved to the University of New Mexico where she received a B.A. in Anthropology in 1948. In the early 50's she had two mystery novels for girls published and co-authored a third novel for early teenagers.

He was a veteran of World War II, the youngest of six children born on a farm in the Ozarks. After his graduation from the University of New Mexico, he received his M. A. degree from UCLA and returned to the University of New Mexico for his Ph. D. in Anthropology. He spent some time working for the United States Department of Justice doing Indian Land Claims research, then taught one year each at the University of Colorado and the University of North Carolina. He became a permanent member of the faculty of Southern Illinois University in Carbondale, Illinois in 1955.

He has authored one book, "Origins of Civilization", published by the SICU press and has edited or co-edited a number of others, including the four volume series with Charles H. Lange, "The Southwestern Journals of Adolph F. Bandelier".

Children in 11th Generation

12250   BENJAMIN LOCKE, b. Boulder, Colo., May 2, 1954.
           He is a senior at Southern Illinois University, Carbondale, Illinois and is a University Studies major. He has many interests including writing science fiction.

12251   VICTORIA SMITH, b. Carbondale, Ill., Oct. 10, 1955, m. Aug. 7, 1976, RICHARD LEOPOLD SASICKI, b. Chicago, Ill., April 2, 1955.
           She is attending John A. Logan Junior College, Carterville, Illinois, working toward an A. A. degree in Child Care which will prepare her to be a nursery school teacher. He is now attending Southern Illinois University, working for a B. A. degree.

12252   CYNTHIA WINNINGHAM, b. Carbondale, Ill., May 28, 1960. She is a junior in high school with interests in drama and writing.

F11427   ELIZABETH HAYGOOD LOCKE, born in Corpus Christi, Texas, June 19, 1935, married in New York, N.Y., May 1955, DAVID OLIVER HENRY CRILLY CLARKE, born in Dublin, Ireland, Aug. 25, 1920.

Betsy attended Stephens College in Columbia, Missouri and Corpus Christi Junior College. David is the son of the late painter Margaret Crilly Clarke and stained glass artist of note and illustrator, the late Harry Clarke of Dublin. David, himself, is an artist and has used his talents in the art department of Pinewood Motion Picture Studios in London and with theatrical companies in Dublin. For many years he worked in the Harry Clarke stained glass studios in Dublin, started by his father whose own father was an importer of stained glass. After the stained glass studios closed their doors in about 1974, David and Betsy moved from Dublin to Texas where they live in Corpus Christi and David is painting, having several exhibits in Texas and other states.

Children in 11th Gen. b. in Dublin, Ireland

12253 ETÁIN MARY REBECCA LOCKE, b. May 15, 1957, m. 1974, RONALD GUY SCOTT and had: 12253a CONAN FERDIA, b. April 3, 1975.

They live in Corpus Christi, where he is employed by a chemical company. Etáin is interested in arts and crafts.

12254 RODERICK CRILLY, b. June 15, 1959. He has just graduated from High School in Corpus Christi and is interested in the U.S. Air Force because of an all-consuming passion for aircraft. He is a member of the U.S. Air Force ROTC.

12255 VERONIQUE ELIZABETH, b. June 2 or 3, 1961. She is in her sophomore year in high school and is interested in arts and crafts.

F11428a GRACE WALKER LOCKE, born in San Antonio, Texas, Sept. 18, 1922, married in San Antonio, Texas, Jan. 25, 1946, FREDERICK BARTON HARVEY, JR., born in Baltimore, Md., 1921.

She graduated 1944 from Vassar as a math major. She is an avid tennis player and loves golf and gardening. She is working for a liberal arts degree at Johns Hopkins University. He graduated from Harvard and served in the Marines in the South Pacific during WW II. He was awarded the Navy Cross and the Purple Heart and was nicknamed "The One Man Army". He is managing partner in Alex, Brown Investment Firm in Baltimore, Md.

Children in 11th Gen. b. in Baltimore, Md.

12257 GRACE WALKER, b. April 12, 1947. She graduated from the University of Pennsylvania and is studying for a Master of Arts degree in Theater at N.Y. Univ.

12258 FREDERICK BARTON, III, b. Mar. 24, 1949. Graduated from Harvard Business School and now with Dean-Witler Investment firm in N.Y.

12259 JOHN LOCKE, b. Dec. 5, 1950. Worked as legislative aid for Sen. Lowell Weicker (R-Conn.) for two years and is working on a law degree at the University of Va.

12260 ROSE HOPKINS, b. Sept. 14, 1954. Graduated from Colorado College, 1977.

F11428b JOHN ROBINSON LOCKE, JR., born in San Antonio, Texas, Aug. 2, 1924, married in San Antonio, Texas, April 1951, BETTY SUE STACY, born in Oklahoma City, Okla., Aug. 1929.

He graduated from the University of Texas and the University of Texas Law School. He served as a First Lieutenant in the Army Air Corps in WW II. With his father, he is a partner in the law firm of Groce, Locke and Hebdon. Hunting, fishing, tennis and photography are his hobbies.

Children in 11th Gen. b. in San Antonio, Texas

12261 JOHN ROBINSON, III, b. Feb. 15, 1952. He graduated from Trinity University in San Antonio.

12262 CAREY PHILLIPS, b. Mar. 29, 1954. He graduated from the University of Texas.

12263 WILLIAM STACY, b. Nov. 19, 1955. He is attending the University of Calif. in Santa Barbara.

12264 PHILIP WALKER, b. Nov. 21, 1957. He is attending the University of Calif. in Santa Barbara.

F11430 ROBERT WITHAM LOCKE, born in Salem, Mass., Nov. 28, 1933, married in South Newfane, Vt., July 25, 1959, MARJORIE ADAMS, born in Brattleboro, Vt., Oct. 5, 1938.

He graduated from Salem Classical High School 1951; Boston Univ. 1961, B.S. degree in engineering management; Univ. of Hartford, 1969, Master's in business administration. Served in U.S. Air Force 1954-58 and attained rank of Captain. He has had continuous service with the Boy Scouts of America and is an Eagle Scout and has received several Scouting awards. He became a Master Mason in 1975 and is an engineer for Pratt & Whitney Aircraft Co. in E. Hartford, Conn.

Children in 11th Generation

12265 DAVID ADAMS, b. Cambridge, Mass., July 23, 1960.

12266 JENNIFER SUSAN, b. Manchester, Conn., Dec. 14, 1961.

12267 JANET ANN, b. Manchester, Conn., Mar. 2, 1964.

F11432a FREDERICK VALENTINE HETT, born in Portsmouth, N.H., Dec. 8, 1907, died in Portsmouth, N.H., April 19, 1955, married in Portsmouth, N.H., Sept. 30, 1940, ANNA E. SCOTT.

Children in 11th Generation

12268 ANN E., b. July 20, 1943. She is a registered nurse and graduate of Central Maine General Hospital, Lewiston, and a 1975 graduate of Boston College School of Nursing. She is presently co-ordinator of operating room at Peter Bent Brigham Hospital in Boston, Mass.

F12269 WILLIAM FREDERICK (twin), b. May 24, 1945, m. Meredith, N. H., Jan. 25, 1969, BEVERLY WOODMAN of Center Harbor, N. H.

12270 MARY MARGARET (twin), b. May 24, 1945. She is a 1967 graduate of Georgetown University, Washington, D.C. and is studying for a Ph.D. at Free University of Berlin, Germany. Her field is Political Science and East German studies.

F11433 ANNA MARY LATHAM, born in Portsmouth, N. H., Dec. 30, 1914, married in Atlanta, Ga., Feb. 4, 1943, LOUIS SHERFESEE, JR., born in Charleston, S.C., Feb. 4, 1910, died in Old Greenwich, Conn., Aug. 31, 1953.
She graduated 1936 from Simmons College, Boston with a B.S. degree in Secretarial Studies. Enjoys traveling. He earned a B.A. degree at Univ. of No. Carolina 1932 and an M.S. degree at Harvard Univ. School of Business Administration, 1934. He was a partner in H.C. Wainwright & Co. on Wall St., New York City.

Children in 11th Gen. b. in Portsmouth, N. H.

F12271 LOUIS, III, b. April 12, 1946, m. Spicer, Minn., June 18, 1971, CAROL LYGRE.

12272 JOHN, b. Feb. 29, 1948. Attended the Univ. of Arizona earning a B.S. in Aerospace Engineering and a B.S. in Mechanical Engineering, 1971 and M.S. in Aeronautical Engineering, 1972. Presently a Captain in U.S. Air Force Reserve and pilot of an F4E Phantom Jet Fighter.

F11435 SHERMAN STANDISH LOCKE, born in Methuen, Mass., Feb. 2, 1917, married in Frederick, Md., Sept. 28, 1944, BARBARA PHYLLIS KNIGHT, born in Burlington, Vt., April 24, 1922.
He graduated from Phillips Exeter Academy in 1937 and Bowdoin College in 1941. He served with the United States Navy during WW II and was discharged with the rank of Lt. Junior grade.
He entered the family contracting firm of L. E. Locke and Son. He also worked with the Internal Revenue Service and is now retired. He is a Third Degree Mason in the Phoenician Lodge.
She graduated from Westbrook Junior College in 1942 and served with the Waves in the United States Navy during WW II as a Laboratory Technician. She has been active in The North Andover Garden Club, The Shawsheen Village Women's Club and is currently active in the Moultonboro Woman's Club and the Moultonboro Methodist Woman's Group. They both enjoy skiing and sailing.

Children in 11th Gen. b. in Lawrence, Mass.

12273 SHERYL SHERMANE, b. Feb. 10, 1948.

12274 JEFFREY LANGDON, b. Dec. 25, 1951.

F11436 RICHARD GORDON LOCKE, born in Methuen, Mass., Jan. 27, 1918, married in Westford, Mass., Jan. 2, 1942, EVELYN MARY CASEY, born in Manchester, N. H., Sept. 6, 1913.

He attended Methuen Public Schools and graduated from Worcester Academy, Worcester, Mass., 1937. He served as a pilot in the Army in the Pacific Theater during WW II, attaining the rank of Capt. With his brother, he operated the construction firm of L. E. Locke & Son. He is Past Master of the Phoenician Lodge A. F. & A. M. in Lawrence, Mass. and Past President of Kiwanis in Lawrence. Presently, he is co-owner of Far Corner Golf Course in W. Boxford, Mass.

Children in 11th Generation

12275 CAROLE JEAN, b. Manchester, N. H., Dec. 13, 1945, m. DONALD STANKATIS.

12276 RICHARD GORDON, JR., b. Lawrence, Mass., Nov. 1, 1947, m. 1966, GAIL HOWARD.

F11439 ANNE MARISE LOCKE, born in Methuen, Mass., July 8, 1923, married in Three Oaks, Mich., Sept. 20, 1946, HOWARD HAMAN, JR., born in Three Oaks, Mich., Sept. 29, 1921.

She attended Methuen Public Schools and Lasell Junior College, Newton, Mass. and is a graduate of Abbot Academy, Andover, Mass.

Children in 11th Gen. b. in La Porte, Ind.

12277 CARA JO, b. July 17, 1948.

12278 MARK STEFAN, b. Dec. 19, 1950.

F11440 FLORENCE JEANETTE LOCKE, born in Portsmouth, N. H., Jan. 21, 1923, married in Covington, Ky., Jan. 30, 1943, RALPH GEORGE DAVIS.

Children in 11th Generation

12279 RALPH GEORGE, JR., b. Denver, Colo., Jan. 30, 1945, m. Cleveland, Ohio, May 23, 1970, KAREN MAPES and had: 12280 ALLISON, b. Nov. 30, 1971.

12281 STUART LANE, b. July 13, 1951, m. Cleveland, Ohio, Sept. 22, 1973, MARY MALBASA.

12282 PAMELA JEAN, b. Cleveland, Ohio, Oct. 10, 1953.

F11441 PHYLLIS THATCHER, born in Portsmouth, N. H., Sept. 16, 1924, married Dec. 30, 1945, FRED ETHELBERT ELDER, born Feb. 27, 1925.

Children in 11th Generation

12283 ANDREW WILLIAM, b. Indianapolis, Ind., Aug. 25, 1948,
       m. Feb. 9, 1971, JACQUELYN LEE and had: 12284
       NICOLE VANIA, b. Aug. 13, 1972.

12285 BONNIE LYNN, b. Ossining, N.Y., May 5, 1951.

F11450 DAVID HENRY LOCKE, born in Boston, Mass., Aug. 4,
1927, married in Wellesley, Mass., 1952, BARBARA BLOOD, born
May 22, 1930.
       He attended Wellesley schools, U.S. Marine Corps, 1944-45, New
Preparatory School, Cambridge, Harvard University, B.A., 1951,
Harvard Law School, 1954. Elected to public office, Town Meeting
member, Town of Wellesley, 17 years; Board of Selectmen, 3 years;
Massachusetts General Court, 16 years; 8 years, House of Representa-
tives; 8 years in Senate. Currently assistant floor leader. Member of
law firm, Jameson-Locke & Fullerton. Member, Norfolk Bar Associa-
tion and Massachusetts Bar Association.
       She is a graduate Wellesley High School, 1948 and Framingham
State College, 1952. Has maintained interest in education and art.
Is a member of Junior Service League of Wellesley.

Children in 11th Gen. b. in Newton, Mass.

12286 DAVID BYRON, b. Sept. 19, 1952.

12287 JEFFREY ALLEN, b. Dec. 22, 1953.

12288 JENNIFER, b. Nov. 30, 1955.

12289 AMY BETH, b. Feb. 19, 1958.

12290 JOHN ADAM, b. Nov. 27, 1962.

F11451 JOHN ALLEN LOCKE, born Nov. 9, 1928, married in
Brookfield, Mass., 1949, EVELENE KILMAIN, born Mar. 25, 1939.
       He attended Wellesley schools, B.A. Dartmouth, 1951, Master
Public Health, University of Michigan, 1959. Employed in field of
Public Health since 1951. Currently with Federal Product Safety
Commission.
       She is a graduate of St. Bernards School, Newton. Did secretarial
work at Babson Reports, Wellesley before marriage.

Children in 11th Generation

12291 JOHN ALLEN, JR., b. Newton, Mass., July 22, 1949,
       m. 1974, JANICE TAYLOR.

12291a THOMAS JOSEPH, b. Newton, Mass., Oct. 28, 1954.

12292 KEVIN VERNON, b. Philadelphia, Pa., Sept. 15, 1959.

12293   ANNE MARIE, b. Philadelphia, Pa., April 13, 1963.

12294   BRIAN, b. Philadelphia, Pa., Jan. 3, 1965.

F11452   ALLEN WILLIAM LOCKE, born in Waltham, Mass., Aug. 24, 1938, married in Washington, D.C., Aug. 20, 1966, ELIZABETH GENTRY HEUN, born in Fort Sill, Oklahoma, Oct. 2, 1942.
He attended public schools of Wellesley, Mass., graduated, 1961 from the University of Mass. with a B.A. degree. Received M.A. in history, 1965 from the University of Mass. Presently employed as a foreign affairs analyst, U.S. Department of State, Wash., D.C.
She graduated from the Madeira School, Greenway, Va. Earned a B.A. degree at Wellesley College, Wellesley, Mass., 1964 and M.A. in art history, 1971 from the American University, Wash., D.C.

Children in 11th Gen. b. in Washington, D.C.

12295   EMILY GENTRY, b. Nov. 28, 1969.

12296   CAROLINE FULLER (twin), b. Aug. 3, 1972.

12297   WILLIAM HOWARD (twin), b. Aug. 3, 1972.

F11453   KENNETH A. BATTEN, born in Corinth, Vt., April 14, 1899, married in Corinth, Vt., Oct. 27, 1921, ANNABELLE CHALMERS WOODCOCK, born in Corinth, Vt., 1893.
He was a very successful farmer in Waits River, Vt. In addition to this he served as mail man on the Bradford to Barre route.
On Oct. 23, 1976 Mr. and Mrs. Batten celebrated their 55th wedding anniversary. In addition to their children, the couple have 20 grandchildren and 12 great grandchildren.

Children in 11th Gen. b. in Waits River, Vt.

F12298   JEANETTE ELEANOR, b. Oct. 18, 1922, m. July 19, 1944, RAYMOND TILLOTSON.

F12299   GARDINER, b. Dec. 8, 1924, m. MARGARET HARTLEY.

F12300   RUSSEL KENNETH, b. Oct. 12, 1927, m. Oct. 8, 1948, ELINOR JOHNSON.

F12301   LOUISE ANABELLE, b. Jan. 29, 1930, m. F. WILLIAM DOE, JR.

F11456   LEWIS WILLIAM BENNETT, born in Milford, Mass., Nov. 17, 1926, married in Stamford, Conn., May 5, 1957, MARY LOUISE ODISEOS.

Children in 11th Generation

12302   DANAE LOUISE, b. Mar. 8, 1959.

12303 LEWIS ANDREW, b. Feb. 7, 1961, d. Jan. 24, 1964.

12304 THOMAS CONSTANTINE, b. Sept. 25, 1964.

F11457 MARY EVELYN BENNETT, born in Milford, Mass., Aug. 16, 1928, married in Grafton, Mass., June 9, 1956, WARREN SCAMMAN.

Children in 11th Generation

12305 JUDITH LEE, b. Oct. 8, 1960.

12306 JANE DIANE, b. Mar. 6, 1962.

12307 STEPHEN HENRY (adopted), b. May 10, 1966.

F11458 FRANCES ALICE BENNETT, born in Worcester, Mass., April 20, 1936, married in Grafton, Mass., Nov. 23, 1962, FREDERICK C. LAING.

Children in 11th Generation

12308 DEIRDRE JEAN, b. Oct. 7, 1964.

12309 JAMES AINSLEY, b. June 11, 1967.

12310 KRISTIN ALICIA, b. Nov. 11, 1972.

F11459 MARGARET JEAN LOCKE, born in Manchester, N. H., Nov. 12, 1936, married in High Point, N. C., Aug. 27, 1957, J. LAWRENCE McCOLLOUGH, born in Birmingham, Ala., Aug. 26, 1935.

He has an A. B. from Wake Forest University, M. A. and Ph. D. from Emory University. Instructor in Philosophy, Wilamette Univ., Salem, Oregon, 1961-63; Assistant Professor of Philosophy, Wake Forest Univ., Winston Salem, N. C., 1963-68; Professor of Philosophy, Clemson, S.C., 1968——— .

She received an A. B. from Duke University and an M. R. E. from Emory University. Director of Christian Education, Methodist Church, Salem, Oregon, 1961-63; teacher in public schools, Clemson, S.C., from 1974.

Children in 11th Generation

12311 LORIN BRADFORD, b. Salem, Ore., July 31, 1962.

12312 LIANE ELAINE, b. Winston Salem, N.C., Feb. 13, 1966.

F11460 MARJORIE SARAH LOCKE, born in Whitefield, N. H., Sept. 28, 1941, married in High Point, N.C., June 14, 1963, DAVID R. BROOKS, born in Evanston, Ill., June 26, 1941.

228   LOCKE GENEALOGY

He received an A. B. from Duke University, an M. A. from College of William and Mary, and is a physicist with the National Aeronautics and Space Administration. She received an A. B. from Greensboro College and was a teacher in public schools, Hampton, Va., 1963-66.

Children in 11th Gen. b. in Yorktown, Va.

12313 GREGORY WILLIAM, b. Aug. 1, 1968.

12314 KARIN ANNETTE, b. Mar. 23, 1971.

F11462 ELIZABETH CHASE, born in Coatsville, Pa., Jan. 17, 1928, married in Oakland, Md., BYRON EARL BESSE, JR.

Children in 11th Generation

12315 BYRON LOCKE, b. Salt Lake City, Utah, June 3, 1951.

12316 ROBERT CHASE, b. Rochester, Minn., Oct. 3, 1952.

12317 ALLISON LOCKE, b. Washington, D.C., Jan. 14, 1957.

F11502 DAVID LESTER JONES, born July 14, 1912,   married HELEN ELIZABETH STARR.

Children in 11th Generation

12318 JANET PEARL, b. Oceanside, Calif., Jan. 22, 1941, m. 1st, LARRY GILL, and had: 12319 LORI RENE, b. 1962; 2nd, SIEGFRIED HORAKH.

12320 DAVID EDWARD, b. Jan. 24, 1945, m. GLENDA ——.

F11503 BARBARA JEAN WILSON, born in Riverside, Calif., Aug. 19, 1917, married in Las Vegas, Nev., April 16, 1954, AUGUSTUS LEE RENNER, JR.
She graduated with A. B. degree from Univ. of Calif. at Berkeley, 1939.

Children in 11th Gen. b. in Oceanside, Calif.

12323 RETA ALICE, b. Mar. 3, 1955.

12324 JERRY LEE MARIA, b. Mar. 16, 1957, m. Las Vegas, Nev., April 25, 1975, ALAN BRUCE CUTSINGER.

F11506 HUGH DANIEL WALLACE, born in Bard, Calif., May 26, 1925, married in Fort Worth, Texas, June 27, 1950, EVELYN WILLIAMS, born in Eagle Pass, Texas, Dec. 24, 1922.
He graduated from Oakdale High School in 1942. Served in the U.S. Navy during WW II, and the U.S. Air Force 1947-1954. Graduated from Fresno State College 1956 with a degree in Physics. Has

worked for Hughes Aircraft since then. Active in the Democratic Party on local and state levels. Active in the Unitarian Churches and a principal founder of churches in Los Angeles area and Lancaster, Calif.

She graduated from Eagle Pass High School, 1940 and Texas State College for Women, Denton, Texas in 1948 with a degree in social work. Also received a Master of Social Work from Univ. of Southern California, 1967.

Children in 11th Generation

12325 KENNETH ALAN, b. Del Rio, Texas, Mar. 27, 1952.
Graduate of Mira Costa High School, Manhattan Beach, Calif. 1970. Attended El Camino Jr. College and Long Beach State Univ. studying structural geology.

12326 KATHRYN LEE, b. Oakdale, Calif., Jan. 11, 1954.
Graduate of Mira Costa High School, 1971. Attended El Camino Jr. College and Long Beach State Univ. where she studied Art Librarianship.

F11507 ROBERT JERI WALLACE, born in Glendale, Calif., Nov. 13, 1931, married in Benidji, Minn., Nov. 28, 1959, BEVERLY JOANNE BLUTH, born in Grey Eagle, Minn., Dec. 24, 1932.

He attended Oakdale, Calif. public schools and Modesto Jr. College. Served in U.S. Air Force. Graduate of Fresno State College, 1957 as electro-mechanical engineer. Attended Stanford University Graduate School of Engineering. Has worked at Jet Propulsion Laboratories since 1961. Active in the direction of the Pasadena Art Museum. She attended public schools in Little Falls, Minn. Graduated as a surgical nurse from St. Scholastica College, Duluth, Minn., 1954. Active in community affairs in La Canada, Calif.

Children in 11th Generation

12327 WILLIAM JERI, b. Palo Alto, Calif., Dec. 21, 1960.

12328 MICHAEL STEVEN, b. Palo Alto, Calif., Dec. 3, 1961.

12329 ELIZABETH JOANNE, b. Pasadena, Calif., June 3, 1967.

12330 THERESA DIANE, b. Pasadena, Calif., June 28, 1968.

F11510 PHYLLIS ANNE WHEAT, born in Fulton, Mo., Oct. 30, 1925, married EDWARD STARR.

Children in 11th Generation

12331 ANNE, b. Jan. 22, 1954.

12332 CHARLES EDWARD, b. Jan. 22, 1954.

12333 SUSAN, b. Jan. 22, 1954.

12334 NELL ELIZABETH, b. Feb. 4, 1959.

12335 RICHARD, b. 1962.

F11515 GRAYDON REED LOCKE, born in St. Johnsbury, Vt., Aug. 20, 1915, married in Sharon, Mass., Feb. 23, 1940, ELEANOR MAY ROTTE, born in Needham, Mass., Sept. 7, 1917.

He attended Medford, Somerville and Needham, Mass. public schools and graduated from the Mass. School of Art. He served in the U.S. Navy during WW II and worked as a draftsman in the aircraft manufacturing business. After sustaining severe injuries in an aircraft accident he and his wife moved to Clearwater, Fla. They operate a ladies-wear consignment shop in Sarasota.

Children in 11th Generation

12336 SHARON ELEANOR, b. Boston, Mass., Sept. 5, 1944, m. Carson City, Nev., June 27, 1964, JAMES CLARENCE SUMMERS.

12337 WENDY GAY, b. Norwood, Mass., Aug. 13, 1951, m. Santa Clara, Calif., Oct. 24, 1970, STEVEN JAY GUST.

F11516 KERMIT ALBION LOCKE, born in St. Johnsbury, Vt., Aug. 28, 1916, married in Arlington, Mass., Feb. 14, 1942, VIRGINIA MARGARET KEEFE, born in Cambridge, Mass., Oct. 30, 1919.

He attended Needham Public Schools and Northeastern University evening classes. He served in the U.S. Army during WW II and is a member of the American Legion. He is presently president of Vanguard Supply, Inc. in No. Grafton, Mass. and resides in Harvard.

Children in 11th Gen. b. in Boston, Mass.

12338 MARTHA JEAN, b. April 13, 1943, m. Harvard, Mass., May 6, 1966, MICHAEL J. TOTARO, M.D.

12339 CAROLE ANNE, b. Aug. 28, 1945, m. Dallas, Texas, Aug. 1, 1967, LEWIS E. VAUGHT.

12340 RALPH CHRISTOPHER, b. Feb. 10, 1953.

F11517 MAURICE SINCLAIR LOCKE, born in St. Johnsbury, Vt., May 27, 1918, married in Newton Highlands, Mass., Sept. 3, 1940, DOROTHY LOIS BANKS, born May 12, 1918.

He graduated from Needham High School and Scott Carbee Art School, Boston. Now semi-retired he works in art and home construction.

Children in 11th Generation

F12341 GILBERT EVERETT, b. Brooklyn, N.Y., July 2, 1941, m.
        Sept. 2, 1959, GLENDA DELORES CLARK.

F12342 MARJORIE CAROLE, b. Newton, Mass., Jan. 14, 1943,
        m. Denver, Colo., Sept. 1, 1963, ROBERT JACKSON
        BAIR.

F12343 GERALDINE DIANE, b. Newton, Mass., April 23, 1945,
        m. Mountain View, Calif., Dec. 18, 1965, CHRISTO-
        PHER LEE CARTER.

F12344 JANICE ELAINE, b. Boulder, Colo., July 21, 1951, m.
        Redding, Calif., Nov. 18, 1972, DAVID JAMES
        EGGEN.

12345   VERNON GEORGE, b. Boulder, Colo., Feb. 5, 1953.

F11518 CORINNE LUCILLE LOCKE, born in Medford, Mass.,
Aug. 20, 1920, married in Needham, Mass., Oct. 1, 1942, KENNETH
WILLIAM GLAZEBROOK.
    She is a graduate of Needham, Mass. High School and Jackson
Von Ladau School of Fashion Design. She is interested in art,
antiques, and interior design.

        Children in 11th Gen. b. in Newton, Mass.

12346   KENNETH WILLIAM, JR., b. Jan. 5, 1944, m. June 17,
        1970, MARSHA GALBACH.

12347   DEBORAH BETH, b. Oct. 19, 1945, m. May 20, 1972,
        GEORGE EVANS CLARK, JR.

F11519 WILLIAM GIFFIN LOCKE, JR., born in Medford, Mass.,
April 29, 1929, married 1st in Bethesda, Md., Oct. 6, 1951, MARY
MARTINEZ, born in Boston, Mass., Oct. 23, 1928, divorced in
Canandaigua, N.Y., July 29, 1976; 2nd, in Rochester, N.Y., Sept.
30, 1976, ANN SWIGART SWAIN, born in Boston, Mass., Nov. 20,
1930.
    He is a graduate of Northeastern Univ., 1958 with a B. B. A.
degree. He resides in Rochester, N.Y.

        Children in 11th Gen. b. in Boston, Mass.

12348   KATHY JEAN, b. Nov. 27, 1954.

12349   JOHN CHARLES, b. July 10, 1959.

F11522 ELMER GEORGE WENHOLD, born in Portsmouth, N.H.,
April 19, 1917, married 1st, 1941, HELEN JOHNSON; 2nd, 1961,
NANCY THAYER; 3rd, May 1, 1976, ALICE (LECERT) WELCH.

He was owner and captain of charter schooners "Flying Cloud III" and "Courageous" out of Newport, R. I. and Nassau, Bahamas. He operated his own shipyard and later was national sales manager for Colonial Pine Craft, Haverhill, Mass. He lives in So. Berwick, Me.

Children in 11th Gen. b. in Portsmouth, N. H.

12350 ROBERT JOSEPH, b. 1941.

12351 SHIRLEY ANNE, b. 1942.

12352 GEORGE ELMER, b. 1943.

12353 JOSEPH, b. 1948.

12354 JANICE, b. 1952.

F11528 NANCY RUTH DISBROW, born in Schenectady, N. Y., April 6, 1953, married in Stockton, Calif., Mar. 10, 1972, JAMES MORGAN BUSHAW, born in Oakland, Calif., Jan. 26, 1952, son of Clyde and Irene (Demas) Bushaw.

Children in 11th Generation

12355 ERIC NATHAN, b. Stockton, Calif., Aug. 8, 1975.

F11548 WHITNEY SIMONDS, born in Providence, R. I., April 28, 1935, married July 25, 1959, LEONARD AUGUSTUS YERKES III, born Aug. 11, 1936.

Children in 11th Generation

12356 AMY BALDWIN, b. Providence, R. I., Mar. 1, 1962.

12357 FAITH MALTBY, b. Providence, R. I., May 5, 1965.

12358 PHILIP E., b. Calif., June 11, 1972.

F11554 PRISCILLA LILLIAN MOQUIN, born in Holyoke, Mass., June 7, 1940, married in Holyoke, Mass., June 30, 1962, ROLAND JEAN-BERCHMANS GODDER, born in Holyoke, Mass., Aug. 1, 1936. She graduated from Holyoke High School, 1958 and College of Our Lady of the Elms, Chicopee, Mass., 1962. Her husband has a Master of Education degree from the University of Mass. and a Doctor of Education from Harvard University, 1966. He had been Dean of the School of Education, Catholic University of America, Washington, D.C. before coming to Durham, N. H. as Executive Director, New England Program in Teacher Education in 1968. They are active in church work, environmental programs, community projects, and athletic programs involving their children.

Children in 11th Generation

12359 CHRISTOPHER ROLAND, b. Sharon, Conn., April 23, 1963.

12360 TERESA ALICE, b. Holyoke, Mass., June 18, 1964.

12361 CAROLINE IRENE, b. July 8, 1966.

F11556 LEON B. MEADER, JR., born in Charleston, Maine area, 1940, married in Acton, Mass., by his father, to RUTH LEE GRAY, born in Rochester, N.H., July 15, 1944.

He owns Bud Meader General Contractors which operates from the Meader Heritage Farm which they now own. This is the farm where Elizabeth Meader Locke was born. Her father bought the farm in 1769 which has been owned by Meaders since.

Children in 11th Gen. b. in Rochester, N.H.

12362 LORRAINE SUSAN, b. Sept. 2, 1961.

12363 LINDA MARY, b. June 20, 1963.

12364 ROBERT PAUL, b. Oct. 12, 1964.

F11618 KENNETH EDWARD MARSTON, born in Manchester, N.H., Sept. 28, 1940, married 1st, in Manchester, N.H., Nov. 1959, BETTY JANE SPAULDING; 2nd, in Bedford, N.H., Aug. 23, 1964, ELIZABETH ANN MURRAY, born in Cambridge, Mass., Feb. 23, 1942.

He was active in Cub and Boy Scouts and Church. Finished schools in Manchester, N.H. Was in engineering corps for two years while in the service. Hobbies were bowling, drag racing and won trophies. Has always been interested in mechanics.

Children in 11th Generation

12365 TAMMY JANE, b. Nashua, N.H., April 14, 1960.

12366 ROBIN ELIZABETH (adopted), b. Weymouth, Mass., Oct. 13, 1962.

F11619 JOE RUSSELL MARSTON, born in Manchester, N.H., Sept. 22, 1942, married in Manchester, N.H., Sept. 16, 1967, LINDA JEANE LECLERC, born in Manchester, N.H., Nov. 19, 1942.

"I was an ugly baby, but now one of the best looking. Activities include bowling, scouting, church and sex. Finished school in Merrimack, N.H., took an Aviation Correspondence course and was in the Air National Guard for four years. Traveled all over the world with the Guard. Right now am the manager of an Insurance Company. "

(direct quote)

Children in 11th Gen. b. in Manchester, N.H.

12367 CHRISTIAN JOHN, b. May 30, 1969.

12368 CRAIG DAVID, b. Jan. 6, 1971.

12369 CARYN BETH, b. Feb. 17, 1972.

F11620 JEFFERY STEPHEN MARSTON, born in Manchester, N. H.,
Sept. 24, 1949, married in Manchester, N. H., Oct. 3, 1970, LINDA
ELIZABETH VIEIRA, born in Manchester, N. H., Aug. 19, 1951.
 Finished school in Manchester, N. H. Was a little dare-devil as a
teenager, but nothing serious. As a kid, loved hobbies such as fishing,
hunting. Is interested in snow mobiling.

Children in 11th Gen. b. in Manchester, N. H.

12370 KEVIN ALLEN, b. Oct. 20, 1971.

12371 JENNIFER LYNN, b. July 3, 1974.

F11622 EDITH FRANCES FLINT, born in Lowell, Mass., July 10,
1879, died in Lowell, Mass., Jan. 10, 1965, married in Lowell,
Mass., Oct. 20, 1903, WALTER NEEDHAM BURTT, born in Lowell,
Mass., died in Lowell, Mass., Sept. 29, 1938.
 He was a division Station Accountant and worked for N. Y. N. H. &
H. Railroad for 42 years. Belonged to the Masons and church.
 She was a member of the Daughters of the American Revolution-
regent and state officer, Colonial Dames, Patriots and Founders, Lady
Gunner, Ancient & Honorable Artillery, Daughters of the Colonial
Wars, Mayflower Ancestors, Colonial Clergy, King's Daughters, etc.
She was a professional genealogist.

Children in 11th Gen. b. in Lowell, Mass.

12372 RICHARD FLINT, b. Sept. 12, 1904, m. Lowell, Mass.,
 Oct. 12, 1935, RUTH MOREY MEERSMAN.

F12373 JOSEPH FREDERIC, b. April 4, 1908, m. Derry Village,
 N. H., July 16, 1938, MARGUERITE T. RICHARDS.

12374 CATHERINE NEEDHAM, b. Jan. 5, 1917.

F11631 JoANN JUNE CALHOUN, born in Des Moines, Iowa,
June 11, 1935, married in Des Moines, Iowa, Nov. 19, 1954, JACK
HARVEY, born in Des Moines, Iowa, Jan. 24, 1933.

Children in 11th Generation

12375 JAMES DOUGLAS, b. Des Moines, Iowa, June 15, 1955.

12376 CAROLYN KAY, b. Des Moines, Iowa, Sept. 21, 1956.

12377 DIANE, b. San Jose, Calif., April 5, 1963.

F11632 JOHN RICHARD CALHOUN, born in Des Moines, Iowa, Dec. 17, 1937, married in Winnebago, Minn., July 29, 1963, LEORA LOUISA GRIFFITH, born in Amboy, Minn., June 24, 1939, daughter of Harold E. and Dorothy Ferne (Phipps) Griffith.

Children in 11th Gen. b. in Des Moines, Iowa

12378 JOHN DANIEL, b. Jan. 28, 1965.

12379 CHRISTOPHER ANDREW, b. Dec. 6, 1971.

F11633 LINDA CAROL CALHOUN, born in Des Moines, Iowa, Dec. 25, 1942, married in Des Moines, Iowa, Aug. 21, 1965, LARRY RAY COOK, born in Des Moines, Iowa, Dec. 30, 1942.

Children in 11th Generation

12380 MICHAEL RAY, b. Fort Bragg, N.C., Aug. 21, 1968.

12381 JEFFREY LAURENCE, b. St. Paul, Minn., April 9, 1971.

F11637 ELLEN MAY ELLIS, born in Des Moines, Iowa, July 20, 1943, married in Camp Zama, Japan, Mar. 4, 1964, DARIELL WAYNE MILLER.

Children in 11th Generation

12382 VERA LYNN, b. Camp Zama, Japan, Jan. 21, 1965.

12383 JOHN DAVID, b. Camp Zama, Japan, Oct. 26, 1967.

12384 POLLY, b. Carmichael, Calif., Nov. 14, 1970.

F11639 CHARLOTTE BOOTH, born in Evanston, Ill., Dec. 25, 1941, married in Glencoe, Ill., Sept. 16, 1961, CHARLES BARNETT, born in Chicago, Ill., Jan. 10, 1937, son of Gayle S. and Lillian (Wilson) Barnett.

Children in 11th Generation

12385 SHEILA, b. Evanston, Ill., May 5, 1962.

12386 PHILLIP, b. Evanston, Ill., June 21, 1963.

12387 CYNTHIA, b. Clinton, Iowa, Nov. 12, 1966.

F11644 ROBERT KENT HOUSER, born in Oberlin, Ohio, Nov. 9, 1946, married in Lancaster, Penna., June 1, 1968, SYLVIA MARIE PFAFFLE, born in Lancaster, Penna., June 8, 1946.

Children in 11th Generation

12388 KAREN ELIZABETH, b. Binghamton, N.Y., Jan. 1, 1969.

12389 JUSTIN DANIEL, b. Chicago, Ill., Oct. 27, 1970.

F11646 DAVID CLOSE HOUSER, born in Vancouver, Wash., Dec. 20, 1950, married in Valdosta, Ga., June 6, 1971, CONNY LOUISE VONK, born in Amsterdam, Holland, Jan. 9, 1950.

Children in 11th Generation

12390 THEADORA, b. West Palm Beach, Fla., Jan. 10, 1971.

F11651 DORIS THELMA EDGCOMB, born in Pasadena, Calif., July 21, 1925, married 1st in San Diego, Calif., 1943, ROBERT SMITH, born in Grand Junction, Colo., April 4, 1918; 2nd, in Las Vegas, Nev., 1946, EMMETT GOLDEN, born in Los Angeles, Calif., Feb. 17, 1917, son of Joseph Michael and Berdinah (Dykstra) Golden; 3rd, in Pasadena, Calif., Oct. 21, 1960, JOHN LESLIE BUCHANAN, born in Kennewick, Wash., May 9, 1919, son of John C. and Gussela Buchanan.

Children in 11th Gen. b. in Pasadena, Calif.

F12391 CORILEE DORIS SMITH, b. April 30, 1944.

F12392 DENNIS MICHAEL GOLDEN, b. Aug. 4, 1946.

F12393 THOMAS PATRICK GOLDEN, b. Aug. 17, 1947.

12394 JANICE MARY GOLDEN, b. May 10, 1951, m. Pasadena, Calif., AMIR H. KOJOURY, b. Tehran, Iran, Mar. 25, 1935, son of Ali and Zahra Kojori.

F11657 ROBERTA LEE CULVER, born in Melrose, Mass., Sept. 17, 1933, married in Melrose, Mass., Mar. 19, 1955, DONALD ROBERT JOHNSON, born in Everett, Mass., June 13, 1935, son of Henry A. and Winifred (Littlewood) Johnson.

Children in 11th Gen. b. in Melrose, Mass.

12395 STEVEN ROBERT, b. Mar. 28, 1956.

12396 KRISTIN LEE, b. Aug. 29, 1958.

12397 SUSAN MARY, b. June 5, 1961.

12398 SHARON ELEANOR, b. Sept. 9, 1962.

F11658 JUDITH MARILYN CULVER, born in Melrose, Mass., Sept. 22, 1936, married in Melrose, Mass., Dec. 27, 1958, JAMES SHANNON WHITE, SR., born in Kansas City, Mo., Jan. 5, 1935, son of Shannon Vincel and Bernice (Maxwell) White.

Children in 11th Generation

12399 JAMES SHANNON, b. Melrose, Mass., Aug. 28, 1962.

12400 JENNIFER SUSAN, b. Melrose, Mass., May 9, 1965.

12400a JONATHAN KIETH, b. Danvers, Mass., Feb. 23, 1973.

F11659 ROBERT DeWITT CULVER, JR., born in Melrose, Mass.,
Dec. 10, 1943, married in Grove City, Penna., Aug. 23, 1969,
MARY JANE YOUNG, born in Grove City, Penna., May 21, 1944,
daughter of Edward and Mabel (McNeish) Young.

Children in 11th Generation

12401 CYNTHIA LEE, b. Melrose, Mass., June 14, 1970.

12402 KIMBERLY ANNE, b. Woburn, Mass., May 11, 1973.

F11699 WYLIE FOSTER VERGE, born in Barss' Corners, N. S.,
married Sept. 24, 1955, MARGARET MacKENNON.

Children in 11th Generation

12403 WYLIE HUGH, b. Aug. 6, 1956.

12404 JANE ELIZABETH (twin), b. Jan. 17, 1958.

12405 ALEXANDER GORDON (twin), b. Jan. 17, 1958.

12406 ALICE MARGARET, b. June 29, 1963.

F11702 ALTHEA LUCILLE FORD, born in Danbury, N. H., April
20, 1921, married in Danbury, N. H., Sept. 22, 1945, ROYCE
ALISON HASKELL.
  She graduated from Plymouth Teacher's College, 1943 and pres-
ently teaches 3rd grade in Littleton, N. H. He has been a jeweler in
Littleton for more than 20 years.

Children in 11th Gen. b. in Littleton, N. H.

12407 ANNE JOYCE, b. July 17, 1948, m. Littleton, N. H.,
       July 22, 1974, JOSEPH TIMMERMAN. She is a teacher
       in Tempe, Ariz.

12408 PAUL FORD, b. Oct. 19, 1951. Graduate of Ariz. State
       Univ. as an Architecture major.

12409 JEANNE ALTHEA (twin), b. Oct. 31, 1955. Attending
       the University of New Hampshire.

12409a CAROL DORIS (twin), b. Oct. 31, 1955. Attending the
       University of New Hampshire.

F11703 CHARLES RUSSELL FORD, born in Harrison, Maine, Jan.
17, 1927, married in Saratoga Springs, N. Y., Mar. 14, 1953,
ANNAMAY TAYLOR.
  He served in the Air Force during WW II. Graduated from Burdett
Business College and works for Prudential Insurance Co.

Children in 11th Gen. b. in Pittsfield, Mass.

12410 MARK TAYLOR, b. Sept. 7, 1955. He is a sophomore at
       A. I. C. in Springfield, Mass.

12411 ELIZABETH ANN, b. Dec. 6, 1957.

12412 GAIL MARIE FORD, b. Dec. 21, 1960, d. Pittsfield,
       Mass., April 11, 1961.

F11704 ARTHUR SUTHERLAND FORD, born in Harrison, Maine,
Feb. 17, 1928, married in Barnstead, N. H., July 21, 1951,
MARJORIE EQUI.
He enlisted in the Army and was stationed at Fort Belvoir, Va. He
attended Univ. of New Hampshire and is Construction Supervisor for
Ebasco Services.

Children in 11th Generation

12413 PEGGY LOUISE, b. Wolfboro, N. H., Oct. 17, 1952.
       She is on the staff of the Eureka Springs, Arkansas
       weekly newspaper and is a 1974 graduate of the Univ.
       of So. Florida.

12413a PATRICIA RUSSELL, b. Littleton, N. Y., Nov. 25, 1954.
       She is a sophomore at the University of Louisiana, Baton
       Rouge.

12414 PETER EQUI, b. Sand Point, Idaho, May 1, 1957.

12415 PAMELA TERESA, b. Lewiston, N. Y., Jan. 13, 1959.

F11705 JOHN BROOKS FORD, born in Danbury, N. H., Aug. 8,
1932, married in Wilder, Vt., Sept. 15, 1956, JANET LEAVITT.
He served in the Navy during WW II on the aircraft carrier Mid-
way. Works for N. Y. Life Ins. Co. in Manchester as Ass't Manager.

Children in 11th Gen. b. in Lebanon, N. H.

12416 RAND LEAVITT, b. April 11, 1957.

12417 ROBIN LEE, b. July 15, 1963.

F11706 KIRKE CURRIER JORGENSEN, born in San Jose, Calif.,
July 26, 1945, married in Riverside, Calif., Nov. 1, 1969, VENITA
JEAN McPHERSON, born in Arizona, Nov. 25, 1945.
Holds a B. A. in Economics from Univ. of Calif. in Santa Barbara.
Served two years as a Lieutenant in the U.S. Army Signal Corps in
Germany. Now employed by Sears, Roebuck and Co. and living in
Riverside. She holds B. A. from Univ. of Calif. in Santa Barbara and
M. A. in Library Science from Univ. of Calif. at Los Angeles.

Children in 11th Generation

12418 ERIK CURRIER JORGENSEN, b. Riverside, Calif., Jan. 20, 1974.

F11709 JOHN MALCOLM LOCKE, born in Rochester, N. H., Oct. 15, 1931, married Dec. 10, 1950, EVELYN TASKER.

Children in 11th Generation

12419 MAE, b. Wolfeboro, N. H., July 1, 1951, m. Concord, N. H., Aug. 1971, WAYNE LENNON and had: 12420 WAYNE MATTHEW, b. Dec. 13, 1972; 12421 ELIZABETH ANN, b. Oct. 17, 1974.

12422 RICHARD MALCOLM, b. Wolfeboro, N.H., July 20, 1952, m. Bow Lake, Northwood, N. H., June 21, 1975, CAROL SMITH.

12423 NATHAN JEFFREY, b. Concord, N. H., Jan. 1, 1958.

12424 GEORGE MALCOLM, b. Wolfeboro, N. H., Oct. 4, 1966.

F11711 SHARON KATHLEEN LOCKE, born in Rochester, N. H., Mar. 7, 1944, married in Barnstead, N.H., Feb. 4, 1964, ROGER TREMBLAY.

Children in 11th Generation

12425 ELLEN MARIE, b. Aug. 13, 1964.

12426 DAVID ALLEN, b. Nov. 1, 1966.

12427 STEPHAN MICHAEL, b. Mar. 24, 1969.

F11712 KENT DREW LOCKE, JR., born in Wolfeboro, N. H., Oct. 10, 1936, married Sept. 27, 1958, JEAN AUDREY POWERS.

Children in 11th Generation

12428 SUSAN ANDREA, b. Fort Lewis, Wash., June 28, 1960.

12429 NANCY JEAN, b. Laconia, N. H., May 9, 1962.

12430 ANDREW KENT, b. Medfield, Mass., April 9, 1968.

F11713 JAMES NUTTER LOCKE, born in Wolfeboro, N. H., Dec. 21, 1937, married in Gilmanton Iron Works, N. H., Nov. 14, 1959, NATALIE JEAN PRICE.

Children in 11th Generation

12431 JAMES NUTTER II, b. Exeter, N. H., April 27, 1960.

12432   MARGARET JEAN, b. Concord, N. H., Nov. 2, 1964.

F11714   THOMAS GEORGE LOCKE, born in Wolfeboro, N. H., Feb. 14, 1940, married in North Barnstead, N. H., Oct. 15, 1966, JOANNE DEE MEUNIER.

Children in 11th Gen. b. in Concord, N. H.

12433   SARA ANN, b. April 6, 1967.

12434   JEREMEY THOMAS, b. Mar. 22, 1964.

F11715   DEBORAH LANE, born in Keene, N. H., Aug. 31, 1942, married in Wash., D. C., Nov. 17, 1962, EARL WALTER ESCH-BACHER, born in Wash., D. C., Aug. 31, 1939.
She is a graduate of the Univ. of Maryland with a B. A. degree. She is a teacher in Prince George's County, Md. and has been active in Girl Scouts and recreational activities in her community.

Children in 11th Gen. b. in Washington, D. C.

12435   KIMBALL COSTINA, b. Dec. 24, 1963.

12436   JULIA MARIA, b. April 27, 1967.

F11716   JOHN TIMOTHY LANE, born in Richmond, Va., Feb. 15, 1945, married in Wash., D. C., Aug. 16, 1967, SUZANNE HAIRFIELD, born in Wash., D. C., Sept. 11, 1948.
He is a graduate of Augusta Military Academy, Staunton, Va. and attended Monatee Jr. College, Bradenton, Fla. He is employed by American Air Lines.

Children in 11th Gen. b. in Washington, D. C.

12437   JOHN TIMOTHY, b. Nov. 14, 1967.

12438   JUSTIN PATRICK, b. Nov. 27, 1969.

F11717   PENELOPE LANE, born in Wash., D. C., Sept. 16, 1949, married in Wash., D. C., June 19, 1971, EUGENE WILLIAMS, JR., born in Wash., D. C., June 14, 1948.
She is a graduate of the Univ. of Maryland and a member of Delta Delta Delta, a national sorority and the D. A. R.

Children in 11th Generation

12439   JEFFREY RYAN, b. Jacksonville, Fla., Mar. 31, 1975.

F11719   RONALD McDUFFEE, born in Waits River, Vt., April 27, 1915, married Mar. 10, 1939, DAISY HALL, born June 19, 1918.

Children in 11th Gen. b. in Plymouth, Mass.

F12440 BETTY, b. July 26, 1945, m. 1st, DWIGHT PIERCE, (divorced); 2nd, LAWRENCE STRASSEL.

12441 NANCY, b. Nov. 11, 1941.

F11723 CHARLES ARTHUR BODKIN, born in Evanston, Ill., April 25, 1937, married in Evanston, Ill., Oct. 14, 1961, PRISCILLA JEAN VOIGT, born in East Troy, Wis., Sept. 9, 1937.

Children in 11th Generation

12444 LINDA LORI, b. Evanston, Ill., June 13, 1962.

12445 ROSE MARIE (adopted), b. Chicago, Ill., July 20, 1963.

F11725 DAVID CLARENDON WRIGHT, born in Haverhill, Mass., June 28, 1925, married in Haverhill, Mass., Sept. 1, 1946, HARRIET LOUISE PARKS, born in San Diego, Calif., Mar. 8, 1926.

Children in 11th Gen. b. in San Diego, Calif.

12446 DAVID PRESCOTT, b. May 20, 1951, m. El Cajon, Calif.,
June 13, 1976, STEPHANY GENE GLASSON.

12447 BRADFORD WILSON, b. Mar. 14, 1953.

12448 CARON LOUISE, b. May 2, 1956, m. Las Vegas, Nev.,
Jan. 17, 1976, ROBERT E. NEFF, JR.

12449 THOMAS CLARENDON, b. April 17, 1959.

12450 REBECCA SUE, b. July 29, 1960.

F11726 DOUGLAS REID HOWARD, born in Pittsburgh, Penna., June 8, 1931, married Dec. 19, 1952, LARUE CREPPS, born in Chicago, Ill., Sept. 7, 1931.

Children in 11th Gen. b. in Chicago, Ill.

12451 LINDA SUE, b. Dec. 7, 1953, m. Dalton, Ill., Feb. 20,
1973, PETER BARCLAY.

12452 DOUGLAS STANTON, b. July 21, 1956.

F11727 JANET ELIZABETH HOWARD, born in Pittsburgh, Penna., July 28, 1935, married Aug. 17, 1957, VERYL DRUMMOND JOHNSON, born in Niagara Falls, N.Y., May 24, 1933.
She is a graduate of Northwestern University with a B.S. degree. Member of Alpha Phi Sorority. Works with pre-school children, and is a member of the Northminster United Presbyterian church in Dallas, Texas.

He is a graduate of Northwestern University with a B.A. degree. Member of Theta Delta Chi Fraternity. Employed by Union Carbide Corp. in Sales Department. Member and officer of Northminster United Presbyterian church of Dallas, Texas.

Children in 11th Generation

12453   KENNETH DAVID, b. Staten Island, N.Y., June 6, 1959.

12454   SARAH LYNN, b. Staten Island, N.Y., June 24, 1960.

12455   STEPHEN MICHAEL, b. Dallas, Texas, Jan. 10, 1965.

12456   JANEL SUZANNE, b. Dallas, Texas, Oct. 25, 1968.

F11728 RONALD ALBERT HOWARD, born in Biddeford, Maine, Mar. 16, 1937, married in Brunswick, Maine, Feb. 10, 1962, JOLEEN PATRICIA BARKER, born in Brunswick, Maine, Feb. 16, 1940.

He is a graduate of Biddeford High School and the Univ. of Maine at Orono, receiving his Bachelor of Science degree in Chemical Engineering. While in Biddeford he was Master Councillor in the Order of DeMolay. Refusing to teach third year chemistry at the Univ. of Maine, he chose instead to be employed by the Union Carbide Corp. He is holder of several inventions, the best known being—when only at the age of 20—developed the so-called "heat shield" on space vehicles for use at the reentry period into the earth's atmosphere; and shortly thereafter the invention of a fuel element for use in nuclear reactors, patented in the United States (Pat. #3 438 858)Great Britain, Germany, France, Italy and Japan. He is a member of the Masonic fraternities and the Congregational church in Cleveland, Ohio.

She is the daughter of Frank and Etta Barker of Brunswick, Maine. A graduate of Brunswick High School and the University of Maine at Orono, receiving the Bachelor of Arts degree in Sociology, and since has received her masters in Education at Cleveland, Ohio. She is a member of the Congregational church and Eastern Star at Cleveland.

Children in 11th Generation

12457   WENDY JEAN, b. Lawrenceburg, Tenn., Nov. 9, 1964.

12458   SHERYL ANN, b. Cleveland, Ohio, May 19, 1969.

F11729 BERYL ANN HOWARD, born in Biddeford, Maine, Aug. 17, 1942, married June 22, 1963, CHARLES EDGAR HOBART, born in Edmunds, Maine, April 20, 1931.

She is a graduate of the Biddeford High School and Boston University as Medical Technologist. She was employed by University Hospital for several years and at that time a central figure in the development of estrogen hormones for women. She is a medical technologist in Biddeford. She is a member of the United Methodist church and Eastern Star of Biddeford.

He is a direct descendant of Vice Pres. Garrett A. Hobart who served under President McKinley, was graduated from the Machias High School, and served in the U.S. Army with distinction. Later he was a buyer for Sears, Roebuck in Boston and presently an executive for Stultz Electric Co. of Portland, Maine.

Children in 11th Gen. b. in Biddeford, Maine

12459 HOLLY MARIE, b. Mar. 16, 1969.

12460 AARON LOCKE, b. Aug. 18, 1975.

F11734 DIANE ALICE HAYES, born in Lawrence, Mass., July 23, 1951, married in Andover, Mass., June 27, 1970, DENNIS MICHAEL TRAYNOR, born in Lawrence, Mass., May 26, 1949, son of Francis and June (Crowley) Traynor.

She graduated from Andover High School, 1969, and Forsythe School for Dental Hygienists in 1972. During her high school years she was a member of the girls gymnastics team and played the trombone in the band. Her interests include gardening, sewing and the domestic arts.

He graduated from Central Catholic High School, Lawrence, Mass. and attended St. Anselms College. He is an insurance salesman and they live in Chester, N.H.

Children in 11th Generation

12461 NOELLE MARIE, b. Lawrence, Mass., Jan. 14, 1971.

12462 LOUISE MARTHA, b. Methuen, Mass., Aug. 26, 1975. She is named for her great grandmother Louise Martha.

12463 SARAH GRACE, b. Methuen, Mass., Jan. 16, 1978. She is named for her great-great-grandmother Sarah Atlanta Pratt Morse and her grandmother, #F11066 Grace Esther Moore Hayes.

F11736 GEORGE EARLE LUCY, JR., born in Amesbury, Mass., July 5, 1928, married in Las Vegas, Nev., June 15, 1954, GLADYS F. VERGAS, born in Haverhill, Mass., June 9, 1934.

He served 4 years in Navy World War II. College 2 years after High School. Studied Electronics and is now an industrial electrician working in Woodland Hills, Calif. at present.

Children in 11th Gen. b. in Hollywood, Calif.

12463a GEORGE EARLE, 3rd, b. Oct. 11, 1955.

12463b KEVIN E., b. Aug. 17, 1957.

F11737 BARBARA MAE LUCY, born in Amesbury, Mass., Oct. 14, 1930, married in Newburyport, Mass., Sept. 17, 1949, LOUIS J. BEAULIEU, born in Ipswich, Mass., Mar. 17, 1926, died in North Andover, Mass., Jan. 24, 1974.

She attended grade and high schools. Is now employed for past 15 years at Western Electric.

Children in 11th Gen. b. in Newburyport, Mass.

F12464 JOSEPH LOUIS, b. Oct. 23, 1950, m. Newburyport, Mass., June 12, 1971, SHARON M. KELLEY.

12465 ROBERT E., b. July 9, 1952.

12466 BRUCE N., b. May 4, 1957.

12467 DEBORA A., b. Dec. 1, 1959.

F11738 ELLEN JANE LUCY, born in Haverhill, Mass., Aug. 9, 1944, married second, in Plaistow, N.H., Mar. 7, 1969, MICHALE WALSH, born in Lynn, Mass., May 13, 1940.

Children in 11th Generation

12468 PATRICIA ANN WALSH (adopted), b. Haverhill, Mass., Oct. 25, 1962.

F11739 DOROTHY MAY LUCY, born in Haverhill, Mass., Aug. 10, 1944, married second, PAUL CHRIONE, divorced, 1964.

Children in 11th Generation

12469 BARBARA E., b. Haverhill, Mass., May 15, 1965.

F11740 ANDREA ELIZABETH CALEF, born in Rochester, N.H., Sept. 16, 1949, married in Barrington, N.H., July 25, 1970, MARTIN W. CONLEY.

Children in 11th Generation

12470 NATHAN CALEF, b. Jan. 31, 1973.

12471 ARIANNE CALEF, b. July 15, 1976.

F11744 BARNEY LINCOLN LOCKE, born in San Mateo, Calif., Dec. 14, 1947, married in Cliffside Park, N.J., Aug. 29, 1971, SUSAN PHILLIPS, born in Jersey City, N.J., Aug. 24, 1949.

His most remarkable feature is an almost carbon copy resemblance to his father, grandfather, and great-grandfather. He attended public schools in Joseph, Ore., and Menlo Park, Calif. He had a youthful interest in music playing the base guitar in "rock" groups he and his friends organized. He graduated from San Mateo Jr. College, 1967 where he majored in aeronautics. He traveled in Europe by thumb and motorcycle for cultural expansion. He graduated from San Jose State in 1971 in Aeronautics and enlisted in the U.S. Air Force where he was commissioned a Lieutenant. Hobbies include skiing, motor-cycling, and nursing an antique Jaguar. He is a pilot for Air West.

Children in 11th Generation

12472 CODY AARON, b. Scott's Air Force Base, Bellville, Ill., April 13, 1973.

12473 KELLY ALYSSON, b. Enterprise, Ore., June 28, 1977.

F11745 MARTIN TAPPAN LOCKE, born in San Mateo, Calif., Oct. 26, 1949, married in Enterprise, Ore., Dec. 28, 1972, CAPRICE SHORTRIDGE, born in Spokane, Wash., Sept. 8, 1955.

He attended public schools in Joseph, Ore. graduating from high school there in 1967. His height of 6 feet 6 inches made basketball a natural sport for him. Following his early desire to be a farmer he studied agriculture technology at Blue Mountain Community College graduating 1970. He joined the Peace Corps and worked a year in Colombia and then managed his parent's farm while they were in Ecuador. Hobbies include skiing and motorcycle riding.

Children in 11th Generation

12474 NATHAN AUGUSTUS, b. Enterprise, Ore., June 26, 1973.

F11751 GARLAND SHAW ALCOCK, born in Coral Gables, Fla., Feb. 10, 1948, married in Tahoe, Calif., June 28, 1975, LAWRENCE PRITCHARD.

She attended Wellesley College, graduated McGill University in Montreal, B.S. degree. Graduated from Boston University, School of Medicine, 1974, Doctor of Medicine. Interned in pediatrics at Mt. Zion Hospital, San Francisco, 1974-75.

Children in 11th Generation

12475 JENNIFER GAEL, b. San Francisco, Calif., June 7, 1976.

F11888 SANDRA PAULINE EMMINGER, born in Kittanning, Pa., Aug. 25, 1946, married 1st, in Vancouver, Wash., June 6, 1963, TOM TRIPLETT, born McMinnville, Ore., April 24, 1943, divorced; 2nd, in Crescent City, Calif., May 19, 1969, JAMES MYERS, born in Albuquerque, N. Mex., Nov. 18, 1942, son of James and Mary Myers.

Children in 11th Gen. b. in Lebanon, Oregon

12476 MARK ALLEN, b. Nov. 16, 1963.

12477 VICKIE ELAINE, b. Nov. 13, 1964.

F11890 SHARON LOUISE DAILY, born in Lebanon, Ore., Sept. 16, 1947, married in Mesa, Wash., July 11, 1967, KERRY LEWIS, born in Caldwell, Idaho, July 22, 1945, son of Bevens F. and Gertrude I. (Latteral) Lewis.

Children in 11th Generation

12478 CHRISTOPHER KERRY, b. Portland, Ore., June 4, 1970.

F11891 GENE RODERICK DAILY, born in Lebanon, Ore., July 11, 1949, married in Camas, Wash., June 14, 1969, DIANNE JORDAN, born in Portland, Ore., Sept. 18, 1950, daughter of Jack and Mildred June (Gilpin) Jordan.

Children in 11th Generation

12479 BRENT JORDAN, b. Portland, Ore., Nov. 20, 1969.

12480 TODD STEPHEN, b. Portland, Ore., Nov. 20, 1969.

12481 JAY MICHAEL, b. Portland, Ore., Nov. 20, 1969.

12482 MARC ALAN, b. Astoria, Ore., July 10, 1974.

F11893 NORMAN DUANE SCHERTENLEIB, born in Tonasket, Wash., Mar. 31, 1952, married in Coeur d'Alene, Idaho, Mar. 20, 1972, VIRGINIA GAIL PRIVITT, born June 20, 1952, daughter of Jack and Helen Privitt.

Children in 11th Gen. b. in Grand Forks, B.C., Canada

12483 SHANE RYAN, b. Jan. 30, 1973.

12484 ROBERT CARL, b. Feb. 12, 1974.

F11897 DEBRA MAXINE CLARK, born in Republic, Wash., Oct. 3, 1956, married in Spokane, Wash., July 13, 1974, WAYNE W. BERGER.

Children in 11th Generation

12484 JAMIE LYNN, b. Spokane, Wash., Dec. 9, 1974.

F11906 JERRY JEROME MILLER, born in Colfax, Wash., April 8, 1948, married in Colfax, Wash., July 8, 1967, PAMILLA JANE GARDNER, born in Spokane, Wash., Feb. 23, 1949.

Children in 11th Generation

12485 DARIN JEROME, b. Spokane, Wash., Dec. 22, 1967.

12486 DAVID THOMAS, b. Pullman, Wash., Jan. 10, 1969.

F11907 THOMAS ELERY MILLER, born in Colfax, Wash., Feb. 17, 1950, married in Steptoe, Wash., May 1, 1970, CHRISTINE KINSINGER, born in Colfax, Wash., Jan. 27, 1951, daughter of Wayne Arnold and Nora Mae (Suess) Kinsinger.

Children in 11th Generation

12486a APRIL HEATHER, b. Colfax, Wash., July 10, 1972.

F11957 DOREEN ADELL HILDRETH, born in Portland, Ore., Aug. 5, 1957, married in Provo, Utah, July 25, 1975, BRENT STUBBS, born in Provo, Utah, Mar. 1956, son of Wayne and ——(Revas) Stubbs.

Children in 11th Generation

12486b STEPHEN RICHARD, b. Provo, Utha, June 12, 1976.

F11980 RACHEL JANE LOCKE, born in Augusta, Maine, Mar. 28, 1932, married in Augusta, Maine, Sept. 19, 1953, LESTER NICHOLS ODAMS, JR., born in Scotts Bluff, Nebr., April 5, 1929.

Children in 11th Generation

12486c CAROLYN ELIZABETH, b. Schenectady, N.Y., Feb. 7, 1959.

12487 LESTER NICHOLS III, b. Bryn Mawr, Penna., June 22, 1960.

12488 STEVEN ANDREW, b. Sept. 21, 1961.

12489 JEFFREY LOCKE, b. Oct. 7, 1963.

F11981 ROBERT HEWINS LOCKE, born in Augusta, Maine, Mar. 30, 1940, married in Boston, Mass., Sept. 14, 1962, JANICE NANCY HAYDEN, born in Boston, Mass., Mar. 31, 1943, daughter of William Andrew and Doris (Paradis) Hayden.

He graduated 1963 Cum Laude from Boston University with a B.S. degree. Earned a Masters in Business Administration from Harvard, 1965. Until 1972 he held marketing management positions. Since 1972 he has taught at college and graduate level. Has his own nautical carving business and has a marketing position with W. R. Grace & Co., Cambridge, Mass.

She graduated 1965 Cum Laude from Boston University with a B. A. degree. Worked as a social worker.

Children in 11th Generation

12490 JONATHAN HAYDEN, b. Dearborn, Mich., Dec. 28, 1967.

12491 CHRISTOPHER HEWINS, b. Dover, N.H., July 10, 1972.

248 LOCKE GENEALOGY

12492 SUSANNAH NANCY, b. Dover, N.H., Nov. 11, 1977.

F11985 JOYCE ELAINE REYNOLDS, born in Lynn, Mass., May 6, 1933, married in Marblehead, Mass., Dec. 28, 1954, EDWARD ARTHUR LUDWIG of Gardiner, Maine, son of Edward Irving and Florence Marshall Ludwig.
They both graduated from the Univ. of Maine, Orono, Maine. He is a chemical engineer for Monsanto Chemical Co., Springfield, Mass.

Children in 11th Generation

12493 LAURA JEANNE, b. Bangor, Maine, Dec. 24, 1955.

12494 RICHARD ALAN, b. Springfield, Mass., Nov. 2, 1957.

12495 LINDA JOYCE, b. Springfield, Mass., Dec. 19, 1961.

F12009 JAMES KENNETH LOCKE, born in Ft. Fairfield, Maine, Aug. 20, 1903, died in East Corinth, Maine, July 11, 1949, married in Gorham, Maine, April 26, 1926, GERTRUDE HARRIET PRATT, born in Fairfax, Manitoba, Canada, July 15, 1907.
She is living in East Corinth, Maine.

Children in 11th Generation

F12496 MARGARET ETHEL, b. Pownal, Maine, Oct. 30, 1927, m. East Corinth, Maine, Aug. 2, 1941, RONALD BEAN.

F12497 JAMES DONALD, b. Ft. Fairfield, Maine, Sept. 1, 1928, m. Bolton Landings, N.Y., Mar. 26, 1959, LILLIAN HASTINGS.

F12498 ROBERT CARLETON, b. Caribou, Maine, April 3, 1933, m. Bath, Maine, April 30, 1955, DELORES JACQUE-LINE SEELEY.

F12010 MARY PHYLLIS ANN LOCKE, born in Ft. Fairfield, Maine, Sept. 24, 1909, married in Portland, Maine, Nov. 7, 1953, JOEL A. CARGILL, born in East Charleston, Vt.
She is a housewife and chaplain, American Legion Aux. Post No. 80, Vt. and member No. Star Chapter No. 25, O.E.S., J.P., Vt., B.F.R.T. Aux. Evangeline Lodge No. 146, Portland, Maine, A.A. R.P., Long Beach, Calif. Living in Island Pond, Vt.
He served in U.S. Army, Staff Sergeant and is now a conductor, Canadian National R.R. Member of American Legion Post No. 80, V.F.W. Post No. 789, A.F. & A.M. Lodge No. 44, U.T.U. No. 719.

Children in 11th Generation

12498 PETER F. DUMSER (given up for adoption), b. Portland, Maine, Jan. 28, 1926.

F12499 JOYCE A. IRELAND, b. Caribou, Maine, Nov. 1, 1929,
        (daughter of John I. Ireland who died May 20, 1950),
        m. Exeter, N. H., Sept. 3, 1949, DOYLE CARLETON
        RUDD.

F12012 CHARLES EUGENE LOCKE, born in Ft. Fairfield, Maine,
Nov. 22, 1912, died in New Sweden, Maine, Jan. 20, 1969, married
in Presque Isle, Maine, May 10, 1930, MARION AVERILL STONE,
born in Ft. Fairfield, Maine, July 9, 1908.
    "Gene" Locke was a successful small farmer. Worked himself to
death to get crops in so he could get to fishing; and harvested, so he
could get hunting. He was active in Ft. Fairfield United Parish
Church Administrative Board and was active in Ft. Fairfield Fish and
Game Club.
    Marion was active in the Women's Clubs at U. P. Church and
taught Sunday School. She was a graduate of Presque Isle Normal
School, taught 8 grades, one year, in a one room school, then married
had her family and did substitute teaching at Maple Grove School,
hospital volunteer at Ft. Fairfield, and School for Retarded Children
Aide.
    After Gene suffered several heart attacks, they sold the farm and
moved to Brewer, Maine, 1966. Marion has worked in many capacities for the First United Methodist Church of Brewer, was an Aide at
Washington Street School in Brewer for 2 years, and an Adult Volunteer for Eastern Maine Medical Center, Bangor, for 6 years with over
600 hours in service.

Children in 11th Generation

12500   CHARLES EUGENE, JR., b. Presque Isle, Maine, Nov. 23,
        1930, married in Andover, New Brunswick, Canada,
        Aug. 30, 1958, ELSIE WRIGHT.

F12501 MILDRED ELAINE, b. Ft. Fairfield, Maine, July 24, 1933,
        m. Brewer, Maine, Feb. 5, 1953, JOHN FRANCIS
        GOODNESS.

12502   STEPHEN WAYNE, b. Ft. Fairfield, Maine, May 30, 1940,
        m. Andover, New Brunswick, Canada, Nov. 25, 1957,
        JOSEPHINE ANNE RAFFERTY.

F12013 EDGAR CLEMENT LOCKE, born in Ft. Fairfield, Maine,
Dec. 20, 1913, married DORIS SEVERANCE, born in Topsfield,
Maine, May 24, 1918.
    He works at Pratt-Whitney, Southington, Conn. Lives in Bristol,
Conn. First Ass't Watch Engineer, Power House. He can't wait to
retire and come back to Maine to hunting and fishing. She works at
Gould Allied Control doing assembly work.

Children in 11th Generation

12503 JUDITH ANN, b. Bristol, Conn., Nov. 17, 1942. She
graduated from high school in Conn., 1 year of Pre-Med
in college and worked for an insurance company. Now
a child care worker at Residence for Tennage Girls.
Active in church work.

F12015 EILEEN THOMPSON EASTMAN, born in Woodsville, N.
H., Aug. 11, 1917, married in Rye, N. H., Oct. 15, 1938, HARRIS
MARTIN ROGERS, born in Portsmouth, N. H., Feb. 14, 1915.

Children in 11th Gen. b. in Portsmouth, N. H.

F12504 PRISCILLA LaFLEUR, b. Sept. 20, 1941, m. Portsmouth,
N. H., Aug. 14, 1959, CLINTON BROOKS MAGOUN.

F12505 ABIGAIL GARLAND, b. Aug. 23, 1943, m. Rye Beach,
N. H., July 25, 1964, O. RAHMAN KHAN.

F12506 MARY ANN, b. Sept. 20, 1944, m. Portsmouth, N. H.,
May 16, 1964, FRANCIS WALTER SAWTELLE.

F12020 ROBERT CARLTON BURT, born in Melrose, Mass., July
17, 1918, married Aug. 4, 1939, ELSIE McELROY.

Children in 11th Generation

12507 ROBERT GEORGE, b. Feb. 10, 1941.

12508 PENELOPE IRENE, b. Feb. 14, 1944.

12509 DEBORAH ELSIE, b. Aug. 17, 1951.

12510 STEVEN CARLTON, b. Sept. 29, 1954.

12511 BONNIE MAY, b. Feb. 14, 1957.

F12023 MARION GODDARD STICKNEY, born in Fort Benning,
Ga., Feb. 7, 1923, married in Boston, Mass., April 30, 1949, ROBERT
HENKLE RENO, born in Macomb, Ill., Mar. 24, 1917.

Children in 11th Generation

12512 ROBERT HENKLE, JR., b. Boston, Mass., May 1, 1950.

12513 REBECCA STICKNEY, b. Concord, N. H., July 29, 1952.

12514 RICHARD CARLTON, b. Concord, N. H., April 10, 1956.

F12029 GEORGE DENNY COBB, born in Wash., D. C., April 24,
1944, married in New Orleans, La., Mar. 18, 1967, SUZANNE
DALLAS CARROLL, born in New Orleans, La., May 1, 1946.

Children in 11th Generation

12515 JEANNIE CARROLL, b. Hammond, La., Nov. 21, 1967.

12516 BARBARA ELISABETH, b. St. Augustine, Fla., May 13, 1970.

12517 STEVENS DENNY, b. Tallahasse, Fla., May 10, 1973.

12518 KENDALL RYAN, b. Tallahassee, Fla., Jan. 29, 1976.

F12033 SHARLA LENAIRE TRINE, born in Eureka, Calif., Mar. 17, 1942, married 1st, Nov. 1964, ROBERT AUGUSTINE; 2nd, Mar. 1967, INGOLF WILSON, JR.

Children in 11th Generation

12519 LONITA LENAIRE, b. Aug. 19, 1965.

12520 ERIK NELS, b. Mar. 23, 1968.

F12034 CANDACE SHERRILL TRINE, born in Oakland, Calif., June 18, 1944, married June 1967, DENNIS INMAN.

Children in 11th Generation

12521 MELISS ANN, b. Oct. 28, 1972.

F12035 ROBIN LYNNE TRINE, born Eureka, Calif., Oct. 31, 1946, married Oct. 1965, ROBERT B. BURDICK.

Children in 11th Generation

12522 JANERA LYNNE, b. Oct. 21, 1966.

12523 MARK ALLEN, b. Jan. 17, 1968.

F12045 PAMELA IRENE ALLEN, born in Fallon, Nev., Sept. 5, 1945, married in Evanston, Wyo., May 2, 1966, SHERMAN DAVID BLANCK, born in Salt Lake City, Utah, Jan. 5, 1940, son of David Thomas and Helen (Richardson) Blanck.

Children in 11th Gen. b. in Salt Lake City, Utah

12524 REBEL ANN, b. Feb. 7, 1967.

12525 DAVID WARD, b. Nov. 13, 1970.

F12046 JACQUELYN LYNN ALLEN, born in Salt Lake City, Utah, May 31, 1948, married in Evanston, Wyo., July 6, 1966, ALAN HOWARD GILLIES, born in Salt Lake City, Utah, Oct. 27, 1946, son of Howard Joseph and Bernice Marie (Van Wagner) Gillies.

Children in 11th Generation

12526 ANNDENIA GAY, b. Norfolk, Va., Aug. 3, 1968.

12527 THOMAS ALAN, b. Salt Lake City, Utah, Jan. 2, 1970.

12528 ANDREW JOHN, b. Salt Lake City, Utah, May 30, 1972.

12529 ALAN HOWARD, JR., b. Salt Lake City, Utah, Dec. 19, 1973.

12530 SUSAN MARIE, b. Salt Lake City, Utah, April 22, 1975.

F12047 MARCELLA JEAN ALLEN, born in Salt Lake City, Utah, Mar. 30, 1955, married in Evanston, Wyo., Dec. 14, 1972, LARRY ORVIL GRESSMAN, born in Payson, Utah, Aug. 1, 1937, son of Orvil T. and Utahna Belle (Peterson) Gressman.

Children in 11th Generation

12531 MICHAEL WARD, b. Rock Springs, Wyo., May 13, 1973.

F12048 APRIL KAY ALLEN, born in Pocatello, Idaho, Aug. 21, 1956, married in Evanston, Wyo., Oct. 18, 1973, MICHAEL STAFFORD CARNAHAN, born in Sydney, Australia, Mar. 30, 1945, son of Burton Carlos and Audray Phyllis (Stafford) Carnahan.

Children in 11th Gen. b. in Salt Lake City, Utah

12532 BRANDY ESTELLE, Oct. 17, 1974.

12533 JOHNATHAN STAFFORD, July 28, 1975.

F12052 STEVEN SCOTT URQUHART, born in San Rafael, Calif., Oct. 28, 1954, married LAURIE HENSHAW.

Children in 11th Generation

12534 CRYSTAL LYNN, b. Feb. 1974.

F12060 EARLE RAYWORTH GOWELL, JR., born Dec. 24, 1934, married VIVIAN SNEAD.

Children in 11th Generation

12535 EARLE RAYWORTH III, b. Nov. 8, 1961.

12536 SCOTT TYLER, b. Dec. 30, 1963.

12537 STACEY ELIZABETH, b. Aug. 1, 1967.

F12068 CECIL GEORGE FRANCIS, born in Lewiston, Maine, Dec. 5, 1911, married in Farmington, Maine, May 29, 1931, MARION ADELAIDE TURNER, born in Farmington, Maine, Nov. 29, 1912.

Children in 11th Generation

12538 CECIL GEORGE, JR., b. Farmington, Maine, July 17, 1932, m. 1st, Sept. 29, 1951, JANE FAYE HODGMAN; 2nd, Nov. 1974, BONNIE MARSH.

F12539 BEVERLY JEAN, b. East Livermore, Maine, Mar. 3, 1934, m. 1st, Oct. 19, 1952, WILLIAM RICHARD COREY; 2nd, Aug. 26, 1961, GEORGE JOHNATHAN HOVANEC, JR.

12540 RICHARD WENDELL, b. Livermore Falls, Maine, Feb. 20, 1936, m. Dec. 28, 1952, GRACE ISABELLE PATRICK.

TWELFTH GENERATION

F10483 WILLIAM ALBERT MOULTON, born in Rye, N.H., June 7, 1911, married in Hampton, N.H., Dec. 23, 1950, AUDREY E. KING, born Oct. 17, 1918.

Children in 12th Generation

12541 KENNETH ELMER, b. Jan. 23, 1948, m. Aug. 15, 1970, SUZANNE LeROY.

F12087 LAURENCE EDWARD GOSS, JR., born in Greenfield, Mass., Dec. 9, 1944, married in Springfield, Mass., June 9, 1968, SHARON MARGARETT RIPP, born in Madison, Wis., Sept. 26, 1944.
He is a graduate of West Springfield, Mass. High School, 1962, and Dartmouth College, 1966. Received an M.A., 1969 and Ph.D., 1973, degrees from the University of Washington at Seattle. Previously employed as an administrative officer at Dartmouth College and a department chairman (geography) at the State University of New York at Oswego. Presently appointed by the Governor as Director of the Coastal Resources Management Program for the State of N.H.
She is a graduate of Middleton, Wis. High School, Salutatorian, 1962, and the University of Wisconsin at Madison, 1966. Received an M.A.T. degree, 1969, from the University of Washington at Seattle. Presently public information director for the N.H. Heart Association.

Children in 12th Gen. b. in Syracuse, N.Y.

12542 LAURA MARIE, b. Feb. 1, 1972.

12543 PETER EDWARD, b. Mar. 6, 1974.

F12090 CAROLYN FRANCES GOSS, born Oct. 1, 1932, married June 9, 1957, PETER G. BROOKS, born May 30, 1932.

Children in 12th Generation

12544 LEE GOSS, b. April 13, 1959.

12545 SUSAN ANN, b. Aug. 20, 1963.

F12097 ROBERT FRANCISCO ESTES, JR., born in Boston, Mass., June 11, 1937, married in Farmington, Conn., ANONE PEARL GETCHELL.

Children in 12th Generation

12546 DEBRA ANONE, b. Fort Sill, Okla., Aug. 24, 1962.

12547 KIMBERLAY ERET, b. Mineral Wells, Texas, Nov. 26, 1967.

12548 DEREK SCOTT (twin), b. Mineral Wells, Texas, Nov. 5, 1969.

12549 DANA KIRK (twin), b. Mineral Wells, Texas, Nov. 5, 1969.

F12098 ELIZABETH PRAY ESTES, born in Hodge, La., July 9, 1940, married in Madison, Maine, Sept. 7, 1962, DAVID FRANCIS MARTIN, born in Waterbury, Conn., Feb. 5, 1942.

She graduated Madison High in 1958. Attended Univ. of Maine, graduated 1962, B.S. Physical Education and Biology. Taught last half of senior year of college at Hanover, N. H., kindergarten through high school. Taught Madison High School (Phys. Ed.), and Lincoln Academy in Damariscotta, Maine. Started to build home in Norridge-wock in 1968. Hobbies are sewing, all handicrafts, gardening and coaching basketball, track, gymnastics, and field hockey.

He graduated from Skowhegan High School, 1961. Attended Colby College, graduated 1965. Taught at Erskine Academy, Lincoln Academy and Lawrence High School in Fairfield, Maine. Coached football, track and soccer. Hobbies are fly tying, coaching, woodworking, farming, and building home.

Children in 12th Gen. b. in Skowhegan, Maine

12550 ROBERTA RUTH, b. April 12, 1963.

12551 DAVID FRANCIS, JR., b. Aug. 13, 1965.

F12101 MARTHA ANNE TOWNE, born in Burlington, Vt., Mar. 8, 1942, married in Richmont, Vt., Oct. 3, 1962, ROGER LOUIS BOMBARDIER, born in Burlington, Vt., June 16, 1940.

Children in 12th Gen. b. in Burlington, Vt.

12552 BRUCE LELAND, b. Aug. 18, 1963.

12553 ROGER LOUIS, b. Sept. 19, 1967.

F12102 RAYMOND STANDLICK LOCKE, born in Hillsdale, Mich., Aug. 17, 1938, married in Barrington, R.I., July 14, 1962, SALLY PAGE RAYMOND, born in Providence, R.I., July 18, 1940.

He attended the University of Michigan, two years Physical education, two years Business Administration. Three years in the Army, Officers Candidate school, Fort Sill, Okla., Paymaster Panama Canal Zone. Graduated from Northeastern University, B.S. in Business Administration. Masters in Business Administration from Northeastern University.

256   LOCKE GENEALOGY

She received a B.A. from Connecticut College and worked as a Biologist for Dr. Hay at the Harvard Medical School. They reside in Newton, Massachusetts where he is a Research Computer Analyst for Digital Corporation.

Children in 12th Generation

12554   STEVEN SANBORN, b. Fort Sill, Okla., Jan. 4, 1964.

12555   DANA PAGE, b. Boston, Mass., Aug. 24, 1967.

12556   REBECCA KINGSBURY, b. Boston, Mass., Dec. 2, 1968.

F12103   RANDOLPH KINGSBURY LOCKE, born in Attleboro, Mass., Oct. 6, 1944, married in Cambridge, Mass., Oct. 16, 1966, MARTHA ANDREWS, born in Boston, Mass., Oct. 30, 1944.
He received the B.A. degree from Trinity College, Hartford, Conn. Three years in the Army, Officers Candidate School, Fort Sill, Okla. Stationed at Salt Lake City, Utah as a recruiter in Colleges for the Officers Candidate Program.
She is a graduate of Colby Junior College. Worked as Executive Secretary for the President of I.B.M. in Boston. They live in Burnsville, Minn. where he is a Manager for the Reinhard Corporation of Minneapolis.

Children in 12th Gen. b. in Boston, Mass.

12557   KIMBERLY, b. Oct. 20, 1969.

12558   ERICA, b. May 17, 1972.

F12104   RICHARD JENNESS LOCKE, JR., born in Portsmouth, N.H., Aug. 1, 1925, married in Boston, Mass., Sept. 22, 1947, ALMA PASQUALE, born in Lewiston, Maine, Nov. 29, 1925.
He served with the U.S. Navy on the battleship "Santa Fe" during World War II. He is a heavy equipment mechanic, employed as a civilian with the U.S. Air Force at Pease A.F.B., Portsmouth, N.H.
She is a triplet. She was a professional singer and a member of the American Theatre Wing, Boston, Mass. Performed with many name bands and had her own radio program at the age of 16. Left the theatre when she married and studied at the University of New Hampshire. She is presently a librarian at the Rye Jr. High School.

Children in 12th Gen. b. in Exeter, N.H.

F12559   ELIZABETH ANNE, b. June 24, 1949, m. Oklahoma City, Okla., Aug. 18, 1972, WILLIAM A. BONTLY.

F12560   JUDITH ALMA, b. Nov. 2, 1950, m. Hampton, N.H., Jan. 17, 1969, KENNETH D. McBRAYER.

12561   KATHY RUTH, b. April 17, 1954, m. July 10, 1976, CHARLES B. SCHMIGLE.

12562 RICHARD JENNESS, III, b. July 9, 1956.

F12107 ROBERT DECATUR PARSONS, born in Boston, Mass., Oct. 25, 1923, married in Springfield, Penna., June 21, 1947, ANNA CAROLYN DETZ, born Dec. 22, 1924.
He earned a B. S. at Penn. State College, a M.S. at Univ. of Maine in Chemical Engineering in Pulp and Paper and is a research engineer in specialty papers. His interests include boating, tennis, woodworking and photography. He is active in the church choir and Boy Scouts.

Children in 12th Generation

12563 JOHN DECATUR, b. June 15, 1956.

12564 ANNE PINE, b. April 22, 1959.

F12108 DONALD GLADWIN PARSONS, born in Portsmouth, N.H., July 14, 1927, married in Ambler, Penna., May 14, 1955, ETHEL SHIRLAW, born June 3, 1932.
He is President of United Investment Council and Vice President of United Business Service, Boston, Mass.

Children in 12th Generation

12565 WILLIAM LANGDON, b. Mar. 19, 1956.

12566 DOUGLAS BOYD, b. Feb. 12, 1961.

12567 EDWARD SHIRLAW, b. July 2, 1967.

F12109 PRISCILLA LOCKE PARSONS, born in Erie, Penna., Sept. 9, 1930, married in Rye, N. H., June 6, 1953, ARTHUR ERNEST FINGER, JR., born April 15, 1932.
She graduated from Coburn Classical Inst., Waterville, Maine, 1948; Westbrook Jr. College, Portland, Maine, 1950; and Syracuse Univ., N. Y., 1953 with a dual degree in Liberal Arts and Library Science. She is secretary to the Vice President of Traffic and Distribution Services, Inc. in Lexington, Mass. She is active in church and community organizations and for 19 years active in the Girl Scouts of America. She likes traveling and talents include piano and chorus work. He is President of Traffic and Distribution Services, Inc., Lexington, Mass.

Children in 12th Generation

12568 JAMES ARTHUR, b. June 20, 1956.

12569 CYNTHIA LOCKE, b. Nov. 1, 1959.

F12111 NORMAN EUGENE BERRY, born June 17, 1919, married Dec. 18, 1942, ELIZABETH ANN GRUBB, born Oct. 27, 1920.

Children in 12th Generation

F12570 LAURENCE EARL, b. April 20, 1938, m. Feb. 10, 1964, KATHELEEN ANNE TULLY.

F12571 PATRICIA ANN, b. July 20, 1946, m. May 16, 1970, DAIRD ALFRED NICKERSON.

F12112 NANCY ELIZABETH BERRY, born Aug. 27,.1925, married Oct. 18, 1947, ADOLPH LOUIS BEROWNSKY, born May 6, 1920.

Children in 12th Generation

12572 DENNIS RICHARD, b. Nov. 6, 1955.

F12114 JOHN LLOYD WENTZELL, born in Somerville, Mass., June 1, 1919, married in Boston, Mass., June 28, 1941, ELIZABETH KINSMAN, born Jan. 18, 1920.
He graduated from Somerville, Mass. High School and Univ. of N.H., 1941 with B.A. degree. He is Manager of Claims for Liberty Mutual Ins. Co. in Worcester, Mass. He is a member of the Masons and enjoys tennis, jogging, woodworking, skiing and sailing. She shares his activities and teaches English at the high school in Westwood, Mass. where they reside.

Children in 12th Generation

F12573 JOHN LLOYD, JR., b. Oct. 7, 1942, m. June 26, 1965, LINDA IRENE FLINT.

12574 STEPHEN PHILBRICK, b. Dec. 12, 1946. He works for Digital Equip. Co. and enjoys skiing, sailing, woodworking and traveling.

F12575 JULIANNE, b. Dec. 12, 1946, m. Aug. 6, 1966, JOHN DAVID MORRISON, b. Feb. 23, 1946.

F12115 DOROTHY WENTZELL, born July 1, 1922, married in Medford, Mass., Sept. 17, 1946, DONALD MARTIN BUTCHER, born in Newton, Mass., Sept. 9, 1922.
She attended Colby Jr. College and graduated from Univ. of New Hampshire. Now resides in Pittsford, N.Y. with her husband, Donald, who is employed by The Andover Companies of Andover, Mass.

Children in 12th Gen. b. in Syracuse, N.Y.

12576 LAURIE, b. Nov. 17, 1950, m. Lewisburg, Penna., Sept. 9, 1972, EDWARD HARRISON MARSTON.
She is a National Merit Scholar. A.B. from Bucknell

University and M. A. from University of Chicago.
Worked as an Assistant Planner in Skokie, Ill.

12577 EDWARD SINNETT, b. Nov. 13, 1952. He graduated from
University of Virginia, College of Architecture, 1974.
Now employed as an architect's apprentice in Roches-
ter, N. Y.

12578 CAROLYN, b. Oct. 5, 1956. She is a student at State
University College — Geneseo in Geneseo, N. Y.

F12117 OTIS DIXON PHILLIPS, JR., born in Newport News, Va.,
Sept. 30, 1912, died in Atlanta, Ga., Sept. 24, 1966, married in
West Palm Beach, Fla., Aug. 10, 1937, HATTIE ADA BOURN, born
Aug. 23, 1914.
He was a hotel manager in Augusta, Ga., was a brilliant man and
well liked by many of Augusta's citizens including the Governor. She
is a Federal employee at Camp Gordon, Ga. She is very witty, a
devoted grandmother and mother and enjoys traveling.

Children in 12th Generation

12579 OTIS DIXON, III, b. Aug. 2, 1938, m. Mar. 16, 1968,
CAROL PHYLLIS GEORGE, and had: 12580 STACY
SUZANNE, b. June 6, 1969.
He works for the U. S. government in Washington,
D. C. He is a Georgia Tech graduate and inherited his
father's love of books and reading.

12581 PATRICIA DELL ANNE, b. July 25, 1943, m. Monroe,
Ga., Mar. 7, 1964, JOHN TROY PRESTON, III, and
had: 12582 JOHN TROY PRESTON IV, b. Jan. 13,
1972.

12583 CHARLES GEOFFREY, b. April 14, 1949.

F12118 CHARLES HARRY PHILLIPS, born in Statesville, N. C.,
July 9, 1914, married in Greensboro, N. C., Oct. 14, 1939, VIR-
GINIA BEVERLEY REAVES, born Dec. 29, 1916.
He is business manager for a large Presbyterian Church. He at-
tended Univ. of North Carolina at Chapel Hill. At the time of his
engagement to his future wife, his picture appeared in the newspaper
with hers saying he was the city's handsomest bachelor! She is a
Hollins College graduate.

Children in 12th Generation

12584 PAMELA ALLEN, b. Greensboro, N.C., Mar. 18, 1942,
m. Nov. 11, 1964, FRANCIS ROBERTSON ILER, JR.,
and had: 12585 VIRGINIA ANN, b. Dec. 10, 1966;
12586 FRANCIS ROBERTSON, III, b. Feb. 9, 1968.

F12587 VIRGINIA PAGE, b. June 29, 1945, m. 1966. HARRY JAMES HILL (divorced 1973).

12588 BEVERLY REAVES, b. Dec. 13, 1954. She was chosen one of the Youth Brain Trust of the state and is attending Duke University.

F12119 JACK BEVERLY PHILLIPS, born in Richmond, Va., Aug. 11, 1917, married in Wetumpkia, Ala., Sept. 12, 1942, KATHERINE ANN RAVESIES, born Dec. 21, 1922.
He served in India during WW II. He attended Georgia Tech and works for Du Pont in Augusta, Ga. where he lives.

Children in 12th Generation

12589 JACK BEVERLY, JR., b. Greensboro, N. C., Oct. 27, 1943, m. Augusta, Ga., Dec. 31, 1966, MARY CATHERINE STURGIS, and had: 12590 JONATHAN SCOTT, b. Mar. 10, 1973.
He attended Clemson Univ. and is a physicist living in Augusta.

12591 STEVEN McKELL, b. Greensboro, N. C., Aug. 14, 1946, m. Feb. 7, 1970, MARGARET DIANNE MITCHELL and adopted: 12592 TIFFANY NICOLE, b. Dec. 3, 1966.
He graduated from Clemson Univ. and served two years in Thailand in the U. S. Army.

12593 KATHERINE ANN, b. Jan. 15, 1961. She is a very good student and is interested in genealogy.

F12120 MARTHA ANNE MOORE, born in Greensboro, N. C., Sept. 2, 1925, married in Greensboro, N.C., June 4, 1946, CHARLES DAVIS MIZE.
She is a graduate of the Univ. of North Carolina and he is an Annapolis graduate and Major General USMC (Ret.).

Children in 12th Generation

12594 DAVID MOORE, b. Detroit, Mich., May 4, 1947, m. Ft. Devens, Mass., April 1971, JANE IRZYK. He is an Annapolis graduate and officer in the Marine Corps.

12595 ANNE LOCKE, b. Greensboro, N. C., July 4, 1949, m. Camp Pendleton, Calif., Dec. 21, 1975, WILLIAM CHARLES CUSEO. She majored in Art at Mary Washington College.

12596 SALLY WATSON, b. Quantico, Va., Oct. 17, 1954, m. Quantico, Va., May 16, 1976, JACQUES JOSEPH

MOORE. She is a graduate of Mary Washington College.

12597 WILLIAM RANDALL, b. Bethesda, Md., Feb. 24, 1960.

F12121 WILLIAM LOCKE MOORE, born in Greensboro, N. C., Feb. 18, 1926, married in Reidsville, N. C., Aug. 17, 1957, DOROTHY ELLEN CHEEK. He is a prominent pediatrician and graduate of Univ. of North Carolina and Harvard University.

Children in 12th Gen. b. in Greensboro, N. C.

12598 THOMAS HENRY, b. Nov. 13, 1958.

12599 SUSAN RICHARDSON, b. Dec. 25, 1962.

12600 ELIZABETH LOCKE, b. Oct. 30, 1965.

F12122 ADA JANE MOORE, born in Greensboro, N. C., Jan. 17, 1929, married in Greensboro, N. C., Mar. 31, 1959, ARMISTEAD WRIGHT SAPP, JR.
She graduated from University of North Carolina and was a private secretary. He is an attorney. She paints portraits. Their sons are honor students at Oak Ridge Military Academy, Oak Ridge, N. C.

Children in 12th Gen. b. in Greensboro, N. C.

12601 ARMISTEAD WRIGHT, III, b. Nov. 2, 1960.

12602 HENRY KING, b. Dec. 27, 1961.

12603 WILLIAM MOORE, b. May 7, 1963.

F12123 ROBERT MOORE ARMFIELD, born in Greensboro, N. C., Feb. 5, 1927, married in Greensboro, N. C., Sept. 16, 1949, BEVERLY FRANCES BELL, born Oct. 31, 1926.
He is a state college graduate in engineering and they live in Mooresville, N. C.

Children in 12th Generation

12604 ELLEN WATSON, b. Winston-Salem, N. C., June 5, 1951, m. Greensboro, N. C., Mar. 17, 1973, ROBERT EARL BOLICK, b. May 10, 1952. She is a graduate of Univ. of North Carolina. They live in Philadelphia.

12605 LAURA LOCKE, b. Burlington, N. C., April 5, 1954, m. Greensboro, N. C., May 31, 1975, CHARLES LEROY TUCKER, III, b. July 29, 1954. She is a graduate of Univ. of North Carolina. They live in Medford, Mass.

F12124   RICHARD LOCKE ARMFIELD, born in Greensboro, N.C., Nov. 7, 1929, married in Easley, S.C., April 4, 1953, CATHERINE LENOIR DAVIS, born Aug. 11, 1929. He is a state college graduate in engineering and lives in Maryville, Tenn.

Children in 12th Generation

12606   ELAINE LOCKE, b. Columbia, S.C., Mar. 1, 1955. Graduated from Butler Univ. majoring in choreography and has opened a dance studio.

12607   CYNTHIA LOCKE, b. Maryville, Tenn., July 29, 1958 Attending Georgia Tech. in Atlanta, Ga., majoring in engineering.

12608   RICHARD LOCKE, b. Sept. 6, 1962.

F12125   GEORGE SHAFFER WOOD, JR., born in Kittery, Maine, Dec. 4, 1915, married in Charlottesville, Va., NANCY GRAY LEE, born in Charlottesville, Va., Mar. 24, 1918.

Children in 12th Generation

F12609   ELIZABETH MARSHALL, b. Chicago, Ill., m. Nov. 4, 1961, ROBERT JOHN ELIAS.

F12610   GEORGE SHAFFER, III, b. Charlottesville, Va., m. Columbia, S.C., April 18, 1970, LINDA CANNON.

F12126   CALVIN WARNER DUNBAR, born in Los Angeles, Calif., Dec. 16, 1924, married in Los Angeles, Calif., June 28, 1954, JANICE HORLICK ROMNEY, born April 23, 1923.

Children in 12th Generation

12611   ELIZABETH DUSTIN, b. June 16, 1956.

12612   NORMAN ROMNEY, b. May 16, 1958.

F12127   BETTIE LU DUNBAR, born in Los Angeles, Calif., May 9, 1926, married in Los Angeles, Calif., June 4, 1949, ROBERT OLNEY THORN, born Aug. 3, 1922.

Children in 12th Generation

12613   RICHARD DUNBAR, b. Feb. 12, 1952.

12614   STEPHEN GIDDINGS, b. Sept. 21, 1954.

12615   ROBERT WARNER, b. Aug. 27, 1956.

F12128   ADALYN HELEN DUNBAR, born in Los Angeles, Calif., Aug. 19, 1930, married in Los Angeles, Calif., May 30, 1953, LEONARD EVERETT, born Dec. 12, 1922.

Children in 12th Generation

12616 KENNETH, b. Feb. 10, 1955.

12617 JAMES, b. Feb. 18, 1957.

12618 SANDRA, b. May 8, 1963.

F12135 LISA ANN MARSTON, born in Exeter, N. H., June 24, 1955, married in Hampton, N. H., Mar. 10, 1972, RICHARD JOSEPH OSBORN.

Children in 12th Generation

12619 GREGORY WAYNE, b. Exeter, N. H., Sept. 21, 1972.

F12156 NANCY ANN WELLS, born in Concord, N. H., April 13, 1941, married in Concord, N. H., Oct. 30, 1965, HOMER VENCIL HORTON, born in Jefferson County, Ky., Aug. 6, 1940.

She graduated from Eastern Nazarene College, Wollaston, Mass., 1963. Was librarian for short time at Quincy, Mass. and at Washington, D.C. prior to marriage. She and husband are members of Trinity Church of the Nazarene, Colorado Springs, Colorado. Her interests are homemaking, church, music and reading. She is a La Leche League leader.

The family is presently residing in Colorado Springs, Colorado, where he is studying for the Nazarene ministry at Nazarene Bible College. He is a member of the official college Trio and on the Freshman basketball team. He is a former member of the Amalgamated Meatcutter's Union. Plays guitar.

Children in 12th Generation

12620 REBECCA LYNN, b. Fort Belvoir, Va., May 12, 1966.

12621 JAMES VENCIL, b. Concord, N. H., May 20, 1968.

12622 JERRY JAY, b. Concord, N. H., Nov. 23, 1970.

12623 SARA-LEE BETH, b. Concord, N. H., May 23, 1972.

F12157 HERBERT DANIEL WELLS, born in Concord, N. H., Oct. 17, 1943, married in Wolfeboro, N. H., Aug. 26, 1967, BARBARA JEAN PRESTON, born in South Weymouth, Mass., Aug. 16, 1944.

He was graduated from Concord, N. H. High School and attended Eastern Nazarene College, Wollaston, Mass. one year. He left to serve in U.S. Naval Reserves, training as electrician's mate at the Naval School in San Diego, Calif. He was student instructor in the night school, and at his graduation was presented a gold seal certificate as honor man of his class. He was assigned to the destroyer USS Wedderburn off Vietnam. Upon discharge, he was employed by IBM

Corporation of Lawrence, Mass. as customer service engineer. He is presently proprietor of Wells Appliance Service, Wolfeboro, N. H. He is a member of Electrical Contractor Association, serving as Director for Carroll County. His hobbies are his work and animals. They are very active in Church of the Nazarene in Wolfeboro, N. H., where they reside.

She attended Burlington, Vt. schools and was graduated from Burlington High School in 1962. She graduated from Concord, N. H. Hospital School of Nursing in 1966 and was employed at the hospital. She also attended Calvary Bible College, Kansas City, Mo., one year, studying for missions. She is presently employed part time as Registered Nurse at Huggins Hospital, Wolfeboro, N. H. Her hobbies are needlework and project organization and scheduling.

Children in 12th Gen. b. in Wolfeboro, N. H.

12624 STEPHEN DANIEL, b. Nov. 11, 1970.

12625 MARK ANDREW, b. Feb. 4, 1972.

F12158 PETER HARRY WELLS, born in Waltham, Mass., April 19, 1943, married in Portland, Ore., Nov. 22, 1969, ELRAE LOUISE SADRING, born April 26, 1950.

He was educated in Portland, Oregon public schools and earned Life Scout award in Boy Scouts of America. He graduated from Claremont, Calif. Men's College in 1965, winning prize for best Mathematics Thesis. Currently he is attending Law School at University of Oregon.

He was employed for several years with Boise Cascade Corporation, Palo Alto, California.

His special interests are sailing and church work. He has served on Board of Directors, Oregon Conference United Church of Christ.

She was educated in Portland, Oregon public schools and attended Portland Community College. Her special interests are homemaking, sailing, and church work.

Children in 12th Generation

12626 RAYMOND PETER, b. Palo Alto, Calif., July 10, 1972.

12627 MARY SARA, b. Eugene, Ore., Dec. 28, 1974.

F12159 MICHAEL WINTHROP WELLS, born in Newton, Mass., Jan. 8, 1945, married in Bremerton, Wash., Sept. 3, 1966, ELAINE MORRIS.

He was educated in Portland, Oregon public schools; earned Boy Scouts of America Eagle award; attended Wesleyan University, Middletown, Conn.; Portland Community College, and graduated from Seattle Pacific University, Seattle, Washington, class of 1968.

He is employed in the new Energy Department for the State of Oregon in charge of forecasting all the petroleum usage for the state. His special interests are sailing and woodworking.

She was educated in the public schools of Bremerton, Wash. and attended Linfield College, McMinville, Oregon. Her interests are her home and church.

They reside in Salem, Oregon.

Children in 12th Generation

12628 JULIE CHRISTINE, b. Seattle, Wash., Feb. 6, 1968.

12629 THOMAS MICHAEL, b. Seattle, Wash., Mar. 3, 1970.

12630 DIANE ELISABETH, b. Kennewick, Wash., Jan. 14, 1974.

F12161 ANNALEE WELLS, born in Franklin, N.H., Dec. 12, 1942, married in Concord, N.H., Oct. 27, 1962, CARLETON SAGER MACK, born in Brewer, Maine, May 26, 1940.

She was educated in Concord, N.H. public schools and is a beautician. She teaches Oriental dancing.

He is District Manager of Equitable Assurance Society, with headquarters in Portsmouth, N.H. He is a member of the Masons. Interested in coin collecting skiing.

Children in 12th Gen. b. in Concord, N.H.

12631 ALAN CARLETON, b. July 13, 1963. He is a Boy Scout and plays clarinet in school band in Portsmouth.

12632 JAY DAVID, b. Mar. 24, 1968.

F12193 JOSHUA ADAMS SIMONTON YOUNG, born in Cambridge, Mass., June 26, 1939, married in Cambridge, Mass., June 17, 1961, MARION HOLLIS McCOWN, born in Bryn Mawr, Penna., Sept. 1, 1940.

Children in 12th Generation

12633 JOSHUA ADAMS SIMONTON, II, b. Boston, Mass., Dec. 5, 1966.

12634 ANDREW SNOWMAN, b. Brookline, Mass., Nov. 26, 1968.

F12198 PETER RONBECK BENSON, born in Everett, Mass., Mar. 28, 1949, married in Roslindale, Mass., Oct. 4, 1969, JUNE ANNE CRAVEN, born in Winchester, Mass., June 26, 1949.

He attended Truro and Brighton, Mass. public schools and served on the USS Forresstal while in the U.S. Navy. He is a licensed heavy equipment operator and rigger and has a Class I driver's license.

Hobbies include woodworking. She attended Roslindale public schools and was a stock and bonds clerk for John Hancock in Boston, Mass. She is active in the Democratic Party and civic organizations in Roslindale where they reside.

Children in 12th Generation

12635 HEIDI ANNE, b. Hyannis, Mass., Oct. 19, 1970. She is member #113204 of the National Society of the Children of the American Revolution. (N.S. of the C.A.R.)

12636 ERIN JUNE, b. Hyannis, Mass., Nov. 17, 1971. She is member #113203 of the N.S. of the C.A.R.

12637 WENDY MARIE, b. Brighton, Mass., Mar. 3, 1974. She is member #114173 of the N.S. of the C.A.R.

F12230 ELIZABETH JEAN ELLIS, born in Somerville, Mass., June 2, 1930, married Oct. 14, 1950, CHARLES LITTLEFIELD SEAMAN, born in Melrose, Mass., April 15, 1930.

Children in 12th Generation

12638 ALLISON RUTH, b. Maine, Feb. 18, 1962.

12639 MERIDITH JEAN, b. Portland, Maine, Sept. 14, 1966.

F12231 RICHARD MacKAY LOCKE, JR., born Feb. 24, 1941, married KATHLEEN E. KEYES, born Nov. 14, 1950.

Children in 12th Generation

12640 RICHARD STANLEY, b. Calif., Aug. 20, 1971.

12641 CAROLINE KATHLEEN, b. Jan. 26, 1976.

F12243 GLORIA JUNE LOCKE, born in Lockeport, N.S., May 14, 1929, married in Lockeport, N.S., July 28, 1950, STUART LAWRENCE MORSE, born in Montreal, Que., Dec. 22, 1926.

She graduated from Lockeport, N.S. High School, 1945 and Acadia Univ. in Wolfville, Nova Scotia with a B.S. in home economics, 1949. She returned to teaching in 1959 and was Supervisor of home economics for the city of Dartmouth, N.S., 1965-68.

He is a graduate of Acadia Univ. and was a technical officer in the Defense Research Establishment until 1954 when he joined the Navy as an instructor officer. He is a Master Mason and Past Master of Composite Lodge in Halifax, Nova Scotia.

Children in 12th Gen. b. in Halifax, N.S.

12642 SUSAN ANNE, b. Dec. 7, 1951.

12643 WILLIAM LOCKE, b. June 25, 1954.

F12244 PAULA CORRINE LOCKE, born in Liverpool, N.S., April 10, 1934, married in Toronto, Canada, Dec. 14, 1956, NEIL NIMMO, born in Stirling, Scotland, Sept. 4, 1934.

She attended Lockeport High School. In 1952 she went to Toronto and took a short course in dress designing. She worked as a bank teller and as a cashier for the Toronto Star for a number of years. In 1956 she married Neil Nimmo, a teacher. She is still very interested in art and design and she does oil painting for her own amusement.

Children in 12th Gen. b. in Toronto, Canada

12644 BELINDA ANN, b. May 7, 1963.

12645 DIANA JUNE, b. May 29, 1966.

F12245 CAROL ANNE EATON, born in Conway, N.H., Mar. 19, 1940, married in Gray, Maine, Aug. 22, 1958, RUSSELL MORRIS KEENE, born in Buxton, Maine, June 19, 1940.

She grew up in Gray, Maine and graduated from Pennell Institute. He is employed at Pratt and Whitney Aircraft and she is an office worker.

Children in 12th Generation

12646 TAMMY FAYE, b. Manchester, Conn., Oct. 10, 1961.

12647 LISA ANNE, b. Manchester, Conn., Feb. 14, 1963.

F12246 JAMES LESLIE EATON, born in Gray, Maine, Dec. 9, 1947, married in Gray, Maine, Aug. 5, 1967, SANDRA RAY PARSONS, born in Lewiston, Maine, Feb. 3, 1946.

He attended Gray public schools and graduated from Gray–New Gloucester High School in 1967. Following graduation went to work for Pratt and Whitney Aircraft in Conn. and attended their training program, becoming a machine tool technician.

Children in 12th Gen. b. in Manchester, Conn.

12648 JAMES LESLIE, JR., b. Oct. 30, 1970.

12649 STACY ANNE, b. July 23, 1974.

F12247 DONALD LOCKE JOHNSTON, born in Norwood, Mass., Oct. 19, 1932, married Mar. 15, 1958, ROBIN DIXON. (divorced)

Children in 12th Generation

12650 ROBIN DENISE, b. Feb. 9, 1954.

12651 IVAN MILLER, b. Phoenix, Airz., Oct. 1, 1958.

F12248 DARYL ANN JOHNSTON, born in Norwood, Mass.,
Aug. 30, 1935, married in Buckeye, Ariz., Dec. 2, 1955, CARL
BABCOCK, born in Blythe, Calif., Sept. 17, 1928.

Children in 12th Gen. b. in Mesa, Arizona

12652 DAVID KEITH, b. July 6, 1956.

12653 SUSAN JANE, b. Sept. 14, 1959.

12654 CHARLES HENRY, b. April 3, 1964.

12655 EDWARD ALLAN, b. Feb. 20, 1966.

12656 MICHAEL BENJAMIN, b. Jan. 22, 1970.

F12249 ELEANOR FRASER JOHNSTON, born in Norwood, Mass.,
Oct. 30, 1938, married in Tempe, Ariz., Dec. 24, 1958, ROBERT
AUSTIN HAMILTON, born in Springfield, Mass., Jan. 12, 1936.
She received a B.S. in Elementary Education from Arizona State
College at Flagstaff, Ariz. She does substitute teaching at all levels.
Is active as a leader in children's Bible Study, Fellowship and is a
member of the Congregational Church. Hobbies are music, back-
packing and camping.

Children in 12th Gen. b. in Stockton, Calif.

12657 DEAN ANDREW, b. Mar. 29, 1961.

12658 JOHN FRASER, b. Jan. 14, 1963.

12659 BONNIE BETHIA, b. Jan. 21, 1968.

F12269 WILLIAM FREDERICK HETT, born May 24, 1945, married
in Meridith, N. H., Jan. 25, 1968, BEVERLY WOODMAN of Center
Harbor, N. H.
He attended Bainbridge Naval Prep. School, graduated, 1966 from
Plymouth, N. H. State College with a B. S. degree. In 1971 he re-
ceived a M. S. degree in Math from the University of N. H.

Children in 12th Gen. b. in Laconia, N. H.

12659a HEATHER ANN, b. Mar. 14, 1971.

12659b WILLIAM FREDERICK, JR., b. July 24, 1973.

F12271 LOUIS SHERFESEE III, born in Portsmouth, N.H., April 12,
1946, married in Spicer, Minn., June 18, 1971, CAROL LYGRE,
born in South Africa, Dec. 12, 1945.
After High School graduation he went on The University of The
Seven Seas - a "floating" college around the world. Graduated from
University of Washington in Seattle with a B.S. in Geology and B.S.

in Oceanography in 1969. Lt. in U.S. Navy. On Aircraft Carrier Hancock during Viet Nam War.

She graduated from Luther College, Iowa and did graduate work at University of Washington. She was international hostess for Trans World Airlines and was born in South Africa - daughter of a Lutheran missionary.

Children in 12th Generation

12660 LOUIS, IV, b. Washington, D.C., April 28, 1974.

12661 DAVID MICHAEL, b. Andrews A.F.B., Washington, D.C., Mar. 19, 1976.

F12298 JEANETTE ELEANOR BATTEN, born in Waits River, Vt., Oct. 18, 1922, married in Waits River, Vt., July 19, 1944, RAYMOND TILLOTSON.

Children in 12th Generation

12662 DORIS ELAINE, b. Waits River, Vt., April 19, 1945.

12663 STEPHAN ARTHUR, b. Waits River, Vt., April 15, 1948, m. LINDA SALAMAAR, b. Corinth, Vt., July 10, 1948.

F12664 RACHEL JEANETTE, b. Feb. 19, 1952, m. MARK KNAPP.

F12299 GARDINER BATTEN, born in Waits River, Vt., Dec. 8, 1924, married MARGARET HARTLEY, born July 1, 1924.

Children in 12th Gen. b. in Waits River, Vt.

12665 LESLIE ERWIN, b. July 4, 1945, m. July 1, 1972, CYNTHEA BIGLOW, b. April 12, 1946.

F12666 LINDA, b. Aug. 4, 1948, m. ROLAND PUTNEY.

12667 VIRGINA, b. Oct. 10, 1955.

12668 RANDALL, b. Sept. 25, 1959.

12669 MARY, b. Dec. 6, 1963.

F12300 RUSSELL KENNETH BATTEN, born in Waits River, Vt., Oct. 12, 1927, married Oct. 9, 1948, ELIN JOHNSON, born Feb. 8, 1930.

Children in 12th Gen. b. in Waits River, Vt.

12670 MIKAEL, b. Aug. 19, 1949.

12671 JUDITH ANN, b. Jan. 5, 1951, m. ANTHONY CITRO, b. Clinton, Mass., July 12, 1950.

12672 AVA JUNE, b. May 21, 1952, m. STEPHEN McKINNEY, b. Springfield, Mo., Feb. 29, 1950.

12673 ALETTA, b. Feb. 20, 1954, m. Waits River, Vt., ROBERT BURNS, b. Gloucester, Mass., Jan. 29, 1950.

12674 KENNETH RUSSELL, b. Oct. 6, 1956.

F12301 LOUISE ANABEL BATTEN, born in Waits River, Vt., Jan. 29, 1930, married F. WILLIAM DOE, JR., born in Bradford, Vt., April 4, 1930, divorced in 1967.

Children in 12th Gen. b. in St. Albans, Vt.

12675 F. WILLIAM, III, b. April 4, 1953.

12676 VANNESSA, b. May 1, 1956.

12677 MATHEW, b. July 25, 1958.

12678 ALLISON, b. Jan. 25, 1960.

F12341 GILBERT EVERETT LOCKE, born in Brooklyn, N.Y., July 2, 1941, married 1st, Sept. 2, 1959, GLENDA DELORES CLARK; 2nd, in San Francisco, Calif., Jan. 22, 1970, LYNDA RAE GOODMAN.

Children in 12th Generation

12679 DEBORAH LYNNE, b. Feb. 21, 1960.

12680 THOMAS MICHAEL BANKS, b. Mar. 11, 1961.

F12342 MARJORIE CAROLE LOCKE, born in Newton, Mass., Jan. 14, 1943, married in Denver, Colo., Sept. 1, 1963, ROBERT JACKSON BAIR.

Children in 12th Generation

12681 KATHERINE JO, b. Feb. 21, 1964.

12682 ROBERT JACKSON, JR., b. July 9, 1966.

12683 JANA KAY, b. Jan. 20, 1970.

F12343 GERALDINE DIANE LOCKE, born in Newton, Mass., April 23, 1945, married in Mountain View, Calif., Dec. 18, 1965, CHRISTOPHER LEE CARTER.

Children in 12th Generation

12684 JEFFREY MAYNE, b. Oct. 19, 1967.

12685 ANN ELIZABETH, b. July 25, 1969.

F12344 JANICE ELAINE LOCKE, born in Boulder, Colo., July 21, 1951, married in Redding, Calif., Nov. 18, 1972, DAVID JAMES EGGEN.

Children in 12th Generation

12686 JENNIFER DAWN, b. Dec. 28, 1974.

F12373 JOSEPH FREDERIC BURTT, born in Lowell, Mass., April 4, 1908, married in Derry Village, N.H., July 16, 1938, MARGUERITE T. RICHARDS, born in Lowell, Mass., July 28, 1912.

He is a graduate of Lowell High School 1926, Hebron Academy 1927, Lowell Technological Institute 1931 with B.S. degree, Boston University 1942 with A.B.A. degree, MIT 1958 with M.S. degree in mechanical engineering, Saint Lawrence Univ., N.Y. 1971 with a Ph.D. in anthropology. Has been Associate Professor at Lowell Tech. Dept. of Mechanical Engineering since 1950. Was a Fulbright Lecturer 1965-67 at Alexandria Univ., Egypt. That university awarded him a medallion of merit. Listed in Who's Who in the East. His talents and professional accomplishments and associations are numerous.

Children in 12th Gen. b. in Lowell, Mass.

12687 JOSEPH FREDERIC, JR., b. July 21, 1939.

12688 JOHN ROBERT, b. April 29, 1943, m. Lowell, Mass., Aug. 27, 1965, KAREN ELIZABETH BRAUN.

F12689 RICHARD FRISBIE, b. Oct. 23, 1944, m. Lowell, Mass., Jan. 27, 1968, GERTRUDE MARIE COTE.

F12391 CORILEE DORIS SMITH, born in Pasadena, Calif., April 30, 1944, married in Las Vegas, Nev., June 16, 1960, THOMAS GASTON, born in Pasadena, Calif., Dec. 26, 1943, son of Thomas and Doris Gaston.

Children in 12th Gen. b. in Pasadena, Calif.

12690 KERRI, b. Mar. 31, 1961.

12691 KRISSY, b. Sept. 5, 1963.

F12392 DENNIS MICHAEL GOLDEN, born in Pasadena, Calif., Aug. 4, 1946, married MARSHA MASTAIN, born in Glendora, Calif., Nov. 3, 1946 or 1947.

Children in 12th Generation

12692 NICOLE, b. Glendora, Calif., May 4, 1969.

12693 COLIN, b. Hanover, N.H., May 20, 1975.

F12393 THOMAS PATRICK GOLDEN, born in Pasadena, Calif., Aug. 17, 1947, married 1st, LOUISE DENOTT, born in Los Angeles, Calif., (?), 1948 (?), daughter of Al and Phyllis Denott; 2nd,

DIANNE KELLERMAN, born in Desert Center, Calif., (?), Feb. 1947, daughter of Ted and Amy Kellerman; 3rd, SALLY GUSTAVSON, born in Glendora, Calif., Nov. 10, 1951, daughter of Ken and Ann Gustavson.

Children in 12th Generation

12694 DAMON, b. Blythe, Calif., July 1, 1970.

12695 DERRICK, b. Wheatridge, Colo., Sept. 12, 1972.

12696 JENNIFER SUNSHINE, b. Covina, Calif., Aug. 11, 1975.

F12440 BETTY McDUFFEE, born in Plymouth, Mass., July 26, 1945, married 1st, DWIGHT PIERCE, divorced; 2nd, LAWRENCE STRASSEL.

Children in 12th Generation

12696a DAREEN, b. July 22, 1969.

12696b EVAN, b. Oct. 6, 1971.

F12464 JOSEPH LOUIS BEAULIEU, born in Newburyport, Mass., Oct. 23, 1950, married in Newburyport, Mass., June 12, 1971, SHARON M. KELLEY.

Children in 12th Generation

12697 DAVID MICHALE, b. Newburyport, Mass., Nov. 15, 1971.

F12496 MARGARET ETHEL LOCKE, born in Pownal, Maine, Oct. 30, 1927, married in East Corinth, Maine, Aug. 2, 1941, RONALD BEAN, born in East Corinth, Maine, Nov. 30, 1927.
    She graduated from Higgins Classical Institute, Charleston, Maine. She and son David are very active in the Pentecostal Church, singing in choir. Her hobbies are singing and playing the organ. They live in East Corinth, Maine.

Children in 12th Generation

12698 DAVID RONALD, b. Bangor, Maine, July 2, 1948, m. June 10, 1967, PHYLLIS LORD.

12699 KENDALL BERNARD, b. Milo, Maine, Nov. 27, 1950, m. Nov. 1, 1969, CARLENA WYMAN.

12700 STEPHEN WAYNE, b. Milo, Maine, June 25, 1955, m. Sept. 20, 1974, GUYLENE BURPEE.

12701 PAUL EUGENE, b. Milo, Maine, July 6, 1956, m. East Corinth, Maine, Aug. 7, 1976, KAREN ANN LeCLAIR.

12702 KATHRYN INEZ, b. Milo, Maine, May 17, 1953, m. Mar. 26, 1971, DUANE DANA LOVELY.

F12497 JAMES DONALD LOCKE, born in Ft. Fairfield, Maine, Sept. 1, 1928, married in Bolton Landing, N. Y., Mar. 26, 1959, LILLIAN LORRAINE HASTINGS, born in Poughkeepsie, N. Y., Feb. 14, 1932. He is a chef at the Arnold Palmer Restaurant in Miami, Fla.

Children in 12th Generation

12703 DARLENE SHIRLEY, b. Glens Falls, N. Y., Oct. 5, 1960.

12704 DOREEN MARJORI, b. Glens Falls, N.Y., Oct. 26, 1961.

12705 JAMES DONALD, JR., b. Ft. Ticondongi, N. Y., Sept. 13, 1964.

F12498 ROBERT CARLETON LOCKE, born in Caribou, Maine, April 3, 1931, married in Bath, Maine, DELORES JACQUELINE SEELEY, born in Houlton, Maine, Oct. 6, 1936.

He graduated from Ricker Classical Institute, Houlton, Maine in 1950. Went into the Marine Corps for 3 years. Graduated from Ricker College with B. S. in education. Was in Federal Youth Corp. for 5 or 6 years. Is now principal of Smyrna Mills, Maine Consolidated High School.

Children in 12th Generation

12706 ROBERTA CARLENE, b. Houlton, Maine, July 17, 1955. She is a senior at the Univ. of Maine at Machias.

12707 REBECCA, b. Houlton, Maine, June 25, 1957, m. Hermon, Maine, Aug. 14, 1976, ANTHONY RALPH REYNOLDS.

12708 KENNETH WILLIAM, b. Houlton, Maine, May 28, 1956. He is in the U. S. Air Force.

12709 MICHAEL WAYNE, b. Houlton, Maine, Oct. 19, 1958.

12710 KEVIN JOHN, b. Houlton, Maine, July 21, 1960.

12711 ROXANNE, b. Houlton, Maine, Nov. 4, 1961.

12712 RUTHANNE, b. Houlton, Maine, July 8, 1964.

12713 MICHELLE, b. Houlton, Maine, Dec. 17, 1965.

12714 MARK JAMES, b. Houlton, Maine, Dec. 14, 1967, d. Hermon, Maine, July 23, 1971.

12715 MARY ANNE, b. Bangor, Maine, Jan. 12, 1971.

12716 CARRIE ANNE, b. Bangor, Maine, May 8, 1974.

F12499 JOYCE ALICE IRELAND, born in Caribou, Maine, Nov. 7, 1929, married in Exeter, N. H., Sept. 3, 1949, DOYLE CARLETON RUDD, born in Graceville, Fla., Feb. 20, 1931.

She is a high school graduate, secretary of Hemphill Lutheran Church, past president of Lutheran Church Women's Auxiliary, past secretary of PTA, co-owner of Western Auto Assoc. Store, Houston, Texas. Worked with husband in business about 20 years.

He is a high school graduate, electronics technician graduate from Univ. of Houston. President of Hemphill Lutheran Church, member of Lions Club International about 18 years, past president of Northeast Houston Lions Club, member of Coast Guard Aux. Owner of Western Auto Associate Store in Hemphill, Texas. Veteran of Korean War.

Children in 12th Generation

12717   LINDA I., b. Portland, Maine, Feb. 19, 1950. She is a high school graduate and 2 years college. Director of Park in Houston Parks and Recreation Dept. Has been dental assistant, office receptionist, member of Lutheran Church, Houston, Texas, telephone operator.

12718   SUSAN C., b. Houston, Texas, Sept. 3, 1951. She is a high school graduate and 2 years college, telephone operator. Has been dental assistant, office receptionist, member of Lutheran Church.

F12501   MILDRED ELAINE LOCKE, born in Ft. Fairfield, Maine, July 24, 1933, married in Brewer, Maine, Feb. 5, 1953, JOHN FRANCES GOODNESS, born in Brewer, Maine, Dec. 20, 1932.

She graduated Ft. Fairfield High School, class of 1950 and Husson College, Bangor, 2-year medical secretarial diploma in Jan., 1953. She is "mostly a housewife", helping husband whose office is at home. Served as secretary of the First United Methodist Church of Brewer. Girl Scout Leader, 7 years. Active PTA member for 15 years, Co-President with husband of Washington-Capri PTA, Brewer. Member of Brewer Music Parents Assoc. and secretary of Brewer Public Library Assoc. Corp. Member of Brewer Booster Club and assistant Den Leader for Cub Scouts.

He graduated Brewer High School, Class of 1951, and Husson College, Bangor, B. S. degree in accounting, 1957. Served 2 years in U. S. Army as active National Guardsman, as cook and company clerk and Postmaster. He is a Notary Public, State of Maine Registered Public Accountant, past president of the Bangor-Waterville Chapter of National Assoc. of Accountants, member of the Maine Society of Public Accountants, PTA member for 15 years, Cadette Girl Scout leader 2 years, treasurer of Brewer Booster Club and past president. Treasurer of Brewer Library Assoc. Corp. Member and president of Parish Council of St. Joseph's Catholic Church, Brewer.

Children in 12th Generation

12719   VICKIE SUE, b. Bangor, Maine, April 28, 1956.
She graduated Brewer High School, Class of 1974,

National Honor Society. Dirigo Girls State. Flutist in
Brewer High Band, in Girl Scouts 8 years. Freshman at
Lewiston, St. Mary's School of Nursing.

12720 JEANNE MARIE, b. New Haven, Conn., April 15, 1959.
She graduated Brewer High School, Class of 1977.
Clarinet in Brewer High Band, Saxaphone, Dance Band.
Girl Scout, 7 years.

12721 KATHY ELLEN, b. Portland, Maine, Nov. 3, 1960. She
is a sophomore Brewer High School, chorus, violin in
orchestra. Active in girls field hockey, pillow polo and
track. Girl Scout, 6 years.

12722 JON THOMAS, b. Brewer, Maine, Oct. 11, 1967. He is
a Cub Scout and in P. A. L. Basketball.

F12504 PRISCILLA LaFLEUR ROGERS, born in Portsmouth, N. H.,
Sept. 20, 1941, married 1st, in Portsmouth, N. H., Aug. 14, 1959,
CLINTON BROOKS MAGOUN, born in Exeter, N. H., Oct. 6,
1940; 2nd, in Rutland, Vt., Dec. 26, 1971, GEORGE METALIOUS.

Children in 12th Generation

12723 ELIZABETH BROOKS, b. Denver, Colo., Jan. 5, 1960.

12724 MARTIN GRANT, b. Marysville, Calif., Dec. 30, 1961.

F12505 ABIGAIL GARLAND ROGERS, born in Portsmouth, N. H.,
Aug. 23, 1943, married in Rye Beach, N. H., July 25, 1964, O.
RAHMAN KHAN, born in Bhopal, India, April 3, 1934.

Children in 12th Generation

12725 SARINA YASMINE, b. Exeter, N. H., July 31, 1965.

12726 FELICIA NASIM, b. Exeter, N. H., Oct. 4, 1966.

12727 SALIM RAHMAN, b. Laconia, N. H., Nov. 20, 1968.

F12506 MARY ANN ROGERS, born in Portsmouth, N. H., Sept.
20, 1944, married in Portsmouth, N. H., May 16, 1964, FRANCIS
WALTER SAWTELLE, born in Brewer, Maine, Nov. 10, 1940.

Children in 12th Generation

12728 SCOTT FRANCIS, b. Cambridge, Mass., Aug. 25, 1964.

12729 TIMOTHY OLIVER, b. Exeter, N. H., Dec. 8, 1965.

12730 CHRISTOPHER ROGERS, b. Ipswich, Mass., Oct. 30, 1967.

12731 AMANDA MARIETTA, b. Ipswich, Mass., Jan. 28, 1969.

F12540 <u>BEVERLY JEAN FRANCIS</u>, born in East Livermore, Maine, Mar. 3, 1934, married in Portsmouth, N. H., Oct. 19, 1952, WILLIAM RICHARD COREY, born in Skowhegan, Maine, Dec. 18, 1912, son of Richard and Cecelia (Haddad) Corey.

Children in 12th Gen. b. in Lewiston, Maine

12732 WILLIAM RANDALL, b. Jan. 5, 1954, m. BELINDA REED TODD.

12733 RHONDA LYN, b. Feb. 19, 1956.

THIRTEENTH GENERATION

F12559 ELIZABETH ANNE LOCKE, born in Exeter, N. H., June 24, 1949, married in Oklahoma City, Okla., Aug. 18, 1972, Capt. WILLIAM BONTLY, U.S.A.F., born in Tennessee, Dec. 26, 1949.

Children in 13th Generation

12734 TRENT ANTON, b. Abilene, Texas, Jan. 16, 1975.

F12560 JUDITH ALMA LOCKE, born in Exeter, N. H., Nov. 2, 1950, married in Hampton, N. H., Jan. 17, 1969, KENNETH D. McBRAYER, born in Shrevesport. La., Dec. 31, 1950.

Children in 13th Generation

12735 CAREY ANN, b. New Britain, Conn., July 26, 1970.

12736 MINDY LOCKE, b. Valrico, Fla., May 18, 1975.

F12570 LAURENCE EARL BERRY, born April 20, 1938, married Feb. 10, 1969, KATHLEEN ANNE TULLY, born May 1, 1943.

Children in 13th Generation

12737 SHAYLA TULLY, b. July 5, 1965.

12738 BRETT OWEN, b. Oct. 28, 1971.

F12571 PATRICIA ANN BERRY, born July 20, 1946, married May, 16, 1970, DAVID ALFRED NICKERSON, born July 24, 1946.

Children in 13th Generation

12739 LAURA ANN

F12573 JOHN LLOYD WENTZELL, JR., born Oct. 7, 1942, married June 26, 1965, LINDA IRENE FLINT, born Jan. 26, 1942.
He works for State Mutual in Worcester, Mass. and enjoys tennis and skiing. They live in Northboro, Mass.

Children in 13th Generation

12740 SCOTT PRENTICE, b. Dec. 10, 1966.

12741 JAMES JOHN, b. Nov. 25, 1969.

F12575 JULIANNE WENTZELL, born Dec. 12, 1946, married Aug. 6, 1966, JOHN DAVID MORRISON, born Feb. 23, 1946.

She is a radiological technician at Cooley Dickenson Hospital in Northampton, Mass. and he is a partner in the Pleasant St. theater there. They are interested in arts and crafts of all kinds.

Children in 13th Generation

12742 JILL ELIZABETH, b. Mar. 21, 1967.

12743 ALETHEA, b. Feb. 3, 1971.

F12587 VIRGINIA PAGE PHILLIPS, born June 29, 1945, married 1st, 1966, HARRY JAMES HILL, divorced 1973; 2nd, Dec. 7, 1974, JOE NORMAN PARKER.

She graduated from Univ. of North Carolina School of Nursing. She lives in Georgetown, South Carolina.

Children in 13th Generation

12744 HOLLAND PAGE HILL, b. Sept. 30, 1966.

12745 HARRY JAMES HILL, III, b. April 6, 1970.

12746 JOE NORMAN PARKER, JR., b. Aug. 29, 1976.

F12609 ELIZABETH MARSHALL WOOD, born in Chicago, Ill., married Nov. 4, 1961, ROBERT JOHN ELIAS.

Children in 13th Generation

12747 JOHN MARSHALL, b. Sept. 1, 1962.

12748 SUSAN DuBOIS, b. Nov. 14, 1963.

F12610 GEORGE SHAFFER WOOD, III, born in Charlottesville, Va., married in Columbia, S.C., LINDA CANNON.

Children in 13th Generation

12749 ANNE MARSHALL, b. Aiken, S.C., Aug. 19, 1973.

F12664 RACHEL JEANETTE TILLOTSON, born in Waits River, Vt., Feb. 19, 1952, married MARK KNAPP, born in Corinth, Vt., Feb. 8, 1950.

Children in 13th Generation

12750 ANGELA, b. Oct. 29, 1969.

12751 ALLISON, b. April 17, 1972.

F12666 LINDA BATTEN, born in Waits River, Vt., Aug. 4, 1948, married ROLAND PUTNEY, born Sept. 11, 1947.

Children in 13th Generation

12752 BRIAN, b. Dec. 9, 1971.

F12689 RICHARD FRISBIE BURTT, born in Lowell, Mass., Oct. 23, 1944, married in Lowell, Mass., Jan. 27, 1968, GERTRUDE M. COTE, born in Lowell, Mass.

He graduated 1968 from Lowell Tech., Lowell, Mass. with B.S. and M.S. degrees in chemical engineering. Worked for W. Va. Paper and Pulp Co. and IBM. Now President of Andover Medical Associates, Andover, Mass.

Children in 13th Generation

12753 KRISTYN MARIE, b. Lowell, Mass., Dec. 3, 1971.

SOME ADDITIONS TO THE GENEALOGY OF
WILLIAM LOCKE OF WOBURN, MASS.

William Locke and John Locke were contemporaries in history. Born in London a year apart, and thereby possibly related, they both came to the New World at early ages: William at age six in 1634 and John well before he reached his majority. Their reasons for removal to a new land quite possibly were the same — religious and political persecution. Both men were successful and respected pioneers who established families whose members were industrious, dependable, intelligent, and hard working. The two families are similar in that, while neither can claim high dignitaries in church, state, or military service, they helped form the backbone of a great democracy.

It is lamentable that the William Locke genealogy has not been updated in over a hundred and twenty-five years. Perhaps one of William's descendants will see it is done completely. What follows is all that was submitted to the Association plus information published in pamphlet form in 1900 by Rev. Samuel L. Gerould.

EIGHTH GENERATION

1021 HERBERT LOCKE, (3590) born in Boston, Mass., March 8, 1849, died in Boston, Mass., June 5, 1874, married in Boston, Mass., Dec. 8, 1870, LUCY A. JEWETT, born in Roxbury, Mass., died in Auburndale, Mass., Jan., 1927.

VIII Children

6328 HERBERT CHARLES, b. Boston, Mass., Sept. 12, 1874.
1034

6329 EUGENIA F.

1022 CATHERINE URANIA GRISWOLD, (4135) born in Greenfield, Mass., Sept. 12, 1831, died in Townsend, Mass., Jan. 26, 1914, married in Townsend, Mass., Oct. 13, 1858, OLIVER PROCTOR, born in Townsend, Mass., July 2, 1823, died in Townsend, Mass., Jan. 13, 1917. She was educated at Goodale Academy in Bernardston and Sanborn Academy in Washington, N. H. She studied music in Brattleboro, Vt. as well as with Prof. Henry Wilson of Greenfield. Music was important to the Griswold family as all of them were musical, four being known in Greenfield as the Griswold Quartet. She possessed a soprano voice of considerable power and never withheld its use where it could benefit or please. While quite young she began teaching school beginning at Wapping, in Deerfield, and including various towns and states including Maine, and Illinois and finally Townsend, Mass. She was active in the Townsend Congregational Church.

VIII Children born in Townsend, Mass.

6330 NILLO GRISWOLD, b. April 4, 1861, d. Townsend, Mass., Oct., 1949, m. Townsend, Mass., April 29, 1920, HESTER HOWE BURDETT.

6331 EDWARD OLIVER, b. March 21, 1869, d. Ayer, Mass., m. WINIFRED DIX.

6332 GALEN ABNER, b. Sept. 19, 1871.   1035

6333 a girl, b. Nov. 15, 1866, d. young.

1023 LUTHER FRANKLIN LOCKE, M. D. (4185) born in Langdon, N. H., Nov. 3, 1820, married first, Nov. 28, 1850, SARAH FOLLANSBEE WILLIAMS of Groton, Mass. who died May 5, 1861. Married second, March 29, 1865, CAROLINE DIANA BARRETT of Langdon, N. H. He graduated from Middlebury College, 1845, Har-

vard Medical College, 1849. He was a physician, surgeon and dentist in Nashua, N. H. where he died Feb. 14, 1892. He was a member
of the Pilgrim Congregational Church.

VIII Children

6334 SARAH GRACE, b. May 17, 1866, d. May 11, 1889.

6335 ANNA WILLARD, b. April 7, 1868, graduated from Wel-
      lesley College, 1892, and the University of Michigan,
      1897, with the degrees of A. M. and M. D. She was a
      practicing physician in New York City and taught
      physiology in the Girl's High School.

6336 CARRIE GERTRUDE, b. Aug. 9, 1869, graduated from the
      Boston Dental College, 1895, with the degree of D.D.S.
      She practiced dentistry in Nashua, N. H.

6337 HARRIET FRANCES, b. Nov. 24, 1870, studied architec-
      ture at M. I. T., 1897, and was an architect in Nashua,
      N. H.

6338 EVA MAY, b. Jan. 20, 1874, graduated from Michigan
      University, 1899, with an M. D. degree.

6339 BESSIE EMMA, b. Sept. 25, 1876, d. Nov. 22, 1885.

1024 DEAN JEWETT LOCKE, (4186) born in Langdon, N.H.,
April 16, 1823, married May 8, 1855, DELIA M. HAMMOND of
North Abington, Mass. He graduated from Bridgewater, Mass. State
Normal School, taught school for four years, then studied at Harvard
Medical College until 1849 when he joined the "Boston and Newton
Joint Stock Assn. " with which he crossed the plains, as physician, to
California, arriving Sept., 1849. He laid out the town of Lockeford
in 1862 where his father, Luther Locke, became the first postmaster,
whom he succeeded. He erected a number of the principal buildings
and was engaged in farming, the keeping of a general store, and the
practice of medicine until he died on May 4, 1887.

VIII Children

6340 LUTHER JEWETT, b. April 16, 1856.   1036

6341 ADA, b. Dec. 16, 1857.   1037

6342 NATHANIEL HOWARD, b. July 19, 1859.   1038

6343 HORACE MANN, b. Dec. 31, 1860.   1039

6344 IDA, b. April 10, 1862.   1040

6345 MARY, b. April 6, 1864, d. Lockeford, Calif., Jan. 31,
      1894, m. March 8, 1887, WILLIAM PATTERSON
      MOORE of Redwood City, Calif. She attended Mrs.
      Perry's Young Ladies' Seminary in Sacramento, Calif.

6346 WILLIAM WILLARD, b. Nov. 19, 1865, m. Nashua, N.H., Sept. 14, 1898, ETTA MAY OBER, D.D.S., a graduate of Boston Dental College. He graduated from the State Normal School, San Jose, Calif., 1885, taught two years, attended Phillips Exeter, N. H. Academy, and graduated from M.I.T., 1892, as a civil and sanitary engineer. He was chief sanitary engineer of Brooklyn, N.Y. and held positions on the Massachusetts Metropolitan Water Board and lived in Framingham, Mass. where his wife practiced dentistry.

6346a HANNAH, b. Nov. 19, 1867, m. Aug. 24, 1893, JOHN C. DEMANGEOT of Lockeford, Calif. She graduated from the New England Conservatory of Music, Boston, Mass. department of piano forte and reed organ tuning, 1889. He was a farmer and she was engaged in music teaching and the tuning of instruments. They adopted 6346b HORACE CELESTE, b. Lockeford, Calif., April 19, 1896.

6346c JOHN CALVIN, b. May 30, 1869, m. Brooklyn, N. Y., Nov. 22, 1899, LILLIAN GREEN, daughter of Clarence S. Green. He graduated, 1894, from M. I. T. as a civil and sanitary engineer and held positions on Boston Subway, Brooklyn, N. Y. Board of Health and Brooklyn Navy Yard as expert aid civil engineer. They lived in Brooklyn.

6347 EDWARD MOORE, b. Oct. 30, 1871.   1041

6348 EUNICE, b. Aug. 13, 1874.   1042

6349 GEORGE HAMMOND, b. Oct. 19, 1877 and graduated from the University of Calif. dept. of Veterinary Surgery, 1898 and served as a veterinary surgeon in the U. S. Army in the Philippine Islands.

6350 THERESA, b. Sept. 8, 1879 and graduated from the Stockton, Calif. High School, 1897 and trained as a nurse in the Women's Hospital, San Francisco, Calif.

1025 GEORGE SHEPLEY LOCKE, (4188) born in Langdon, N.H., Oct. 30, 1830, married May 15, 1859, SUSAN L. HAMMOND of North Abington, Mass. He went to California in 1852 and settled in Lockeford where he remained as a farmer until he died in San Francisco, Dec. 10, 1895. He was a member of the Lockeford Congregational Church.

VIII Children

6351 SARAH ANN JANE, b. Aug. 5, 1860.   1043

6352 ELMER HAMMOND, b. Oct. 22, 1862, d. May 20, 1875.

6353 GEORGE FRANKLIN, b. Aug. 22, 1864, d. Nov. 14, 1868.

6354 WALLACE HUNTINGTON, b. May 8, 1867. 1044

6355 AMY, b. Feb. 4, 1869, d. same day.

6356 LILLA, b. May 26, 1871, m. Oct. 18, 1899, JAMES A. JORY of Lockeford, Calif. She graduated from the training school for nurses at the Women's Hospital, San Francisco, Calif., 1891 and resided in Lockeford where he was engaged in farming.

6357 JOHN GEROULD, b. Sept. 20, 1873, d. San Francisco, Calif., Feb. 10, 1886.

6358 MERTICE, b. June 4, 1876. 1045

6359 FRANKLIN HAMMOND, b. Aug. 5, 1878, attended the College of Physicians and Surgeons, San Francisco, California.

6360 ALMA GRACE, b. Jan. 5, 1882, d. Dec. 2, 1882?.

1026 MARY ABBY LOCKE, (4190) born in Ipswich, Mass., March 4, 1833, married in Marshall, Texas, Nov. 23, 1855, REUBEN KNIGHT. He was a wholesale and retail grocer and was an Odd Fellow and deacon in the Presbyterian Church where his fine business abilities contributed to the financial strength of the church. She died July 19, 1876 and he died Nov. 27, 1879.

VIII Children

6361 CHARLES, b. Sept. 5, 1856, d. Sept. 9, 1859.

6362 KATIE, b. Oct. 6, 1857. 1046

6363 MARY CHRISTINE, b. March 2, 1859. 1047

6364 WILLIAM FITZ, b. Oct. 2, 1860, d. July 21, 1861.

6365 infant, b. and d. Jan. 12, 1862.

6366 REUBEN CLINTON, b. Dec. 28, 1862. 1048

6367 HARRY, b. Oct. 2, 1864, d. Nov. 11, 1871.

6368 RICHARD SHANNON, b. March 10, 1866, d. March 18, 1866.

6369 LUCY ANN, b. April 2, 1867, d. Oct. 29, 1867.

6370 ELLEN CLINTON, b. June 13, 1869, m. Nov. 27, 1888, WILLIE W. BATTLE of Caddo Parish, La. He was employed in the U. S. Custom House, New Orleans, La.

where they lived and she attended the Presbyterian
Church.

1027 SARAH JEWETT LOCKE, (4191) born in Ipswich, Mass.,
Feb. 24, 1835, married Jan. 20, 1858, JOHN DYKE of Greenfield,
N. H. He was a merchant in Jefferson, Texas where he died April 9,
1869. She resided in Marshall, Texas and attended the Presbyterian
Church.

VIII Children

6371 LIGGETTE AUSTIN, b. Feb. 22, 1859, d. June 17, 1859.

6372 MARY ANNA, b. May 26, 1861, d. Nov. 9, 1868.

6373 CATHERINE AUSTIN, b. Oct. 4, 1863.   1049

6374 CLINTON ADAMS, b. May 26, 1865   1050

6375 ABBY ABBOTT, b. July 10, 1868, d. Nov. 15, 1873.

1028 ANNA ABBOTT LOCKE, (4193) born in Ipswich, Mass.,
Dec. 26, 1849, married first, March 8, 1886, WILLIAM LONG
KETCHAM of Rock Island, Ill. who died in Marshall, Texas, June 15,
1891. He was a railroad engineer and resided in Natchitoches, La.
She married second, March 8, 1894, FRANK McCLARAN in Marshall,
Texas where he was a farmer and elder of the Cumberland Presbyterian
Church.

VIII Child

6376 FREDERICK LOCKE, b. Oct. 26, 1890.

1029 CLEMENTINE MARIA LOCKE, (4194) born in Acworth,
N. H., Aug. 17, 1824, married Aug. 23, 1849, Rev. WILLIAM
PORTER, of Lyme, N. H. She graduated from Mt. Holyoke Seminary,
1845 and taught in St. Charles and Troy, Mo. until her marriage. He
was a graduate of Dartmouth College, 1840 and Andover Theological
Seminary, 1845. He was ordained a Congregational minister April 12,
1846. He preached, taught and edited a paper in Illinois and
Missouri, 1845-1872 when they moved to Ivanhoe, Prospect Park, a
suburb of Los Angeles, Calif.

VIII Children

6377 CALVIN LOCKE, b. St. Francisville, Mo., July 26, 1853,
       d. Westminister, Calif., March 22, 1879. He was a
       graduate of the Homeopathic Medical College, Cleve-
       land, Ohio, 1878.

6378　MARY STOUGHTON, b. Port Byron, Ill., April 29, 1855, m. June 10, 1889, CHARLES STEWART HAINES, d. Los Angeles, May 10, 1892. He was a graduate of the Germantown, Penna. Agricultural College and raised thoroughbred stock of all kinds.

1030　CALVIN STOUGHTON LOCKE, (4197) born in Acworth, N. H., Oct. 11, 1829, married June 5, 1855, ANNE LINCOLN of Northboro, Mass. He was a graduate of Amherst College, 1849, Harvard Divinity School, 1854, and was ordained Unitarian that year. He served as minister in West Dedham (now Westwood) and Dover, Mass. He maintained a private school in Westwood, which opened in 1863 and was superintendent of schools. He traveled extensively in Europe and the United States.

VIII Children

6379　MARY STOUGHTON, b. May 5, 1856. She graduated from the Girls' High School in Boston, 1874, Smith College, 1880, and Radcliffe College, 1892, with a A. M. degree. She taught in schools in Boston and Baltimore, Md.

6380　HARRIET PROCTOR REYNOLDS, b. July 16, 1857, d. July 9, 1870.

6381　WILLIAM WARE, b. Dec. 14, 1858, m. June 16, 1900, SARAH KENDALL SAVARY of Groveland, Mass. He was a graduate of Worcester Polytechnic Institute, 1877, Harvard Divinity School, 1885 and was ordained Unitarian in 1886. He served at the Barnard Memorial Chapel in Boston and then taught in New York City, Dedham and Concord, Mass.

6382　HENRY LINCOLN, b. July 12, 1860, graduated from Cornell University, 1880 and was a farmer in Brighton, Colorado.

1031　SAMUEL LANKTON GEROULD, (4199) born in East Alstead, N. H., July 11, 1834, married first, Sept. 20, 1860, LUCY ABBY MERRIAM of Greenville, N. H. who died Jan. 12, 1867. He married second, Dec. 5, 1867, LAURA ETTA THAYER of Acworth, N. H. He graduated from Dartmouth College, 1858, studied at Union Theological Seminary, 1858-1860, and was ordained Congregational, Oct. 2, 1861. Served as minister in Stoddard, N. H., Goffstown, N. H. and Hollis, N. H. Served in the Union Army, 1862-65, in Company G, 14th N. H. Volunteers. He received the honorary degree of D. D. from Dartmough College in 1897.

VIII Children

6383 MARY CLEMENTINE, b. Stoddard, N. H., Dec. 3, 1861. She studied at Mt. Holyoke Seminary until her health gave way. She was employed as a clerk in the office of the Secretary of State and of the Adjutant General in Concord, N. H.

6384 JOHN HIRAM, b. Stoddard, N. H., Oct. 2, 1868. He graduated from Dartmouth College, 1890 and Harvard College, 1892, with A. M. and Ph. D. degrees. He was an instructor in zoology at Dartmouth College.

6385 EMMA, b. Dec. 8, 1869, d. Dec. 24, 1869.

6386 JAMES THAYER, b. Oct. 3, 1872 and graduated from Dartmouth College, 1895. He was a librarian at General Theological Seminary in New York City and Library of Columbia University and was appointed chief librarian at the University of Missouri, Columbia, Mo.

6387 HARRIET DUPEE, b. Oct. 26, 1874 and graduated from Middlebury College, 1897 and taught in Westwood, Mass.

6388 GORDON HALL, b. Oct. 4, 1877. Graduated, 1899, from Dartmouth College and studied at Oxford University, England.

6389 MARION LOCKE, b. Sept. 11, 1880 and studied at Mt. Holyoke College.

6390 LEONARD STINSON, b. March 20, 1883.

1032 SARAH AZUBAH GEROULD, (4201) born in East Alstead, N. H., April 13, 1839, married May 24, 1861, Hon. ISAAC N. BLODGETT of Canaan, N. H. She was a graduate of Mt. Holyoke Seminary, 1859. They lived in Franklin, N. H. and he was Chief Justice of the Supreme Court of New Hampshire.

VIII Child

6391 ANNA GERALDINE, b. Canaan, N. H., Aug. 13, 1862 and was educated at Wellesley College.

1033 WARREN SHADRACH SHATTUCH, (5117) born in New York City, Jan. 14, 1833, died in New York City, March 29, 1906, married May 21, 1856 to HENRIETTA CAROLINE FROST, born in Massachusetts, March 31, 1835 and died in Brooklyn, N. Y., April 14, 1914. He was a Presbyterian minister and is listed in "Who's Who in America, 1850-55".

VIII Child

6392 MARGUERITE, b. Brooklyn, N. Y., Dec. 13, 1878, d.
Landsdowne, Penna., July 7, 1965, m. May 12, 1906,
GEORGE WELLS ARMS, JR.

NINTH GENERATION

<u>1034   HERBERT CHARLES LOCKE</u>, (6328) born in Boston, Mass.,
Sept. 12, 1874, died in New Haven, Conn., Dec. 5, 1958, married
first, in Jamaica Plain, Mass., June 25, 1901, CHRISTINE WILHEL-
MINA MAIS, born in Boston, Mass., Oct. 3, 1872, died in Long
Island City, N. Y., April 21, 1935. He married second, in Boston,
Mass., Oct., 1939, GERTRUDE McINTOSH.

IX Children

6393   GERTRUDE IRENE, b. Boston, Mass., Nov. 5, 1907, m.
Matawan, N.J., June 25, 1933, DAVID E. BIGWOOD,
M.D. who d. 1970. She graduated from Newton, Mass.
High School, attended Wellesley College, graduated
from the University of Michigan and earned a Master's
Degree at Yale. She lives in Syracuse, N.Y.

6394   MARION FRANCES, b. Chicago, Ill. She graduated from
Newton, Mass. High School, attended LaSalle Junior
College, graduated from the University of Michigan and
earned a Master's Degree at New York University. She
lives in Hamden, Conn. and teaches in the Sleeping
Giant Jr. High School.

6395   HERBERT CHARLES, JR., b. Indianapolis, Ind., Sept. 2,
1914, m. St. Albans, Vt., Sept. 1, 1940, LAURA ANNE
MITCHELL. He graduated from the Matawan, N.J. High
School and attended University of Michigan High School
and Rutgers University, N. J. He was employed for 36
years by F. W. Woolworth Co. and managed stores in
Buffalo, N. Y., Danielson, Conn., Chicopee, Mass.,
and Lantana and Pompano Beach, Fla. He served in the
Quartermaster Corps during World War II and was sta-
tioned in the Pacific. He is a member of A. F. & A. M.
Lodge of Masons and lives in Pompano Beach. He is a
Vice President of the Locke Family Association.

<u>1035   GALEN ABNER PROCTOR</u>, (6332) born in Townsend, Mass.,
Sept. 19, 1871, died in Townsend, Mass., Feb. 17, 1964, married in
Townsend, Mass., April 14, 1917, MELORA ELLA WARNER, born in
Townsend, Mass., May 6, 1883, died in Townsend, Mass., April 26,
1955. He attended Townsend High School and Worcester Academy.
He helped organize the Townsend Grange where he was active all his
life holding various offices including Master. He did general farming,
ran a dairy, a saw mill, drove a school bus and was active in town

affairs where he served as assessor and selectman. After taking elocution lessons he gave oral renderings of poetry for the enjoyment of his friends. He was small physically but strong, a teetotaller, non-smoker; the personification of Calvinistic morality. His hay fields were classroom or cathedral as philosophical, natural science, or religious discussions accompanied the work there, a practice begun by his father. She was a teacher.

IX Children born in Townsend, Mass.

6396 CATHERINE WARNER, b. Sept. 18, 1918.   1051

6397 ROBERT GALEN, b. July 29, 1921, m. Rochdale, Mass., April 26, 1947, MARY ELIZABETH IRWIN.

6398 DAVID MANNING, b. Nov. 27, 1925, d. in a tractor accident in Townsend, Mass., Aug. 9, 1941.

1036 LUTHER JEWETT, (6340) born in Lockeford, Calif., April 16, 1856, married June 3, 1884, ALICE JOSAPHINE LIPP. They lived in Lockeford where he was a wholesale and retail dealer in livestock and ran a meat market.

IX Child

6399 NELLIE, b. Feb. 2, 1885.

1037 ADA LOCKE, (6341) born in Lockeford, Calif., Dec. 16, 1857, married Oct. 30, 1882, Rev. WILLIAM HENRY COOKE. She was graduated from the State Normal School, San Jose, Calif., 1876 and taught five years. Her husband is a graduate of the Oakland Theological Seminary (Congregational), 1880, and was pastor of the Fourth Congregational Church of that city, 1881-1892, when his health failed. He then became assistant State Sunday School mission-ary for California and resided in Sunol Glen, Calif. where he served the church as pastor and preached at stations at Dublin and Mission San Jose.

IX Children

6400 WELDON BAGSTER, b. Lockeford, Calif., June 28, 1884.

6401 WINNIE, b. Oakland, Oct. 22, 1885, d. June 27, 1886.

6402 ALMA, b. Oakland, Calif., May 2, 1887.

6403 ROBERT LOCKE, b. Brockton, Mass., Oct. 21, 1889.

6404 HESTER, b. Oakland, Calif., Feb. 19, 1894.

1038 NATHANIEL HOWARD LOCKE, (6342) born in Lockeford, Calif., July 19, 1859, married Dec. 25, 1884, LUCINDA M. CLAPP of Lathrop, Calif. He was graduated from the State Normal School, San Jose, Calif., 1880 and taught a number of years. He was a farmer and dairyman in Lockeford.

IX Children

6405 CHESTER CLAPP, b. Dec. 19, 1885.

6406 LOTTIE CLAPP, b. Oct. 9, 1887.

6407 ALMA CLAPP, b. March 1, 1891.

6408 HOWARD CLAPP, b. Jan. 9, 1894.

6409 MYRLE CLAPP, b. July 3, 1895.

6410 NATHANIEL CLAPP, b. April 30, 1897.

1039 HORACE MANN LOCKE, (6343) born in Lockeford, Calif., Dec. 31, 1860, married Dec. 12, 1888, EUNICE C. BLANCHARD of Brockton, Mass. He graduated from Harvard College, Medical Dept. 1886, and practiced medicine in Mokelumni Hill, Calif., Somerville, Mass., Brockton, Mass. and Sturbridge, Mass.

IX Children born in Brockton, Mass.

6411 DEAN JEWETT, b. Feb. 14, 1890.

6412 LOUIS, b. June 12, 1892.

1040 IDA LOCKE, (6344) born in Lockeford, Calif., April 10, 1862, married first, May 8, 1883, Rev. WILLIAM HENRY PASCOE. He served in the U.S. Navy through the Civil War and graduated from the Oakland Theological Seminary (Congregational), 1879. He served the churches of Lockeford, Redwood City, Rio Del, and Scotia, Calif. until he died Aug. 5, 1889. She married second, Sept. 12, 1893, BENJAMIN MARSTON PARKER of Scotia, Calif. She graduated from the State Normal School, San Jose, Calif., 1881 and resided in Eureka, Calif.

IX Children

6413 SUSIE, b. Lockeford, Calif., Feb. 1, 1884.

6414 JOSEPH AUGUSTINE BENTON, b. Lockeford, Calif., June 14, 1885.

6415 WEBSTER LOCKE, b. Scotia, Calif., April 29, 1894.

6416 IRVING KEITH, b. Scotia, Calif., July 22, 1895.

6417 GEORGE HERBERT, b. Scotia, Calif., Dec. 26, 1896, d. Sept. 18, 1897.

6418 DELIA, b. Eureka, Calif., Oct. 31, 1899.

1041 EDWARD MOORE LOCKE, (6347) born in Lockeford, Calif., Oct. 30, 1871, married April 7, 1893, AGNES M. STEWART of Lockeford. He was a farmer and dairyman in Lockeford.

IX Children

6419 EDNA STEWART, b. Lockeford, March 19, 1894.

6420 AGNES MARIE, b. Los Angeles, Oct. 20, 1895.

1042 EUNICE LOCKE, (6348) born in Lockeford, Calif., Aug. 13, 1874, married in Eureka, Calif., March 17, 1895, EDWARD WARREN WEBSTER. She graduated from the State Normal School, San Jose, Calif., 1894 and taught before her marriage. They resided in Scotia, Calif. where he was chief sawyer in the Pacific Lumber Company mills.

IX Children born in Scotia, Calif.

6421 DEAN BENJAMIN, b. May 14, 1896.

6422 EDWARD LOCKE, b. Oct. 24, 1898.

1043 SARAH ANN JANE LOCKE, (6351) born in Lockeford, Calif., Aug. 5, 1860, married Dec. 25, 1882, WILLIAM THOMAS SMITH of Ferndale, Calif. She graduated from the State Normal School, San Jose, Calif., 1880. They lived in Ferndale, Calif. where he was a farmer and she was a member of the M. E. Church.

IX Children

6423 ELMER WILLIAM, b. Oct. 21, 1883.

6424 HARRY JAMES, b. June 17, 1885.

6425 WARREN LOCKE, b. Nov. 8, 1886.

6426 ETHEL, b. Sept. 28, 1888.

6427 MILDRED, b. June 10, 1891.

6428 GERTRUDE, b. Nov. 24, 1898.

1044 WALLACE HUNTINGTON LOCKE, (6354) born in Lockeford, Calif., May 8, 1867, married Dec. 13, 1891, MAUD M. MISENER of Elliot, Calif. They resided in Lockeford where he was a rancher.

IX Children

6429 ERMA GRACE, b. Nov. 18, 1894.

6430 CARLTON GEROULD, b. Dec. 24, 1897.

1045 MERTICE LOCKE, (6358) born in Lockeford, Calif., June 4, 1876, married Aug. 20, 1898, JAMES S. GILL of Kettle Falls, Wash. She graduated from the State Normal School, San Jose, Calif., 1897. They lived in Kettle Falls where he was in the hotel business and she was a member of the Congregational Church.

IX Child

6431 GEROULD LOCKE, b. Lockeford, Calif., Aug. 21, 1899.

1046 KATIE KNIGHT, (6362) born in Marshall, Texas, Oct. 6, 1857, married March 27, 1883, THOMAS P. YOUNG, an attorney at law in Marshall, Texas and deacon in the Presbyterian Church.

IX Children

6432 MARY KATHERINE, b. July 17, 1884.

6432a THOMAS P., b. June 17, 1886, d. Sept. 5, 1887.

6433 ANNA CHRISTINE, b. Jan. 25, 1888.

6433a WILLIAM FRANKLIN, b. Feb. 16, 1891.

6434 MARY P., b. Nov. 27, 1892.

6434a LOUISE CLOUGH, b. May 7, 1894.

6435 REUBEN KNIGHT, b. March 28, 1896, d. Dec. 24, 1896.

6435a CALVIN LOCKE, b. Feb. 27, 1899.

1047 MARY CHRISTINE KNIGHT, (6363) born in Marshall, Texas, March 2, 1869, married Nov. 11, 1882, MILTON LOTHROP, who was a wholesale grocer in Marshall, Texas, a deacon and treasurer of the Presbyterian Church.

IX Children

6436 HUGH REUBEN, b. Oct. 30, 1885.

6437 MILTON, b. Oct. 29, 1887.

6438 KATIE GARLAND, b. Oct. 13, 1889.

6439 GRAFTON, b. Jan. 21, 1891.

6440 MARY, b. July 11, 1894.

6441 NELLIE, b. July 19, 1897, d. July 22, 1897.

6442 CONSTANCE, b. Nov. 29, 1899.

1048 REUBEN CLINTON KNIGHT, (6366) born in Marshall, Texas, Dec. 28, 1862, married first, Jan. 19, 1884, LIZZIE HOWARD of Marshall, Texas, married second, Sept. 19, 1894, QUEENIE ANDERSON of Nacogdoches, Texas, having obtained a divorce from his first wife. He was a baggage master in San Antonio, Texas.

IX Children

6443 HARRY HOWARD, b. July 14, 1885.

6444 MARGUERITE, b. Nov. 29, 1889, d. Jan. 7, 1890.

1049 CATHERINE AUSTIN DYKE, (6373) born in Marshall, Texas, Oct. 4, 1863, married first, June 18, 1879, GEORGE R. WILCOX, a painter. She was divorced from him with custody of her children and married second, July 11, 1888, GEORGE L. McALLISTER of Bedford, N. H. He was a merchant and sewing machine agent and died in Marshall, Texas, Jan. 12, 1896.

IX Children

6445 MARY VAUGHN, b. June 19, 1880, studied at the State Sam Houston Normal Institute in Huntsville, Texas.

6446 CHARLES RICHARDS, b. July 16, 1882.

1050 CLINTON ADAMS DYKE, (6374) born in Marshall, Texas, May 24, 1865, married Jan. 7, 1890, LEONORA A. ALLBRIGHT of Colliersville, Tenn. He was a commercial traveller, living in Pittsburg, Texas.

IX Children

6447 CLINTON ALLBRIGHT, b. Marshall, Texas, Oct. 27, 1890.

6448 FRED MILLS, b. Dangefield, Texas, Oct. 2, 1895.

6449 ————, b. May 26, 1900.

TENTH GENERATION

  1051 CATHERINE WARNER PROCTOR, (6396) born in Townsend, Mass., Sept. 18, 1918, married first, in Townsend, Mass., Sept. 24, 1941, RAYMOND BOYES, JR., married second, in Townsend, Mass., June 20, 1964, RALPH BRACKETT WILSON, She graduated from Spaulding School and attended teacher's college. She belonged to the Four-H Club, the Grange and enjoyed swimming and skating. After finishing college she taught at Townsend, Littleton and New Bedford.

X Children

6450 JANE CATHERINE PROCTOR, b. Groton, Mass., May 16, 1940.   1052

6451 RAYMOND PROCTOR, b. Townsend, Mass., Sept. 20, 1942.   1053

6452 CAROL REBECCA, b. Townsend, Mass., Oct. 11, 1944.
                                                                        1054

ELEVENTH GENERATION

1052 JANE CATHERINE PROCTOR BOYES, (6450) born in Groton, Mass., May 16, 1940, married in Norwood, Mass., May 26, 1962, JOHN THOMAS STONEFIELD, born in Norwood, Mass., June 20, 1939. She attended Keene State College after graduating from high school. She was active in 4-H Club, Girl Scouts and for a while worked at the home of Charles Hopkins, portrait artist. He attended Northeastern University and is an engineer for Fitchburg Paper Co. She is active in the historical society, the Manning Family Assoc. and the Congregational church. They live in Townsend, Mass. where they are rebuilding the family homestead.

XI Children

6452 JOHN GALEN, b. Ft. Carson, Colo., March 4, 1964.

6453 JAMES DAVID, b. Townsend, Mass., Feb. 17, 1967.

6454 JEREMIAH BELL, b. Townsend, Mass., June 16, 1970.

6455 JOSHUA SAMUEL, b. Townsend, Mass., March 18, 1972.

1053 RAYMOND PROCTOR BOYES, (6451) born in Townsend, Mass., Sept. 20, 1942, married in Townsend, Mass., May 5, 1964, JOYCE EVELYN CUTLER, born in Barre, Vt., Aug. 13, 1945. He served in the U. S. Navy and works at New England Business Service. They live in Townsend where they enjoy swimming and skating.

XI Children born in Fitchburg, Mass.

6456 DONITA RAE, b. Nov. 1, 1964.

6457 RAYMOND PROCTOR, JR., b. March 14, 1969.

1054 CAROL REBECCA BOYES, (6452) born in Townsend, Mass., Oct. 11, 1944, married in Leominster, Mass., Oct. 12, 1962, DAVID SAWTELLE WRIGHT, born in Leominster, Mass., Feb. 14, 1938. She graduated from North Middlesex High School which she had named as winner of a contest. She is active in the Highland Baptist Church in Fitchburg. They operate a small farm and are active in Grange activities. He is an electronics technician for Mosler Safe Co.

XI Children

6458 GEORGE RONALD MACK, JR., b. Fitchburg, Mass., June 1, 1961.

6459 CYNTHIA ANN WRIGHT, b. Fitchburg, Mass., July 20, 1964.

6460 MATTHEW JEREMY WRIGHT, b. Townsend, Mass., Feb. 14, 1970.

SOME DESCENDANTS OF
GEORGE AND SARAH (HIETT OR HIATT) LOCKE
OF VIRGINIA

The Locke families of New Hampshire and Massachusetts are not, of course, the only Lockes who have settled in America. Recent research has revealed other Locke families in Virginia, Tennessee, Pennsylvania, and Wisconsin.

The following sketch of descendants was submitted by Richard V. and Marian (Bennett) Locke of Chelmsford, Mass. Much of their information is based on a larger work compiled by Dorothy L. W. Brown in 1959-61 for the DAR and is supplemented by their own research. Due to its brevity, this section is not indexed.

Hopefully, one day someone will compile and publish a complete genealogy for this family.

GEORGE LOCKE, born possibly in Berkeley or Frederick Co., Va., April 25, 1747, died in Frederick Co., Va., Sept. 28, 1823. His parents are not known. He married first, SARAH HIETT (or HIATT), born Oct. 9, 1753 and died July 7, 1827. She was the daughter of John Hiett (or Hiatt), born in England in 1696 and Margaret (Stephens) Edwards. George and Sarah Locke are buried on the Old Locke Farm one mile east of Wadesville, Va. in what is now Clarke Co., Va.

Children of George and Sarah (Hiett or Hiatt) Locke:

(I)   WILLIAM, b. March 3, 1773, d. Oct. 20, 1839, m. Frederick Co., Va., Feb. 28, 1799, CATHERINE MOODY.

MARY, b. Oct. 23, 1774, d. June 14, 1847, m. Jan. 2, 1792, JOHN HIATT. They lived Jefferson Co., Va. and had twelve children.

JOHN, b. July 26, 1776, d. probably Feb. 7, 1795.

SARAH, b. Feb. 1778, d. Brown Co., Ohio, June 28, 1854, m. Dec. 9, 1799, JOHN HIATT.

ELIZABETH, b. about 1780, d. June 15, 1827, m. Frederick Co., Va., July 10, 1807, ISAAC THACKER. They had three daughters: Martha, Sally and Elizabeth.

GEORGE, b. Berkeley Co., Va., Sept. 7, 1782, d. German Township, Clark Co., Ohio before April 26, 1838, m. before 1811, SARAH ――――, b. July 4, 1790, d. Clark Co., Ohio before March 19, 1838. They had twelve children.

BETY, b. Feb. 1787.

NANCY, b. Aug. 6, 1784, d. Nov. 1784 or 1794.

NEAL, m. Berkeley Co., Va., Aug. 7, 1809, RACHAEL MERCHANT.

THOMAS, b. about 1788, m. Berkeley Co., Va., Dec. 27, 1809, CYNTHIA HALL.

BENJAMIN,

JOHN, b. March 24 or 29, 1795, d. March 7, 1877, bur. Brucetown Methodist Cemetery, m. REBECCA ――――, d. Dec. 9, 1867 aged 76, bur. Brucetown Methodist Cemetery. They had six children. His will dated Nov. 23, 1874 is recorded in Clarke Co., Va.

I   WILLIAM LOCKE, born on March 3, 1773, died on Oct. 20, 1839, married in Frederick County, Va., Feb. 28, 1799, CATHERINE MOODY, died Oct. 23, 1860.

Children of William and Catherine (Moody) Locke:

(II)   JOHN, b. Feb. 1, 1800.

MARIA, b. April 26, 1801, d. July 20, 1875, m. ABRAM CRIM, b. Oct. 27, 1797, d. Feb. 4, 1875. Both bur. Brucetown Methodist Cemetery.

HARIETTE, b. Jan. 8, 1803, d. March 10, 1825, m. March 30, 1824, JOSHUA JOHNSTON.

NEAL, b. probably Dec. 6, 1804, d. Jan. 15, 1805.

GEORGE, b. Dec. 25, 1805, d. March 30, 1862, m. Frederick Co., Va., Aug. 24, 1824, WINIFRED WILCOX, d. April 10, 1866, aged 60 yrs. 2 mos. 26 da. Both bur. Brucetown Methodist Cemetery.

SARAH or SALLY, b. May, 1807, m. Frederick Co., Va., Jan. 23, 1828, GEORGE L. DUNN.

ELIZA, b. Feb. 20, 1809, d. July 1, 1879, m. JACOB CRIM.

FRANKLIN, b. Feb. 24, 1811, m. Clarke Co., Va., Dec. 5, 1837, MARY ANN HOUT.

JULLETTE or JULIA ANN, b. July 16, 1813, m. Frederick Co., Va., Dec. 23, 1834, WILLIAM AMBROSE.

WILLIAM CHAMBERS, b. May 28, 1815, m. Clarke Co., Va., Jan. 26, 1839, LUCINDA GATES.

JACOB LINZA, b. Oct. 19, 1817, m. Oct. 13, 1845, ELINOR CUNNINGHAM.

BENJAMIN, b. Sept. 25, 1819, m. Clarke Co., Va., Dec. 12, 1845, RUHANNA VAN CLEAVE.

WASHINGTON, b. Nov. 8, 1821, d. Feb. 17, 1824.

II   JOHN LOCKE, born on Feb. 1, 1800, marriage and death records not located. A John Locke listed in the 1850 Federal Census in Jefferson County, 28th district is believed to be this John Locke.

Family unit described in 1850 Federal Census:

JOHN LOCKE, age 50 years.

ANN LOCKE, age 45 years.

JOHN W. LOCKE, age 21 years.

WASHINGTON P. YOUNG, age 40 years.

SARAH C. YOUNG, age 20 years. (A marriage is recorded in Washington County, Md., Aug. 6, 1849 and in Jefferson Co., W. Va., Dec. 30, 1849 of Sarah Catherine Locke and Washington P. Young.)

JOSHUA H. LOCKE, age 17 years. (b. 1834, d. June, 1890, bur. Greenhill Cemetery, m. Washington Co., Md., April 8, 1858, MATILDA S. MERCER, d. 1928. They had eight children.)

(III)   FRANKLIN H. LOCKE, age 14 years.

LUCY A. LOCKE, age 12 years.

III   FRANKLIN HOWARD LOCKE, born in Jefferson County, West Virginia, about 1836, buried in Greenhill Cemetery, Berryville, Clarke Co., Virginia, Jan. 21, 1903, married first before 1860, ELIZABETH LANHAM died on Aug. 22, 1875 in childbirth. Married second, in Clarke Co., Va., on Jan. 6, 1876, HANNAH WILLING-HAM, buried in Greenhill Cemetery, April 27, 1912, the daughter of William and Matilda Willingham.

Children of Franklin and Elizabeth (Lanham) Locke:

PIERCE J., b. 1861/62, d. March 22, 1936, m. first, widow SARAH A. (BELL) RUTTER, d. May 27, 1914. Married second, Feb. 17, 1917, MINNIE L. GLAIZE.

THOMAS, b. Feb. 29, 1864, d. Jan. 25, 1940, m. Jan. 1, 1895, ROSA N. GRUBBS.

BENJAMIN, b. July 4, 1866, m. Aug. 30, 1897, LILYAN GRACE WILLINGHAM, daughter of Jacob Willingham.

(IV)   ARTHUR H., b. Berryville, Clarke Co., Va., Feb. 15, 1867, m. Sept. 12, 1889, AMELIA ELIZABETH STICKLES.

EDWARD, b. 1870, m. first, Jan. 1, 1894, MARY ELLEN GRUBBS, m. second, March 7, 1906, MARTHA E. MORGAN.

GEORGE, b. Jan. 23, 1871.

WILLIAM FRANKLIN, b. 1873, m. Dec. 28, 1898, MARY E. L. WILLINGHAM, daughter of Jacob and Martha (Cooper) Willingham.

KEMP, b. Aug. 22, 1875, m. first, May 18, 1898, MARY BROWN, m. second, Oct. 7, 1914, MATTIE SOWERS.

Children of Franklin and Hannah (Willingham) Locke:

ROBERTA LILLY, b. Clarke Co., Va., July, 1878.

LULY ROBERTA, b. Clarke Co., Va., July, 1878.

LUCY, b. 1879, m. Dec. 24, 1902, EDWARD LOCKE, son of Howard and Matilda Locke.

ELIZABETH, b. Feb. 1882, m. Clarke Co., Va., Feb. 24, 1902, WALTER TUMBLINE.

NANCY, b. Feb. 1879, d. 1949, m. March 26, 1910, CHARLES LACEY BREY, a grandson of Howard and Matilda Locke.

IV   ARTHUR H. LOCKE, born in Berryville, Clarke Co., Va., Feb. 15, 1867, died on June 14, 1947, buried in Edgehill Cemetery, Charlestown, W. Va., married on Sept. 12, 1889, AMELIA ELIZABETH STICKLES, born in Clarke Co., Va., Nov. 15, 1866, died on Nov. 12, 1935, the daughter of Henry C. and Susan (Writ) Stickles. He was a carpenter by trade and they were affiliated with the Baptist Church in Charlestown, W. Va. where they lived.

Children of Arthur and Amelia (Stickles) Locke:

IDA ELIZABETH, b. June 19, 1890, d. Oct. 17, 1968, bur. in Charlestown, W. Va., m. Charlestown, W. Va., Feb. 6, 1908, JOSEPH BAKER McCAULEY. They had five children.

EFFIE ROBERTA, m. first, Sept. 1, 1917, CARL MORRIS. They had a son, Carl. M. second, Mr. Saylor.

HENRY, b. 1895, d. Sept. 1943, changed his name to OSCAR RILEY and m. MARY E. ROGERS. They lived in Dorchester, Mass.

(V)   RICHARD VENNING, b. Charlestown, W. Va., May 11, 1896.

VIRGINIA, b. May 17, 1898, d. Waynesboro, Penna., April 11, 1950, m. Charlestown, W. Va., Oct. 18, 1919, SAMUEL McDONOUGH. They had five children. She m. second EARL WELTY.

V   RICHARD VENNING LOCKE, born in Charlestown, W. Va., May 11, 1896, died in Ormond Beach, Fla., Jan. 5, 1972, married first in the Canal Zone, STELLA MAY JOHNSON from Armstrong, Mo. He married second in Springfield, Mass., July 31, 1926, GLADYS EVELINE BAINES, born in East Longmeadow, Mass., April 20, 1898, the daughter of Francis H. and Helen Madge (Robertson)

Baines. He married third in Elkton, Md., Jan. 10, 1944, HAZEL (McDONALD) PENNIMAN.

Children of Richard and Gladys (Baines) Locke:

(VI)   RICHARD VENNING, JR., b. Springfield, Mass., July 12, 1931.

MARIAN LOUISE, b. Nov. 28, 1937, m. first, Feb. 22, 1958, RAYMOND BLACKSTONE. Their children are:

TERI, b. Feb. 28, 1959.
JOHN LAWRENCE, b. March 22, 1960.
GREGG STUART, b. June 8, 1964, d. May 8, 1967.
ROBERT, b. Sept. 17, 1965.

She m. second in Nashua, N. H., Dec., 1972, WILLIAM WOOD, they live in Mountain View, Calif.

VI   RICHARD VENNING LOCKE, JR., born in Springfield, Mass., July 12, 1931, died in Boston, Mass., May 8, 1977, married in Springfield, Mass., April 5, 1952, MARIAN HELEN BENNETT, born in Springfield, Mass., March 12, 1932, the daughter of Wallace E. and Helen (Diamond) Bennett. He graduated from Technical High School and the University of Houston, Houston, Texas. He served in the U. S. Army Signal Corps, 1952-1954. From 1954 to 1958 he was employed in the Electrical Engineering development section of the Schlumberger Well Surveying Corp. in Houston, Texas. In January, 1959 he became a staff member at Lincoln Laboratory, a research and development facility operated by the Massachusetts Institute of Technology. They lived in Chelmsford, Mass. from 1950 until his death. She married second in Houston, Texas, March 24, 1979 to Jimmy S. Drew of that city.

Children of Richard V., Jr. and Marian (Bennett) Locke:

DAVID R., b. March 21, 1956, m. Chelmsford, Mass., Dec. 21, 1974, DONNA MARIE ARCHAMBEAULT. They had: James Robert, b. Sept. 7, 1978.

BARBARA E., b. Houston, Texas, April 23, 1958.

LINDA H., b. Lowell, Mass., Jan. 23, 1961.

CAROLYN P., b. Lowell, Mass., Oct. 9, 1968.

Jeffrey Allen	225	Leona	118,217
Jeffrey Langdon	223	Leona Elizabeth	52,102
Jennifer	225	Leonard Morse	30
Jennifer Susan	222	Lida Madeline	53
Jeremey Thomas	240	Lillian May	120
Jesse	25,32	Lloyd Granville	75
Jesse Sumner	53	Lydia Susanna	30,42
Jessica Elizabeth	84	Mabel Margaret	63,146
Jessie Edna	64	Mabel Robertson	118
Joan Constance	124	Madaleine Dale	75,155
Joanna	81	Mae	239
John	25,32	Margaret	70,134
John Adam	225	Margaret Chase, Jr.	128
John Allen	127,225	Margaret Ellen	147
John Allen, Jr.	225	Margaret Ethel	248,272
John Berry	125	Margaret Jean	128,227,240
John Charles	231	Margaret June	124,203
John Crawford	124,204	Margaret Louise	44,95
John F.	45	Margaret Sarah	73
John Fernando	97	Maria H.	48
John Glenwood	187	Maria Lorraine	43
John Gordon	82,166	Marian Hardy	120
John Hugh	67,117	Marion	47
John Malcolm	153,239	Marion Fiske	67
John Robert	37,81,96	Marjorie	70
John Robinson	68,121	Marjorie Carole	231,270
John Robinson, Jr.	121,221	Marjorie Ruth	37,85
John Robinson III	222	Marjorie Sarah	128,227
John Stephen	167	Marjorie Sylvia	98,185
John Stuart	147	Mark James	273
Jonathan	68	Martha Jean	230
Jonathan Hayden	247	Martin Tappan	161,245
Joseph Arthur	84,168	Mary Anita	83
Josephine Jones	67,117	Mary Anne	273
Joyce	215	Mary Bell	30,44
Judith Alma	256,277	Mary Bruce	82,165
Judith Ann	217,250	Mary Elizabeth	32,53
Judith Anne	82,166	Mary Estella	64
Judith May	73,127	Mary Kelley	70,154
Julia Ann	96	Mary Linna	112,214
Julia Garland	79	Mary Phyllis Ann	187,248
Julie Ann	168	Mary Rubena	73,128
Justin Charles	84	Maurice Sinclair	133,230
Kathleen Anne	146	Merritt Caldwell	53
Kathleen Frances	70	Michael David	167
Kathy Jean	231	Michael Wayne	218,273
Kathy Ruth	256	Michelle	273
Kelly Alysson	245	Mignon	68,121
Kenneth William	273	Mildred	78
Kent Drew	70,153	Mildred Elaine	249,274
Kent Drew, Jr.	154,239	Mildred Josephine	118,217
Kermit Albion	133,230	Mildred Sarah	73
Kevin John	273	Myrta Belle	44,96
Kevin Sidney	218	Nancie	46
Kevin Vernon	225	Nancy	97
Kimberly	256	Nancy Elisabeth	124
Langdon Elvin II	124	Nancy Jean	239
Lela Sylvina	45,97	Nancy Theresa	166
Leon Leonard	29,52	Nathan Augustus	245

www.ingramcontent.com/pod-product-compliance
Lightning Source LLC
Chambersburg PA
CBHW070547270326
41926CB00013B/2232